THE PETROFF DEFENSE

THE PETROFF DEFENSE

Gyözö Forintos and
Ervin Haag

Collier Books
Macmillan Publishing Company
New York

Maxwell Macmillan Canada
Toronto

Collier Books   Maxwell Macmillan Canada, Inc.
Macmillan Publishing   1200 Eglinton Avenue East
  Company   Suite 200
866 Third Avenue   Don Mills, Ontario M3C 3N1
New York, NY 10022

Macmillan Publishing Company is part of the Maxwell
Communication Group of Companies.

Library of Congress Cataloging-in-Publication Data

Forintos Gyözö.
    The Petroff defense / Gyözö Forintos and Ervin
  Haag. -- 1st Collier Books ed.
          p.   cm.
    Rev. ed. of: The Petroff defence. 1983.
    Translated from Hungarian.
    ISBN 0-02-028561-2
    1. Chess--Openings. I. Haag, Ervin. II. Forintos, Gyözö.
  Petroff defence. III. Title.
  GV 1450.2.F67 1991
  794.1'22--dc20   91-17568
                                                                CIP
Macmillan books are available at special discounts for
bulk purchases for sales promotions, premiums, fund-
raising or educational use. For details, contact:

        Special Sales Director
        Macmillan Publishing Company
        866 Third Avenue
        New York, NY 10022

First Collier Books Edition 1991

10   9   8   7   6   5   4   3   2   1

Printed in Great Britain

Contents

3 ... d6

Preface to the Second Edition

The Petroff Defence, **1 e4 e5 2 ♘f3 ♘f6** (known in some countries as the Russian Defence) has been increasingly used in major tournaments over the last decades. Among others, World Champion Kasparov and ex-World Champion Karpov have included it in their repertoire.

The fact that Black may often choose between a sharp, tactically rich line and a solid, positional variation depending on his style or mood adds to the attractiveness of the defence.

Often, from the very nature of the Petroff Defence, the variations transpose into each other. By taking the trouble to look up all lines we appreciated the importance of the differences in move order. The Petroff Defence is strongly recommended for young players – partly because the sharper variations cultivate tactical awareness and partly because the typically simple positions are easy to understand.

We hope this book will command interest among a large number of chess players. Not only is it essential for players of the Petroff Defence to be familiar with new ideas and assessments; it is also important for White players of 1 e4 to examine the Petroff Defence and choose lines most suited to their style.

History

The Petroff Defence is one of the oldest defences. It was mentioned by Lucena in *Repeticion de Amores e Arte de Axedrez con el juegos de Partido* ..., the first known textbook dealing with modern chess, published in Salamanca around 1497. Damiano's book of 1512 *Libro da Imparare Giocare a Scachi et de bellissimi Partiti* provided valuable contributions to the defence and it was analysed in detail by Ruy Lopez in his book *Libro de la invencion liberal y arte del juego de Axedrez* in 1561. After that the defence was forgotten and mentioned only in outline in Cozio's book in 1766 and Ponziani's book in 1769. New attention was drawn to the defence by Carl Jaenisch, a Russian master, who published detailed analysis in *La Palaméde* in 1842, mainly the work of his compatriot, Alexander Petroff, at that time the strongest Russian master. Earlier, in his *Shakmatnaya Igra,* published in 1824, Petroff had condemned the defence! But he went on to prove its viability in practice and the defence was thus named after him, although it is known as the Russian Game in some languages.

The interest of great chessplayers of that age was soon attracted by Petroff's Defence, in which Black tries to initiate a counter-attack as early as the second move. Analyses and studies followed each other: Bilguer 1846, Walker 1846, Allgaier 1847, Staunton 1847. The reputation of the defence suffered after the correspondence game Pest-Paris (1843-46) became known - and this shadow continued until 1871 when new ideas for the defence were developed.

Steinitz tried to disprove the soundness of the Petroff

Defence by 3 d4 in his work *The Modern Chess Instructor* in 1889, however, without any success. Nevertheless, his analyses contributed greatly to the theory. At the turn of the century great masters of attack, Pillsbury, Marshall, Blackburne and Teichmann popularised the defence by using it as their favourite weapon.

In 1924 the Russian master, Sozin, collected the works which had been published on the Petroff Defence and augmented them with his own analyses. Later on Euwe, Keres and Polugayevsky did similarly valuable work.

The first monograph was written by David Hooper in 1966, while many others contributed important work by exploring and explaining new ideas.

Some famous chessplayers have often played the Petroff Defence and made theoretical contributions — Alexander, Kashdan, Holmov, Trifunovic, Lilienthal, Bronstein, Petrosian, Smyslov, Spassky, Hort, Hübner, Larsen, Timman, Yusupov, Nunn, Salov, Chandler, Belyavsky, Ivanchuk, not to forget the great names of World Champions Kasparov and Karpov.

E.J. Haag and G.J. Forintos

Symbols

+	check
=	balanced position
±	some advantage to White
∓	some advantage to Black
±	clear advantage to White
∓	clear advantage to Black
±±	winning advantage to White
∓∓	winning advantage to Black
∞	unclear position
∞̄	with compensation
!	good move
!!	excellent move
!?	interesting move
?!	dubious move
?	weak move
??	blunder
△	with the idea
⌒	better is
(m)	match
(ol)	olympiad
(izt)	interzonal tournament
Ch.	Championship
corr.	correspondence game

1) 3 d4 ed: Introduction

1	e4	e5
2	♘f3	♘f6
3	d4	ed *(1)*

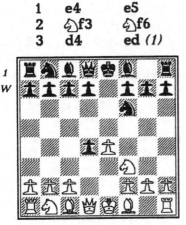

3 ... ♘**xe4** is discussed in Chapters 8-13.

3 ... d5 — Chapter 14.

3 ... d6 is not advisable for Black. White may transpose into the normal variations of the Philidor Defence (1 e4 e5 2 ♘f3 d6 3 d4 ♘f6). We give a "tight" repertoire, being enough to get some advantage from the opening: after 4 de ♘xe4 5 ♕d5! ♘c5 (5 ... f5!? 6 ♗c4 ♕e7 7 0-0± — Keres) 6 ♗g5! Black has tried:

a) **6 ... f6?** 7 ef gf 8 ♗e3 ♗e6 9 ♕h5+ ♗f7 10 ♕h4 ♘bd7 11 ♘c3 c6 12 0-0-0±± Maroczy - Bogoljubov, Bled 1931.

b) **6 ... ♕d7** 7 ed ♗xd6 (7 ... ♕xd6 8 ♘c3±) 8 ♘c3 0-0 9 0-0-0 ♕g4 10 h3 ♕h5 11 ♗e2± (Keres).

c) **6 ... ♗e7** 7 ed ♕xd6 8 ♘c3 and now:

c1) **8 ... 0-0** 9 0-0-0± L Steiner - Holzhausen, Berlin 1928.

c2) **8 ... c6** 9 ♕xd6 ♗xd6 10 0-0-0± (Polugayevsky).

c3) **8 ... ♕xd5** 9 ♘xd5 ♗d6 10 0-0-0 0-0 11 ♗e7± (Polugayevsky).

c4) **8 ... h6** 9 ♗e3 c6 10 ♕xd6 ♗xd6 11 0-0-0 ♗e7 12 ♘c4± Smit - Peterson, Riga 1972.

If **3 ... ♗e7** 4 de! ♘xe4 5 ♕d5 ♘c5 6 ♘c3± or 5 ... ♘g5?! 6 ♗xg5 ♗xg5 7 ♗c4 0-0 8 ♘c3± (8 e6 ♗f6 9 ef+ ♔h8 10 ♘c3 ♕e7+! △ c6 - d5∞).

4   e5

4 ♗c4 is studied in Chapter 7, or:

a) If **4 c3?** ♘xe4 is the simplest.

b) **4 ♕xd4** and now:

b1) **4 ... ♘c6** 5 ♕e3 ♗b4+ 6 ♘c3 (6 c3 is met by ... ♗a5 – b6) 6 ... 0-0 7 ♗d2 ♗xc3 8 ♗xc3 ♘xe4 shows White has chosen an unfavourable line of the "Centre Game".

b2) **4 ... d5** 5 e5 ♘e4 6 ♕a4+ c6 7 ♘bd2 f5 (7 ... b5 8 ♕b3 ♘c5=) 8 ef ♘xf6 9 ♕h4 ♗d6 10 ♗e2 0-0 △ ... ♘bd7 and Black had excellent play in Nikolic – Taruffi, Rovigo 1976.

4   ...   ♘e4

Other ideas are inadequate:

a) **4 ... ♘d5?** 5 ♕xd4 ♘b6 6 ♘c3 ♘c6 7 ♕e4 ♗e7 8 ♗f4 0-0 9 ♗d3 g6 10 0-0-0 △ h4± Dückstein – Huber, Vienna 1961.

b) **4 ... ♕e7?** 5 ♗e2± e.g.

b1) **5 ... ♘g4** 6 0-0 (6 ♕xd4 is also good) 6 ... ♘c6 7 ♖e1±.

b2) **5 ... ♘e4** 6 0-0 (6 ♕xd4 ♕b4+ 7 ♘bd2± Mieses – Grob, (m) Zürich 1934) 6 ... ♘c6 7 ♖e1 h6 8 ♗b5! △ ♘xd4±.

5   ♕xd4

For **5 ♕e2** see Chapter 5.

5 ♗b5 is discussed in Chapter 6.

The weak **5 ♘xd4** can be strongly met by 5 ... d6, or even 5 ... ♗e7, e.g. 6 ♕g4 d5 7 ♕xg7 ♖f8 8 ♕xh7 (⌐ 8 ♗d3) 8 ... ♗c5 9 ♗e3? (9 c3 ♕e7=) 9 ... ♗xd4 10 ♗xd4 ♕g5!∓ S Kantor – E Kahn, Budapest 1987.

White's other try – **5 ♗d3** – has the disadvantage of allowing Black to seize the initiative at once:

a) **5 ... ♗b4+!** 6 c3 (6 ♘bd2 is more careful) 6 ... dc 7 bc (7 0-0? cb is weaker 8 ♗xb2 ♘c5 9 ♗c2 ♘e6 10 ♘c3 Ciocaltea – Radulov, Romania 1953; 10 ... ♗xc3∓) 7 ... ♘xc3 8 ♕b3 ♘d5+ 9 ♔e2 c6 10 ♗e4 ♕a5 and White cannot hope for any advantage.

b) **5 ... ♘c5**, planning ... ♘c6, is also good.

5   ...   d5

6   ed

For 6 ♕a4+ see b2) 4 ♕xd4 d5.

6   ...   ♘xd6

Now:

a) 7 ♗f4, 7 ♗g5, and 7 ♕e5+ are discussed in Chapter 2.

b) 7 ♗d3 – Chapter 3.

c) 7 ♘c3 – Chapter 4.

2) 3 d4 ed:
7 ♗f4/ 7 ♗g5/ 7 ♕e5+

4	e5	♘e4
5	♕xd4	d5
6	ed	♘xd6

Here we consider:

A: 7 ♗f4
B: 7 ♗g5

Other possible moves include:

a) 7 ♗d3 – discussed in Chapter 3.

b) 7 ♘c3 – see Chapter 4.

c) 7 ♕e5+ ♕e7 8 ♘c3 ♗e6! 9 ♘d4 ♘d7 10 ♕e3 ♗c4= e.g. 11 ♘db5 ♘xb5 12 ♘xb5 ♗xf1! 13 ♖xf1 ♔d8!

A

7 ♗f4 (2)

7	...	♘c6
8	♕e3+	

Or 8 ♕d2 and now:

a) 8 ... ♗g4 9 ♘c3?! (9 ♗e2) 9 ... ♕e7+! 10 ♕e3 ♕xe3+ 11 fe 0-0-0 12 0-0-0 ♗e7 ½-½ Sznapik – Smyslov, Berlin 1979.

b) 8 ... ♗e6 9 ♘c3 ♕d7 10 0-0-0 0-0-0 11 ♕e3 a6 (⌐ 11 ... ♕e8) 12 ♘e4± Kudriasov – Maslov, Cheliabinsk 1972.

c) 8 ... ♕e7+! 9 ♗e2 ♘e4 10 ♕e3 (10 ♕c1) 10 ... ♘b4 (10 ... ♗f5 △ ... 0-0-0) 11 ♕c1 ♕c5 12 0-0! and not now 12 ... ♘xc2? 13 ♘c3! ♘xc3 14 ♕xc2 ♘xe2+ 15 ♕xe2+ ♕e7 16 ♕c2±, L Schmid – Kinzel, Siegen (ol) 1970, but 12 ... ♗e6! 13 c4=.

8	...	♕e7
9	♘c3	♕xe3+

10 ♗xe3 ♗g4 11 ♘d4 ♘xd4 12 ♗xd4 ♘f5! =, the game Hübner – Timman, Tilburg 1986 went 13 ♗e5 ♗d6 14 ♗xd6 ♘xd6 15 f3 ½-½.

B

7 ♗g5 (3)

Now Black has tried:

B1: 7 ... ♕d7?!
B2: 7 ... f6
B3: 7 ... ♘c6

B1

    7   ...   **♕d7?!**
    8   **♘c3**   **♘c6**
    9   **♕a4!**

This is the best place for the white queen as from there she can best support the team-work of all the white pieces. It is more precise than 9 ♕d2 when, after 9 ... f6!, the black queen can get to f7 without loss of tempo.

B2

    7   ...   **f6**
    8   **♗f4**

Or 8 ♗d2 is also possible, e.g. 8 ... ♘c6 9 ♕a4 ♗d7 10 ♗e2 ♕e7 11 ♘c3 0-0-0 12 0-0-0 ♕f7= Shishkov - E

Kahn, Budapest 1987.

    8   ...   **♘c6**

8 ... ♕e7+ 9 ♗e2 ♘c6 10 ♕a4 g5?! (better is 10 ... ♗d7, transposing into the main line) 11 ♗xd6 ♕xd6 12 ♘c3 ♕b4 13 ♕b5 ♗d7, Romanishin - Smyslov, Lvov 1978, 14 h4!± — Romanishin.

    9   **♕a4**

Other tries:

a) 9 ♕d1 ♕e7+ 10 ♗e2 ♗g4 11 0-0 0-0-0 12 ♖e1 g5 13 ♗d2 ♕g7 14 ♘c3 ♘f5∓ Smyslov - Mats, Moscow 1963.

b) 9 ♕d2 ♗f5 10 ♗e2 ♕e7 11 0-0 0-0-0 12 ♖e1 ♘e4?! 13 ♕c1 g5 14 ♗d3! ♗h6!= Steinitz - Pillsbury, St. Petersburg 1895/96; 12 ... ♕f7!∓.

c) 9 ♕e3+ ♕e7 and now:

c1) 10 ♕xe7+ ♗xe7 11 ♘c3 ♗f5 12 0-0-0 0-0-0 13 ♘d4 ♘xd4 14 ♖xd4 ♘f7 15 ♖xd8+ ♖xd8∓ Spielmann - Marshall, Baden-Baden 1925 and Zubaryev - Marshall, Moscow 1925. Bogoljubov considers 12 ♘d5! 0-0-0 13 ♘xe7+ ♘xe7 14 ♘d4= to be better.

c2) 10 ♘c3 ♗g4 11 ♗e2 ♕xe3 12 ♗xe3 ♘f5 13 ♘d5 0-0-0 14 0-0-0 ♘xe3 15 ♘xe3 ♗d7 16 ♗d3 ♗c5∓ Stoltz - Alekhine, Munich 1941.

    9   ...   **♕e7+**

This equalizes.

10	♗e2	♗d7
11	0-0	♕xe2!

12 ♖e1 ♘e5! 13 ♕xd7+ ♔xd7 14 ♖xe2 ♘xf3+ 15 gf ♘f5 with good chances.

B3

7 ... ♘c6

The simplest move.

8 ♕e3+!

Others:

a) 8 ♗xd8? ♘xd4 9 ♘xd4 ♔xd8 10 ♘c3 c6 11 0-0-0 ♔c7∓ Butcher - Hooper, London 1954.

b) 8 ♕d2 ♗e7= △ 9 ♘c3 ♘e5!

c) 8 ♕c3 f6! 9 ♗f4 ♕e7+ 10 ♗e2 ♗e6 11 ♘bd2 0-0-0 12 0-0 ♕f7 Bogoljubov, Ilyin-Zhenevsky and Rabinovich - Kubbel, Levenfish and Romanovsky, a training game in Leningrad 1924; 13 ♖fe1!=.

8 ... ♗e7

9 ♘c3

Now White does not gain anything by trading bishops and queens: 9 ♗xe7 ♕xe7 10 ♕xe7+ ♔xe7 (10 ... ♘xe7 11 ♘c3 ♗g4 12 ♗e2 0-0-0 13 0-0-0 ♖he8= Kostic - Kashdan, Bled 1931) 11 ♘c3 ♗g4 12 0-0-0 ♖he8 13 ♗b5 ♔d7 14 ♗xc6+ bc 15 ♖d3 ♗xf3 16 ♖xf3 ♖e5 17 ♖d1 f6 18 b3 ♖fe8 19 ♖d4 ♔c8!= Braga - Hartoch, Amsterdam 1986.

9 ... ♘f5

9 ... 0-0?! 10 0-0-0 ♖e8 11 ♘d5!±.

10	♗xe7	♘cxe7
11	♕e5	0-0
12	♖d1	♘d6
13	♗d3	♘g6
14	♕g3	♖e8+

Planning 15 ... ♕f6 with balanced chances. Feeble is 14 ... ♕e7+ 15 ♔d2 ♘f5 16 ♗xf5 ♗xf5 17 ♔c1 ♖ad8 18 ♘d4 ♗c8 19 ♖he1± Konstantinopolsky - Smyslov, Sverdlovsk 1943.

3) 3 d4 ed: 7 ♗d3

4	e5	♘e4
5	♕xd4	d5
6	ed	♘xd6
7	♗d3	

We consider:

A: 7 ... ♕e7+ (Bronstein)
B: 7 ... ♘c6

A

7	...	♕e7+ *(4)*

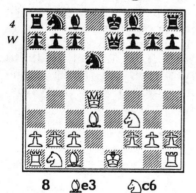

8	♗e3	♘c6

Others:

a) **8 ... ♘f5?!** 9 ♗xf5 ♗xf5 10 ♘c3! ♘c6 (10 ... ♗xc2? 11 ♖c1 △ ♘d5±; 10 ... ♕b4 11 ♕e5+ ♗e6 12 0-0-0 ♘c6 13 ♕xc7 ♖c8 14 ♕f4 ♕a5 15

♕g5!± Bonch-Osmolovsky – Baronov, Moscow 1954) 11 ♕f4 ♕b4 12 0-0-0±.

b) **8 ... ♗f5** and now:

b1) **9 ♗xf5** ♘xf5 10 ♕a4+ ♘c6 11 0-0 ♕b4! Petrusiak – Borisenko, Riga 1968.

b2) **9 ♘c3** ♘c6 10 ♕f4 (10 ♕a4 ♗xd3 11 cd ♕d7 12 d4± Bronstein – Holmov, Vilnius 1958) 10 ... ♗xd3 11 cd ♕d7 (11 ... 0-0-0 would be too risky after 12 0-0; 11 ... ♕e6 12 0-0-0 ♗e7 13 d4 ♕f5 14 d5± Spassky – Holmov, USSR 1960) 12 ♘e5! ♘xe5 13 ♕xe5+ ♕e6 14 ♕a5 b6 15 ♕a4+ ♕d7 16 ♕d4± Suetin – Mikenas, USSR 1959.

9	♕f4	

9 ♕a4 ♗d7 △ ... ♘e5.

9	...	g6

Or:

a) **9 ... f6?** 10 ♘c3 ♗e6 11 0-0-0 0-0-0 12 ♕a4 ♔b8 13 ♗c5! ♕f7 14 ♘d4±± Bonch-Osmolovsky – Kamishov, USSR 1949.

b) **9 ... h6** 10 ♘c3 ♗e6 11

♕a4±.

10 ♘c3

and now:

A1: 10 ... ♗e6
A2: 10 ... ♗g7

A1

10 ... ♗e6
11 ♘d4

Or 11 0-0 ♗g7 12 ♖fe1 0-0 13 ♗c5± Matanovic - Kieninger, Hamburg 1955.

11 ... ♗g7
12 ♘xc6

Keres regards 12 ♘xe6 as better.

12 ... bc
13 0-0

13 ♕a4 also deserves attention, e.g. 13 ... ♗d7 14 0-0 0-0 15 ♕a5± △ ♘a4 Korchnoi - Averbakh, USSR 1957/58.

13 ... 0-0
14 ♗d4±

A2

10 ... ♗g7
11 ♘d5

Or 11 0-0-0 ♗e6=.

11 ... ♕d8
12 0-0-0 0-0
13 ♗c5

If 13 c3 then ♘e7! (13 ... ♗e6? 14 ♗c2!) △ ♘xd5 or ♘f5.

13 ... ♗e6!

Black's tactical counter chances must not be disregarded:

a) Keres warns against 14 ♘xc7 and in the game Lutikov - Shaposhnikov, USSR 1954, after 14 ... ♕xc7 15 ♗xd6 ♕b6! 16 c3 (16 ♗xf8? ♗xb2+ 17 ♔d2 ♕xf2+) 16 ... ♖fc8 Black had a strong attack for the pawn. 15 ♕xd6 offers no improvement after 15 ... ♕a5 16 ♗a3 ♖fc8!

b) 14 ♗e2 ♖e8! 15 ♖he1 ♗xd5 16 ♖xd5 ♘e7 17 ♖dd1 ♘ef5!∓ (Barczay).

B

7 ... ♘c6 *(5)*

8 ♕f4

8 ♕e3+ ♗e7 (simpler is 8 ... ♕e7) 9 ♗d2 ♗e6 10 ♕f4 (10 ♘c3 ♘b4) 10 ... ♗f6 11 ♘c3 ♕d7 12 0-0-0 0-0-0=.

Now Black has:

B1: 8 ... ♗e6
B2: 8 ... ♗e7
B3: 8 ... g6

8 ... ♕e7+ transposes to line A.

B1

8   ...   ♗e6
and now:

B11: 9 ♘c3
B12: 9 ♗d2

9 ♘g5± (Polugayevsky) is the simplest way of gaining an advantage.

B11

9   ♘c3   ♕d7
a) **9 ... ♗e7** transposes to line B2.
b) **9 ... g6** 10 ♘d4 ♗g7? (10 ... ♕d7) 11 ♘xe6! fe 12 0-0 Buljovcic - Ilievsky, Yugoslav Ch. 1965; 12 ♘e4!± Keres.
10   ♗e3
10 0-0 h6? (⌓10 ... ♗e7, see line B2) 11 ♗e3 g5 12 ♕a4 ♗g7 13 ♘e4± Liberson - Plaskeyev, Moscow 1968.
10   ...   ♘f5
Inferior is **10 ... f6?** 11 0-0-0 0-0-0 12 ♗b5 a6 13 ♕a4!± Dobson - Liljak, Belgrade 1969.
11   ♗xf5   ♗xf5

12 ♘e5 ♘xe5 13 ♕xe5+ ♗e6 14 ♘b5 ♗d6 15 ♘xd6+ ♕xd6 16 ♕xd6 cd 17 0-0-0± Adorjan - Kostro, Wijk aan Zee 1971.

B12

9   ♗d2   ♕d7
10   ♘c3
10 0-0 0-0-0 11 ♘c3 ♗e7 12 ♕a4 ♔b8 13 ♗e3 ♘f6 14 ♖ad1±.
10   ...   ♗e7
11   0-0-0
After 11 0-0 Euwe's ... 0-0-0 is best.
11   ...   0-0
The only good move.
12   h4
12 ♖he1 is better for White as it prevents not only ... f6, but also ... ♗f6, e.g.:
a) **12 ... ♗f6** 13 ♘e4 ♘xe4 14 ♕xe4 g6 15 ♗h6 ♖fe8 16 ♕f4± Friedgood - Roux, Tel Aviv (ol) 1964.
b) **12 ... ♗f5** 13 ♗xf5 ♕xf5 14 ♕xf5 ♘xf5 15 g4 ♘h4! 16 ♖xe7 ♘xf3 17 ♖xc7 ♘xh2 18 g5!±.
12   ...   f6!?
13   ♖he1   ♗f5?
Better first 13 ... ♖ae8 ∠ ♕c8.
14   ♗xf5   ♕xf5
15 ♕xf5 ♘xf5 16 g4, Mednis - Horowitz, New York

1955, 16 ... ♘d6 17 ♘d5 ♗d8 18 ♗f4±.

B2

8 ... ♗e7
9 ♘c3

9 0-0 is also good. Mostly it transposes into later variations.

9 ... ♗e6

9 ... 0-0 10 ♗e3 (also possible is 10 ♘d5) 10 ... ♕d7 11 0-0-0 ♕g4 (11 ... ♘f5? 12 g4! ♘xe3 13 ♗xh7+!) 12 ♘d5! ♗d8 13 ♘g5! h6 14 ♘e4 ♕xf4 15 ♗xf4 ♘e8 16 ♗b5± Adorjan – Androvitzky, Budapest 1971.

10 0-0

Or:

a) 10 ♗d2 transposes into the previous line B2 except after 10 ... 0-0, which proved strong in Murey – Vasyukhin, USSR 1967: 11 0-0 ♗f6 12 ♖fe1 ♕d7 13 ♖ad1 ♗f5! 14 ♘d5 ♗xb2 15 ♗xf5 ♕xf5 16 ♘xc7 ♖ad8=.

b) 10 b3 ♗f6 11 ♗b2 and now:

b1) 11 ... g5!? 12 ♕e3 g4 13 ♘d2 ♗d4 14 ♕e2, Bisguier – Steinmeyer, USA 1956, 14 ... ♕e7! with good play for Black.

b2) 11 ... 0-0 12 0-0 (12 0-0-0 is also good) 12 ... ♕c8 (12 ... ♘e7 13 ♖ad1±

Gunston - MacDonald, corr. 1937) Paris – Bern, corr. 1921, 13 ♖fe1!±.

c) 10 ♗e3 when:

c1) 10 ... ♕c8? 11 0-0-0 0-0 (11 ... ♗f5 12 ♘d5 0-0? 13 ♘d4 1-0 Stanciu – Weissmann, Craiova 1957) 12 ♘d4 (12 h4 is also good) 12 ... ♘xd4 13 ♗xd4± Ivkov – Keller, Moscow 1956.

c2) 10 ... ♗f6! transposes to the next note.

10 ... ♕d7

Best.

10 ... 0-0 is also to be considered when besides 11 ♖d1 (Euwe), 11 ♖e1 is good, and naturally 11 ♗d2 as well. After 11 ♗e3:

a) 11 ... h6? 12 ♖fe1 ♕c8 13 ♕g3 ♔h8 14 ♘d4! ♘xd4 15 ♗xd4 ♘e8 16 ♘d5!± Udovcic - Bertok, Yugoslavia 1954.

b) 11 ... ♕d7 12 ♖ad1± Nezhmetdinov - Zukhovitsky, USSR 1955.

c) 11 ... ♗f6 12 ♖ad1 when:

c1) 12 ... ♕c8? 13 ♗c5 ♖d8 14 ♘g5± is Unzicker - Keller, Lugano 1959.

c2) 12 ... ♘e7 13 ♗c5 ♘g6 14 ♕g3 (14 ♗xg6 fg!=) 14 ... ♗xc3! 15 bc ♕f6 16 ♘g5, Nezhmetdinov - Damsky, Kazan 1964, 16 ... ♕xc3 17 ♘xe6 fe 18 ♗xd6 cd 19 ♗xg6

♕xg3=.

11 ♗e3

11 ♘e4 does not promise anything, e.g. 11 ... ♘xe4 12 ♗xe4 0-0-0 13 ♗xc6 ♕xc6 14 ♘d4 ♕d5 15 ♘xe6 ♕xe6 16 ♗e3 a6 ½-½ Milic - Rabar, Novi Sad 1945.

11 ... 0-0

Inferior are:

a) **11 ... ♘f5?** 12 ♗xf5 ♗xf5 13 ♘b5± Barry - Showalter, (m) 1896.

b) **11 ... h6?!** 12 ♖ad1 0-0 (12 ... 0-0-0? 13 ♕a4!±±) 13 ♘e4±.

c) **11 ... ♗f5** 12 ♖ad1 ♗xd3 13 ♖xd3 ♕f5 14 ♘d5! ♕xf4 15 ♗xf4 0-0-0 16 ♘e5 ♖he8 17 ♘xc6 bc 18 ♘xe7+ ♖xe7 19 ♗e3± Schlick - Zisk, Germany 1986.

12 ♖ad1

Now:

B21: 12 ... ♗f6
B22: 12 ... ♖ad8

If 12 ... ♕c8?! 13 ♘d4± Trapl - Schubert, Czechoslovakia 1959.

B21

12 ... ♗f6
13 ♘e4! ♗xb2
14 ♘xd6

Another possibility is 14 ♘c5±.

14 ... cd

a) **15 ♗xh7+?!** ♔xh7 16 ♖xd6 ♕e7 17 ♘g5+ ♔g8 18 ♕e4 g6 19 ♕h4 f6!∞ Darga - Lieb, Berlin 1957.

b) **15 ♘g5** g6! 16 ♕h4 h5 17 ♘xe6 ♕xe6 18 ♗c4±.

B22

12 ... ♖ad8

and now White can try:

a) **13 ♗c5 ♕c8** 14 ♘g5 ♗xg5 15 ♕xg5 ♖fe8 16 ♗xd6 (△ 16 ♖fe1) 16 ... ♖xd6 17 ♘e4 ♕d8! 18 ♕h5 ♖d5∓ Broadbent - Hooper, London 1954.

b) **13 ♘g5 ♗xg5** 14 ♕xg5 f6! 15 ♕h4 ♗f5 16 ♗c5 ♗xd3 17 ♖xd3 ♕e6 18 ♘d5 ♖f7!= Smyslov - Kan, Moscow 1939.

c) **13 ♘e4** is good, e.g. 13 ... ♘xe4 14 ♕xe4 f5 15 ♕a4±.

B3

8 ... g6 (6)

White has:

B31: 9 0-0
B32: 9 ♘c3

Other possibilities:

a) **9 ♗d2** (△ 9 ... ♗g7 10 ♗c3±) 9 ... ♕e7+! and now:

a1) **10 ♔f1?!** ♗g7 11 ♗c3 0-0 12 ♗xg7 ♔xg7 13 ♘c3 ♗e6 14 ♖e1 ♕f6∓.

a2) **10 ♗e2** ♘e4! (Mikenas) 11 ♘c3 ♘xd2 12 0-0-0! ♗e6 13 ♘d4 ♘xd4 14 ♕xd4 ♘xb3+ 15 ab ♗h6+ 16 ♔b1 0-0= Kotkov - Vistanetsky, Vilnius 1961.

b) Euwe's **9 ♘d4** can be met by 9 ... ♘b4 10 0-0 ♘xd3 11 cd ♗e7=.

B31
9 0-0 ♗g7
Now White has a choice:

B311: 10 ♗d2
B312: 10 ♘c3
B313: 10 ♖e1+

B311
10 ♗d2 ♗xb2
Black can prevent all the complications with:

a) **10 ... ♕f6** 11 ♕xf6 ♗xf6 12 ♘c3 ♗e6 13 ♘g5 ♗xg5 (13 ... ♗c4? 14 ♘ge4) 14 ♗xg5 0-0 or 14 ... ♘h4=/±

b) **10 ... 0-0** 11 ♗c3 (11 ♘c3 ♗e6 - see line B1, note b in Chapter 4) when:

b1) **11 ... ♗f5** 12 ♖d1! ♕e7 13 ♗xg7 ♔xg7 14 ♘c3 ♗e6 15 ♗b5!± Matsukevich - Chesnauskas, Leningrad 1964.

b2) **11 ... ♗e6!** can be taken into consideration.

11 ♘c3 ♗xc3
11 ... ♗xa1? 12 ♕xa1 0-0 13 ♗f6! ♕d7 14 ♕h6 ♘e8 15 ♗g7!! ♘xg7 16 ♘g5± Keres.
12 ♘xc3 0-0!
White's attack can hardly compensate the lost pawn, Neumann - Spala, corr. 1958.

B312
10 ♘c3 0-0
11 ♗e3
11 ♗d2 transposes into line B1, note b to 10 0-0-0 in Chapter 4.
11 ... ♗e6

a) **11 ... ♕f6??** 12 ♘d5 ♕d8 13 ♗c5 ♖e8 14 ♘xc7±± F Olafsson - Lopez Garcia, Berg en Dal 1960.

b) **11 ... ♖e8(!)** 12 ♖ad1 ♘e5! 13 ♗b5 ♗d7 14 ♗d4 ♘xf3+ 15 ♕xf3 ♗xd4= Geller - Smyslov, Biel 1976.

12 ♗c5
Or:

a) **12 a4** a5 (⌐ 12 ... a6) 13 ♗c5 ♕f6!? 14 ♕xf6 ♗xf6 15 ♘b5! ♖fc8 16 ♗xd6! cd 17 ♘xd6 ♖c7 18 ♗c4 ♖d8 19

♘b5 ♖cd7 20 c3 ♘e5 21 ♘fd4 ♗c4 22 ♖fe1 ♘d3 23 ♗xd3 ♗xd3 ½-½ Darga - Donner, Amsterdam 1969. The bishop pair and the occupied d-file will equalize.

b) **12 ♖ad1** and now:

b1) **12 ... ♕c8** 13 ♘g5 ♗f5 14 ♘ge4 ♗e5 15 ♘xd6 ♗xf4= Ivkov - Beni, Tel Aviv (ol) 1964.

b2) **12 ... ♕f6** 13 ♕xf6 (13 ♕g3 or 13 ♕a4 must be met by 13 ... ♘e5) 13 ... ♗xf6 14 ♘g5 ♘b4! 15 ♘xe6 fe 16 ♗c5 ♘xd3 17 ♖xd3 ♖fd8 18 ♖e1 b6 19 ♗d4 with an even ending in Short - Murey, Hastings 1982/3.

c) **12 ♖fe1 ♖e8** 13 ♖ad1 Simagin - Vesovich, corr. 1966, 13 ... ♕f6!

d) **12 ♘g5!?** ♖e8 13 ♖ad1 ♕f6 14 ♕xf6 ♗xf6 15 ♘xe6 fe 16 ♘b5, Larsen - Trifunovic, Dortmund 1961, 16 ... ♖ac8±.

12 ...   ♖e8

Inferior are:

a) **12 ... ♕f6?** 13 ♕xf6 ♗xf6 14 ♘b5!± Unzicker - Jimenez, Leipzig (ol) 1960. Now 14 ... ♖fc8 is the best, compare Darga - Donner, var. a at White's 12th.

b) **12 ... b6?** 13 ♗a3 ♘e7 14 ♖ad1 ♗xc3 15 bc ♘d5 16 ♕h6 ♕f6 17 ♘g5 ♕g7 18 ♕xg7+ ♔xg7 19 ♘e4± Yanofsky - German, Stockholm 1962.

13   ♖ad1   ♕f6!
14   ♗xd6   cd
15   ♕xd6   ♖ed8

15 ... ♗f8 16 ♕g3 ♗b4 is also good.

16   ♕g3   ♕e7

17 ♘g5 ♗xc3! 18 bc ♗xa2= Hermlin - Maslov, USSR 1970.

B313

10   ♖e1+   ♗e6
11   ♘c3

Or:

a) **11 ♕a4?!** 0-0 12 ♗g5 ♕d7 13 ♘c3 h6 14 ♗f4 a6!∓ Milic - Trifunovic, Yugoslav Ch. 1958.

b) **11 ♘g5?!** 0-0! 12 ♘xe6 fe 13 ♕g4 (13 ♕g3? ♗d4 14 ♖f1 ♘e4!∓ Kurtesch - B Toth, Budapest 1969. The knight cannot be taken because of ... ♗xf2+), when:

b1) **13 ... ♕f6** 14 ♕xe6+ (14 ♕g3 ♘b4!∓ Hübner - Segal, Dresden 1969) 14 ... ♕xe6 15 ♖xe6 ♗d4 16 ♖e2 ♖xf2!∓.

b2) **13 ... ♗d4!** 14 ♕xe6+ ♔h8 15 ♖e2 ♕h4 16 g3 ♕h5∓∓ Analysis by Bonch-Osmolovsky.

11   ...   0-0
12   ♗e3

Less powerful is 12 ♗d2.

12 ... ♖e8

12 ... ♕f6 13 ♕a4 Nezhmetdinov-Kakabadze, USSR 1955, 13 ... h6=.

13 ♖ad1 ♕f6!=

13 ... ♕c8? 14 ♗c5± Simagin - Vesovich, corr. 1963-66.

B32

9 ♘c3 ♗g7

a) **9 ... ♗e6?** is too early here, for 10 ♘d4 ♗g7 11 ♘xe6 fe Buljovcic - Ilievsky, Belgrade 1965, 12 ♘e4± (Keres).

b) **9 ... ♕e7+** 10 ♗e3 ♗g7 has been mentioned, by transposition, in line A2.

10 ♗e3

Or:

a) **10 h4?** ♗e6 (also 10 ... 0-0, 10 ... h6) 11 h5 ♕e7 12 ♗e3 0-0-0 13 0-0-0? ♗xc3! 14 bc ♘b5!∓∓ Klavin - Maslov, USSR 1957.

b) **10 ♗d2** ♕e7+! Yudovich - Gusakov, Perm 1960.

c) **10 0-0** 0-0 11 ♗e3 ♖e8 12 ♖ad1 ♘e5 13 ♗b5 ♗d7 14 ♗d4 ♘xf3+ 15 ♕xf3 ♗xd4− Geller - Smyslov, Biel (izt) 1976.

10 ... ♗e6

11 0-0-0

Inferior are:

a) **11 0-0** ♕f6 12 ♖ad1 0-0 13 ♕a4 ♘e5= Unzicker -

Alexander, Hastings 1954/55.

b) **11 h4** and now:

b1) **11 ... ♘f5!?** 12 ♗c5 ♗xc3+ 13 bc ♕d5 14 ♗a3 0-0-0 15 0-0 ♘d6 16 ♖fe1 h6∞ Sax - Solomon, Australia 1987.

b2) **11 ... h6** or **11 ... ♕e7** haven't been tried yet.

11 ... ♕f6

Or 11 ... 0-0 12 ♗c5! ♖e8 (12 ... ♕f6? 13 ♕xf6 ♗xf6 14 ♘b5±± Matanovic - Trifunovic, Yugoslav Ch. 1958) 13 ♗b5! (13 ♘b5 a6!=) 13 ... a6 14 ♗xc6 bc 15 ♘e4± Zuckermann - Balshan, Dresden 1969.

12 ♘g5

Or:

a) **12 ♕xf6** ♗xf6 when:

a1) **13 ♘e4** ♗g7 14 ♘fg5! 0-0 (14 ... ♗xa2 15 ♘xd6+ cd 16 ♗b5±) 15 ♘xe6 fe 16 ♘g5 ♖fe8 17 ♖he1± Parma - Trifunovic, Bled 1961.

a2) **13 ♘b5** ♘xb5 14 ♗xb5 0-0 15 ♗xc6 bc 16 ♗d4 ♗e7 with compensation for the isolated pawns.

a3) **13 ♘g5** ♗xc3! 14 ♘xe6 ♗xb2+ 15 ♔xb2 fe=.

b) **12 ♕a4** h6 13 ♘d4 (13 ♗d4 ♕f4+!) 13 ... 0-0! 14 ♘xc6 (14 ♘xe6 fe! △ b7 - b5) 14 ... bc 15 ♕xc6 ♗xa2! with attacking chances.

12   ...   ♛xf4

12 ... 0-0-0 13 ♛xf6 ♗xf6 14 ♘xe6±.

13   ♗xf4   ♗xc3

13 ... 0-0-0 14 ♘xe6 fe 15 ♖he1 ♗xc3 transposes to the main line.

14   bc

14 ♘xe6 ♗xb2+ 15 ♔xb2 fe 16 ♖he1 ♔d7 △ ... ♖hf8 and ... ♖ae8 with a later ...

e5 and Black has no worries.

14   ...   0-0-0

14 ... ♗xa2? 15 ♖he1+ ♔f8 (15 ... ♗e6 16 ♘xe6 fe 17 ♗xd6! cd 18 ♖xe6+ ♔d7 19 ♗c4±) 16 c4! ♘xc4 17 ♘e4 ♘4e5 18 ♘c3! ♘xd3+ 19 ♖xd3 ♗e6 20 ♗h6+ then 21 ♘d5± Keres.

15   ♘xe6   fe

16 ♖he1± Polugayevsky.

4) 3 d4 ed: 7 ♘c3

4	e5	♘e4
5	♕xd4	d5
6	ed	♘xd6
7	♘c3	

This knight move is more flexible than developing the bishop which has various options while c3 is the correct square for the knight.

| 7 | ... | ♘c6 (7) |

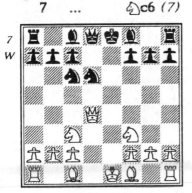

If 7 ... ♗f5 White gains the advantage after both:

a) **8 ♕e5+** ♕e7 9 ♘d5 ♕xe5+ 10 ♘xe5 f6 11 ♘f3 (11 ♘xc7+? ♔d8 12 ♘xa8 fe∓) 11 ... ♕d7 12 ♗f4 ♘c6 13 0-0-0

Bronstein – Borisenko, Moscow 1961.

b) **8 ♗g5** f6 (8 ... ♘c6 9 ♕e3+ ♗e7 10 ♘d5 ♗e6 11 0-0-0±) 9 ♗f4 ♘c6 10 ♕a4 ♗e7 11 0-0-0 0-0 12 ♘d5± Stein – Zakharov, USSR 1960.

| 8 | ♕f4 |

Or:

a) **8 ♕a4** when:

a1) **8 ... ♗f5?!** 9 ♗b5! ♕e7+ 10 ♗e3 ♘xb5 11 ♕xb5! ♕b4 12 0-0-0± threatening ♕xf5 and ♘d5.

a2) **8 ... ♗e7** 9 ♗d2 (9 ♗f4 ♗f6) 9 ... 0-0 10 0-0-0 ♗e6 11 ♗d3 a5 12 a3 ♘b4!! 13 ab ab 14 ♕xb4 ♖a1+ 15 ♘b1 ♗a2 16 c3 ♘c4! 17 ♗g5! ♕xd3 18 ♖xd3 ♗xb1 19 ♕xc4 ♗xd3+ ∓ Simagin – Grushevsky, USSR 1958.

b) **8 ♗b5** ♕e7+ 9 ♕e3 ♗d7 10 0-0 ♕xe3 11 ♗xe3, Suer – Estrada, Varna (ol) 1962, 11 ... 0-0-0=.

Now Black has three main choices:

A: 8 ... g6
B: 8 ... ♗e6
C: 8 ... ♗f5

Less impressive are:

a) **8 ... h6** 9 ♗d3 g5 10 ♕a4± Polugayevsky.

b) **8 ... ♕e7+** 9 ♗e3 ♗e6 10 0-0-0±.

c) **8 ... ♕d7** 9 ♗d3 ♕g4 Janosevic – Radulov, Vrsac 1971, 10 ♘d5 ♕e6+ 11 ♕e3±.

d) **8 ... ♗e7** 9 ♘d5 ± Polugayevsky. 9 ♗b5± Romanishin. 9 ♗d3 transposes to line B2 Chapter 3 or 9 ♗e3 ♗e6 10 0-0-0 0-0 11 ♘g5 (11 h4) 11 ... ♘xg5 12 ♕xg5 ♕e7 Sveshnikov – Oll, USSR 1987, and now 13 ♕xe7 ♘xe7 14 ♗c5±.

e) **8 ... ♘f5** 9 ♗b5! ♗d6 10 ♕e4+ ♕e7 and now:

e1) **11 ♗xc6+** bc 12 0-0 0-0! 13 ♕xc6 ♖b8 △ ... ♗b7∞.

e2) **11 ♗d2** ♗d7 12 0-0-0 ♕xe4 13 ♘xe4 ♗e7 14 ♖he1 0-0-0! 15 ♗c4!?± Azmaiparashvili.

e3) **11 ♗g5** (11 g4!?) 11 ... f6! (11 ... ♕xe4+ 12 ♘xe4 ♗e7 13 ♗xc6+ bc 14 ♗xe7±) 12 ♗d2 ♗d7 13 0-0-0 ♕xe4! (13 ... 0-0-0? 14 ♗xc6±; 13 ... 0-0?! 14 ♕xe7 ♘fxe7 15 ♘e4±) 14 ♘xe4 ♗e7 15 g4!? a6? (⌐ 15 ... ♘d6! 16 ♘xd6+ ♗xd6 17 ♖he1+ ♔f8! 18 g5

♗g4=; 17 ♖de1+ ♔f8 [17 ... ♘e7!? Makarichev] 18 ♖hg1 ♖e8= Azmaiparashvili) Kasparov – Karpov (m/10) New York 1990; 16 ♗xc6! ♗xc6 17 ♖he1 ♗xe4 18 ♖xe4 ♘d6 19 ♖e2 △ ♘d4 – e6± Azmaiparashvili.

A

    8   ...   g6 *(8)*

Now White has:

A1: 9 ♘d4
A2: 9 ♗b5
A3: 9 ♗e3
A4: 9 ♗d2

For 9 ♗d3 see line B32 Chapter 3.

A1

    9   ♘d4   ♗g7
Alternatives after Mikenas' 9 ... ♗d7:

a) **10 ♘xc6** ♗xc6 11 ♕d4 ♖g8 12 ♘d5 ♗g7 13 ♕e3+

♔f8!∞.

b) **10 ♘db5** a6 11 ♘xd6+ ♗xd6 12 ♕e4+ ♗e6 (12 ... ♕e7 13 ♗g5!) 13 ♗h6 ♕f6! 14 ♕e3 ♗e5 15 ♘e4 ♕e7 16 0-0-0 ♖d8! (△ ... ♗xb2+, ♗d4 or ♗xa2) 17 ♖xd8+ ♔xd8 18 ♘c5 ♔c8= Perenyi – Halasz, Budapest 1984.

c) We suggest **10 ♗b5!±**.

10 ♘xc6 bc

11 ♗e2 0-0 12 0-0 ♗f5 13 ♕a4 ♖b8! 14 ♗f3! ♘b5?! 15 ♘e2± Halifman – Zysk, Groningen 1985/6. Better is 14 ... ♖b6 △ 15 ♗xc6 ♗xc2= Halifman.

A2

9 ♗b5 (Bronstein)
9 ... ♗g7(!)

Inferior are:

a) **9 ... ♘xb5?** 10 ♘xb5 ♗d6 11 ♘xd6+ (11 ♕a4 ♕d7 12 ♗f4 ♗xf4 13 ♕xf4 0-0= Boleslavsky – Maslov, Moscow 1963) 11 ... ♕xd6 12 ♕xd6 cd 13 ♗f4±.

b) **9 ... ♗d7?** 10 ♗xc6 ♗xc6 11 0-0 ♗g7 12 ♖e1+ ♔f8 13 ♘d4 ♕f6 14 ♘xc6 ♕xf4 15 ♗xf4 bc 15 ♗e5±.

10 ♗xc6+ bc
11 0-0 0-0
12 ♗e3 ♖b8!

Feeble is 12 ... a5?! 13 ♗d4! ♖e8 14 ♗xg7 ♔xg7 15 ♖fe1± Bronstein – Maslov, Mos-

cow 1959.

13 ♖ab1 a5
14 a3

Or:

a) **14 ♗d4** ♖b4! 15 a3 ♖c4∓.

b) **14 ♗c5** ♖e8 15 ♘d4 ♗e5 16 ♕f3 ♕h4 17 g3 ♕h3 18 ♖fe1 ♗b7 19 ♘ce2 (19 ♘b3 ♘c4) 19 ... ♘e4! 20 ♘f4 (20 ♕xe4 ♗d6!) 20 ... ♗xf4 21 ♖xe4 ♖xe4 22 ♕xe4 ♗d6 23 ♘b3 ♕h5∓ Smilov – Grewlund, corr. 1977.

14 ... ♖e8

15 ♗a7 (⌐ 15 ♖fd1) 15 ... ♖b7 16 ♗c5 ♗f5 17 ♕a4 ♘e4!∓ Romanishin – Smyslov, USSR Ch. 1977.

A3

9 ♗e3 ♗g7
10 0-0-0

11 ♗d3 transposes to line B32 Chapter 3.

10 ... 0-0

If 10 ... ♗e6?!:

a) **11 h4** h6 (⌐ 11 ... h5) 12 ♘d4 ♘e5 13 ♕f3 ♘xd4 14 ♗xd4 ♗xd4 15 ♖xd4 ♕e7 16 ♘e4± Kapengut – Anikayev, Moscow 1969.

b) **11 ♗b5** ♕f6 (11 ... 0-0 12 ♗xc6 bc 13 ♘d4±) 12 ♗xc6 bc 13 ♕xf6 ♗xf6 14 ♘d4± Bertok – Rabar, Yugoslav Ch. 1962.

c) **11 ♘b5** 0-0 12 a3 a6 (⌐

12 ...   ♖e8) 13 ♘xc7± (13 ♘bd4 is also good) Alexandria – Rubtsova, USSR 1969.

11	h4	h6
12	♘b5	

Or 12 ♗c4 ♗f5 13 ♗b3 ♖e8 14 ♘d4 ♘xd4 15 ♗xd4 ♗e6 16 ♖he1 g5!= Gligoric – German, Stockholm 1962.

12	...	♗e6
13	a3	♖e8!

14 ♘xc7 ♕xc7 15 ♕xd6 ♕a5 16 ♕c5 ♕xc5 17 ♗xc5 ♗g4 with some compensation for the sacrificed pawn.

A4

9	♗d2

Black has two reasonable defences:

A41: 9 ... ♗g7
A42: 9 ... ♕e7+

A41

9	...	♗g7
10	0-0-0	0-0(?)

Better is 10 ... ♗e6 transposing to line B1.

11	h4!

11 ♗d3 is feeble and can be met by 11 ... ♗f5 or 11 ... ♗e6=.

11	...	h6!

The only correct move. Others:

a) 11 ... ♕f6? 12 ♕xf6 ♗xf6 13 ♘d5±.

b) 11 ... ♖e8 12 h5 ♗f5 13 g4 ♗e4 14 hg fg 15 ♘g5! ♗xh1 16 ♗c4+ ♔h8 17 ♖xh1 h6 18 ♘b5 ♖f8 19 ♖xh6+ ♗xh6 20 ♗c3+ 1-0 Kucera – Binder, Czechoslovakia 1966.

c) 11 ... h5 12 ♘d5 ♗e6 13 ♗c3 ♗xd5 14 ♖xd5 ♖e8 15 ♗d3 ♗xc3 16 bc ♕e7 (16 ... ♖e6) 17 g4 hg 18 h5! ♘e4 19 hg! 1-0 Klovan – Kärner, Riga 1965.

d) 11 ... ♗e6? too late! 12 h5 when:

d1) 12 ... ♕f6 13 ♕xf6 (13 ♕h2 and 13 ♘g5 are also good here) 13 ... ♗xf6 14 ♘g5 ♖fe8 15 hg hg 16 ♘xe6, Zakharov – Holmov, USSR 1958, 16 ... fe±.

d2) 12 ... ♖e8 13 ♕h2 ♗f5 14 hg hg 15 ♗g5 ♕d7 16 ♕h7+ ♔h8 17 ♘d5 f6 18 ♕h8+! ♗xh8 19 ♖xh8+ ♔f7 20 ♖h7+ 1-0 Zhilin – Gusakov, Perm 1960.

12	♗d3

Also good is 12 ♘d5 ♗e6 13 ♗c3 ♗xd5 14 ♖xd5 ♗xc3 15 bc ♔g7 16 h5 ♖h8 17 hg± Gufeld – Rabar, Moscow 1961.

12	...	♗e6
13	♖he1	

Or 13 ♔b1?! a5 14 a3 ♖b8 15 ♘b5? ♘xb5 16 ♗xb5 ♕d5 17 c4 ♕d3+ 18 ♔a2 ♕c2 19

♗c1 ♘b4+ 0-1 Kinnmark - Ek, Sweden 1963.

13 ... ♖e8

Slightly better than 13 ... a5 14 a3 ♖b8 15 ♘e4 ♗f5 16 ♗c3± Zakharov - Furman, Kiev 1957.

14 a3 ♕f6

Better is 14 ... a6!

15 ♕xf6 ♗xf6

16 ♗xh6 ♗xc3 17 bc ♗g4 18 ♗f4 ♔g7 Boleslavsky - Trifunovic, Zagreb 1958, 19 c4± (Keres).

A42

9 ... ♕e7+!
10 ♗e2 ♗e6
11 0-0

Other tries:

a) 11 ♘g5? ♗h6 12 0-0-0 f6 13 ♘xe6 ♗xf4 ∓ Geller - Trifunovic, Bled 1961.

b) 11 0-0-0 ♗g7 12 h4 (on 12 ♖he1! not 12 ... ♕f6? 13 ♘g5! Vujic - Nedeljkovic, corr. 1978 but 12 ... 0-0) 12 ... h6 13 ♖he1 ♕f6 14 ♗d3 (14 ♕a4? 0-0 15 g4 b5) 14 ... ♕xf4 15 ♗xf4 0-0-0= Keres - Trifunovic, Bled 1961.

c) 11 ♘d4 ♗h6! and now:

c1) 12 ♕xh6? ♘xd4 when:

c11) 13 ♕g7? ♘xc2+ 14 ♔d1 0-0-0 15 ♔xc2 ♘f5∓∓ Yudovich.

c12) 13 0-0-0 0-0-0 14 ♖he1 ♘xe2+ 15 ♖xe2 ♘f5∓.

c2) 12 ♘xc6 ½-½ Geller - Smyslov, Leningrad 1971.

11 ... ♗g7

12 ♖ae1 0-0-0 13 ♕a4 ♔b8 14 ♗d3 ♘c8= Geller - Smyslov, Lvov 1978.

B

8 ... ♗e6 (9)

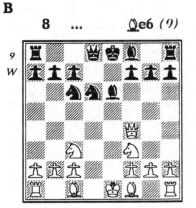

This is aimed to take the sting out of ♗b5.

Now White has:

B1: 9 ♗d2
B2: 9 ♗e3

Or:

a) 9 ♗d3! is best here transposing to line B1 Chapter 3.

b) 9 ♗b5 ♘xb5 (9 ... ♘d7? 10 0-0±) 10 ♘xb5 ♗d6 11 ♘xd6+ ♕xd6 12 ♕xd6=.

B1

9 ♗d2 g6

9 ... ♗e7 10 0-0-0 0-0 is

also playable, i.e. after 11 ♗d3 White's attack on the kingside is not that powerful, and there is no pressure on the d–file.

10   0-0-0

Or:

a) **10 ♘d4?!** ♘xd4 11 ♕xd4 ♘c4! and Black equalizes at least.

b) **10 ♗d3** when the usually strong ... ♕e7+ is obviously unavailable ... ♗e6; after 10 ... ♗g7 11 0-0 (If White wants to castle long then he can usually do without ♗d3, see column) 11 ... 0-0 (11 ... ♕f6 12 ♕a4!) 12 ♕a4 ♘e5 (△ 12 ... a6) 13 ♘xe5 ♗xe5= Platonov – Vistanetsky, USSR 1964.

10   ...   ♗g7

White has explored many possibilities trying to exploit his initiative, both in the centre and on the kingside.

B11: 11 ♘b5
B12: 11 ♘g5
B13: 11 ♗d3
B14: 11 h4

Or:

a) **11 ♗b5** is less successful: 11 ... 0-0 12 ♗xc6 bc 13 ♘d4 ♗d5 (13 ... ♗d7 14 ♘b3 with complications) 14 ♘xd5 cd 15 ♗b4 ♖e8!=.

b) If **11 ♖e1** h6! keeps the balance.

B11

11   ♘b5 (Bronstein)
11   ...   a6!

Other ideas are less precise:

a) **11 ... ♘xb5** 12 ♗xb5 ♕d6 13 ♕a4±.

b) **11 ... ♕e7** 12 ♗c3 ♗xc3 13 ♘xc3 0-0-0 and now:

b1) **14 a3** ♗f5= Sakharov – Maslov, Vilnius 1959.

b2) **14 ♗d3** f6! 15 ♖he1 ♕f7=.

12   ♗c3

12 ♘xd6+ cd∓.

12   ...   ab!

12 ... ♗xc3 13 ♘xc3 ♕e7 14 ♗d3 0-0-0 15 ♖he1 ♕f8 16 ♘g5!± Krogius – Trifunovic, Varna 1960.

13   ♗xg7   ♖xa2!
14   ♖xd6!   cd
15   ♗xh8

15 ♔b1 ♕a5 16 b3 ♘b4! △ ... ♖a1+ with mate (16 ... ♖g8 17 ♗f6∞ Schwarz) 17 ♗xb5+ ♕xb5 18 ♗xh8 ♘xc2∓∓.

15   ...   ♕a5

White must look urgently for a perpetual check, e.g. by 16 b3 ♘b4 17 ♕xd6! (17 ♗b2 ♖xb2!) 17 ... ♖xc2+ 18 ♔d1 ♗xb3 19 ♕e5+! ♔f8 (the only move) 20 ♕g7+.

B12

11 ♘g5

This leads to complications and may meet with more loss than benefit.

11 ... 0-0!

11 ... ♕f6 12 ♕xf6 ♗xf6 13 ♘xe6 fe 14 ♖e1± Klovan - Chesnauskas, Voroniez 1969.

12 h4

12 ♗d3 transposes into line B13. See also Chapter 3.

12 ... h6
13 ♘ge4

13 ♘xe6?! fe 14 ♕g4 ♕f6 15 ♗d3 ♘e5 16 ♕h3 b5∓ Pintsuk - Chesnauskas, USSR 1969.

13 ... ♕e7!

13 ... ♘xe4?! 14 ♘xe4 ♕e7 15 ♗c3 ♗f5=.

14 ♘xd6?! cd

15 ♗c4 ♖ac8 16 ♗b3 is Nikolayevsky - Vistanetsky, USSR 1959, 16 ... ♘d4∓. 14 ♖e1 is slightly better.

B13

11 ♗d3   0-0

The queen moves are inferior:

a) 11 ... ♕d7? 12 ♘a4±.

b) 11 ... ♕f6?! 12 ♕xf6 (12 ♕a4 h6) 12 ... ♗xf6 13 ♘g5 0-0-0(!) (13 ... ♘b4) 14

♘xe6 fe 15 ♖he1 ♖he8 16 ♘e4 ♘xe4 17 ♖xe4± Tal - Rossetto, Amsterdam 1964.

12 h4

Feeble is 12 ♘e4 ♘xe4 13 ♗xe4 ♗xa2 - unclear.

12   ...   ♕f6

For 12 ... h6 see lines A41 and B24, by transposition.

If 12 ... b5? 13 h5 b4 14 ♘e4 ♗c4 (14 ... ♘c4 15 ♗xc4 ♗xc4 16 ♗c3! ♕e7 17 ♗f6±) 15 hg+ Heintze - Kovalevsky, Germany 1985.

13   ♕h2

Better than either:

a) 13 ♕g3? ♘b4 14 ♗g5 ♘xa2+ 15 ♔d2 ♘xc3!∓∓.

b) 13 ♕xf6 ♗xf6 14 ♘g5 ♘b4=.

13   ...   ♘e5

Not 13 ... h6?? 14 ♗g5!

14   ♗g5

Or 14 ♘xe5 ♕xe5 15 ♕xe5 (15 ♗f4 ♕a5 16 h5 g5 or 15 f4 ♕h5!) 15 ... ♗xe5 16 h5 ♖fe8= Boleslavsky - Alatortsev, Moscow 1945.

14   ...   ♘xf3
15   gf

15 ♗xf6 ♘xh2 16 ♗xg7=.

15   ...   ♕xf3
16   h5

The preparation of 16 ♖dg1 can also be considered.

16   ...   ♕xh5

17 ♕xh5 gh 18 ♖xh5 f5! 19

♖g1 ♖f7 (19 ... ♗f7 △ ... ♗g6
— Schwarz) 20 ♘e2 Medina
- Miagmasuren, Skopje (ol)
1972, 20 ... ♗c4!=.

B14

11 h4   h6(!)

Better than:

a) 11 ... 0-0? see var. d in
line A41 by transposition.

b) 11 ... ♕f6 when:

b1) 12 ♕a4 gains a pawn
e.g. 12 ... h6 13 ♗a6 0-0 14
♗xb7 ♘xb7 15 ♕xc6 ♘a5!
but the c4 square is weak,
Mnatsakanian - Maslov,
Moscow 1963.

b2) 12 ♘g5 ♕xf4 13 ♗xf4
♗xc3 14 ♘xe6 ♗xb2+ 15
♔xb2 fe=.

b3) 12 ♕xf6 ♗xf6 13 ♘g5
0-0 (13 ... ♗c4? 14 ♘ce4!) 14
♘xe6 (14 h5) 14 ... fe 15 h5±
Magrini - Toth, Italy 1972.

12 ♗d3

For 12 ♘b5 compare line
B21.

12 ...   0-0

12 ... ♕f6?! 13 ♕xf6 ♗xf6
14 ♖he1 ♔d7 15 ♘e4±.

The column transposes
to A41.

13 ♖he1   ♖e8

With mutual chances.

B2

9 ♗e3

Now Black's best way is
to benefit from the pecul-
iarity of the position that
presents itself, i.e. ♘c3 has
been played instead of ♗d3.

9 ...   ♘f5!
10 ♘b5

Or:

a) 10 ♖d1 ♗d6 11 ♕e4
♘xe3 12 ♕xe3 ♕f6 13 ♗d3=
Shianovsky - Vistanetsky,
Vilnius 1958.

b) 10 ♗d3 ♗d6 11 ♘e4
♘xe3 12 ♕xe3 ♕f6= Simagin
- Vistanetsky, Moscow 1961.

10 ...   ♗b4+

10 ... ♗d6 can also equalize.

11 ♗d2

If 11 c3 ♗a5=.

11 ...   ♗xd2+
12 ♘xd2   0-0

12 ... ♘d6 equalizes without complications.

13 0-0-0

If 13 ♘xc7? ♘fd4! and
now:

a) 14 ♗d3 ♘b4!

b) 14 ♘xe6 ♘xc2+! 15 ♔d1
fe∓.

c) 14 0-0-0 ♖c8 and Black
has excellent chances.

13 ...   ♖c8

14 ♘f3 ♕e7 15 ♗d3 a6 16
♘c3 ♕b4= Fuderer - Bron-
stein, Kiev 1959.

C

8 ...   ♗f5

Holmov and Bronstein have played an important part in modernizing this variation.

9 ♗b5! *(10)*

Now Black has a choice:

C1: 9 ... ♗d7
C2: 9 ... ♗e7
C3: 9 ... ♕e7+

Much inferior are:

a) **9 ... ♘xb5?** 10 ♘xb5 and one of the double threats (♕xf5 and ♘xc7+) canot be prevented.

10...♕e7+ and not 11 ♗e3?! when ♕b4+ transposes into line C32 but 11 ♔f1!±± .

b) **9 ... ♗xc2?** 10 ♘e5 (also good is 10 ♗xc6+ bc 11 ♘d4±) Geller – Nahlik, Szczawno Zdroj 1957, 10 ... ♕e7 11 ♗xc6+ bc 12 ♗e3± .

C1

9 ... ♗d7(?)

10 ♗e3 a6
Better is 10 ... ♗e7.
11 ♗xc6 ♗xc6
12 ♘e5!
Or 12 0-0-0 Capelan – Sagadin, Detmold 1967, 12 ... ♗e7 13 ♘e5 0-0± .
12 ... ♗xg2
13 ♖g1 ♗h3
14 0-0-0 ♗e6
15 ♘e4 f6?
Better is 15 ... ♕e7.
16 ♗c5!! ♗g8
16 ... fe 17 ♕xe5 ♕d7 18 ♗xd6±± .
17 ♖ge1 ♗e7
18 ♘c6! bc 19 ♘xd6+ cd 20 ♗xd6±± Honfi – Kardos, Budapest 1949.

C2

9 ... ♗e7
10 ♘d4
Or:
a) **10 ♗e3** 0-0 11 0-0-0 ♕c8 12 ♗a4 ♗e6, Matanovic – Holmov, Sochi 1968, 13 ♘d5!±
b) **10 ♗xc6+** bc 11 ♘c5! 0-0 (11 ... ♗xc2 12 ♗e3 0-0 13 ♘xc6 ♕e8 is only transposition) 12 ♘xc6 ♕e8 13 ♘xe7+ ♕xe7+ 14 ♗e3 ♗xc2 15 ♖c1 ♗d3 16 ♘d5 ♕d8 17 ♕d4 ♗a6! 18 ♘xc7 ♖b8 19 ♖c6 (19 ♕xa7 ♗c4∞) 19 ... ♗b7 20 ♖xd6 ♕xc7= Sax – Yusupov, Rotterdam 1988

We suggest 15 0-0, e.g. 15 ... ♗g6 16 ♘d5 ♕d7 17 ♖fd1 (△ ♘xc7) 17 ... ♖fd8 18 ♖ac1 winning a pawn (18 ... c6 19 ♖xc6!).

> **10   ...   ♗d7**
> **11   ♗xc6   ♗xc6**

Or 11 ... bc 12 ♕f3!± Blau - Kinzel, Adelboden 1969.

> **12   ♘xc6   bc**
> **13   ♕a4!**

13 0-0 0-0 14 ♗e3 ♕b8?! (14 ... ♖b8) 15 ♗d4± Ghizdavu - Cunnigham, USA 1974.

> **13   ...   ♕d7**

14 0-0 0-0 15 ♘d5± was Gligoric - Bajec, Sarajevo 1951.

C3

> **9   ...   ♕e7+!** *(11)*

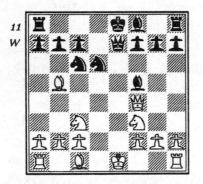

11
W

White's choice is narrowed:

C31: 10 ♔f1
C32: 10 ♗e3

C31

> **10   ♔f1 (Tal)**
> **10   ...   ♗e4**

The only serious attempt to solve most of Black's problems. If 10 ... ♗xc2? 11 ♘d5 ♕d8 12 ♘e5± or 11 ♗d2±.

Now White has:

C311: 11 ♗xc6+
C312: 11 ♗d2
C313: 11 ♗a4

11 ♘xe4 is met by 11 ... ♘xb5

C311

> **11   ♗xc6+   ♗xc6**
> **12   ♘e5   0-0-0**

12 ... ♗d7? 13 ♘d5±.

12 ... ♗b5+? 13 ♘xb5 ♘xb5 and 14 ♗d2 or 14 ♗e3±.

> **13   ♘xc6   bc**
> **14   ♕a4**

14 ♗e3 ♕e6! with counterplay, e.g. 15 ♗xa7 ♘c4 16 ♗e3 ♗b4.

> **14   ...   ♘b5!**
> **15   ♗e3   ♕b4**
> **16   ♕a6+**

Or 16 ♕xb4 ♗xb4 and now both

a) 17 ♘xb5 cb 18 ♗xa7 ♖d2 and

b) 17 ♘a4 ♗d2 18 ♗c5 ♗g5 give Black adequate counterplay.

16   ...   ♔b8

16 ... ♔d7? 17 ♘xb5 ♕xb5
18 ♕xb5 cb 19 ♗xa7 c5 20
♖d1+ ♔c8 21 ♖xd8+ ♔xd8 22
♗b8±.

17   ♕xc6

Or:

a) 17 a3 ♕c4+ 18 ♔g1 ♗c5
19 ♕xc6 ♘d4 with active
play for Black.

b) 17 ♘xb5 ♕xb5+ 18
♕xb5+ cb 19 a4 and White's
advantage can hardly be
realized, e.g. 19 ... ba 20
♔e2 a3!

17   ...   ♘d4
18   ♗xd4   ♕xd4
19   g3

19 ♖d1 (19 ♘b5 ♕c5!−) 19
... ♕xd1+ 20 ♘xd1 ♖xd1+ 21
♔e2 ♖xh1 22 ♕e8+ ♔b7 23
♕b5+ ♔c8 24 ♕e8+ ♔b7 ½-½
Suetin - Holmov, Moscow
1964.

19   ...   ♗c5

and Black can generate
enough counterplay after
20 ♕f3 ♕c4+ 21 ♔g2 ♖d2.

C312

11   ♗d3   ♘xb5
12   ♘xb5   0-0-0
13   ♖e1   f5
14   ♘c3

14 ♘g5 ♕d7 15 ♘e6 g5! 16
♘xg5 ♗h6∓ (Szabo).

14   ...   ♕c5
15   ♘xe4   fe

16   ♕xe4   ♕b5+!

Not 16 ... ♗d6? 17 ♗c3
♖hg8 18 h4 h6 19 h5 ♕b6 20
♖h4! ♕a6+ 21 ♕c4± Szabo
- Strand, Budapest v Stockholm, tele-game 1965.

17   ♔g1

Or 17 c4 ♕xb2 18 ♗g5
♗b4! 19 ♖b1 ♕xa2 20 ♗xd8
♖xd8 (threatens ... ♗c5)
and Black had clear com-
pensation for the sacrificed
material in Mukhin - Borisenko, Tashkent 1968.

17   ...   ♕xb2

18 ♗g5 ♖d7 19 ♕e8+ ♘d8
20 ♘e5 ♖d4 21 ♗xd8 ♖xd8
22 ♕e6+ ♔b8 23 ♘f7 ♗b4!
with excellent counterplay
- Szabo. However, we re-
commend 20 h4 with good
coordination of the white
pieces, e.g. 20 ... h6 21 ♘e5
♖d4 22 ♗xd8 ♖xd8 23 ♕e6+
♔b8 24 ♖h3 (△ ♘c6+ and
♖b3)±.

C313

11   ♗a4   0-0-0
12   ♗e3   ♗xf3

More accurate than 12 ...
f6? when:

a) 13 h4 ♗xf3 14 gf! ♘e5
15 ♗b3 ♔b8, Suetin - Borisenko, Riga 1968, 16 ♕a4!? a6
17 ♖e1± (Suetin).

b) 13 ♘xe4 ♕xe4 14 ♖d1±
(Keres).

13   ♕xf3

Or 13 gf ♘e5 14 ♖e1 ♕e6! △ ... ♕h3+ or ... ♕c4+.

13   ...   ♘e5

With balanced chances.

C32

10	**♗e3**	**♘xb5**
11	**♘xb5**	**♕b4+**
12	**♕xb4**	**♗xb4+**
13	**c3** *(12)*	

Black now faces a choice:

C321: 13 ... ♗a5
C322: 13 ... ♗d6

C321

13	**...**	**♗a5**
14	**b4**	**♗d3!**
15	**a4**	**a6**
16	**♘bd4(!)**	

Euwe's suggestion; in-adequate are:

a) **16 0-0-0** allowing ♗e2, when:

a1) **17 ♖d2 ♗xf3**, Matan-ovic - Antunac, Zagreb 1964,

18 gf ab 19 ♘c5 ♘e5! 20 ♖e1 f6 21 f4 ♗b6 22 fe!⩱.

a2) **17 ♖de1 ♗xf3 18 ♗c5+ ♔d7 19 gf ♖ae8** △ ... ♗xb4= Kotkov - Yefimov, USSR 1958.

a3) **17 ba ab 18 ♖de1 ♗xf3 19 ab ♘d5 20 bc ♗xc6 21 ♗g5+ ♔f8 22 ♗e7+ ♔g8 23 ♗b4 b6=** Stein - Holmov, Moscow 1964.

b) **16 ♘a3** (Mikenas) 16 ... ♗b6 17 ♗xb6 cb 18 0-0-0 0-0-0 and Black's position can be held (Keres).

16	**...**	**♗b6**

Not 16 ... ♘xd4? 17 ♗xd4 ♗b6 18 0-0-0!± Parma - Trifunovic, Amsterdam 1965.

17	**♘xc6**	**bc**
18	**♗xb6!**	

After 18 a5 ♗xe3 19 fe ♗e4! Black defends effectively.

18	**...**	**cb**

19 0-0-0 0-0-0 20 ♘e5 ♗e4 21 ♘xf7 ♗xg2 22 ♖xd8+ (22 ♘xd8 ♗xh1 is only equal) 22 ... ♖xd8 23 ♘xd8 ♗xh1 24 ♘e6± leaves White a pawn up (Holmov).

C322

13	**...**	**♗d6(!)**
14	**♘xd6+**	

Not 14 0-0-0 0-0-0 when:

a) **15 ♗xa7? ♘xa7 16 ♘xa7+ ♔b8 17 ♘b5 ♗f4+ 18**

♘d2 c5! 19 g3 ♗h6 20 f4 g5∓ (Holmov).

b) Naturally **15 ♘xd6+** ♖xd6! 16 ♖xd6 cd 17 ♘d4 ♘xd4 18 ♗xd4 ♔c7=.

14 ... cd
15 0-0-0

♖xd6 is threatening. Less promising are:

a) **15 ♗f4** 0-0-0 16 0-0-0 d5 17 ♘d4 ♘xd4 18 ♖xd4, Ristoja - Xinogalas, Haifa 1970; 18 ... ♖he8=

b) **15 ♘d4** ♘xd4 16 ♗xd4 0-0 17 a4 ♖fe8+ 18 ♔d2 d5 19 ♖he1 a6 20 ♖xe8+ ♖xe8 21 ♖a3 ♗d7 ½-½ Szabo - Holmov, Ordzhonikidze 1964.

15 ... ♔e7

A suggestion of Spassky's. Other tries:

a) **15 ... ♖d8?** 16 ♘d4 ♘xd4 17 ♖xd4±.

b) **15 ... ♘e5?** 16 ♘h4 ♗e6 17 ♖xd6 0-0 18 b3 ♘g4 19 ♖e1 ♖fd8 20 ♖xd8+ ♖xd8 21 ♘f3±± Kuijpers - Blau, Brunnen 1966.

c) **15 ... 0-0-0** 16 ♘d4! ♗e6! 17 ♘b5! ♗xa2 18 ♗f4!±± *Schach Archiv*.

d) **15 ... ♗e6** is worthy of attention, especially if White loses time defending his a-pawn:

d1) **16 ♔b1**, Alexandria - Kobaidze, USSR 1970, 16 ... 0-0-0 keeps the balance.

d2) **16 b3** when:

d21) **16 ... d5?** 17 ♖he1 f6 18 ♘g1! 0-0 19 ♘e2 ♗f7 20 ♘f4 ♖fd8 21 h4± Kapengut - Rumiantsev, Riga 1968.

d22) The right move is **16 ... ♔e7** 17 ♖d2 (17 ♖he1!? Schwarz) 17 ... ♖hd8 18 h3 b6! 19 ♖hd1 d5= Zhuravlev - Borisenko, Riga 1968.

d3) **16 ♖xd6 ♗xa2** and now not

d31) **17 ♘d4?!** ♘xd4 18 ♗xd4 0-0 19 ♖d7 ♖fb8 20 ♖e1 a5 21 ♖e5 ♗c4 22 h4 b5 23 ♖g5 g6 24 h5 ♖d8∓ Gurgenidze - Holmov, Grozny 1969.

d32) **17 ♖e1** 0-0= Vechet - Tichy, CSSR 1978.

d33) **17 ♗c5!** 0-0 18 ♖xc6 (18 ♖d7 ♖fb8=) 18 ... bc 19 ♗xf8 ♔xf8 20 ♘d2 ♗d5 21 f3± Matulovic - Holmov, Sochi 1968.

16 ♖he1 ♗e6=

Not 16 ... ♘e5?? which is met by 17 ♗c5!±±.

Black's position can be held, e.g. 17 ♗f4 ♖hd8 18 ♗g5+ f6 19 ♘d4 ♘xd4 20 ♖xd4 ♔f7!

5) 3 d4 ed: Steinitz's 5 ♕e2

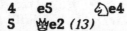

	4	e5	♘e4
	5	♕e2 (13)	

This move was revived by Fischer in 1962. Black has two good continuations:

A: 5 ... ♗b4+
B: 5 ... ♘c5

A

	5	...	♗b4+

White also faces a choice:

A1: 6 ♔d1 (Steinitz)
A2: 6 ♘bd2 (Modern)

Not 6 c3? dc 7 bc ♘xc3 8 ♕c4 ♘d5+!

A1

	6	♔d1

The king move is dubious, exposing itself to the attack of the black pieces.

	6	...	d5

6 ... ♘c5?? 7 ♗g5 wins.

	7	ed	f5

And now:

A11: 8 dc
A12: 8 ♘g5

A11

	8	dc?	♕xc7
	9	♘xd4	

Gaining the pawn is risky.

	9	...	♘c6!
	10	♘xc6	

Or 10 c3 ♘xd4 11 cd Steinitz – Pillsbury, St. Petersburg (m) 1895-96 11 ... ♗d7! 12 ♗e3 ♖c8∓ (Morgan).

	10	...	bc
	11	c3	

Weaker are:
a) 11 f3? ♗a6! 12 ♕xa6 ♘f2+ 13 ♔e2 ♕e5+ 14 ♗e3 f4∓∓ or

b) 11 ♗e3 a5 12 c3 ♘a6 13 ♕e1 0-0-0+ 14 ♔c2 ♘xf1 15 ♕xf1 ♗c5 16 ♗xc5 ♘xc5 17 ♘d2 ♖xd2+! 18 ♔xd2 ♕f4+ 19 ♔c2 ♕e4+∓∓ Norway – Scott, 1935.

11 ... ♗e7

Feeble are:

a) 11 ... ♗a6? 12 ♕xa6 ♘xf2+ 13 ♔c2±.

b) 11 ... ♗c5? 12 f3 ♗a6 13 ♕xa6 ♘f2+ 14 ♔c2! ♘xh1 15 ♗f4± Gleeson – Rowley, corr. 1971

After 11 ... ♗e7 White's king remains a continuing target, outweighing the sacrificed pawn.

A12

8 ♘g5! 0-0

8 ... ♗xd6? 9 f3 ♗e7 10 fe ♗xg5 11 ♕h5+±.

9 ♕c4+

9 dc?! ♕xc7 10 ♕c4+ ♕xc4 11 ♗xc4+ ♔h8 12 ♖f1 h6∓ (Bilguer).

9 ... ♔h8 *(14)*

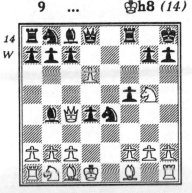

The moment of truth.

This subject might be adapted from any of Shakespeare's histories: bloody sacrifice, violent murders, hidden relatives as the source of conspiracy; and nearing the end, the plot has become clear and truth will out. That means catharsis for the audience but tragedy for the survivors – if any remain. Let us remain only spectators!

10 ♘xe4

Or:

a) 10 dc? ♘xf2+ 11 ♔e2 ♕e7+ 13 ♔xf2 ♕e1+∓∓ (Steinitz).

b) 10 ♘f7+? ♖xf7 11 ♕xf7 ♘xf2+ (11 ... ♘xd6 is also good) 12 ♔e2 ♘xh1 13 dc ♕d7! 14 cb(♕) ♕xf7 15 ♕f4 ♗d7∓∓ (Steinitz).

c) 10 ♕xb4 ♘c6 11 ♕a3 (11 dc? ♘xf2+!) 11 ... ♘xf2+ 12 ♔e1 ♘xh1 13 dc ♕e8+ 14 ♗e2 f4 15 ♔f1 ♗d7 16 ♘d2 ♘e5 17 ♘df3 ♘g4 18 ♗d3 Steinitz – Pillsbury, St. Petersburg (m) 1895-96; 18 ... h6!∓.

10 ... fe

11 dc

Weaker is 11 ♕xb4? when:

a) 11 ... ♗g4+ 12 ♗e2 ♗xe2+ 13 ♔xe2 ♘c6 14 ♕e1 ♕xd6 15 ♘d1 ♖ac8 16 b3 e3 17 ♘a3 ♕f4! 18 ♗xf8 e2+∓∓ Lipschutz - Showalter, (m) 1896.

b) 11 ... ♘c6 and now:

b1) **12 dc?** ♗g4+ 13 ♗e2 ♗xe2+ 14 ♔xe2 ♖xf2+! 15 ♔e1 ♕h4 16 g3 ♖xh2! 17 ♖g1 ♕g4 18 ♕c4 d3 19 ♘c3 ♖e2+ 20 ♔d1 dc mate, Mayer - A Steiner, Temesvar 1896.

b2) **12 ♕e1** ♗g4+! 13 ♗e2 ♗f5 gives Black excellent chances for the sacrificed material.

11 ... ♕e7∞

- Porreca.

Feeble are:

a) 11 ... ♕f6? 12 cb(♕) ♕xf2 Kharush - Gurevich, Riga 1975, 13 ♕g3! ♗g4+ 14 ♗e2 ♕f1+ 15 ♕e1±±.

b) 11 ... ♗g4+?! 12 ♗e2 (12 f3? ef!) 12 ... ♗xe2+ 13 ♔xe2 ♕h4 14 c8(♕)! ♕xf2+ 15 ♔d1 Black's attack has lost its wind. However 5 ... ♗b4+ went out of fashion because of the following simple yet modern idea.

A2

6 ♘bd2 ♘xd2

6 ... d5? (6 ... ♘g5? 7 ♘xd4 △ c3±) 7 ed f5 (7 ... 0-0? 8 dc ♕xc7 9 ♕xe4±±) 8 dc ♕xc7 9 ♘xd4 and Black has no compensation such as after 6 ♔d1.

7 ♗xd2 ♕e7!

Or 7 ... ♗xd2+ 8 ♕xd2 d5! 9 ♕xd4 0-0 10 0-0-0 ♗e6 11 ♗e2±.

8 0-0-0

8 ♘xd4? ♗xd2+∓.

8 ... ♘c6
9 ♗g5 ♕e6
10 ♔b1 ♗c5

Grechkin - Nikitin, USSR 1964. Black has preserved his pawn advantage, but White has compensation in development.

B

5 ... ♘c5
6 ♘xd4 ♘c6!

6 ... ♗e7 is weak, viz. 7 ♘c3 0-0 8 ♗f4 d5(6) 9 0-0-0± (Steinitz).

Now White has:

B1: 7 ♘xc6
B2: 7 ♗e3

7 ♘f5 ♘e6∞

B1

7 ♘xc6

With two recaptures:

B11: 7 ... bc
B12: 7 ... dc

B11

7 ... bc

Black had to choose between two general principles; recapturing towards the centre or opening up the c8-bishop. The first is the more difficult way of playing. It resembles a variation of the Scotch Game (1 e4 e5 2 ♘f3 ♘c6 3 d4 ed 4 ♘xd4 ♘f6 5 ♘xc6 bc 6 e5 ♘d5) except that the knight is on c5 instead of d5. The difference is advantageous for White.

8 ♘c3

Or 8 ♗e3 ♕h4 (8 ... ♖b8?!) 9 ♕c4 ♕xc4 10 ♗xc4 ♘a4 11 ♗b3 ♘b6 (easier to reach in the Scotch Game — ♘d5 - b6)± Spassky - Vistanetsky, Tallinn 1959.

8 ... ♖b8

△ 9 ... ♗a6 10 ♕g4 ♖b4!

Less effective are:

a) 8 ... ♗a6 9 ♕g4 or

b) 8 ... ♗e7 9 ♗e3! 0-0 10 0-0-0±.

9 f4

Better than 9 a3 when:

a) after **9 ... ♗a6** 10 ♕g4 ♗xf1 11 ♖xf1 d6 (⌐ 11 ... d5) we suggest 12 ♗e3!, e.g. 12 ... ♖xb2 13 0-0-0 ♕b8 14 ♗xc5! dc 15 e6±±.

b) **9 ... ♗e7** 10 ♗e3 and now:

b1) **10 ... ♖xb2?** fails to 11 ♗xc5 ♗xc5 12 ♘a4 ♖b5 13 ♕g4+.

b2) **10 ... d5** 11 ed cd 12

♗xc5 dc 13 ♕e5 ♕d6 14 ♕xg7, Keres - Bolbochan, Buenos Aires 1964, 14 ... ♘f6! 15 ♘e4 ♗xg7 16 ♘xd6+ ♔e7= (Keres).

c) **9 ... ♘e6** is playable, e.g. 10 f4 c5∞.

9 ... ♗e7
10 ♕f2 d5

Not 10 ... d6 11 ♗e3!± when 11 ... ♖xb2? would be met by 12 0-0-0.

11 ♗e3 ♘d7(!)
12 0-0-0 0-0
13 g4

Fischer preferred this move to either:

a) **13 ♗xa7?** ♖a8 14 ♗e3 ♗b4 when Black has succeeded in seizing the initiative.

b) **13 ♘a4** ♖b4 14 b3 ♖xa4!∞.

13 ... ♗b4
14 ♘e2 ♘b6

15 ♘d4 ♕e8 16 c3 ♗e7 (16 ... ♗c5) 17 f5 c5 18 ♘b5 d4! 19 ♗f4 (19 cd c4 20 ♘c3 ♘a4∞), Fischer - German, Stockholm (izt) 1962, 19 ... ♗b7 20 ♖g1 a6∞.

B12

7 ... dc(!)

The way for Black's bishop and queen has been opened, making a healthy development possible and promising equality.

8 ♘c3   ♗f5
9 ♗e3

Better than:

a) **9 g4?** ♗e6! 10 ♗g2 ♕h4 11 h3 h5∓ Figler - Borisenko, USSR 1971, breaking up the pawn formation.

b) **9 g3** ♘e6! 10 ♗e3 ♘d4 11 ♗xd4 ♕xd4 12 a3 ♗g4 13 f3 ♗e6 14 f4 ♗e7 15 ♕e4 ♗c5 = /∓ Tal - Szabo, Havana (ol) 1966.

9 ...   h5!

Less effective are:

a) **9 ... ♗e7?** 10 g4! ♗g6 11 ♖d1 ♕c8 12 ♗g2± Litvinov - Borisenko, USSR 1971.

b) **9 ... ♕d7?!** 10 f3 h5 11 ♕f2 0-0-0 12 ♖d1± Kudriashov - Chesnauskas, USSR 1964.

c) **9 ... ♘e4?** 10 ♘xe4 ♗xe4 11 ♖d1 ♕e7 12 ♗d4±.

d) **9 ... ♕e7** 10 g4 ♗d7 11 0-0-0 (Keres) sacrificing the pawn is strong, e.g. 11 ... ♕xe5 12 f4 ♕e7 13 ♗g2 0-0-0 15 ♖he1 ♕h4 16 h3 with the initiative.

10 ♖d1

Or 10 ♕c4?! b5 11 ♕f4 ♗xc2 12 ♖c1 ♘d3+ 13 ♗xd3 ♗xd3 14 ♖d1∞ Horton. We suggest 14 ... ♕d7!?

10 ...   ♕e7
11 ♖d2   ♘d7

11 ... ♕xe5?? 12 ♗xc5.

12 f4   0-0-0∓

Klavin - Vistanetsky, Tbilisi 1962. If 13 ♗xa7 ♕b4! The shortcomings of Steinitz's system appear again.

B2

7 ♗e3 *(15)*

7 ...   ♘xd4

The only good move, and not:

a) **7 ... ♘xe5?** 8 ♘b5! ♘a6 (8 ... ♘e6 9 f4 △ f5±±) 9 ♗d4 d6 10 f4±±.

b) **7 ... ♗e7(?)** White may transpose advantageously into the above game Litvinov - Borisenko: 8 ♘xc6 dc 9 ♘c3 ♗f5 10 g4! ♗g6 11 ♖d1 ♕c8 12 ♗g2±; or 8 ♘xc6 bc 9 ♘c3 0-0 10 0-0-0±.

c) **7 ... b6?** 8 ♘xc6 dc 9 ♘c3 ♕e7 10 f4 h5 11 ♕f3 ♗b7 12 0-0-0 ♕h4 13 ♗xc5 ♗xc5 14 ♗a6 1-0 Horton - Clarke, England 1973.

8 ♗xd4   ♕h4!

The best move promising equality.

Other tries after 8 ... ♘e6 9 ♗c3:

a) **9 ... ♗e7** 10 ♘d2 (△ ♘e4±) 10 ... d5 11 ed ♕xd6 12 ♘c4 ♕c5 13 0-0-0 0-0± G Popov - Gorenstein, corr. 1969.

b) **9 ... ♗c5** (Fuchs) 10 ♘d2 ♗d4 11 ♗xd4 ♘xd4 12 ♕d3 ♘c6 13 0-0-0 0-0 14 f4 f6 15 ef ♕xf6 16 g3±.

9 ♗e3

9 ♗c3 is not forceful enough 9 ...♘e4! 10 g3 (10 ♗d4 ♘g3) 10 ... ♘xc3 11 ♘xc3 ♕d4!=.

9 ... ♕b4+

9 ...♕e4?! is risky 10 ♘c3 ♕xe5 11 0-0-0 and White has a development advantage.

10 c3 ♕e4

10 ... ♘d3+? 11 ♕xd3 ♕xb2 is bad: 12 ♕b5! ♕xa1 13 ♘c4 ♕a3 14 ♕b3±±.

11 f4 d5

12 ♘d2

12 ed ♗xd6 13 ♘d2 ♕e6 or ♕e7 evens things up.

12 ♕g6

13 ♘f3 c6

14 0-0-0 ♗e7

Holmov thinks 14 ... a5 is better.

15 ♖g1 h5

16 ♕f2 ♘e4 17 ♕c2 b5 18 ♗d3 Tal - Holmov, Alma Ata 1969. Now 18 ... a6 and ... c5 retain equality (Petrosian and Suetin).

Conclusion: Black can obtain sufficient counterplay against Steinitz's 5 ♕e2.

6) 3 d4 ed: Spanish 5 ♗b5

4	e5	♘e4
5	♗b5 *(16)*	

Tal surprised the chess world with the Spanish 5 ♗b5 in 1963.

A: 5 ... ♘c6
B: 5 ... ♗b4+
C: 5 ... c6

Also 5 ... a6 6 ♕xd4 ab (6 ... ♘xf2?! 7 ♕xf2 ab 8 0-0±; or 6 ... ♘c5 7 ♗c4 ♘c6 8 ♕f4 ♘e6 9 ♗xe6±) 7 ♕xe4± Nunn – Taruffi, Ostend 1975.

A

5	...	♘c6

Though this is objectively good, we suggest some other continuations that do not transpose into the Spanish (Ruy Lopez) for the friends of the Petroff. See lines B and C.

6   0-0

6 ♘xd4? ♘xf2!; 6 ♕e2 ♘c5 7 0-0 ♗e7 8 ♖d1 0-0 9 ♗xc6 Tal – Furman, Riga 1958, 9 ... d3!= (Petrosian).

6   ...   ♗e7

If 6 ... a6:

a) 7 ♗c4? d5 8 ed ♘xd6 9 ♗b3 ♗g4∓.

b) 7 ♗a4 transposes into the Spanish.

c) 7 ♕e2 ♘c5 8 ♗c4 ♗e7 9 ♖d1 d5! 10 ed ♕xd6= Shamkovich – Smyslov, USSR 1971.

d) 7 ♗xc6 dc and now:

d1) 8 ♕e2 ♗f5 9 ♖d1 ♗c5 10 ♗e3 (10 c3 d3!) 10 ... ♕e7 (10 ... ♕d5? 11 ♘c3±) 11 ♘xd4 ♗xd4 12 ♗xd4 0-0-0, Kuindshi – Zeitlin, USSR 1977, 13 ♘c3=.

d2) 8 ♖e1 ♘c5 9 ♘xd4

♘e6 10 ♗e3=.

7   ♖e1

7 ♘xd4 transposes to the Spanish.

7   ...   ♘c5

7 ... d5? 8 ed ♘xd6 9 ♗xc6+ bc 10 ♘xd4± Tal – Darga, Havana 1963.

8   ♘xd4   0-0!?
9   ♘f5   d5!

10 ♗xc6 and now:

a) **10 ... ♗xf5** 11 ♗xd5 c6 gives counterplay for the pawn.

b) **10 ... bc** is also good, transposing into the Spanish.

B

5   ...   ♗b4+
6   c3

6 ♔f1!? – ECO. 6 ♘bd2 is of no consequence.

6   ...   dc
7   0-0!   ♗e7!

After 7 ... cb 8 ♗xb2 White has excellent attacking chances. If 7 ... ♘c6? 8 ♗xc6 dc 9 ♕a4! a5 10 ♖d1 ♕e7 11 a3 ♘c5 12 ♕c2 ♗e6 13 ♘d4±.

8   ♖e1   cb

9 ♗xb2 ♘c5 10 ♘c3 c6 11 ♗c4 b5 12 ♗f1 0-0 △ ... d5∞ Shamkovich.

C

5   ...   c6

6   ♕xd4 *(17)*

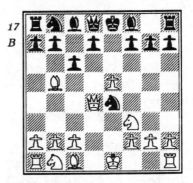

6 ♗d3 ♘c5= (Euwe).
Now Black has:

C1: 6 ... ♘c5
C2: 6 ... ♕a5+

C1

6   ...   ♘c5
7   ♗c4   b5

Or 7 ... ♘e6 8 ♕e4 ♘a6 9 ♗xa6± (Keres).

8   ♗b3   ♗e7

8 ... d5 9 ed ♕xd6 can also be considered.

9   ♕g4   g6
10 ♕f4   d5

If 10 ... ♘xb3 11 ab 0-0 12 ♕h6 f6 13 h4! ♖f7 (△ 13 ... ♕e8) 14 h5 ♗f8 15 hg!! ♗xh6 16 gf+ ♔xf7 17 ♖xh6 fe 18 ♘c3 d5 19 ♗g5 ♕g8, Jansa – Kolarov, Bad Luhacovice 1971, 20 ♘xe5+ ♔f8 21 f4± Hort.

11 ed   ♘xb3

12 ab ♕xd6 13 ♘c3± Hort.

C2

6	...	♕a5+
7	c3	♘xf2

7 ... ♕xb5?! 8 ♕xe4 ♘a6 9 c4 (Also 9 ♘d4 Jonsson) 9 ... ♕b4+ 10 ♘bd2± Vaskan - Maslov, Riga 1964.

8 ♕xf2

Or:

a) **8 ♗c4?!** ♘xh1 (8 ... ♗c5? 9 ♕f4±) 9 ♘g5 (9 ♕f4? fails to 9 ... d5 10 ed ♕f5) ♕b6!∞ (9 ... ♕c5?? 10 ♗xf7+ wins the queen).

b) **8 0-0** ♘h3+± (Euwe).

8	...	♕xb5
9	a4!?	

Or 9 ♗e3 and now:

a) **9 ... d5?** 10 ♘g5 ♗e6 11 ♖f1 ♘d7 12 ♘xe6 fe 13 ♕f7+ ♔d8 14 ♕xe6± Jansa - Pithart, Harrachov 1966.

b) **9 ... ♗e7** 10 ♘d4 (10 b3 0-0 11 c4 is also possible) 10 ... ♕xe5 11 0-0 with attacking chances.

9	...	♕d5

9 ... ♕d3(?) 10 ♘g5 ♕d5! (10 ... ♕g6 11 h4!±) 11 0-0!±.

10	♗e3	d6

11 0-0 h6 (⌓ 11 ... ♗e6) 12 ♘a3 de 13 ♖ad1 ♕b3 (13 ... ♕e4 14 ♘xe5!) 14 ♘c4!± ♗e6 (14 ... ♕xc4 15 ♘xe5 △ ♘xf7) 15 ♘cxe5 ♗e7 16 ♘d4 ♕d5 (16 ... ♕a2 17 c4! ♗xc4 18 ♖a1) 17 ♘dxc6 ♘xc6 18 ♖xd5 ♗xd5 19 ♘xc6 bc 20 ♗c5 ♗f6 21 ♕e2+ ♗e6 22 ♕a6 1-0 Kosten - Miralles, Lyon 1988.

7) 3 d4 ed: 4 ♗c4
(Urusoff Gambit)

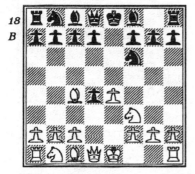

18
B

This interesting gambit was named after Prince Sergei Urusoff, who was born in 1827. He was the second strongest Russian chessplayer after Petroff who was 33 years older. The gambit named after him was worked out in 1857. In the evening of his life he presented his chess books to S L Tolstoy, the writer's son, and had also been attached in long friendship to the great writer himself.

Black has tried:

A: 4 ... ♗c5
B: 4 ... ♘xe4

Or:

a) **4 ... c5** The main idea is that 5 e5 can be met strongly by 5 ... d5. However, there can come a surprise, viz. 5 ♕e2! d6? 6 e5 de 7 ♘xe5 ♗e6 8 ♘xf7! ♕e7 9 ♕xe6 1-0, Akos - P Csaszar, Hungary corr. 1968. Now 5 ... d5 can also be considered, e.g. 6 ed+ ♗e7 7 ♗b5+ ♔f8 (7 ... ♗d7? 8 d6!) △ ... a6 and ... ♘xd5. 5 0-0, suggested by Bilguer, is a good, solid move. After that, best is 5 ... d5 6 ed ♗e7.

b) **4 ... ♘c6** transposes to the Two Knights Opening (1 e4 e5 2 ♘f3 ♘c6 3 ♗c4 ♘f6 4 d4 ed) or to the Scotch Opening - rather complicated but good "stock play".

c) **4 ... d6** 5 e5 ♗b4+ 6 c3 ♕e7+ 7 ♗e2 dc 8 bc ♗c5 9

0-0 0-0 10 c4 ♖e8= Pills-
bury - Marshall, Paris 1900,
11 ♗d3 ♗g4 (threatening
... ♗d4) 12 ♗b2 ♘bd7 planning ... ♘e5. See also Chapter 14.

d) **4 ... ♗b4+?!** 5 c3 dc 6
bc(!). A change from the
well-known variation! In
case of 6 ♘xc3 Black would
stand very comfortably,
but after 6 bc the bishop is
forced to withdraw and
then the knight is chased
away by e4 - e5, gaining
important tempi for White's
attack.

A

4 ... ♗c5

The intention is similar
to the Max Lange attack
after 5 e5 d5 6 ef dc 7 ♕e2+
♗e6 8 fg ♖g8 but the position is even better.

5 0-0 d6

a) **5 ... ♘c6** transposes
into Max Lange attack.

b) One had better avoid **5
... ♘xe4?**, e.g. 6 ♖e1 d5 7
♗xd5 ♕xd5 8 ♘c3 ♕h5 (△
♕d8) 9 ♖xe4+ ♗e6 10 ♖e5
♕g6 11 ♘d5 ♗d6 12 ♘h4±
Sozin.

6 c3 d3!

6 ... dc cannot be recom-
mended - the bishop at c5
is missing from the defence.

7 ♕xd3 ♘c6=
- Keres.

B

4 ... ♘xe4
5 ♕xd4 *(19)*

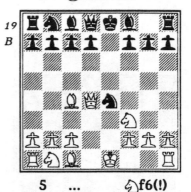

5 ... ♘f6(!)

Other tries are inade-
quate:

a) **5 ... d5?** 6 ♗xd5 ♘f6 7
♗xf7+ ♔xf7 8 ♕xd8 ♗b4+ 9
♕d2± Euwe.

b) **5 ... ♘d6?** 6 0-0 ♘c6 7
♖e1+ ♘e7 8 ♗b3±± Prokes -
Zander, Vienna 1925.

c) **5 ... ♘c5** and now:

c1) **6 ♘c3** is good, or

c2) **6 ♗g5!** f6 (6 ... ♘c6? 7
♗xf7+) 7 ♗e3 c6 (better
first 7 ... ♘e6) 8 ♘c3 d5 9
0-0-0 ♗e7 10 ♕h4 ♘bd7 (10
... 0-0 11 ♘xd5±±; 10 ... ♗e6
11 ♖he1±) 11 ♘xd5 cd 12
♕h5+ g6 13 ♕xd5± Estrin -
Taimanov, Leningrad 1949.

6 ♗g5

6 0-0 ♗e7 7 ♘c3 c6!

6 ... ♗e7

6 ... ♘c6!? is interesting.
7 ♕h4 (7 ♗xf6 ♘xd4!) 7 ...
d5 8 ♗xf6 gf 9 ♗b3 ♗e6 10
♘c3 ♗b4 11 0-0-0 ♗xc3 12
bc ♕e7 13 ♗xd5 0-0-0 with
about level chances in Tartakower - Shories, Barmen
1905. However, there is an
even stronger continuation
for Black, viz. 9 ... ♕e7+!
followed by ... ♗e6 and ...
0-0-0. So Black can advantageously avoid the following complicated alterna-
tives.

7 ♘c3 *(20)*

20
B

Now Black has tried:

B1: 7 ... ♘c6
B2: 7 ... c6

And:
a) 7 ... 0-0(?) 8 0-0-0!
and then ... d7 - d5 cannot
be played successfully.
b) 7 ... d5 8 ♘xd5 ♘xd5 9

♕xd5 ♕xd5 10 ♗xd5 c6 11
♗b3?! (11 ♗c4± R Schwarz)
11 ... ♘d7 12 0-0-0 ♘c5 13
♗c4 ♗xg5+ 14 ♘xg5 0-0 15
♖he1 (15 ♘xf7 ♗e6) 15 ... h6
16 ♘e4 (16 ♘xf7 b5!) ♘xe4
17 ♖xe4 ♗e6= Gibbs
- Littlewood, Ilford 1961.

B1

7 ... ♘c6
8 ♕h4

Again Black has a choice:

B11: 8 ... d5
B12: 8 ... d6

B11

8 ... d5
9 0-0-0 ♗e6
10 ♖he1 0-0

Better than 10 ... h6? 11
♗xf6 ♗xf6 12 ♕h5!± Tere-
shenko-Rotlewi, St. Petersburg (m) 1909.

11 ♗d3 h6
and now:
a) 12 ♔b1 This quiet move
can easily be effective:
a1) 12 ... ♕d7? 13 ♗xh6
♘e4 14 ♗g5 ♗xg5 15
♘xg5±± Shmelnitsky - Ev-
entov, corr. USSR 1955-57.
a2) 12 ... ♘e8 (Euwe) 13
♗xe7 ♕xe7 14 ♕xe7 ♘xe7.
Although the attack has
finished White managed to
preserve some develop-

mental advantage.

a3) **12 ... ♘d7!** deserves attention, e.g. 13 ♗xe7 ♕xe7 14 ♕xe7 ♘xe7 and after 15 ♘d4 Black has ... ♘c5!

b) **12 ♗xh6** ♘e4 13 ♕f4 ♗d6 14 ♕e3 ♗c5= Lasker.

c) **12 ♖xe6!?** fe 13 ♗xh6 gh 14 ♕g3+ ♔h8 15 ♕g6 ♖f7 16 ♕xf7 ♕g8! with balanced chances.

d) **12 g4** Black must be careful: 12 ... ♘xg4 13 ♗xe7 ♕xe7 14 ♕g3 and now ♕d6! is best with mutual chances.

B12

8	...	d6
9	0-0-0	♗e6

Better than 9 ... ♗f5? 10 ♖he1 0-0 when:

a) **11 ♕f4** ♗g6 12 g4 ♘a5 13 ♗d3 ♕d7 14 ♗xf6 ♗xf6 15 ♘d5 ♗d8 16 ♗f5± an off-hand game, Keidanski – Lasker, Berlin 1891.

b) **11 ♖xe7?!** ♘xe7 12 ♗xf6 gf 13 ♖e1 ♘g6 14 ♕h6 ♖e8! 15 ♖xe8+ ♕xe8 16 ♘d5 ♕d8 with ... c6 and ... ♕f8 and Black is rather better.

10 ♗d3

Not 10 ♖he1? ♗xc4 11 ♕xc4 0-0 12 ♖e3! ♘d7 and now:

a) **13 h4** ♖e8 14 ♗xe7 ♖xe7 15 ♖xe7 ♘xe7 16 ♘g5 ♘e5 17

♕e4 ♘7g6 18 f4 h6∓ Berlin – Budapest, corr. 1937-38.

b) **13 ♖xe7** ♘xe7 14 ♖e1 ♖e8 15 ♘d5 when Black can reply 15 ... ♘b6.

10	...	♕d7

Or:

a) **10 ... h6** 11 ♖he1 ♕d7 12 ♗b5 0-0-0. One example after Keres' 13 ♕a4!: 13 ... ♘d5 14 ♖xd5! hg 15 ♘d4 1-0 Ushold – Wallinger, corr. 1984. Black may not risk that and feel it necessary to interpolate 11 ... a6, which transposes to the next line.

b) **10 ... a6** 11 ♖he1 ♕d7 (Black could have tried 11 ... h6 here) 12 ♘e4 ♘xe4 13 ♗xe4 0-0-0 14 ♗xc6 ♗xg5+ 15 ♘xg5 ♕xc6 16 ♘xe6 fe 17 ♕g4= (Hooper). Black gave back the pawn for equality.

In the main line Black tries to retain his extra pawn.

11 ♗b5

Keres thinks 11 ♖he1 is also good.

11	...	0-0! *(21)*

Not 11 ... 0-0-0? because of 12 ♘e5! (12 ♕a4 is also good – Keres) 12 ... ♕e8 13 ♘xc6 bc 14 ♗a6+ ♔d7 15 ♘a4± – Tartakower.

Now White can choose:

a) **12 ♘d4** Black had

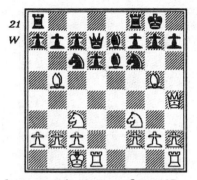

21
W

better chances after 12 ... h6 and 13 ♗xh6 ♘g4! or 12 ... a6 13 ♘d4 h6 14 ♗xh6 ♘g4!∓ (Hooper).

b) 12 ♘e5 when:

b1) 12 ... ♛c8 13 ♘xc6 bc 14 ♗xc6 h6 (14 ... ♖b8?! 15 ♘e4 ♛d8 16 ♖d3± Matrisch - Nikovic, corr. 1972-73) 15 ♗d2 ♖b8 16 ♛a4 ♘g4= Neishtadt - Burlaiev, Moscow 1958.

b2) 12 ... ♛e8 13 ♘xc6 bc 14 ♗d3 h6 and 15 f4! seems perilous, though with 15 ... ♘d5! Black avoids the trap (15 ... hg? 16 fg±) with balanced chances - Estrin.

B2

7	...	c6
8	0-0-0	d5
9	♖he1	

After 9 ♛h4 correct is 9 ... ♗e6 when 10 ♖he1 or 10 ♗d3 transposes to the column.

Now Black has:

B21: 9 ... 0-0
B22: 9 ... ♗e6

B21

| 9 | ... | 0-0 |
| 10 | ♛h4 | |

Not 10 ♗xd5? cd 11 ♖xe7 ♘c6!

| 10 | ... | ♗f5 |

Also:

a) 10 ... h6? 11 ♗xd5!

b) 10 ... ♘bd7? Confuses the cooperation of the black pieces. The activity of the c8-bishop is especially restricted. 11 ♗d3 and now:

b1) 11 ... h6? 12 ♗xh6 ♘e4 and 13 ♛g4± is possible, since the c8-bishop is eliminated. Or 12 ... gh 13 ♛xh6 ♗d6 14 ♖e3! ♛c7 15 ♛g5+ ♚h8 16 ♘e5! ♘xe5 17 ♛xf6+ ♚g8 18 ♖g3+ ♘g6 19 ♗xg6±± Wöber - Druckenthaner, Austrian League 1988.

b2) 11 ... g6 12 ♖e2 (12 ♘d4, threatening 13 ♘f5, promises winning chances) 12 ... ♖e8 13 ♖de1 ♘e4 14 ♘xe4 △ 15 ♖xe4 and White wins.

c) 10 ... ♗e6(!) 11 ♗d3 h6! 12 ♗xh6 ♘e4 13 ♛f4 (13 ♛h5 g6! Estrin) 13 ... ♗d6 14 ♛e3

♗c5 15 ♘d4 ♕f6! is equal.

> **11 ♘d4   ♗g6**
> **12 ♗d3   h6!?**

Against the threat of 13 ♘f5.

Better was 12 ... ♕d7.

> **13 ♗xg6   hg**

14 ♕xg5 ♘e4!? 15 ♗h7+! ♔h8! 16 ♕h5 ♘f6 17 ♕h4 ♘e4 18 ♕h3 ♘g5∞ (Lauterbach).

B22

> **9 ...   ♗e6**
> **10 ♗d3**

Or 10 ♕h4 ♘bd7 (10 ... 0-0 transposes to line B21c) 11 ♘d4?! (11 ♗d3 leads to the column) 11 ... ♘f8 12 ♘f5 ♗xf5 13 ♗xf6 ♗e6 14 ♗xe7 ♕xe7 15 ♕d4 ♕f6 16 ♕e3 with an initiative for the pawn Schlechter - Teichmann, Vienna 1904.

> **10 ...   ♘bd7**

10 ... ♕a5? is refuted by 11 ♗f5.

As for 10 ... 0-0 see line B21 with transposition.

> **11 ♕h4 *(22)***
> **11 ...   ♘c5**

This is the main line in this critical position.

> **12 ♘d4**

Threats 13 ♘f5.

12 ♗f5 ♗xf5 13 ♗xf6 ♘e6 14 ♗xe7 ♕xe7 occurred in Estrin - Hachaturov, Mos-

cow 1943, and after 15 ♘xd5?! cd 16 ♕a4+ ♔f8 17 ♖xd5 ♗g6 is unclear - Keres.

> **12 ...   ♘g8!**

12 ... ♘fd7? and now:

a) 13 ♗xe7 ♕xe7 14 ♕xe7+ ♔xe7 15 f4 ♘xd3+ 16 ♖xd3 (⌂ 16 cd - Polugayevsky) 16 ... g6 17 g4 ♘c5 18 ♖de3 ♔d6 19 b4 ♘e4 20 ♘xe4 de 21 ♘xe6 fe 22 ♖xe4± Neishtadt - Volkovich, Moscow 1958.

b) 13 f4 ♗xg5 14 fg ♘xd3+ 15 ♖xd3 ♘c5 16 ♖h3 a5 17 ♕h5!± Prokes - Spielmann, Vienna 1907.

> **13 ♗xe7**

After 13 f4:

a) Not **13 ... ♔f8?** 14 b4 ♘xd3+ 15 ♖xd3± Torre - Tholfsen, New York 1924, but

b) **13 ... ♗xg5!** 14 fg ♘e7!∓ (Byhovsky).

> **13 ...   ♕xe7**

14 ♕g3   ♕f6!

Planning a later ... ♘e7. Depending on circumstances, Black can also castle either side.

Dubious it 14 ... g6?! when:

a) **15 ♘ce2!?** (Keres) or

b) **15 f4** (Estrin) cause Black many problems.

c) **15 ♘db5!** is also good, e.g. 15 ... ♔f8 (15 ... cb? 16 ♘xd5!) 16 b4!± in Schäfer – Trzeciak, corr. 1985.

We are convinced Black has a fine game in these lines – including accepting Urusoff's gambit.

8) 3 d4 ♞xe4: Introduction

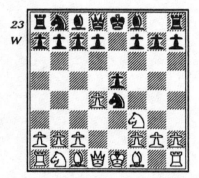

23
W

In essence Black restricts White's chances with this method and, evidently, his own as well. Both sides might march the major pieces on to only one open file and might consider occupying the only central point (e5 for White and e4 for Black).

The line 3 ...♞xe4 is easy to learn and makes a good repertoire.

Now we look at:

A: 4 ♞xe5
B: 4 de
C: 4 ♗d3 Introduction

If 4 ♕e2 d5 5 ♞xe5 ♗e7 6 ♞d2 ♞xd2 7 ♗xd2 0-0 8 0-0-0 ♞c6 9 ♞xc6 bc 10 ♕h5 ♗f6 11 ♗e3 ♖b8 12 h4 c5∞ Mnatsakanjan - Sergievsky, USSR 1963.

A

4 ♞xe5

This is rare, because Black can revert to the Classical Method (3 ♞xe5) by playing 4 ... d6 (5 ♞xf7? ♕e7!) or 4 ... d5.

4 ... ♞f6

The only move of independent importance.

5 ♗c4

Alternatives are:

a) 5 ♗d3 ♞c6 6 c3 (6 ♞xc6 dc=) 6 ... ♗e7 7 0-0 0-0 8 ♖e1 ♞xe5 (Or 8 ... d6) 9 de ♞e8 10 ♕c2 g6 11 ♗h6 ♞g7 12 ♞d2±.

b) 5 c4 ♗b4+ 6 ♞c3 0-0 7 ♗e2 d6 8 ♞f3 ♖e8 9 0-0 ♗xc3 10 bc b6 △ ... ♗b7, ... ♞bd7 controlling the e4 square - about level.

c) **5 h3** (to meet 5 ... d6 with 6 ♘f3, see 5 ... ♘f6 in Chapter 24) 5 ... ♘c6 or 5 ... g6 and decide about ... d6 or ... d5 only after castling and according to White's set up.

d) **5 ♗g5 ♗e7 6 ♗d3 0–0 7 0–0 ♘c6** or 7 ... d6 and the defence can be undertaken safely.

     5 ... d5

5 ... d6 6 ♘xf7 ♕e7+ △ ... d5∞.

     6 ♗d3 ♗e7

7 0–0 0–0 and after 8 ♗g5 White stands slightly better – Hort.

B

     4 de *(24)*

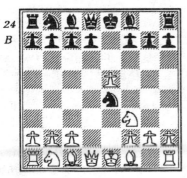

Now Black has:

B1: 4 ... ♗c5
B2: 4 ... d5

    Or:

a) **4 ... d6** transposes to the Philidor Method (1 e4 e5 2 ♘f3 d6 3 d4 ♘f6 4 de ♘xe4) and 5 ♕d5±.

b) **4 ... ♗b4+ 5 ♘d2±.**

B1

     4 ... ♗c5

Black transforms the game into a gambit.

Now White has:

B11: 5 ♕d5
B12: 5 ♗c4

Or 5 ♗e3? ♗xe3 6 fe d5!∓.

B11

     5 ♕d5 ♗xf2+
     6 ♔e2(!)

Not 6 ♔d1 f5 7 ♗c4 ♖f8 8 ♘bd2 c6 9 ♕d3 d5∓ — Mikenas.

     6 ... f5
     7 ♘c3!

The strongest. Other tries:

a) **7 ef ♘xf6 8 ♕e5+** (8 ♕g5 0–0!) 8 ... ♔f8!∓.

b) **7 ♘bd2 c6!** 8 ♕d3 (⌐ 8 ♘xe4, see column) 8 ... d5! 9 ed 0–0!∓.

     7 ... c6

Or 7 ... ♘xc3+ 8 bc ♗h4 9 ♘xh4 ♕xh4 10 g3 ♕e7 11 ♔f2 ♘c6 12 ♗c4! ♘xe5? (⌐ 12 ... ♕e6) 13 ♖e1 ♘g4+ 14 ♔f1! ♘xh2+ 15 ♔g2±±

Adorjan.

8   ♘xe4!

A splendid queen sacrifice for two minor pieces and attacking chances — or rather Black's singular lack of counterplay.

8   ...   cd

9 ♘d6+ ♚f8 10 ♚xf2 ♘c6 11 ♗e3 d4 12 ♗f4 and White stands better.

B12

5   ♗c4   ♘xf2

5 ... ♗xf2+? 6 ♚e2 c6 7 ♗d3 (7 ♖f1 is also good) 7 ... d5 8 ed f5 9 ♗xe4 fe 10 ♚xf2 ef 11 ♖e1+±.

6   ♗xf7+   ♚xf7

Or 6 ... ♚f8?! 7 ♕d5 ♘xh1 8 ♗h5! ♕e7 9 ♗g5 ♗f2+ 10 ♚e2 ♕e6 11 ♘c3! g6 12 ♕xe6 de 13 ♗f6 ♖g8 14 ♗g4 ♗b6 15 ♖xh1 ♘c6 16 ♖d1± Black is unable to develop without material loss - Hachaturov.

7   ♕d5+   ♚e8

8 ♕xc5 ♘xh1 9 ♗g5 d6 10 ♕e3 ♕d7 11 ♘c3 h6 12 ♗h4 Vargha - Ostriker, corr. 1978-79. Now 12 ... d5 was needed and after 13 0-0-0 c6 14 ♘e4 de 15 ♖xd7 ♘xd7 Black can defend his material advantage successfully.

B2

4   ...   d5

5   ♘bd2

Other tries:

For 5 ♗d3 see var. C, 4 ♗d3 d5 5 de.

5 ♗e3 ♗g4! 6 ♘bd2 ♘d7 7 ♗e2 ♕e7 8 0-0 0-0-0 9 ♗xa7 ♘xe5 10 ♘xe5 ♗xe2 11 ♕xe2 ♕xe5 12 c4 (12 f3 ♗d6!) 12 ... ♗d6 13 ♘f3 ♕h5 (△ ... ♗xh2+) 14 ♕c2 ♖he8 15 ♖fd1 dc∓ Westerinen - Bednarski, Eksjö 1976.

5   ...   ♘c5

Or:

a) 5 ... ♗e7?! 6 ♘xe4 de 7 ♕xd8+ ♗xd8 8 ♘g5, Adorjan - Benko, Hastings 1973/74, 8 ... ♗xg5 9 ♗xg5 ♘c6 10 0-0-0 0-0 11 ♗b5!±.

b) 5 ... ♘xd2 and now:

b1) 6 ♕xd2 ♗e7 7 h3 c5 8 c3 ♘c6 9 ♗d3 0-0 10 0-0 f6! 11 ef ♗xf6 12 ♘g5 ♗xg5 13 ♕xg5 ♕xg5 14 ♗xg5 ♗f5= Ilincic - Raicevic, Yugoslav Ch. 1986.

b2) 6 ♗xd2 ♗e7 7 ♗f4 c5! (7 ... 0-0 8 ♕d2± Adorjan, or 8 ♕d3 Kovacevic) when:

b21) 8 c3 ♘c6 9 ♗d3 ♗e6 10 h3 g5! 11 ♗g3 ♕b6∓ Short - Seirawan, Lugano 1986.

b22) 8 ♕d2!? △ ♖d1=.

c) 5 ... ♘c6 6 ♘xe4 (6 ♗b5) 6 ... de 7 ♕xd8+ ♘xd8 8 ♘d4! (8 ♘g5 ♗f5= Keres)

8 ... ♗c5 (8 ... ♘e6 9 ♗e3±) 9
♗e3! (9 ♘b5 ♗b6 10 ♗e3
♗a5+! 11 ♗d2 ♗b6 12 ♗e3=) 9
... 0-0! (9 ... ♗b6 10 ♗c4!±)
10 ♗c4 (10 0-0-0 ♖e8 11 ♘b5
♗xe3+ 12 fe ♘c6 13 ♗c4 a6
or 13 ... ♖e7= Yudasin) 10 ...
♗xd4! 11 ♗xd4 ♗e6 12 ♗xe6
(12 ♗e2 ♗d5=) 12 ... fe (12 ...
♘xe6!?) 13 0-0 ♘c6 14 ♗c3
b5 15 a3 a5 16 ♖fe1 b4 17
♗d2! ♖ad8!= Sveshnikov -
Yudasin, USSR 1990.

d) **5 ... ♗f5** (Adorjan)
when White may get into
difficulties over his e-
pawn, e.g.:

d1) **6 ♗d3** ♘c6 7 ♕e2 ♕e7
8 ♘xe4 de 9 ♗xe4 ♕b4+ 10
♘d2 ♗xe4 11 ♕xe4 0-0-0
with enough play for the
pawn.

d2) **6 ♘xe4** ♗xe4 7 ♗d3
♘c6 8 0-0 ♗e7 9 ♖e1 ♘b4!
10 ♕e2 ♘xd3 11 cd ♗xf3 12
♕xf3 ♕d7= Balashov -
Mihalchishin, Minsk 1985.

e) **5 ... f5** is untested.
      6 ♘b3! ♘xb3

This is best, since 6 ...
♘e6 can be met by 7 ♗e3
♗e7 8 ♕d2 followed by 9
0-0-0± - Adorjan.
      7 ab ♗e7

7 ... ♘c6, Tshalkasuren -
Espinoza, Tel Aviv (ol) 1964,
can be met by 8 ♗b5 or 8 c3
♗e7 9 b4±.

      8 ♗b5+

Or 8 ♗d3 ♘c6 (8 ... 0-0?!
9 c3 △ ♕c2±) 9 ♗f4 ♗g4 10
h3 (10 c3 ♕d7 11 h3 ♗f5=) 10
... ♗h5 when:

a) **11 ♕e2?!** ♘d4∓ Sokol-
sky - Lilienthal, USSR 1938.

b) **11 0-0** 0-0 12 ♖e1 ♕d7
13 c3 ♘d8!, Zivanovic -
Zlaticanin, corr. 1986, 14
♕c2! ♗g6=.

      8 ... c6
      9 ♗d3 ♘d7

10 c3 ♘c5 11 ♗c2 ♗g4 12
b4 ♘d7 13 0-0 0-0 (13 ...
♘xe5 14 ♕d4 ♘xf3+ 15 gf
♗h3!∞) 14 ♖e1 g6= Nunn -
Schüssler, Vienna 1986.

C
      4 ♗d3 d5
      5 de *(25)*

25
B

For 5 ♘xe5 see Chapter
9.

Bronstein suggests 5 de
when analysing one of his
games in his book *200 Open*

Games. The question is whether White can gain any advantage.

5 ♗xe4 de 6 ♘xe5 ♗d6 7 ♕e2 ♗xe5 8 de ♗f5? (8 ... ♕d4=) 9 ♘c3 0-0 10 ♘xe4 ♘c6 11 0-0 ♖e8 12 f4 ♘d4 13 ♕d3 ♘xc2 14 ♕xc2 ♕d4+ 15 ♕f2 ♕xe4 16 ♗e3±/= Capablanca - Redding, New York 1905.

After 5 de Black has:

C1: 5 ... ♘c5
C2: 5 ... ♗e7
C3: 5 ... ♘c6

Or:
5 ... ♗f5!? 6 ♕e2 ♘c6 7 ♘bd2 ♘xd2 8 ♗xd2 ♕d7 9 h3? (△ 9 0-0 △ ... ♗c5? 10 ♗xf5 ♕xf5 11 ♕b5 ±) 9 ... ♗c5 10 c3 0-0∓ Kettner - Hertneck, German League 1986.

C1

	5 ...	♘c5
	6	♗e2

6 0-0 ♗e7 7 ♘d4 ♘xd3 8 ♕xd3 c5 9 ♘f5 ♗xf5 10 ♕xf5 ♕d7 11 ♕f3 ♘c6 = Schlick - Autenrieth, Germany 1985.

	6 ...	♗e7

6 ... ♘e6 △ ... c5 is recommended for Black.

	7	0-0	0-0
	8	♗e3	♗g4

8 ... c6 9 ♘bd2 (9 c4±; 9 ♘c3 see 8 ♘c3) 9 ... ♘e6 10 ♘b3=.

	9	h3	♗xf3

10 ♗xf3 c6 11 c4! dc 12 ♘d2 b5 13 a4! ♘xa4 14 ♘xc4 ♕c7 15 ♘d6 ♘d7 16 ♘xb5! cb 17 ♖ac1± Romanishin - Arhipov, Tbilisi 1986.

C2

	5 ...	♗e7
	6	0-0	0-0

6 ... c5? is feeble, e.g. 7 ♖e1 f5 8 ef ♘xf6 9 b3± Serraillier - Mortimer 1901.

6 ... ♘c5, transposes into the previous note.

	7	c4

7 ♘c3 ♘xc3 8 bc ♘c6 (8 ... c5) 9 ♖e1 f6! 10 e6 (10 ef ♗xf6=) 10 ... f5 (△ ... ♖f6, ... ♕d6) 11 ♗b5 ♕d6 ⩲, T Horvath-Forintos, Budapest 1985.

	7 ...	c6

7 ... ♗e6 is no better:
a) 8 ♘d4± (Horton).
b) 8 ♕c2! as after 8 ... f5 9 ef, ♘xf6 is bad because of 10 ♘g5, while 9 ... ♗xf6 is at best a dubious sacrifice of the pawn.

	8	♕c2±

Zagorovsky - Shamayev, Leningrad 1949.

C3

	5 ...	♘c6

6 0-0

Or:

a) **6 ♘xe4** de 7 ♕xd8+ ♔xd8=.

b) **6 ♕e2 ♘c5** (6 ... ♗f5 7 ♗b5) 7 0-0 ♘xd3 (7 ... ♗g4 8 ♗b5) 8 cd ♗g4 9 ♗e3 d4 (△ 9 ... ♗xf3 10 gf d4∓) Bronstein - Zaslavsky, (m) Kiev 1938.

c) **6 ♗f4 ♗g4** 7 ♘bd2 ♘c5 (7 ... ♘xd2 8 ♕xd2 ♗xf3? {△ 8 ... ♕d7} 9 gf ♘d4 10 0-0-0!±) 8 ♗e2 ♘e6 9 ♗g3 ♗c5 10 c3 0-0= Milic - Trifunovic, Beverwijk 1963.

6 ... ♗e7

A strategy adopted by Karpov. Black postpones developing the c8-bishop in favour of quick castling.

Other lines:

a) **6 ... ♗f5** 7 c3 (7 ♗b5 would be uncomfortable here) 7 ... ♗c5 8 b4 (8 ♕e2) 8 ... ♗b6 9 b5 ♘e7 10 ♕c2 0-0 11 ♘d4 ♗g6= Milner-Barry - Crowl, Australia - Great Britain, radio 1947.

b) **6 ... ♗g4** when:

b1) **7 ♗f4** and now:

b11) 7 ... ♗e7 8 h3 (8 ♘c3 ♘xc3 9 bc g5 10 ♗g3 h5 11 h3 ♗e6 12 ♘d4 ♘xd4 13 cd ♕d7= Belyavsky - Makarichev, USSR 1973) 8 ... ♗f5 9 ♘bd2 g5?! (9 ... ♕d7) 10 ♘h2 h5 (△ 10 ... ♕d7) 11 ♗b5! g4 12 ♘d4 ♗d7 13 e6!± Chelebi - Mazarov, Lebanon 1956.

b12) 7 ... ♘d4 8 c3 ♘e6 9 ♗e3 ♘6c5 10 ♗e2 ♗e7 11 ♘bd2 0-0= (Sozin).

b2) 7 ♘bd2 ♘xd2 8 ♗xd2 ♘d4 9 ♗e2 ♘xe2+ 10 ♕xe2 ♕d7 11 h3 ♗xf3 12 ♕xf3 ♗c5 13 c4 0-0-0= Romanishin - Makarichev, Frunze 1985.

b3) 7 ♘c3!? ♘xc3 (7 ... ♗xf3∞) 8 bc ♗e7 9 ♖e1 ♕d7 10 h3 ♗h5 11 ♖b1 ♘d8 12 ♗e2 c6 13 c4! dc 14 ♕xd7+ ♔xd7 15 e6+! (△ ♘e5+) 15 ... ♔c7 16 ef ♘xf7? (△ 16 ... ♗xf3) 17 ♗xc4 ♗d6 18 ♘d4 ♖he8 19 ♘e6+ ♔d7 (19 ... ♔c8 20 ♘b2) 20 ♖xb7+ 1-0 Romanishin - Ehlvest, Yerevan 1988.

7 ♘bd2 ♘c5
8 ♗e2

8 ♗b5 ♗d7 (8 ... 0-0 9 ♗xc6) 9 c4?! (9 ♗xc6) 9 ... dc 10 ♗xc4 0-0 11 a3 a5 12 ♕e2 ♗f5∓ Sidani - Ferreira, Thessaloniki (ol) 1988.

8 ... 0-0

9 ♘b3 ♘xb3 10 ab f6! 11 ef ♗xf6= Romanishin - Karpov, Moscow 1981.

9) 3 d4 ♘xe4:
5 ♘xe5 Introduction

4	♗d3	d5
5	♘xe5	(26)

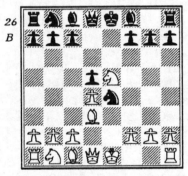

26
B

Now Black has a myriad of choices:

A: Some inaccurate set-ups
B: 5 ... ♘f6
C: 5 ... ♗e6
D: 5 ... ♘c6

For 5 ... ♘d7 see Chapter 10.

For 5 ... ♗e7 see Chapter 11.

For 5 ... ♗d6 see Chapter 12.

A
Some inaccurate set-ups:

a) 5 ... c5? 6 ♕e2 with advantage.

b) 5 ... ♘d6? 6 0-0 ♕h4 (◯ 6 ... ♗e6, see also 5 ... ♗e6, in line C) 7 ♖e1 ♗e7 8 ♘c3 c6 9 ♘f3 ♕h5 10 ♗f4± Szilagyi - Csom, Hungary 1964.

c) 5 ... ♕f6? 6 0-0 ♗d6 7 ♕e2±.

B

5	...	♘f6
6	0-0	♗e7

White now has two ways of obtaining an advantage:

a) 7 c4 and after 7 ... 0-0 or 7 ... c6 8 ♘c3 0-0 see line C523 Chapter 11, by transposition.

b) 7 ♗g5 0-0 8 c3 ♘bd7 9 f4 Waller - Glass, Vienna 1978; ◯ 9 ♕c2!

C

5	...	♗e6
6	♕e2!	

7 ♗xe4 and ♕b5+ are threatened.

| 6 | ... | ♘d6 |

7 0-0   ♗e7
8 ♖e1

Or 8 ♘d2 0-0 9 ♖e1 ♗f5
(9 ... ♘c6 10 c3±) 10 ♘b3
♗xd3 11 ♕xd3 ♘d7 (11 ... f6)
12 ♘c5!± Minic - Rogoff,
Zagreb 1971.

8 ...   ♘d7

Not:

a) **8 ... 0-0?** 9 ♘xf7!±±,
or

b) **8 ... ♕c8** 9 ♘c3 0-0 10
♕h5 g6 (10 ... f5 11 ♘e2±
Steinitz).

9 ♗f4!

Better than:

a) 9 ♘c3 c6 10 ♗f4 ♘xe5=
Unzicker - Malich, Sochi
1965.

b) 9 ♘d2 ♘xe5 10 de ♘f5
11 ♘f3 0-0 12 ♗f4± Lein -
Malich, Sochi 1965.

9 ...   ♘xe5
10 ♗xe5   0-0
11 ♘d2   ♗f6

11 ... ♖e8 (Hooper) also
fails to equalize, viz. 12 ♕h5
g6 13 ♕h6 ♗f8 14 ♕f4.

12 ♕h5   g6
13 ♕h6   ♗xe5

14 de ♘f5 15 ♗xf5 ♗xf5 16
♘f3 f6 17 ♘d4!± Fuchs -
Malich, Leipzig 1965.

Conclusion: 5 ... ♗e6 con-
cedes the e4-square and
leaves Black unable to con-
test the e file with his
rook.

D
5 ...   ♘c6

This move is not really
good because the doubled
pawn can be exploited nowadays in the hands of a
master.

6 ♘xc6

Other moves do not pro-
mise any advantage:

a) **6 ♘c3 ♗b4** 7 ♘xc6
♘xc3!= Gligoric - Trifun-
ovic, Kragujevac 1959.

b) **6 ♘f3?** is pointless
and in the game Mortimer -
Marshall, 1903, after 6 ...
♗g4 7 c3 ♗d6 8 ♗e3 f5 9
♕b3 ♕d7! 10 ♗e2 0-0-0
Black even had the more
active position.

c) **6 0-0 ♘xe5** transposes
to line B Chapter 10.

6 ...   bc
7 ♕e2!

Other ideas include:

a) **7 ♗xe4 de** 8 0-0 g6 9
♖e1 f5 10 f3 ♗g7 11 c3 0-0 12
fe fe 13 ♖xe4 ♗a6 14 ♘d2 c5
and Black has excellent
compensation for the pawn.

b) **7 0-0 ♗e7**, see line C3
in Chapter 11; Better is 7 ...
♗d6 8 ♘d2 0-0 9 ♗xe4 de 10
♘xe4 ♗xh2+= Maljutin -
Rosenkrantz, St. Petersburg
1909.

7 ...   ♕e7
8 0-0   ♘d6

8 ... g6 9 ♗xe4 ♛xe4 10 ♕d2!± Bilguer.

9	♖e1	♛xe2
10	♖xe2+	♗e6

Feeble is 10 ... ♔d8 11 ♘d2 ♗f5 12 ♘b3! ♗xd3 13 cd± Showalter - Marshall, Paris 1900.

11	♘d2	♔d7

Black has a tenable position, e.g. 12 ♘b3 ♘c4! or 12 ♘f3 f6.

10) 3 d4 ♘xe4: 5 ... ♘d7

4	♗d3	d5
5	♘xe5	♘d7 (27)

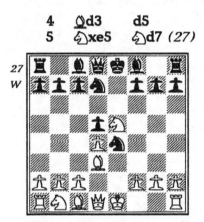

27
W

This move aims to exchange the centralized knight on e5, but without weakening the pawn formation.

White has now tried:

A: 6 ♘xf7
B: 6 0-0
C: 6 ♘c3
D: 6 ♘xd7
E: 6 ♕e2

A

6	♘xf7 (28)

28
B

An unnecessary, and probably not good, sacrifice.

6	...	♔xf7

A good alternative is 6 ... ♕e7 7 ♕e2 when:

a) 7 ... ♔xf7? 8 ♕h5+ ♔f6 9 0-0 ♕f7 10 ♕h4+ g5 11 ♗xg5+! ♘xg5 12 f4± Gurgenidze – Bellin, Tbilisi/Sukhumi 1977.

b) Better is 7 ... ♕xf7!

7	♕h5+	♔e7

7 ... ♔e6 is an adventurous continuation. If:

a) **8 ♕e2 ♗d6** (8 ... ♕h4? 9 g3 △ f3±; 8 ... ♔f7!?) 9 f3 ♕h4+ 10 ♔f1! ♖f8 11 ♘c3

♔f7 12 fe ♔g8+ 13 ♔g1 ♘f6∞
- Raetsky.

b) **8 ♗xe4** de 9 d5+ ♔e7 10
♗g5+ ♘f6 11 ♘c3 ♕e8 12
♕h4 ♗f5 13 0-0-0 ♔f7 and
Black has no more trouble,
Dozorets - Kishnev, Jurmala 1975.

8   ♕e2

Unclear is 8 ♕xd5!?, e.g.
8 ... ♘df6 9 ♕b3! ♗e6 10
♕xb7∞ Nenashev - Baikov,
Moscow 1985.

8   ...   ♔f7
9   ♕h5+

Leads to a draw by repe-
tition, as, for example,
Nunn - Balashov, Malta (ol)
1980.

B

6   0-0   ♘xe5

If 6 ... ♗e7 7 c4 ♘ef6 8
♘c3 dc 9 ♗xc4 0-0 10 ♗g5±
is Peterson - Kristiansen,
Kringsja 1978.

7   de   ♘c5

Or 7 ... ♕h4 8 ♕e2 Sarapu
- Dive, Wellington 1988; ⌐
8 ♗xe4 de 9 ♘c3±.

8   ♗e2

Or 8 ♘c3:

a) **8 ... ♘xd3** 9 ♕xd3 c6 10
♘e2 ♗e7 11 ♕g3 g6 12 c3 0-0
13 ♗h6 ♖e8 14 f4 ♗f5= Ad-
ams - Petrovic, Paris 1989.

b) **8 ... c6** and:

b1) **9 ♘e2 ♗e7** 10 ♘g3 0-0

11 c3 ♘xd3 12 ♕xd3 f6 13 ef
♗xf6 14 ♗e3 ♕c7 15 ♖ae1 b6
16 ♘h5 ♕f7= Velimirovic -
Kapelan, Vrsac 1989.

b2) **9 ♕f3 ♕h4** and now:

b21) **10 h3 ♗e7** 11 ♖e1 ♘xd3
12 cd 0-0 13 ♗f4 ♖e8 14 a3
♗f8 14 d4 g5 16 ♗e3 ♖e6
with mutual chances in
Geller - Smejkal, Moscow
1981.

b22) **10 ♘e2 ♗e7** (a routine move, 10 ... ♗g4 is
better) 11 ♘f4 0-0 12 h3 ♘e6
13 ♗e3 f6 14 ♘xe6 ♗xe6 15
♗f5 ♗xf5 16 ♕xf5 fe 17 ♕xe5
♖ae8?! (⌐ 17 ... ♕f6) 18
♕e6+ ♔h8 19 ♕d7!± Geller -
Plaskett, Sochi 1984.

8   ...   c6

8 ... ♗f5 is premature,
e.g. 9 ♘d2 ♗e7 10 ♘f3 ♘e6
11 ♗e3 0-0 12 c3± P Blatny -
G Hernandez, Thessaloniki
(ol) 1988.

8 ... ♗e7 is good, and
now:

a) **9 f4** f5=.

b) **9 ♘c3** c6 10 f4?! d4!∞
Minic - Eng, Berlin 1984.

c) **9 ♗f3** c6 10 ♘d2 ♗f5
(10 ... ♗e6 △ ♕d7) 11 ♘b3
♘xb3 12 ab d4?! (12 ... 0-0)
13 ♗g4!± Suchan - Grush-
evsky, Moscow 1986.

9   ♗e3

Or 9 ♘d2 f6 10 ef ♕xf6 11
♘f3 ♘e6 12 ♗e3 ♗c5= Kon-

stantinopolsky - Lilienthal, USSR Ch. 1940.

9 ... ♗e7

10 f4 ♘e4 11 ♘c3 ♘xc3 12 bc ♕a5=.

C

6 ♘c3

This acceptance of doubled pawns is all grist to Black's mill.

6 ... ♘xe5

a) **6 ... ♗b4?!** 7 0-0!?∞ ♘xc3 8 bc ♗xc3 9 ♗a3 ♗xa1 10 ♗b5!±.

b) **6 ... ♘xc3** 7 bc ♘xe5 8 de ♗e6 (8 ... ♗e7(!) 9 0-0 0-0 10 f4 f5!=) 9 0-0 f5?! (9 ... ♕d7 10 f4 g6 11 f5 gf 12 ♕h5 0-0-0 13 ♗xf5 ♗c5+ 14 ♔h1 d4=) 10 ♖b1 ♖b8 11 ♗e3 c5, King - Davidovic, Thessaloniki (ol) 1988, 12 f4 ♗e7 13 g4±.

7 de ♗b4

a) **7 ... ♕h4?** is feeble, e.g. 8 ♗xe4! de 9 ♘d5 ♗b4+ 10 c3 (after 10♘xb4 e3 11 ♘d3 Black has 11 ... ♗g4!!) 10 ... ♗a5 11 ♕a4+ c6 12 ♕xa5 cd 13 ♕b5+!± (Keres).

b) **7 ... ♘xc3** is again playable, e.g. 8 bc ♗e7 9 ♕h5 (9 0-0 see 6 ... ♘xc3) 9 ... ♗e6 10 ♖b1 ♕d7!= Kremenetsky - Pripis, Moscow 1977. 10 f4 can also be considered - Sax.

8 0-0 ♗xc3

8 ... ♘xc3 9 bc ♗xc3 10 ♖b1 (10 ♗a3 is not enough) when:

a) **10 ... 0-0** 11 ♗xh7+ (11 ♗a3 ♖e8 12 f4 f5 13 g4∞) 11 ... ♔xh7 12 ♕d3+ ♔g8 13 ♕xc3 b6 14 ♕g3!± (Sax).

b) **10 ... ♕e7** 11 ♖b3 ♗xe5? (the correct course is 11 ... ♗b4! - Sax) 12 ♖e1 0-0 13 ♕h5! f5 14 ♗f4 1-0 Sax - Nunn, Brussels 1985.

9 bc ♗e6

9 ... ♘xc3? 10 ♕e1 d4 12 f4 g6 13 ♗b2 ♘a4 13 ♗a3± (Sax).

10 f4 ♕d7

Also good is 10 ... f5 11 ef ♕xf6 12 ♗xe4 de 13 ♕h5+ ♕f7 14 ♕b5+ c6 15 ♕b4 ♗d5 16 a4 a6 17 a5 c5 18 ♕a4+ ♕d7 19 ab ♕xa4= Palac - Arhipov, Belgrade 1988.

11 ♕f3 g6

12 c4! ♘c5 13 ♗e2 ♕c6! 14 ♖d1 0-0-0= Sax - Pr Nikolic, Brussels 1988. Sax recommended 14 ♕a3 as an improvement.

D

6 ♘xd7 ♗xd7 (29)

There are three lines:

D1: 7 ♘d2
D2: 7 ♕e2
D3: 7 0-0

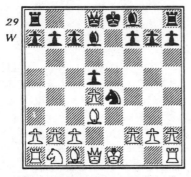

29
W

Or:

a) **7 ♘c3** can be strongly met by ... ♘xc3 △ ... ♛h4, ... 0-0-0.

b) **7 ♗f4 ♛f6!** 8 ♗xe4 ♛xf4 9 ♗xd5 0-0-0∓ Raetsky.

D1

7	♘d2	♛h4

Thematic and correct, but 7 ... ♘xd2 is also playable, viz. 8 ♗xd2 ♛f6 9 ♛e2+ ♗e6 10 ♛e5 ♛xe5 11 de 0-0-0= Simic - Kapelan, Vrsac 1981.

8	0-0	♘xd2
9	♛xd2	♗d6

9 ... ♛xd4!? 10 ♖e1+ Monakov - Chehov, Moscow 1975. Our suggestion is 10 ... ♗e7.

10	♛e2+	

Or 10 ♖e1+? ♔f8! △ 11 f4 ♗xf4∓.

10	...	♗e6
11	f4	0-0-0 =

D2

7	♛e2	♛e7
8	0-0	0-0-0
9	♘d2	

Others:

a) **9 ♗f4?** g5 - Euwe.

b) **9 f3** ♘d6=.

c) **9 c4**∞.

9	...	♘g5!

Also good is 9 ... ♘xd2.

10 ♛xe7 ♗xe7 11 f4 ♘e6 12 ♘f3 ♖df8= Geller - Arhipov, Moscow 1986.

D3

7	0-0(!)	♛h4

Other tries:

a) Smyslov's **7 ... ♘f6** also promises a solid position, e.g.:

a1) Black should not really be afraid of the open e-file, viz. 8 ♖e1+ ♗e7 9 ♛e2 ♗e6! 10 f4 g6 when 11 f5 can be met by 11 ... gf followed by ... ♘f6 - e4.

a2) **8 ♗g5** ♗e7 9 c3 (9 ♘d2 0-0! 10 ♗xf6 ♗xf6 11 ♛h5 g6 12 ♛xd5 ♗c6=; 9 c4!?) 9 ... c6 10 ♘d2 0-0 11 ♛c2 h6 12 ♗h4 ♘h5 13 ♗xe7 ♛xe7 14 ♖fe1 ♛d6 15 ♘f3 with some initiative, Geller - Smyslov, Moscow 1981.

a3) **8 c4!?** ♗e6 9 c5 g6 10 ♛a4+ (10 ♛b3!?) 10 ... ♛d7 11 ♛b3 c6 12 ♗f4 ♘h5= Prasad - Arlandi, Thessaloniki (ol)

1988.

b) After **7 ... ♗d6** 8 ♕h5 is not perilous e.g. 8 ... ♘f6 9 ♖e1+ ♗e7.

Or 8 c4 c6 and now:

b1) **9 ♘c3 ♘xc3** 10 bc Short – Hübner, Wijk aan Zee 1986, and now 10 ... 0-0 11 cd cd 12 ♕h5 g6 13 ♕xd5 ♕c7= (Short).

b2) **9 cd** cd 10 ♘c3 ♘xc3 11 bc, Hellers – Wolff, Baguio 1987, and 11 ... 0-0 12 ♕h5 f5 or 12 ... g6 13 ♕xd5 ♕c7!= (Short).

c) **7 ... ♕f6** when:

c1) **8 c3 0-0-0 9 ♘d2 ♗d6!=** Connolly – E Perez, Thessaloniki (ol) 1988.

c2) **8 c4 ♕xd4(!)** 9 ♘c3, Tseshkovsky – Bareev, Kiev Ch. 1986, and 9 ... 0-0-0 10 ♘xd5 ♘c5=.

c3) **8 ♘c3 ♕xd4** (simpler 8 ... ♘xc3 9 bc 0-0-0=) 9 ♕h5 (9 ♘xe4 de 10 ♗xe4 ♕xd1 11 ♖xd1 0-0-0= Kengis – Rosentalis, Kiev 1984) when:

c31) **9 ... ♘f6** 10 ♖e1+ ♗e7 11 ♕g5 ♘e4!? 12 ♕f4 g5∞.

c32) **9 ... 0-0-0!?** △ 10 ♗e3 ♘f6∞.

c4) **8 ♗xe4** de 9 ♘c3 0-0-0 10 ♘xe4 ♕g6 (10 ... ♕b6? 11 ♖e1!+ A Ivanov – Rosentalis, USSR 1985) 11 f3 and now:

c41) **11 ... h5** 12 ♗f4 h4 13 ♕d3 h3 14 g4 ♕b6 15 a4 ♗e6 16 ♖fd1, A Ivanov – Kochiev, USSR 1985, 16 ... f5!?∓ Raetsky.

c42) **11 ... f5** 12 ♘f2 ♗b5 13 ♖e1 ♗d6, Korolev – Glek, corr. 1986-88, 14 a4∞.

8   c4

Or:

a) **8 ♕e1 0-0-0 9 f3 ♕xe1 10 ♖xe1 ♘d6 11 c3 f6** ½-½ was Timoshchenko – Nogueiras, Havana 1981.

b) **8 ♘c3 0-0-0?** (first 8 ... ♘xc3) **9 ♘xd5 ♗g4!?** 10 ♕e1! ♗f3!? 11 ♕e3! ♖xd5 12 ♕xf3 ♘f6 13 ♗f5+ ♔b8 14 ♗e3±± Dückstein – Navarro, Thessaloniki (ol) 1988.

8   ...   0-0-0
9   c5

9 ♘c3 (9 g3!? is untested – Mihalchishin; 9 cd ♗d6 10 g3 ♘xg3=; we suggest 10 f4!?) when:

a) **9 ... ♗d6** 10 g3 and now:

a1) **10 ... ♘xg3** 11 fg! ♗xg3 12 ♕c2!±.

a2) **10 ... ♘xc3** 11 bc ♕h3 12 c5 ♗e7 13 ♖b1 Peev – Radulov, Bulgarian Ch. 1962.

b) **9 ... ♘f6**, a comprehensive move △ ... ♕xd4, ... ♗d6 or ... ♘g4. If 10 cd ♗d6! 11 f4 g5 12 ♕f3! g4 13 ♕g3 ♕h5∞.

9   ...   g5!

Feeble are:

a) **9 ... Nxf2?** 10 Rxf2 Qxd4 11 b4! (11 c6) 11 ... Qxa1 12 Nb2 Qxa2 13 Nc3± Mihalchishin.

b) **9 ... g6?** 10 Nc3 Bg7 11 Ne2 g5 12 f3 Nf6 13 Be3 g4? 14 g3 Qh5 15 Nf4 Qh6 16 Qd2± Kotkov - Hachaturov, Moscow 1971.

c) **9 ... Nf6** is also bad. 10 Nc3 g6 (10 ... Qxd4 11 c6!) 11 Ne2 Bh6 12 Bxh6 Qxh6, Prasad - Ravikumar, Indonesia Ch. 1987, 13 b4±.

10 Nc3

Or:

a) **10 f3 Nf6!** 11 Be3 when:

a1) **11 ... g4** 12 Nd2 Bh6 13 f4 Nh5∞, Arshenev - Raetsky, USSR 1988, 13 ... g3 14 h3 Ng4 15 Nf3 Nxe3=.

a2) **11 ... Re8** 12 Qd2 (12 Bf2 Qh6∞ Makarichev) 12 ... Rxe3 (12 ... Rg8 13 Bf2 Qh6 14 Qa5 Kb8 15 Bg3 Rc8 16 Nc3 Nh5!∞) 13 Qxe3 Nh5! and now:

a21) **14 Rd1** Bg7 15 Bf1 g4!, Dolmatov - Makarichev, Reykjavik 1990, 16 fg Re8! 17 Qd3! Bxg4 18 Nc3! Bxd1 19 Rxd1= Makarichev.

a22) **14 Nc3** Bg7 15 Ne2 Re8 16 Qf2 Rxe2!? 17 Qxh4 gh 18 Bxe2 Bxd4+ 19 Kh1 Nf4∞ Mihalchishin.

a23) **14 Nd2!?** Bg7 15 Nb3 Re8 16 Qf2 Nf4 17 Rfd1!

Qxf2+ 18 Kxf2 Ba4 19 Bf5+ Kd8 20 Re1!?± Makarichev.

a3) **11 ... Rg8** when:

a31) **12 Bf2** Qh6 13 Nc3 g4 14 Bg3 Qe3+ 15 Bf2 Qh6 16 Bg3 Qe3+ drawn - Bagirov.

a32) **12 Qe1** Re8 13 Qxh4 gh 14 Bd2 (14 Bf2 Nh5!) 14 ... Nh5 15 Na3! f5 16 Nc2 △ 17 Rae1.

a33) **12 Nc3** g4 (12 ... Re8) 13 g3! Qh3 14 f4 Nh5 15 Qe1! Re8 16 Qf2 Nf6 17 Rfe1 Bg7 18 Qc2 Re7 19 Bf2 Rge8 20 Re5 c6, van Riemsdyk - Casafus, Buenos Aires 1990, 21 b4!±.

a4) **11 ... Bg7** 12 Nc3 Rde8 13 Bf2 Qh6 14 g3 Qh3? (⌂ 14 ... Nh5) 15 Qc2 h5 16 Rfe1 h4 17 c6!± van Riemsdyk - Finegold, Dieren 1990.

b) **10 Be3** Re8! (10 ... f5!? 11 f3 Nf6!∞) and now:

b1) **11 Nc3** Re6!

b2) **11 Nd2** f5! equalizes (11 ... Bg7 12 Nf3 Qh5 13 Bxe4!±).

b3) **11 f3** Nf6 12 Bf2 Qh6! 13 Nc3 g4 14 f4! (14 Rc1 Rg8!) 14 ... g3!? (14 ... Qxf4 15 Bh4! Qxd4+ 16 Kh1 Ne4! 17 c6!±) 15 Bxg3 Rg8 (△ 16 ... Rxg3 and Ng4; 15 ... Ng4 is also good)∞ Makarichev -Ye Rongguang, Belgrade 1988.

10 ...   Bg7

a) **10 ... f5** 11 ♘xd5 (11 ♕b3 ♘f6; 11 f4) 11 ... ♘xf2! 12 ♖xf2 ♕xd4 13 ♗xg5 ♗xc5 14 ♘e3 f4! 15 ♗xf4 ♖hf8 16 ♕f1 ♕xe3! 17 ♗xe3 ♗xe3 18 ♕e2 (18 ♗xh7=) 18 ... ♗xf2+ 19 ♔h1 ♖de8 20 ♕c2, Wedberg – L A Schneider, Törshavn 1987, 20 ... h5⩲.

b) **10 ... ♖g8!?** 11 ♘xd5 ♖g6!∞ (Casafus, Morgado) 12 f3 ♖h6 13 fe±/∞.

c) **10 ... ♘f6!?** 11 ♕f3!? (11 g3 ♕h3 12 ♕f3 ♘g4 13 ♕g2 ♕xg2+=; 11 ♘e2 ♘g4!? 12 h3 ♘h6 13 ♗d2 ♖g8 14 f3 f5 15 ♕e1 ♕h5!? 16 b4 ♖e8 17 ♕f2, Am Rodriguez – Arhipov, Belgrade 1988, 17 ... f4!∞) 11 ... ♗g7 12 ♗f5 (12 ♘xd5 ♘xd5 13 ♕xd5 ♗e6=) 12 ... ♔b8 13 g3 ♕xd4 (13 ... ♕h5∞) 14 ♗xg5 ♕e5!= Y Grünfeld – Mihalchishin, Palma de Mallorca 1989.

11 ♘e2

11 g3 ♕h3 and now:

a) **12 ♘xe4!?** de 13 ♗xe4 ♗b5! 14 ♗xg5 ♖xd4 when:

a1) **15 ♕b3** ♖xe4 16 ♕xb5 h6! 17 ♗e3 ♖h4!= Dolmatov – Akopyan, Erevan 1988. 14 ♗g2 ♕f5 15 ♕b3 c6 16 ♖d1= (Akopjan) was less risky.

a2) **15 ♗g2!?**

a21) **15 ... ♕f5** 16 ♕b3 c6! 17 ♗e3 ♗xf1 18 ♖xf1 (18 ♗xd4 ♗xd4 19 ♖f1 ♗xc5=)

18 ... ♖d7? 19 ♕a4!± Geller – Howell, Reykjavik 1990, but 18 ... ♖hd8!∞.

a22) **15 ... ♕e6** 16 ♕f3 ♗c6 17 ♕e3 ♗xg2 18 ♔xg2 ♖e4 19 ♕b3, Nunn – Barua, London 1990, 19 ... ♕xb3 20 ab a6!=.

b) **12 ♘xd5** ♖he8 (12 ... ♗g4? 13 ♗xe4! ♗xd1 14 ♗f5+!±) 13 ♕f3 ♗f5 14 ♘e3 (14 ♘c3 ♖xd4 15 ♗xe4 ♖dxe4!? 16 ♗xg5∞) 14 ... ♗g6 15 c6?! (15 d5 ♘d2! 16 ♗xd2 ♗xd3∞ Ioseliani – Howell, 1989) 15 ... ♖xd4 16 ♗e2 h5 17 cb+ ♔b8 18 ♖e1 ♕d7 with balanced chances in Smagin – H Olafsson, Sochi 1988.

11 ... f5

a) **11 ... ♖de8** and now:

a1) **12 f3** ♘f6 13 ♗d2 ♖xe2!? 14 ♕xe2 ♘h5! 15 ♕f2 ♕xf2+ 16 ♖xf2 ♘f4 17 ♗xf4 gf 18 c6 ♗e6 19 cb+ ♔b8 ⩲ ... ♗xd4⩲ Ulibin – Akopyan, USSR 1988. Also good is 13 ... ♖hg8!?

a2) **12 a4** ♖e6! 13 f3 ♖h6 14 fe de 15 ♗c4 ♕xh2! 16 ♔f2 ♖f6+ 17 ♔e1 ♕xg2 18 ♖xf6 ♗xf6 19 ♗e3 ♗g7∞ Yoseliani – Gaprindashvili, USSR 1990.

b) **11 ... ♖he8!?** 12 f3 ♘f6 13 ♗d2 (13 ♕e1 ♕xe1=) 13 ... ♖xe2! 14 ♗xe2 (14 ♕xe2 ♘h5!∞ Howell – Makarichev, Frunze 1989) 14 ...

♞g4!, Sherzer – Halasz, Budapest 1990, 15 ♗f4! gf 16 fg ♛f6∞ Halasz.

12 f3   ♖hf8!

12 ... ♞f6?!13 ♛e1±.

13 a4!?

Or:

a) **13 fe?** fe 14 ♗c2 ♖xf1+ 15 ♛xf1 ♖f8∓.

b) **13 ♛e1** when:

b1) **13 ... ♛xe1** 14 ♖xe1 ♗c6 (14 ... ♖de8±) 15 ♖d1 f4 16 a4 ♞f6 17 b4 ♗d7 18 b5± Am Rodriguez – H Olafsson, Sochi 1988.

b2) **13 ... ♛h5** and now:

b21) **14 fe** de! 15 ♗c4 f4 16 c6!? ♗xc6 17 ♛a5, Am Rodriguez – G Hernandez, Pinar del Rio 1990, 17 ... f3!? 18 ♗e3∞ Rodriguez.

b22) **14 ♛a5!?** ♔b8 15 ♛b4! ♖f6 16 fe (16 c6? ♖xc6) 16 ... de 17 ♞g3 ♛h4 18 ♗xe4! fe 19 ♖xf6 ♗xf6 20 ♗e3∞ van der Wiel – Sisniega, Thessaloniki (ol) 1988.

13 ...   ♖de8

Less impressive is 13 ... ♖f6 14 ♛e1 ♛h5 15 fe ♖h6 (15 ... de 16 ♗b5 c6 17 ♞f4!± Grünfeld – Davidovic, Tel Aviv 1989) 16 ♛g3 de, Oll – Vladimirov, Tallinn 1988 active chess, 17 ♗c4 △ f4 18 ♗xf4±.

14 ♛e1

Or 14 ♖a3 Sveshnikov –

Makarichev, Moscow 1987, 14 ... ♞f6 15 ♛e1 ♛xe1 16 ♖xe1 f4=.

14 ...   ♛xe1

Or 14 ... ♛h5 15 c6 (15 fe de 16 ♗b5 c6 17 ♗c4 f4∞ Elizarov – Beshukov, USSR 1989) 15 ... ♗xc6 16 fe de 17 ♗b5 ♖e6 18 ♛d1 f4 19 d5 ♖d6 20 ♞c3 f3 21 ♞xe4 ½-½ van der Wiel – Miralles, Lyon 1988, 21 ... ♖xd5∞.

15 ♖xe1   f4!

16 fe de 17 ♗c4 f3 18 ♗e3! fe 19 ♖xe2 c6!= Sax – Salov, Brussels 1988.

E

6 ♛e2 *(30)*

Now Black can try:

E1: 6 ... ♞xe5
E2: 6 ... ♛e7

E1

6 ...   ♞xe5
7 ♗xe4   de

8   ♕xe4   ♗e6
9   ♕xe5
9 de ♗d5 10 ♕g4 h5 11 ♕h3 ♕e7 12 f4 ♕e6! 13 ♕xe6+ fe 14 0-0 ♗c5+ 15 ♔h1 0-0-0∓ (Larsen).
9   ...   ♕d7
10   0-0
Alternatives:

a) **10 c4?** ♗b4+ 11 ♘c3 0-0-0 12 0-0 (12 d5? ♗xd5!) 12 ... ♗xc4∓ is Makarichev - Shmuradko, Vitebsk 1981.

b) **10 c3?!** ♗d6 11 ♕a5 ♗c4∓.

c) **10 ♘c3** 0-0-0 11 ♗e3 ♗b4 12 0-0 f6. See main column (by transposition).

d) After **10 ♗e3**:

d1) **10 ... 0-0-0** 11 ♕a5! ♕c6 (11 ... b6!? 12 ♕xa7 ♗d5! - Raetsky, 13 ♘d2∞) 12 ♘c3 b6 13 ♕a6+! ♔b8 14 ♘b5± Hort - Short, Germany 1987.

d2) **10 ... ♕c6** 11 ♘c3 (11 0-0 ♗d6∞) 11 ... ♗b4 12 0-0 ♗xc3 13 bc 0-0-0= Gurgenidze - Dorfman, USSR Ch. 1981.

d3) **10 ... ♗d6** 11 ♕a5 ♗d5!?∞.

d4) **10 ... ♗b4+** 11 c3 (11 ♘d2? 0-0-0 12 c3 f6 13 ♕g3 ♗d6 14 ♕f3 ♖he8 15 h3 f5!∓ Unzicker - Eng, Germany 1984) 11 ... ♗d6

d41) **12 ♕xg7** 0-0-0 13 ♘d2, Oll - Halifman, USSR

1985, 13 ... ♕c6!∓ 14 0-0-0 ♗f5! △ ... ♕xc3+!

d42) **12 ♕a5** b6 (12 ... ♕c6 13 f3 ♗d5 14 ♘d2 0-0 15 0-0 ♖fe8!∓ Fedoseiev - Raetsky, corr. 1983-84, or 13 0-0 ♗d5 14 f3 b6 15 ♕a6 ♗c4 16 d5 ♕xd5 17 ♕a4 b5 18 ♕d1 ♕e5∓∓ Klinger - Wolff, Baguio 1987) 13 ♕g5 h6 14 ♕h5 ♕c6 15 0-0 g6 16 ♕h4 ♗e7 17 ♕g3 g5 18 ♘d2 f5 19 ♕f3 ♗d5 20 ♕xf5 ♗xg2∓ Shivodov - Kuznetsov, USSR 1987.

d43) **12 ♕g5** f6 13 ♕h5+ ♗f7 14 ♕f3 0-0-0 15 ♘d2 ♕b5 16 a4 ♕d3 17 ♕e4± Lanc - Huba, Prague 1989.

10   ...   0-0-0
11   ♗e3
11 c3 ♗d6 12 ♕a5 ♗d5⩲ - I Zaitsev.
11   ...   ♗b4!?
This is directed against ♕a5 and ♘c3.
12   ♘c3
Alternatives:

a) **12 a4** (△ ♕b5) 12 ... a6! — Larsen.

b) **12 a3** ♗d6 13 ♕a5 ♗d5! with good chances, e.g. 14 ♘c3 ♗xg2! or 14 ♕xa7 ♕g4 15 f3 ♕h4.

c) **12 c3** f6 (12 ... ♗d6 13 ♕a5) 13 ♕g3 ♗e7 14 ♘d2 h5 15 f3 g5 16 c4 f5 17 ♕e5 ♗d6 18 ♕a5± Kir. Georgiev - Salov, Leningrad 1987.

12   ...   f6

Now:

a) **13 ♕f4**, Unzicker - Rogoff, Amsterdam 1980, 13 ... ♗xc3!? - Larsen.

b) **13 ♕e4** ♗xc3 14 bc g5∞.

c) **13 ♕g3?** ♗xc3! 14 bc h5 when:

c1) **15 h4** g5! 16 f3 (16 hg h4∓) 16 ... ♖dg8 17 ♖f2 ♕c6 18 ♗d2 g4∓∓ Karpov - Larsen, Tilburg 1980.

c2) **15 f3** h4 16 ♕f2 h3 17 g3 ♕c6 18 a4 a5 19 ♖fb1 ♗c4 20 ♖e1 ♖he8∓ Gurgenidze - Rosentalis, Harkov Ch. 1985.

E2

6   ...   ♕e7
7   ♗xe4

Or:

a) For **7 ♘xf7** see var. c line A.

b) **7 0-0** ♘xe5 8 de ♘c5 9 b3 ♗e6 10 f4 g6 11 ♗b2 0-0-0 12 ♘d2 ♔b8 13 ♘f3 ♕d7= Timman - Larsen, Bugojno 1980.

c) **7 ♗f4** ♘xe5 8 ♗xe5 f6 9 ♗f4 ♘d6 with two ways:

c1) **10 ♘c3** c6 11 0-0-0 ♕xe2 12 ♘xe2 ♗d7 (12 ...

♔f7!?) 13 h4 ♔f7= Matanovic - Udovcic, Skopje 1962.

c2) **10 ♘d2** ♕xe2+ 11 ♗xe2 ♗f5 12 0-0-0 0-0-0= Dueball - Paoli, Reggio Emilia 1973.

7   ...   de
8   ♗f4   ♘xe5

Better than 8 ... g5 9 ♗g3 ♗g7 10 ♘c3 0-0 11 ♘d5 ♕d8:

a) **12 ♘xd7** ♗xd7 13 ♗xc7 ♕e8 14 ♗d6±.

b) **12 0-0-0±** Bitman - Schwartz, Moscow 1970.

9   ♗xe5   ♗f5!

Hort's improvement.

9 ... f6 10 ♗g3 f5 11 ♘c3 c6 12 0-0-0 ♕g5+ 13 ♔b1 ♗b4 14 ♘b5! f4 15 ♘c7+ ♔f8 16 ♕xe4 1-0 is Dely - Malich, Pecs 1964.

10   ♘c3   0-0-0

11 0-0-0 ♕e6 12 ♕e3! h5 13 h3 f6 14 ♗h2 (14 ♗xc7!? △ ♔xc7 15 d5) 14 ... g6 15 ♔b1 ♗h6 16 ♕g3 ♖h7 17 ♖he1 ♕b6 18 ♘xe4 ♖xd4 19 ♖xd4 ♕xd4 20 ♕b3! ♖d7 21 a3 b6!= Karpov - Hort, Amsterdam 1980.

In spite of all the earlier assessments 6 ... ♕e7 is playable for Black.

11) 3 d4 ♘xe4: 5 ... ♗e7

4	♗d3	d5
5	♘xe5	♗e7 *(31)*

This is a modest continuation.

Now White has:

A: 6 c4
B: 6 ♘d2
C: 6 0-0

The unusual 6 ♘c3 is best met by 6 ... ♘xc3 (6 ... ♗b4 7 0-0! see line c2 to White's 6th, Chapter 12) 7 bc 0-0 8 ♕h5 g6 9 ♕h6 (9 ♘xg6=) 9 ... ♗f6! 10 0-0 ♘c6 11 ♘xc6 bc= van Riemsdijk – Mirza, Thessaloniki (ol) 1988.

A

6 c4

This should be prefaced by 0-0.

6 ... ♗b4+

For 6 ... ♘f6 7 0-0 0-0. see line C523 by transposition.

7 ♔f1

7 ♘bd2 is better, though 7 ... ♗xd2+ 8 ♗xd2 ♘xd2 (8 ... 0-0 is also good) 9 ♕xd2 0-0 10 0-0 ♗e6=.

7 ... 0-0
8 ♕b3

Or 8 c5 c6.

8 ... ♗d6
9 cd ♗xe5

10 de ♘c5 11 ♗xh7+ ♔xh7 12 ♕c2+ ♔g8 13 ♕xc5 b6! (⌐ 14 ♕d4 ♘c6 15 ♕e4 f5) Zlotnik – Ovchinnikov, USSR 1968. White faces a hard defence.

B

6 ♘d2 ♘xd2
The alternatives:
a) 6 ... ♘f6(?) Pointless. 7

0-0 0-0 8 c3 c5 9 dc ♗xc5
10 ♘b3 ♗d6 11 ♘f3 ♘e4 12
♕c2± Kapengut – Roizman,
USSR 1968.

b) **6 ... ♘d6** and 7 ♕h5
gives White the advantage –
Keres, i.e. 7 ... g6 8 ♗xg6!?
fg 9 ♘xg6 hg (9 ... ♗g4! 10
♕xg4 ♖g8∞ Kapengut) 10
♕xh8+ ♔d7 11 ♕g7 ♕e8 12
0-0 ♘c6 13 ♘f3! ♘f5 14
♕h7±.

7   ♗xd2   ♘c6!
Weaker are:

a) **7 ... 0-0(?)** 8 ♕f3 △
0-0-0± – Bronstein.

b) **7 ... ♘d7** 8 f4! ♘xe5 9
de g6 10 ♕f3± Gurgenidze –
Travnicek, Olomouc 1976.

8   ♘xc6
8 c3 (8 ♕h5 ♗e6!) 8 ...
♘xe5 9 de c6=.

8	**...**	**bc**
9	**0-0**	**0-0**
10	**♕h5**	**g6**
11	**♕h6**	**♖b8!**

12 b3 ♗f6 13 c3 ♖e8! Spassky – Hort, (m) 1977.

Bronstein's 6 ♘d2 should
only give a microscopic advantage.

C

6   0-0 *(32)*
Now Black has tried:

C1: 6 ... ♘d7
C2: 6 ... ♘f6

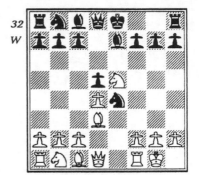

C3: 6 ... ♘c6
C4: 6 ... ♗e6
C5: 6 ... 0-0

C1

6	**...**	**♘d7**
7	**c4**	

Or:

a) **7 ♘xd7** when:

a1) **7 ... ♗xd7** 8 c4± or 8
♗xe4 de 9 ♖e1± – Polugay-
evsky.

a2) **7 ... ♕xd7** 8 ♗xe4 de 9
♖e1 f5 10 f3 ♗f6 11 c3 0-0 12
fe fe 13 ♘d2 b6 14 ♘xe4 ♗b7
and the power of the b7-
bishop offsets being a
pawn down.

b) **Euwe's 7 ♗f4** is posi-
tionally best although it
leads to only a slight advantage:

b1) **7 ... 0-0** 8 c4 c6 9 ♕c2
♘df6?! (△ 9 ... ♘xe5 10
♗xe5± Euwe) 10 ♘c3 ♘xc3
11 bc h6 (△ 11 ... ♗e6 12 c5±)
12 c5 ♖e8 13 ♖fe1± △ ♘xf7.

b2) **7 ... ♘xe5 8 ♗xe5 0-0 9 c4 ♗d6?** (correct is 9 ... c6 10 ♕c2± Euwe) and now the combination 10 cd ♗xe5 11 de ♕xd5 12 ♕c2 ♘g5 13 h4 ♖d8 is refuted by 14 ♘c3! ♕xd3 15 ♖fd1! Zagorovsky – Ovchinnikov, USSR 1969.

c) **7 ♖e1 ♘xe5 8 de ♘c5 9 ♗f1 ♗f5=**.

7 ... ♘xe5
8 de c6

Or 8 ... ♗e6 9 cd ♗xd5 (9 ... ♕xd5?? 10 ♕a4+) 10 ♕c2 ♘c5 11 ♖d1 ♘xd3 12 ♖xd3 c6 13 ♘c3 ♕a5 14 ♗d2 ♗c4 15 ♖d4 ♕a6 16 ♘e4± Ciocaltea – Rogoff, Malaga 1971.

9 cd

9 ♕e2 and 9 ♗c2 can also be considered, though in Tseshkovsky – Ovchinnikov, USSR 1968, Black overcame the threat from the dangerous passed pawn: 9 ♗c2 ♗e6 10 ♕e2 ♘c5 11 ♖d1? (⌂ 11 cd and 12 ♖d1±) 11 ... d4!

9 ... ♕xd5

Feeble is 9 ... cd, see Black's 7th by transposition.

10 ♕f3! f5

Weaker are:

a) **10 ... ♗f5? 11 ♘c3! ♘xc3 12 ♕xf5 g6 13 ♕h3±** Keres.

b) **10 ... ♘c5?! 11 ♕xd5 cd 12 ♗b5+ ♗d7 13 ♘c3±**.

11 ♖e1

11 ef ♘xf6 12 ♕e2 ♗g4! 13 f3±/= Minic – Ostojic, Yugoslavia 1968.

11 ... ♘c5!

Not 11 ... ♕xe5? 12 ♘c3! 0-0 13 ♗f4 ♕e6 14 ♘xe4 fe 15 ♖xe4±.

12 ♕xd5 cd⁻

If now 13 ♗c2 ♔f7! is correct.

C2

6 ... ♘f6

This is premature as 7 ♗xe4 is not a serious threat. For games starting with 6 ... ♘f6 7 c4 0-0 see line C523 with transposition.

7 ♘d2

7 ♗g5 0-0 8 ♘d2 ♘c6 9 ♘df3± Lundin – Makarczyk, Hamburg 1930.

7 ... 0-0
8 ♖e1 ♘c6

9 c3 ♗d6 10 ♘df3 ♗xe5 11 ♘xe5 ♘xe5 12 de ♘e4 13 ♗e3 f5 14 ef ♘xf6 15 ♕c2± with the advantage of a bishop pair in Veröci – Nikolau, Pernik 1972.

C3

6 ... ♘c6
7 ♘xc6 bc

With four continuations:

a) **8 c4 0-0 9 f3 ♘g5 10 c5=** Niephaus – Schüster,

Essen 1948. The d4 pawn provides Black with a target.

b) **8 ♖e1** 0-0?! 9 ♗xe4 de 10 ♖xe4 ♖b8 L Schmid – Bhend, Venice 1953. White should play accurately since Black has almost enough compensation for the sacrificed pawn. 11 ♖e1± is the most elastic.

c) **8 ♗xe4** de 9 ♖e1 can be considered, and

d) **8 ♘d2** as well, despite the exchanges.

C4

6	...	♗e6 (?)
7	♘c3	

The question is whether Black can successfully defend the e4 pawn after 7 ♗xe4 de 8 ♘c3. It seems as if it is possible, e.g. 8 ... f5 9 ♕h5+ g6 10 ♘xg6 ♗f7!∓, or 9 d5 ♗f6!

7	...	♘d6

Clearer is 7 ... ♘xc3.

8	♕f3	c6

If 8 ♕h5 g6 9 ♘xg6 fg 9 ♕e5 △ ♖e1∞.

9	♖e1	♘d7

10 ♕g3 g6 (⌐ 10 ... 0-0 11 ♗h6 ♗f6) 11 ♗h6± Zaselisvili – Sangla, USSR 1967.

C5

6	...	0-0

Now White has:

C51: 7 ♖e1
C52: 7 c4!

Or:

a) **7 ♗xe4** de 8 ♘c3 when:

a1) **8 ... f6?** 9 ♘c4 f5 10 ♗f4± Steinitz.

a2) **8 ... f5** 9 f3 ef 10 ♖xf3 ♘d7=.

b) **7 ♘d2** f6 8 ♘5f3 f5= Matanovic – Udovcic, Yugoslav Ch. 1952.

c) **7 ♘c3** is our untried suggestion. If 7 ... f6? or 7 ... f5? 8 ♘xd5!; 7 ... ♘xc3 8 bc △ ♕h5; 7 ... ♘f6 8 ♗g5±.

C51

7	♖e1	♘d6

Other tries:

a) **7 ... f5?** 8 f3±.

b) **7 ... ♘c6** 8 ♘xc6 bc 9 ♗xe4 de 10 ♖xe4 transposes to line C3.

c) **7 ... ♘f6** 8 ♗g5±.

d) **7 ... f6** 8 ♘f3 f5 9 c4! (9 c3 ♔h8!) 9 ... ♘c6 10 ♘c3 ♗e6 11 cd ♗xd5 12 ♘xd5 ♕xd5 13 ♕e2 ♘d6 14 ♗c2!±.

e) **7 ... c5!?** deserves attention. If 8 ♗xe4 de 9 ♖xe4 then 9 ... f5 with counterplay.

8	♕f3	♗e6
9	♘c3	c6
10	♘e2	♕c8!

Planning ... ♗f5 with an adequate defence.

C52

7   c4! *(33)*

White shakes the e4 base by attacking d5.

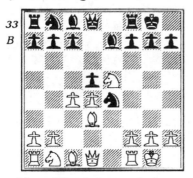

Now Black has tried:

C521: 7 ... ♘c6
C522: 7 ... c6
C523: 7 ... ♘f6

Or 7 ... ♗e6(?) 8 ♕c2!± (△ 8 ... f5 9 c5) 8 ♘c3 is feeble when 8 ... ♘xc3 9 bc dc is best with more or less equality of position, instead of 8 ... ♘f6? (see 8 ... ♗e6 in line C523).

C521

7   ...   ♘c6?

If White does not set up a claim to break it he may gain an opening advantage by 8 ♘xc6 bc 9 ♕c2.

8   cd   ♕xd5
8 ... ♘xe5 9 ♗xe4.

9   ♘xc6

Or 9 ♖e1 ♘xf2 10 ♔xf2 ♕xd4+ 11 ♖e3! ♕f4+ 12 ♘f3 ♗c5 13 ♕c2!±. A general lesson can be drawn from this: the d5 pawn should be reinforced.

9   ...   ♕xc6

9 ... bc 10 ♕e2!±±.

10   ♕e2±±

C522

7   ...   c6
8   ♘c3

Or 8 ♕c2 ♘f6 9 c5!? ♘bd7 (⌐ 9 ... b6) 10 ♘c3 ♘xe5 11 de ♘d7 12 ♗xh7+ ♔h8 13 ♗f5 ♘xe5 14 ♖e1 ♗f6? (14 ... f6 seems to be much better) 15 ♗f4 ♖e8 16 ♖e3!± attacking on the e- or h-file as in Tseitlin - Karasev, Leningrad 1970.

8   ...   ♘xc3
Weaker:

a) **8 ... f6?** 9 cd ♘xc3 10 ♕h5! ♘e2+ 11 ♔h1! f5 12 ♕xe2±.

b) **8 ... ♘f6** 9 ♕b3! see var. 8 ... c6 in line C523 with transposition.

9   bc   ♘d7
9 ... dc 10 ♗xc4 ♘d7 11 f4 when:

a) **11 ... ♘f6?!**, von Popiel - von Gottschall, Hannover

1902, 12 ♕b3! ♘d5 13 f5 gives White a perceptible advantage.

b) 11 ... ♘b6 12 ♗d3 (12 ♗b3!) 12 ... c5! 13 ♔h1 cd 14 cd ♗e6= Kassel - Grag 1942.

> **10 cd**

Or 10 f4!?

> **10 ... cd**
> **11 ♘xd7 ♗xd7=**

Stein - Udovcic, Berlin 1962.

After 7 c4 the position of the knight on e4 cannot be kept except at a disadvantage. So Black should retreat:

C523

> **7 ... ♘f6**
> **8 ♘c3**

Or 8 ♗g5 ♘bd7 9 ♘c3 dc 10 ♗xc4 ♘b6 (Black's knight is better here than on a5) 11 ♗b3 and now Black has several tries:

a) 11 ... ♘fd5 12 ♗xe7 ♘xe7 13 ♕f3!± Gligoric - Gudmundsson, Amsterdam 1950.

b) 11 ... ♘bd5 12 ♕f3! when:

b1) **12 ... c6?** 13 ♘xd5±.

b2) **12 ... ♗e6** 13 ♗xf6 ♘xf6 14 ♗xe6 fe 15 ♕xb7 (15 ♖d1 is also good) 15 ... ♕xd4 16 ♘c6±.

b3) **12 ... ♘xc3** 13 bc c6 14

♖ad1 or 14 ♖fe1 with positional advantage.

c) 11 ... ♗e6 12 ♗xf6! ♗xf6 13 ♗xe6 fe 14 ♕g4 (Capturing on f6 was necessary for this) 14 ... ♕e7 15 ♖ae1 ♖ad8 16 ♘f3! ♖fe8 17 ♖e2 ♘d7, Matulovic - Malich, Lugano (ol) 1968, 18 ♖fe1±.

d) 11 ... c6. A patient defensive player may accept Black's problems, e.g. 12 ♖e1 ♘bd5 13 ♕f3 ♗e6 14 ♖ad1 ♖e8, Jacek - Polakovic, corr. 1981.

> **8 ... ♘c6 (34)**

a) **8 ... ♗e6(?)** 9 c5!±.

b) **8 ... c6** 9 ♕b3± or 9 ♖e1 dc?! 10 ♗xc4 ♘bd7? 11 ♘xf7! ♖xf7 12 ♕b3 ♘d5 13 ♘xd5 ♗d6 14 ♘e7+ 1-0, Mokry - Arlandi, Haifa 1989.

c) **8 ... dc** 9 ♗xc4 when:

c1) **9 ... ♘bd7** 10 ♕b3 ♘xe5 11 de ♘g4 12 ♗f4 c6 (12 ... ♕d4 13 ♘d5) 13 h3± Lasker - Mason, Paris 1900.

c2) **9 ... ♞fd7** (△ 10 ♛b3 ♞xe5 11 de ♞c6, though it is somewhat slow) 10 ♗f4 ♞b6 11 ♗b3 ♞8d7 12 ♛f3 ♞f6 13 ♖fe1 c6 (13 ... a5) 14 ♗g5 a5 15 ♖e3 a4 16 ♗xf7+! ♖xf7 17 ♞xf7 ♚xf7 18 ♖ae1 ♗f8 19 ♞e4± Short – Tempone, World Junior Ch. Mexico City 1981.

c3) **9 ... ♞c6** 10 ♗e3 (better than 10 ♞xc6 bc 11 ♗f4±) 10 ... ♗d6 (10 ... ♞a5 11 ♗d3 b6 12 ♛f3 ♗b7 13 ♛h3 ♖e8 14 ♖ad1 ♞c6 15 f4 or 15 ♞e4±) 11 f4 ♞e7 12 ♛b3! ♛e8 13 ♖ae1 a6 14 a4 ♞c6± Duhrssen – Batik, corr. 1936.

9	♞xc6	bc
10	c5	a5
11	♖e1	♖e8
12	♗f4	♗e6

13 h3 ♛d7 14 ♛f3 ♖eb8 15 b3 ♞e8 16 ♗e5 ♗f6 17 ♗c2 ♗xe5 18 ♖xe5 g6 19 g4 f6 20 ♖e3 ♛f7 21 ♖ae1 ♞g7 with about balanced chances in Sveshnikov – Holmov, Moscow 1987.

12) 3 d4 ♘xe4: 5 ... ♗d6 Introduction

4	♗d3	d5
5	♘xe5	♗d6 *(35)*

The most promising way for Black.

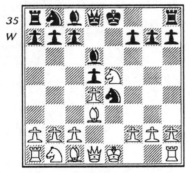

	6	0-0

Or:

a) **6 c4** when:

a1) **6 ... ♗xe5** 7 de ♘c6 8 0-0 ♗e6=.

a2) **6 ... ♗b4+** is also playable (see 5 ... ♗e7 6 c4 variations in line A, Chapter 11).

a3) **6 ... 0-0** 7 0-0 (7 cd ♗b4+ and ... ♕xd5= Holmov) see (by transposition) Chapter 13.

b) **6 ♕e2** ♗xe5! 7 de ♘c5 8 ♘c3 0-0 9 0-0 c6, Mieses - Grob, (m) Zürich 1934, 9 ... ♖e8!=.

c) **6 ♘c3** Either here or after castling is the same. However, there are some variations from the common lines, e.g.:

c1) **6 ... ♗b4?** 7 0-0! ♘xc3 (7 ... ♗xc3 8 bc ♘xc3 9 ♕h5±) 8 bc ♗xc3 9 ♗a3!± e.g. 9 ... ♗xa1 10 ♕h5 ♗e6 (10 ... g6 11 ♘xg6) 11 ♘xf7± or earlier 11 ♖xa1±.

c2) **6 ... ♘xc3** 7 bc ♘d7!? (7 ... 0-0 or 7 ... ♕h4 see, by transposition, line C) 8 0-0 (8 ♘xd7 ♗xd7=) 8 ... ♘xe5 9 de ♗c5 10 ♕h5 ♗e6 11 ♖b1, Polyakov - Komosin, corr. 1983-84, 11 ... ♕d7! △ 12 ♖xb7 ♗b6, Matsukevich.

c3) **6 ... ♘f6** can be found in var. b, line C.

d) **6 ♘d2** when:

d1) **6 ... ♘g5?** 7 ♘df3 ♘xf3+ 8 ♕xf3± Shamai - Berg, 1978.

d2) **6 ... ♘xd2** 7 ♗xd2 ♘d7

(⌐ 7 ... ♕h4) 8 ♕h5! ♕e7 9 0-0-0± Alexandriya - Sul, Riga 1974.

d3) **6 ... ♗xe5!** 7 de ♘c5 when:

d31) **8 ♘f3** with two lines:

d311) **8 ... ♘xd3+** (premature) 9 ♕xd3 ♘c6 10 ♗g5 ♘xe5! 11 ♕e3 f6 12 ♘xe5 ♕e7! 13 0-0-0 ♕xe5 14 ♕xe5 fe 15 ♖xd5 ♔f7 16 ♖xe5 ♗e6 17 ♖he1 ♖he8, Hort - Toth, San Bernardino 1982, 18 f3!±, Hort; 9 ... c6 10 0-0 (10 ♗g5 ♕a5+ 11 ♘d2 ♕a6!, Hort) 10 ... ♗g4 11 ♘g5 h6 12 ♕d4! ♗e6 13 ♘xe6 fe 14 c4 ♕e7 15 ♗d2 (15 ♗e3!?) 15 ... c5 16 0-0 with even chances, Bardin - Peshkov, corr. 1983/84; 9 ... ♗g4 10 ♗g5 (10 ♕b5+ ♘d7 11 ♗g5! is also strong) 10 ... ♕d7 11 0-0-0 c6 12 ♕a3 ♘a6±, Matsukevich.

d312) **8 ... ♗g4** 9 h3 ♗h5? 10 ♗f5 0-0 (⌐ 10 ... ♘e6) 11 g4 ♗g6 12 ♗g5± Gurgenidze - Yusupov, USSR 1982; 9 ... ♗xf3 10 ♕xf3 ♘xd3+ 11 ♕xd3 0-0 12 ♗e3 (12 ♕g3 see below, while Matsukevich's suggestion is 12 0-0 △ ♗d2, ♖ae1) 12 ... ♖e8 13 0-0-0 c6 14 f4 ♘a6 15 c4 ♕a5 16 ♔b1 ♘c7 17 cd ♘xd5∓ Goncharov - Polya-

kov, corr. 1983-84; 9 ... ♘xd3+ 10 ♕xd3 ♗xf3 11 ♕xf3 0-0 12 ♕g3 (12 ♗f4? ♘c6 13 0-0-0 d4 14 ♖he1 ♕e7 15 ♔b1 ♕e6 16 a3 ♖fe8∓ Nunn - Toth, Lugano 1984) 12 ... ♔h8! 13 0-0 ♕d7 14 f4? (better earlier 14 ♗e3 △ ♖ad1) 14 ... ♘c6 15 f5 ♖ae8! 16 f6 gf 17 ♗h6 ♖g8∓.

d32) **8 ♘b3** (= Hort) 8 ... ♘xd3+ 9 ♕xd3 0-0 10 ♗f4 (more careful is 10 0-0 b6 11 ♕g3 ♕d7!? 12 ♗f4 ♕g4 13 e6= Russek - Garcia Gonzales, Bayamo 1987) 10 ... b6 11 0-0-0 ♗e6 12 ♕g3 (12 c4) 12 ... ♕d7 13 ♗h6 f5∓ J Koch - Savva, Groningen 1986/87.

d33) **8 ♗e2** (= Hort) 8 ... ♘c6 9 ♘f3 ♗g4 10 ♗f4 0-0 11 0-0 ♖e8 12 ♖e1 ♕d7 13 h3 ♗h5 14 c3 ♖ad8, Mateu - Yusupov, Skien 1979 15 ♗g5=.

e) **6 ♕f3** when:

e1) **6 ... 0-0?!**∞ Polyakov - Osanov, corr. 1983-84.

e2) **6 ... ♕e7** 7 0-0 0-0 and now:

e21) **8 ♘c3** ♘xc3 9 bc ♗xe5 10 de ♕xe5 11 ♗f4 ♕f6 12 ♕g3 ♘c6 13 ♗g5 ♕d6 14 ♗f4 ♕f6 ½-½ in Zaitzev - Yusupov, Yerevan, 1982.

e22) **8 ♘d2?** ♗xe5 9 de ♕xe5 10 cd ♘c5 11 ♘c3 ♘xd3 12 ♕xd3 ♘a6 — Matsukevich.

e3) **6 ... ♗xe5** 7 de with two alternatives:

e31) **7 ... ♘c6?!** 8 ♗xe4 ♘d4 9 ♕d1! de 10 ♗e3 ♘c6 11 ♕xd8+ ♘xd8 12 ♘c3± with considerable advantage in Polyakov - Posdnikin, corr. 1983-84.

e32) **7 ... ♘c5** 8 ♕g3 (8 ♘c3 ♗e6 9 ♕g3 ♘xd3+ 10 cd ♖g8 11 0-0 {11 d4!} 11 ... ♘c6 12 f4 ♕d7 13 ♕f3 ♗e7± Mokrinski - Chaleyev, corr. 1983-84) 8 ... ♘xd3+ 9 cd ♖g8 10 0-0 ♗e6 11 ♘d2, Polyakov - Orehov, corr. 1983-84, 11 ... ♘c6 △ 12 ♘b3 d4 13 ♘c5 ♕d5 - Matsukevich.

> **6 ... 0-0** *(36)*

Other tries:

a) **6 ... ♘c6** 7 ♘xc6 bc 8 c4 0-0 transpose into var. B1, Chapter 13; while 8 ... ♕h4 or 8 ... ♕f6 can also be considered; 7 ♗b5 ♗d7 8 ♘xd7 ♕xd7 9 c3 0-0= (Pachman), we suggest 9 c4!? △ ... ♘f6 10 ♗g5.

b) **6 ... ♕h4** when:

b1) **7 ♘c3** ♘xc3 8 bc 0-0 transposes into line C1.

b2) **7 g3?!** (unnecessarily weakening) 7 ... ♕h3 8 ♖e1 ♗xe5 9 ♗xe4 de 10 ♖xe4 ♘c6 11 de ♗e6 12 ♘c3 ♖d8 with active Black play in

Maljuga - Komosin, corr. 1983-84.

b3) Our suggestion is 7 ♘f3 △ 8 ♖e1 and c4.

c) **6 ... ♗xe5** 7 de ♘c6 (7 ... ♘c5 8 ♘c3± Fred - Hadziotis, Tel Aviv (ol) 1964; 8 ♕h5!?) 8 ♘d2 ♘c5 9 ♘b3 ♘xd3 10 ♕xd3 0-0 11 f4 g6 (11 ... f5!?∞) 12 f5!? ♘xe5 13 ♕g3 f6 14 fg ♘xg6 15 ♗h6 ♖f7 16 ♖ae1 ♗d7 17 ♘d4 c6? 18 h4 ♕b6 19 c3 ♔h8 20 h5± Wedberg - Jones, Haifa 1989.

d) **6 ... ♘d7** 7 ♘xd7 ♗xd7 8 c4 c6 transposes into var. c 7 ... ♗d6, line D3, Chapter 10.

The rules of symmetry apply here - with correct defence Black should keep the balance. But the imitation should not be overdone:

White has tried:

A: 7 ♘d2

B: 7 ♖e1
C: 7 ♘c3

Or 7 f3 ♗xe5 (7 ... ♘c5=,
Keres) 8 de ♘c5 9 ♘c3
♘xd3 10 ♕xd3 c6 11 ♗e3 b6!
12 ♖fe1 (12 ♖f2) 12 ... ♗e6 3
♖ad1 ♘d7= Muhin - Noah,
Leningrad 1966.

For 7 c4 see Chapter 13.

A

7 ♘d2
Now Black has three
lines:

A1: 7 ... ♘f6
A2: 7 ... ♘xd2
A3: 7 ... ♗xe5

Or:
7 ... f5?! 8 ♘b3 ♘d7 9 ♗f4
♖e8 10 f3± Orehov - Uda-
lov, corr 1983-84.

After 7 ... ♘c6? 8 ♘xe4
de 9 ♗xe4 ♗xe5 10 de ♕xd1
11 ♖xd1 ♘xe5 12 ♗f4 Black
has the worse endgame.

A1

7 ... ♘f6(?)
Black increases the con-
gestion of his pieces, giving
up the e4-square without
countering against the e5-
knight.

8 ♘df3 ♘c6
Weaker 8 ... h6 9 c4 c6 10

♕b3± Richardson - Marsh,
Spain 1969.

9 c3 ♖e8
10 ♖e1 ♗g4 11 ♘xg4 ♘xg4
12 ♖xe8+ ♕xe8 13 ♕c2 h6 14
♗d2 (14 ♕b3 ♗xh2+!) 14 ...
♘f6 15 ♖e1 ♕f8 16 ♕b3 ♖b8
17 ♘h4± Penrose - Milner-
Barry, British Ch. 1966.

A2

7 ... ♘xd2
Suiting Petroff's Defence!
8 ♗xd2 ♘c6
Not better is 8 ... ♕h4 ⌐
9 c3 f6 10 ♘f3 ♕h5; on 9 g3
not 9 ... ♕h3? 10 ♕f3± B
Thipsay - Slavotinek, Thessaloniki (ol) 1988, but 9 ...
♕xd4 10 ♗c3 ♕c5 11 ♕h5
f5∓; we suggest 9 f4 and if
9 ... f6 10 ♗e1! ♕h6 11 ♘g4±.
9 ♘xc6 bc
10 ♕h5 g6
11 ... f5 can also be considered.
11 ♕h6 ♖e8
12 ♖ae1
12 ♗g5!? ♗e7 13 ♖ae1 ♗xg5
14 ♖xe8+ ♕xe8 15 ♕xg5 ♗e6
16 f4 ♕d8 17 ♕g3 ♕d6± is
Nunn - Hort, BBC Master
Game, London 1979.
12 ... ♖xe1
13 ♖xe1 ♗d7 14 ♖e2±
Parma - Toth, Rome 1900
and now 14 ... ♕f0 was the
correct defence.

A3

7 ...	♗xe5
8 de	♘c5
9 ♘b3	

Or:

a) **9 ♗e2 ♘c6** 10 f4 f6 (or 10 ... ♖e8) 11 ♘f3 fe 12 fe ♗f5 13 ♗e3 ♘e6 14 c3 Prieditis - Berger, corr. 1974-75; 12 ... ♗g4 △ 13 b4 ♘e4.

b) On **9 ♘f3**, 9 ... ♗g4 is best, then ... ♘c6, c.f. note d311 to White's 6th.

9 ...	♘xd3
10 ♕xd3	♘c6
11 ♗f4	

Or:

a) **11 ♖e1 ♕d7!** 12 ♗f4 ♕g4 (12 ... ♕f5) 13 ♗g3= Gurgenidze - Dvoretsky, USSR 1979.

b) **11 f4 f6!** 12 ef and now:

b1) **12 ... ♕xf6?!** 13 ♕xd5+ ♗e6 14 ♕c5 ♖ad8 15 ♗d2! (15 c3) 15 ... ♕xb2 16 ♗c3 ♕xc2 17 ♗xg7 ♕xc5+ 18 ♘xc5 ♖fe8 19 ♗c3 (19 ♘xe6 ♖xe6 20 f5 ♖e4! Maeder - Morgado, corr. 1984) 19 ... ♖d5? (19 ... ♗c4!) 20 ♘e4± Ljubojevic - Razuvayev, Amsterdam 1975.

b2) **12 ... ♖xf6** 13 ♗e3 (13 f5 ♘e5! 14 ♕g3 ♘f7=) 13 ... ♗f5 14 ♕d2, Matulovic - Toth, Budapest (m) 1972, 14 ... ♖g6!=. So 11 f4 rarely occurs.

11 ...	♕d7(!)

11 ... ♕h4?! 12 ♕d2 h6 13 c3 a5 14 a4 ♖d8 15 ♘d4 ♕e7 16 ♖fe1± Gufeld - Kochiev, USSR 1978.

12 ♖ad1	

Or 12 ♗g3 ♕f5 13 ♕xd5 ♕xc2 14 f4 ♗e6 15 ♕f3 ♖ad8 16 ♖f2 ♕f5 17 ♘c5 ♗d5= Rabinovich - Siwak, corr. 1983-84.

12 ...	♕g4

12 ... ♕f5, suggested by Yusupov, equalizes.

13 ♕e3	

13 ♕g3 ♕xg3 14 ♗xg3 ♘e7 (14 ... ♗e6 15 f4 ♘e7 ½-½ in Motwani - Yusupov, Skien 1979) 15 c3 c6 16 ♖fe1 ♘f5 17 ♗f4 b6 18 ♘d4 ♗d7= Velimirovic - Knezevic, Maribor 1980.

13 ...	♘e7
14 f3	

a) **14 h3?** ♕g6 15 c3 b6∓ Timoshenko - Yusupov, USSR 1979.

b) **14 ♕c5 ♘g6** 15 ♗g3 h5∞ - Yusupov.

14 ...	♕g6

15 ♕c5 (15 ♕c3 c6 △ ... b6) 15 ... ♕b6! 16 ♗e3 ♖e8 17 ♕c3 ♕c6! 18 ♕d2 ♕g6 19 ♖fe1, Grünfeld - Toth, Biel 1986, 19 ... b6=.

B

7 ♖e1	♗xe5!

8   de   ♘c6
9   ♗f4   ♘c5
9 ... f5 10 f3 ♘c5 11 ♗b5±.
10   ♘c3
10 ♗b5±.
10   ...   ♘b4
Or 10 ... ♗e6 11 ♕d2 △
♖ad1±.
11   ♗f1   d4
12 ♘b5 ♘e6 13 ♗d2 △ c3±
Euwe.

C
7   ♘c3   ♘xc3
a) **7 ... ♗xe5?** is premature. 8 de f5 9 ef ♘xf6 10 ♗g5±, Keres.

b) **7 ... ♘f6(?)** 8 ♖e1 (8 ♗g5!?) 8 ... ♘c6 9 ♗g5 ♗e6 10 ♘b5 ♗e7 11 ♗f4 ♘xe5 12 de± Gligoric – Alexander, Dublin 1957.

c) **7 ... f5** 8 f3 (8 ♘e2) 8 ... ♘xc3 9 bc c5 (9 ... ♗xe5 10 de ♕e7, Geller – Yusupov, Vilnius 1981, 11 ♕e1! ♘c6±) 10 f4 c4 11 ♗e2 ♘d7 12 a4 ♘f6 13 ♗a3 ♗xa3 14 ♖xa3 ♕d6 15 ♖a1 b6 16 ♗f3 ♗d7 17 ♕c1 ♖ab8 18 ♕a3 ♕xa3 19 ♖xa3 ♗e8 20 h3 h5 21 g3 ♖c8 22 ♔f2± Tseshkovsky – Reshevsky, Moscow 1989.
8   bc *(37)*
Now Black has a choice:

C1: 8 ... ♕h4
C2: 8 ... ♘d7

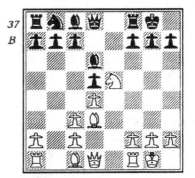

Other tries seem less effective:

a) **8 ... ♕f6(?)** 9 ♖b1 (9 f4 ♗f5 10 ♖b1 is also good) 9 ... ♘c6 10 f4±.

b) **8 ... ♘c6** 9 ♘xc6 (9 f4) 9 ... bc 10 ♕h5 g6 11 ♕h6±.

c) **8 ... ♗xe5(?)** is out of place here. 9 de ♘c6 10 ♖e1±.

d) **8 ... c5** when:

d1) **9 ♖e1** c4 10 ♗f1 ♘d7 11 ♕f3 ♘f6 (11 ... ♘b6! 12 ♗f4 ♗f5 △ ... f6) 12 ♗g5 ♗e7 13 ♖e3± ♗e6 14 ♖ae1 (△ ♘xf7) 14 ... ♕a5! 15 ♘d7!? ♘xd7 16 ♗xe7 ♖fe8 17 ♗b4 ♕b5, Suetin – Gasic, Olomouc 1975, 18 a4 ♕c6 19 a5±.

d2) **9 ♕h5!** and now:

d21) **9 ... f5?!** is weak, viz. 10 ♗g5! ♕c7 11 ♕f3 ♗e6 12 ♖fe1 c4 13 ♗f1, Geller – Yusupov, USSR Ch. 1983, 13 ... ♕c8 14 ♗f4±.

d22) **9 ... g6** 10 ♕h6 ♘c6 11 ♗g5 ♗e7 12 ♗xe7 ♘xe7 13

♘f3 f6 14 dc± - Krogius.

C1

8   ...   ♕h4(?)

This is primarily a preventive move, pre-empting ♕h5. However, the queen is misplaced.

9   ♖e1

a) If **9 f4** ♘d7 — Matsukevich.

b) **9 ♖b1** f6 10 ♘f3 ♕h5 11 c4! dc 12 ♗xc4+ ♔h8 13 ♖b5± J Horvath - Yap, Szirak 1985.

9   ...   ♘c6

a) **9 ... f6?** 10 g3 ♕h3 11 ♗f1 ♕f5 12 g4 ♕e6 13 ♘g6 ♕xg4+ 14 ♕xg4 ♗xg4 15 ♘xf8 and White turned his exchange to account in Krogius - Bremer, Helsinki 1942.

b) **9 ... ♘d7** 10 g3 ♕h3 11 ♗f1 ♕f5 Smyslov - Lilienthal, USSR Ch. 1941. Botvinnik's suggestion 12 ♗g2, with White's slight advantage, should met by 12 ... ♘b6.

10   g3

Or 10 ♖b1 ♘xe5 11 de ♗c5 12 ♗e3 ♗xe3 13 ♖xe3 (△ ♖b4) 13 ... c5 14 ♗e2± Kapengut - Karasev, Leningrad 1971.

10   ...   ♕f6

10 ... ♕h3 11 ♗f1 ♕f5 12

f4±.

11   f4!

11 ♘xc6 bc 12,♕h5 h6 13 h4 (△ ♗g5) is not a crushing attack: 13 ... ♕d8! 14 g4 ♕d7 15 ♗f5 ♕d8 16 ♗g5 ♗xf5! 17 gf ♕d7 18 ♗e3 ♖fe8 (△ 19 f6 ♕h3!∓) — Boleslavsky.

11   ...   ♗f5
12   ♖b1   ♖ab8

13 ♕f3 ♗xd3 (13 ... ♘e7? 14 g4 ♗xd3 15 ♘d7! ♕g6 16 cd) 14 cd ♗xe5 15 de ♕e6 16 ♗a3 ♖fe8 17 d4 g6 18 ♖b5 ♖ed8 19 ♖eb1 b6 20 g4± Boleslavsky.

C2

8   ...   ♘d7
9   f4

Alternatives:

a) **9 ♘xd7** when:

a1) **9 ... ♗xd7** 10 ♕h5 f5 and now:

a11) **11 c4** ♕f6! 12 c3 dc 13 ♗xc4+ ♗e6 14 ♗g5 ♕f7 =.

a12) **11 ♕f3** c6 12 ♗f4 ♕c7 13 ♗xd6 ♕xd6 ½-½ Adorjan - Yusupov, Indonesia 1983.

a13) **11 ♖b1** b6 (11 ... ♖b8?!, Adorjan - Toth, Budapest 1970, 12 c4±) 12 ♖e1 (12 c4 ♕f6) 12 ... c6! 13 ♗g5 ♕c7 14 ♗e7 ♖fe8! 15 ♗xd6 (15 ♗xf5 ♗xh2+!) 15 ... ♕xd6 16 h3 (16 ♕g5!?) 16 ... ♖e7= Geller - Yusupov, USSR Ch. 1979.

a2) **9 ... ♕xd7** 10 ♕h5 (10

♖b1 ♖e8 11 ♕h5 g6 12 ♕f3 ♖b8 13 h3 c6 14 ♗g5 ♕c7 15 ♖be1, A Ivanov - Vladimirov, USSR 1987, 15 ... ♖xe1 16 ♖xe1 ♗e6 △ ... ♖e8=) 10 ... g6 (10 ... f5 11 c4±) when:

a21) **11 ♕f3 ♖e8** and now:

a211) **12 a4** c6 13 ♗f4 ♕c7 14 ♗xd6 ♕xd6 with a tenable position in Adorjan - Petran, Hungarian Ch, 1973.

a212) **12 ♗h6 ♗f8** (12 ... ♕c6 is also good) 13 ♗xf8 ♖xf8 14 ♖fe1 ♕c6! 15 h4 ♕xc3 16 ♕xd5 ♗e6 ½-½ Short - Yusupov, Plovdiv 1983.

a22) **11 ♕h6 ♖e8** 12 ♗d2, Zijatdinov - Tashodzayev, Tashkent 1984, 12 ... ♗f8=.

b) **9 ♖e1** when:

b1) **9 ... ♘xe5** 10 de ♗c5 11 ♗e3 ♗xe3 12 ♖xe3 ♕h4 13 ♖b1! (△♖b4) 13 ... c5 transposes to the game Kapengut - Karasev, 1971. See White's 10th in line C1.

b2) **9 ... ♗xe5** 10 de ♘c5 and now:

b21) **11 ♗f1 ♖e8** 12 ♕h5 (12 ♗e3 b6 13 c4± - Keres; 12 ♗a3 b6 13 c4 d4= Gufeld - Makarichev, USSR Ch. 1973) 12 ... ♕d7!? 13 ♗e3 ♕c6 14 ♖ab1 a6 Chiburdanidze - Schüssler, Haninge 1988, and here we suggest that White should try 15 ♗xc5

♕xc5 16 ♖e3 △ ♗d3.

b22) **11 ♗a3 ♘xd3** 12 cd ♖e8 13 d4±/= Weydrich - Habenschuss, corr. 1978.

b23) **11 ♕h5** (Mikenas) 11 ... ♘xd3 12 cd c5?! 13 d4 ♕a5 14 ♖e3 cd? 15 ♖g3!± Matsukevich - Alexandrov, corr. 1985; 12 ... a5 13 ♗a3 ♖e8, Matsukevich - Mironov, corr. 1985, 14 f4±; 12 ... ♕d7 13 ♕f3! (13 ♗e3 ♕g4= Bracco - Reis, Brazil corr. Ch. 1986) 13 ... d4 14 ♖b1 ♕f5? (⌐ 14 ... dc 15 ♖b3 ♕f5) 15 ♕xf5 ♗xf5 16 ♖xb7± Matsukevich - Skotorenko, corr. 1985.

b3) **9 ... c5** when:

b31) **10 ♘xd7 ♕xd7** 11 dc ♗xc5 12 ♖e5 ♖e8 13 ♖xe8+ ♕xe8 14 ♗f4 ♕e6= Kremenetsky - Makarichev, Moscow 1976.

b32) **10 ♗f4** c4 11 ♗f5 ♘f6 12 ♗xc8 ♕xc8 13 ♖e3 ♕f5 14 ♗g3 ♘e4 15 ♕b1 ♘xg3 16 hg f6 17 g4! ♕c8 18 ♕b5!± Carlsson - Schaufelberger, corr. 1979; 15 ... ♗xe5±. Because 9 f4 seemed so powerful, 7 ♘c3 quickly became a popular line. But since the discovery of ...

9 ... c5! *(38)*

... giving Black excellent play, the 7 ♘c3 line has virtually disappeared.

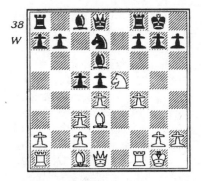

38
W

10 ♕f3

Probably the best try from the multitude of attempts by White to rehabilitate the line:

a) **10 dc** when:

a1) **10 ... ♘xc5** 11 ♗e3, Holmov – Korensky, 11 ... ♕c7=.

a2) The real improvement is **10 ... ♗xc5+** 11 ♔h1 ♘f6= – Tal. Black's play is easier to organize.

b) **10 c4?** cd 11 cd ♘f6 12 ♗c4 ♗c5, Kupreichik – Dvoretsky, USSR Ch. Leningrad 1974, 13 ♘d3 ♗e7 ∓, Dvoretsky.

c) **10 ♗e3?** c4 (10 ... ♕c7 is also good) 11 ♗e2 ♘b6! 12 a4 a5! 13 ♗f3 f6 14 ♘g4 ♗d7 15 ♗d2 ♗c6∓ Haag – Petran, Budapest 1974.

d) **10 ♖f3?** (△ ♗xh7+) 10 ... ♘f6! 11 h3 c4 12 ♗f1

♘e4∓. The knight arriving on e4 is much stronger than the other one on e5.

e) **10 ♖e1** c4 11 ♗f1 ♘f6 12 g3 ♘e4 13 ♖e3 f6∓.

f) **10 ♘xd7** ♗xd7 11 ♕h5 f5 12 ♕f3 ♗c6 13 c4 ♕f6 14 c3 ♕f7= Minic – Treppner, Berlin 1984.

10 ... c4!

An improvement on 10 ... ♘f6? 11 f5? (11 dc±) 11 ... ♕a5 12 ♘g4 ♘xg4 13 ♕xg4 ♕xc3 14 ♗e3 ♖e8!∓ Tseshkovsky – Makarichev, Lvov 1973.

11 ♗e2 ♕a5

11 ... ♘b6 is interesting, e.g. 12 f5 f6 13 ♘g6?! (13 ♘g4 ♗d7∞) 13 ... ♖e8! ⌐ ... ♗xf5.

12 a4

Tal suggested 12 ♗d2 f6 13 ♗xc4 ♘b6 14 ♗d3 fe 15 ♕h5 e4 16 ♗xe4 h6 17 ♖ae1 as an improvement but this is uncertain after 17 ... ♗g4.

12 ... f6

13 ♗xc4?

13 ♘g4 ♘b6 14 f5 ♗d7∓.

13 ... fe

13 ... ♘b6! 14 ♗d3 fe 15 ♕h5 e4 16 ♗xe4 h6!∓, Tal.

14 ♕xd5+ ♕xd5

15 ♗xd5+ ♔h8 16 fe ♖xf1+ 17 ♔xf1 ♘xe5! 18 de ♗xe5= Tal – Benko, Hastings 1973/74.

13) 3 d4 ♞xe4: 5 ... ♝d6
6 0-0 0-0 7 c4

4	♝d3	d5
5	♞xe5	♝d6
6	0-0	0-0
7	c4(!)	*(39)*

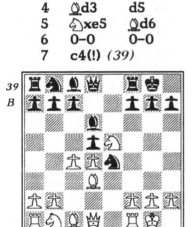

Black should avoid the symmetrical position; after 7 ... c5? 8 cd cd 9 ♝xe4 ♝xe5 White may give check by 10 ♝xh7+ winning a pawn.

Black has now tried:

A: 7 ... c6
B: 7 ... ♞c6
C: 7 ... ♝xe5

And less effective:
a) 7 ... f6? 8 cd± (Keres).

b) 7 ... f5(?) 8 f4 c6 9 ♝e3 ♝e6 10 cd cd 11 ♞c3 ♞c6 12 ♖c1 ♖f6? (◦ 12 ... ♖c8 or 12 ... ♝xe5) 13 ♝xe4 fe 14 ♞b5 ♞e7 15 ♞xd6 ♛xd6 16 g4!±.

c) 7 ... ♞f6 with two alternatives:

c1) 8 ♞c3 dc 9 ♝xc4 ♞bd7 10 ♖e1 (10 f4) 10 ... ♞b6, Ziska – Jones, Thessaloniki (ol) 1988, 11 ♝b3±.

c2) 8 ♝g5 dc and now:

c21) 9 ♞xc4?!, Chigorin – Halprin, Vienna 1898, 9 ... ♝e7=.

c22) 9 ♝xc4 ♝xe5 10 de ♛xd1 11 ♖xd1± (Bilguer), but in this case 9 ... h6 followed by ... ♞c6 was necessary.

A

7	...	c6
8	♞c3	

Other tries worthy of study:

a) 8 cd cd 9 ♛c2 ♞d7!? (the weaker 9 ... ♞f6 could transpose to b1) 10 ♝xe4 de

11 ♕xe4 ♘f6 12 ♕h4 ♖e8 13 ♗f4 ♗e7 Samaiev - Baronov, corr. 1935–36 with sufficient compensation for the pawn. Better is 13 ♘c3! ♗xe5 14 de ♖xe5 15 ♗g5±.

b) **8 ♕c2** and now:

b1) **8 ... ♘f6(?)** 9 cd cd 10 ♗g5 h6 11 ♗h4 followed by 12 f4± (Keres).

b2) **8 ... ♖e8** 9 f3 ♘f6 10 f4 dc 11 ♗xc4 ♗e6 12 ♗xe6 ♖xe6 13 ♘c3 ♘a6= Euwe - Olland, Utrecht 1922.

b3) **8 ... ♕h4** 9 ♘f3 ♕h5 10 c5 ♗c7 11 ♗xe4 de 12 ♕xe4 ♗g4 13 ♘e5 ½-½ was Timman - Hort, Bugojno 1980.

b4) **8 ... ♘d7** transposes into var. a.

b5) **8 ... ♘a6!?** 9 a3 (9 ♗xe4 de 10 ♕xe4 ♖e8∞) when:

b51) **9 ... ♗e6?!** 10 cd cd 11 ♘c3 ♘f6 12 ♗g5 h6 13 ♗h4 g5!? 14 ♗g3 ♘h5 15 ♖ae1 ♘c7 16 ♕d1 ♗g7 (16 ... ♘xg3 17 fg±) 17 f4 f5 18 ♗c2! △ ♗b3± Radulov - Forintos, Berlin 1988.

b52) **9 ... ♘ac5!** equalizes:

b521) **10 dc** ♗xe5 11 ♗xe4 de 12 ♕xe4 ♖e8 with active play for the pawn.

b522) **10 ♘xc6** ♗xh2+!

c) **8 ♕e2** ♘f6 (8 ... ♘d7 9 ♗xe4 de 10 ♘xd7 ♗xd7 11 ♕xe4±) 9 cd cd 10 ♗g5 h6 11 ♗h4 △ f4± (Keres).

d) **8 ♘d2** ♘xd2 9 ♗xd2 dc 10 ♗xc4 ♘d7 11 ♖e1 ♘xe5 (11 ... ♘b6? 12 ♘xf7!) 12 de ♗c5 13 ♕c2 ♕e7 (⌐ 13 ... ♕b6)) 14 ♗d3 g6 15 h4!± Sveshnikov - Kveinis, USSR 1989, 30 minute game.

8   ...   ♘xc3

Most precise. Other tries:

a) **8 ... f6?** 9 cd ♘xc3 10 ♕h5! f5 11 bc±.

b) **8 ... ♘d7?** when:

b1) **9 ♘xe4** de 10 ♗xe4 ♘xe5! 11 de ♗xe5 12 ♗xh7+ ♔xh7 13 ♕h5+ ♔g8 14 ♕xe5 ♖e8 with sufficient compensation for the pawn.

b2) **9 ♘xd7!** ♗xd7 10 cd ♘xc3 11 bc cd 12 ♕h5 f5 13 ♕f3! ♗e6 14 ♖e1± Keemink - Olland, corr. 1932.

c) If **8 ... ♗f5?** we suggest 9 ♕f3±.

9   bc

Now Black can consider:

A1: 9 ... ♗xe5
A2: 9 ... ♘d7

Or:

a) **9 ... f6?** 10 ♕h5.

b) **9 ... ♗e6?** when:

b1) **10 f4** ♗xe5 11 fe dc 12 ♗xh7+!± Steinitz.

b2) **10 ♕h5** and now:

b21) **10 ... g6** 11 ♕h6 ♘d7

12 f4± Schmidt – Reitstein, Wilderness 1964.

b22) **10 ... f5** 11 ♕e2 ♕c8 12 c5 ♗c7 13 a4 ♗a5 14 ♗d2± Endzenins – Garner, corr. World Ch. 1959–62.

c) **9 ... dc** 10 ♗xc4 ♘d7 10 f4 ♘f6± Popiel – Gottschall, Hannover 1912. Comparing to a similar position, but with ... ♗e7, Black has a more favourable situation; he may defend his f7 pawn more easily (... ♕c7) and at the same time prepare his counterplay with ... c6 – c5.

A1

| 9 | ... | ♗xe5 |
| 10 | de | dc! |

10 ... ♗e6? 11 ♕h5! g6 12 ♕h6±.

10 ... ♘d7?! 11 ♗a3! ♖e8 12 f4±.

11 ♗xc4   ♕e7

Other tries also fail to equalize:

a) **11 ... ♕xd1?** 12 ♖xd1±.

b) **11 ... ♗e6** 12 ♗xe6 fe 13 ♕b3 ♕c8 14 ♗a3 c5 15 ♖ad1 b6 16 ♖d6 ♖e8 17 ♕a4± Maroczy – Showalter, Paris 1900.

c) **11 ... ♗f5** 12 ♕f3 ♗g6 13 ♕g3 ♕a5 14 ♗e3!± Schorr – de Loughry, Tel Aviv (ol) 1964.

d) **11 ... ♕a5** 12 a4! ♕xe5

(12 ... ♕xc3 13 ♗a3!±± ♖e8 14 ♗xf7+!) 13 ♖e1 ♕c7 14 ♗a3 c5 (14 ... ♖d8?? 15 ♗xf7+! ♔xf7 16 ♕h5+) 15 ♕f3±.

12   a4

Or:

a) **12 ♕h5 ♕c5!**

b) **12 ♖e1 ♕c5** 13 ♕b3 b5 14 ♗d3 ♗e6 15 ♕c2 h6 16 a4 ♖d8 17 ♗e3!± Botterill – de Veauce, Islington 1971.

12   ...   ♗e6

a) **12 ... ♕xe5?** 13 ♖e1±.

b) **12 ... ♖d8?!** 13 ♕h5± Chigorin – Lebediev, St. Petersburg 1901.

c) **12 ... ♖e8** could be tried.

13 ♗a3   c5

14 ♗d3 ♘c6 15 f4 ♖fd8 16 ♕c2 g6 17 ♖ae1± Pogats – Androvitzky, Budapest 1962.

A2

| 9 | ... | ♘d7 |
| 10 | f4 | |

Or:

a) **10 ♖e1 ♗xe5** 11 de ♘c5 12 ♗c2 Ivanovic – Kurajica, Bor 1980, 12 ... dc! with ... ♘d3 would give Black good counterplay.

b) **10 ♘xd7! ♗xd7** 11 cd cd 12 ♕h5 f5 13 ♕f3!±.

10   ...   ♘f6

Or 10 ... dc 11 ♗xc4 (11 ♘xc4 ♘f6) 11 ... ♕c7 12 a4 c5 13 ♕e2 b6 14 a5, A Rodriguez – Sisniega, Bayamo 1981, 14 ... ba △ ♘b6∞.

11 ♕c2

Also good is 11 f5 c5 12 ♗g5 ♖e8 13 ♖e1± Jansa – Kupka, Czech Ch. 1962.

11	...	dc
12	♘xc4	♗e6
13	♘xd6	♕xd6
14	f5±	

Chigorin – Pillsbury, Paris 1900.

B

    7   ...   ♘c6 *(40)*

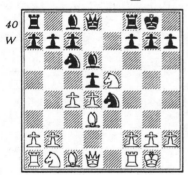

Now White has:

B1: 8 ♘xc6
B2: 8 cd

Or 8 f4 when:
a) **8 ... ♘xd4** 9 ♗xe4 ♗xe5 10 ♗xh7+ ♔xh7 11 fe c5 (11 ... dc 12 ♘c3 △ ♘e4±) 12 ♕h5+ ♔g8 13 ♗g5 ♕d7 14 ♘c3± L Steiner – Rejfir, Maribor 1934.

b) **8 ... ♘b4** 9 cd ♘xd3 10 ♕xd3 ♘f6 11 ♘c3 ♗b4 12 f5±.

c) **8 ... ♗xe5** 9 de f5= See var. b. 9 ... f5 line C21.

B1

8	♘xc6	bc
9	c5	♗e7
10	♘c3	

Or:
a) **10 f3** ♘g5 11 ♘c3 f5!=.
b) **10 ♕c2** f5=.
c) **10 ♘d2** (Maroczy) and now:

c1) **10 ... ♘xd2?** 11 ♗xd2 ♗f6 12 ♗c3 a5 13 ♗c2 ♕d7 14 h3± Geller – Naranja, Palma de Mallorca (izt) 1970.

c2) **10 ... ♗f5**, Aitken – Hooper, Felixstowe 1949, 11 ♘b3 ♕d7=.

c3) **10 ... ♗f6** 11 ♘xe4 (11 ♘b3 a5 12 a4 ♕d7 △ ... ♗a6 and ... ♖fb8=) 11 ... de 12 ♗xe4 ♗a6!? 13 ♗xc6 ♖b8 14 ♖e1 ♗xd4= (Keres).

d) **10 ♘a3** planning b4 – b5 has not been tried in practice.

    10   ...   **f5**

Weaker are:
a) **10 ... ♘f6** 11 ♕a4 ♗d7 12 ♖e1 ♘e8 13 ♖e2± German – Maragliano, Brazilian Ch. 1951.

b) **10 ... ♘xc3** 11 bc f5 12 ♗f4 ♗f6 13 ♕a4 ♕d7 14 ♕a5

♖f7 15 ♖fe1 g5 16 ♗e5± German – Sallamini, Brazilian Ch. 1951.

c) **10 ... ♗f6** 11 ♗e3±.

11 f3

Also good is 11 ♘e2 ♗f6 14 ♕a4± Rumens – Milner-Barry, British Ch. 1978.

    11 ... ♘g5
    12 ♕a4!

Or 12 ♗e3 ♘e6=.

    12 ... ♕d7
    13 ♗f4±

Black's c6 pawn is a definite weakness which White should be able to exploit.

Less effective is 13 ♘e2 ♘e6 14 ♘f4 ♘d8 15 ♖e1 ♗f6= Schmid – Krebs, corr. 1951–52.

B2
    8 cd ♘xd4
    9 ♗xe4

Or:

a) If **9 ♗f4?** ♕f6 Thomas – Hallmark, York 1959.

b) **9 ♘c4** and now:

b1) **9 ... ♘f6(?)** 10 ♗xh7+ ♔xh7 11 ♕xd4 ♘xd5, Szabo – Michell, Mar del Plata 1948, 12 b3! ♖e8 13 ♗b2± (Harding).

b2) **9 ... ♕h4!** 10 ♘xd6 ♘xd6 11 ♘c3 ♗f5= (Euwe).

    9 ... ♗xe5
    10 ♘c3(!)

Feeble are:

a) **10 ♗xh7+?** ♔xh7 11 ♕h5+ ♔g8 12 ♕xe5 ♘c2∓∓.

b) **10 f4 ♗f6** when:

b1)) **11 ♘c3 ♗f5** 12 ♕d3 ♗xe4= Alekhine – Alexander, Hastings 1933/34; 12 ♗e3 ♗xe4 13 ♗xd4=.

b2) **11 ♕d3 ♖e8!** and then:

b21) **12 ♗xh7+?** ♔h8 13 ♘c3 (13 ♗e4? ♖xe4!∓∓) ... g6 14 ♗xg6 fg 15 ♕xg6 ♗f5 with a violent attack for Black.

b22) **12 ♘c3** g6 13 ♗d2 ♗g7 14 ♖ae1 ♗f5= Henley – Wheeler, Bristol 1960.

b3) **11 g4** g6(!) 12 ♘c3 ♗g7 13 ♗e3 c5= Meszaros – Erdy, Budapest, 1955.

    10 ... ♗f5
    11 ♗e3 ♗xe4
    12 ♗xd4 ♗c2

More precise than 12 ... ♗xd4 13 ♕xd4 ♗g6 14 ♖c1 a6 15 ♕b4± Matulovic – Hecht, Belgrade 1969.

    13 ♕d2(!) ♗xd4

14 ♕xd4 ♕d7 15 ♖fe1 a6 16 ♖e2± Tal – Osnos, Kiev 1964.

C
    7 ... ♘xe5! *(41)*

The most active continuation.

    8 de

Now Black can consider:

C1: 8 ... ♗e6
C2: 8 ... ♘c6

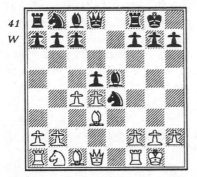

41
W

8 ... c6(?) is a bit passive,
9 ♕c2 f5 10 ef ⬧xf6 11 ♗g5
h6 12 ♗h4 ♗e6 13 ⬧d2 ⬧bd7,
Honfi – Bartos, Budapest
1954, 14 ♖fe1±.

C1

8   ...   ♗e6

That move is no longer
considered adequate.

9   cd!

Or 9 ♗e3?! ⬧c6 10 f3? (10
f4) 10 ... d4 11 ♗xe4 de 12
♕c2, Duckstein–Trifunovic,
Vienna 1962, 12 ... ⬧xe5!∓.

9   ...   ♕xd5

9 ... ♗xd5? 10 ♕c2±.

10   ♕c2!

If 10 ♖e1 ♖d8!

10   ...   f5
11   ef   ⬧xf6
12   ⬧c3   ♕e5

a) **12 ... ♕c6** (Keres) 13
♗g5 ⬧bd7 14 ♖fe1 ♗c4 15
♗f5 Zrzavy – Stefec, corr.
1981, and Black can defend
his position with 15 ... h6.

b) **12 ... ♕h5** 13 ⬧b5 ⬧a6∞.
   13   ⬧e4

Or:
a) **13 ⬧e2 ⬧bd7!** 14 ♗f4
♕c5= Honfi – Malich, Kecskemet 1968.
b) We suggest **13 ♗d2** (∠
14 ♖ae1), e.g. 13 ... ⬧g4 14
f4! ♕c5+ 15 ♔h1 ⬧f2+ 16
♖xf2 ♕xf2 17 ⬧e4 with an
attack.

13   ...   ⬧g4
14   ⬧g3

14 g3? ⬧c6 15 f4 ♕d4+ 16
⬧f2 ♖ad8 (16 ... ⬧b4 17
♗xh7+ ♔h8 18 ♕e4!) 17 ♗d2
h6 18 ♗c3 ♕b6∓ ½–½ Dely –
Malich, Kecskemet 1968.

14   ...   h5?

14 ... h6 is obviously better.

15   ♗d2   ♗d5

16 ♗c3 ♕g5 17 ♗h7+ ♔h8
18 ♕g6±± Liberzon – Henn-
ings, Debrecen 1968.

C2

8   ...   ⬧c6

Counter-attack in the
best tradition of Petroff's
Defence.

Now White has tried:

C21: 9 f4
C22: 9 ♗f4
C23: 9 cd

Other tries:

a) **9 ♖e1?** ♘xe5 10 cd ♘xf2! 11 ♔xf2 (Not 11 ♗xh7+ ♔xh7 12 ♕h5+ ♔g8 when neither knight can be captured) 11 ... ♕h4+ is favourable for Black, e.g. 12 ♔g1 ♘g4! 13 h3 ♘f2 △ ... ♘xd3∓.

b) After **9 f3** there is only one way to keep the balance, viz. 9 ... ♘c5 10 cd ♘xd3! 11 ♕xd3 ♘b4 (11 ... ♘xe5 12 ♕d4 ♖e8 13 ♘c3±) 12 ♕b3 ♘xd5 13 ♖d1 ♗e6!=, 14 ♕xb7 is risky because of 14 ... ♕h4!, while 14 ♘c3 leads to common exchanges.

c) **9 ♗c2** ♗e6 10 cd ♕xd5 11 ♕xd5 ♗xd5 12 f3 ♘c5 13 ♗e3 ♘e6 14 ♖d1 ♘b4 15 ♗a4 ♗xa2 16 ♘d2 ♗xb1 17 ♗xb4 c5 18 ♗c3 ♗f5 19 g4! ♗g6 20 ♖d7∞ Wedberg – Schüssler, Malmö 1987–88.

C21

9 f4

Here Black has a choice:

Or:

a) **9 ... ♘c5?!** 10 cd ♘xd3 11 ♕xd3 ♘b4 12 ♕e4! ♘xd5 13 f5 ♖e8 14 ♘d2! △ ♘c4 or ♘f3±.

b) **9 ... f5** leads to equality e.g. 10 ♘c3 ♘xc3 11 bc d4 (11 ... ♗e6 12 ♕e2 ♘a5 is also good), Kapengut - Stepanov, USSR 1976, 12 ♗b2 dc 13 ♗xc3 ♘d4 or 13 ... ♗e6=.

C211

9 ... ♗f5
10 ♘c3

Other examples:

a) **10 g4?** dc! 11 ♗e2 (11 ♗c2 ♕xd1!) 11 ... ♗e6 12 f5 ♗d5∓∓.

b) **10 cd** ♕xd5 11 ♗xe4 ♕xe4∓, Kostro - Dvoretsky, Polanica Zdroj 1973, if 12 ♘c3 ♕c4 or ... ♕d4+.

c) **10 ♕e1** is not the best either:

c1) **10 ... dc??** 11 ♗xe4 ♕d4+ 12 ♗e3! ♕xe4 13 ♘c3 ♕c2 14 ♖f2 ♕d3 15 ♖d1±±.

c2) **10 ... ♕d7** (B Toth) 11 ♘a3 (11 g4 ♗xg4 12 cd ♘c5∞) 11 ... ♖ad8 with even chances.

c3) **10 ... ♘d6** 11 ♗xf5 ♘xf5 12 g4 ♘fd4 13 cd ♕xd5 14 ♘c3 ♕f3! 15 ♕d1! ♕xd1 16 ♖xd1 ♖ad8= Wikman–Sloth, corr. 1985–86.

d) **10 ♗e3**, Nicevski - Dvoretsky, Polanica Zdroj 1973, 10 ... d4!

10 ...   ♘xc3

10 ... ♘b4? 11 ♗b1! ♕e7 (11 ... ♘xc3 12 bc ♗xb1 13

♖xb1±) 12 cd ♕c5+ 13 ♔h1 ♘xc3 14 bc ♕xc3 15 ♗b2! ♕xb2 16 ♗xf5 ♖ad8 17 ♖b1± Janosevic - Toth, Madonna di Campiglio 1974.

11 bc   ♗xd3
12 ♕xd3   dc
13 ♕xc4   ♕e7

13 ... ♕d7 is also good, Jansa - Makarichev, Amsterdam 1975.

14 ♖b1   ♖ab8

15 ♗e3 ♕e6! with level chances in Valkesalmi - Dolmatov, Groningen 1979.

C212
9 ...   ♘b4
10 cd

10 ♗e3 ♗g4 (10 ... ♗f5 see var. d. line C211) 11 ♗e2 ♗xe2 12 ♕xe2 dc 13 ♖d1 (13 ♕xc4 ♕d3) 13 ... ♘d3 14 ♘a3 ♕d5! 15 ♘xc4 ♖ad8∓.

10 ...   ♕xd5
11 ♗xe4   ♕xe4
12 ♘c3   ♕c4(!)

a) 12 ... ♕f5 13 ♗e3 ♗e6 (13 ... ♘c2 14 ♗c5!) 14 ♕f3 ♖fd8! 15 ♖ad1 ♖xd1 16 ♖xd1 c6= Movcka - Polakovic, corr. 1981.

b) 12 ... ♕g6 13 ♗e3 ♗g4! when:

b1) 14 ♕a4? ♘c2 15 ♘d5 ♕d3! Vanman - Broberger, corr. 1978.

b2) 14 ♘d5 ♗xd1! (14 ...

♘xd5 15 ♕xd5 ♗f5!= Palciauskas - Morgado, corr. 1978-80) 15 ♘e7+ ♔h8 16 ♘xg6+ hg 16 ♖axd1(!) ♖fd8 17 a3 ♘d5= (Matsukevich).

b3) 14 ♕b3 ♘c2 15 ♘d5 ♕e4 16 ♖ac1 ♘xe3 17 ♘xe3 ♗e6 18 ♕c3 (18 ♕a3) 18 ... ♖ad8 with active play in Kraut - Forintos, Kecskemet 1987.

13 ♗e3   ♗f5

14 ♕f3 ♘c2, Sikora - Maroszczyk, Trinec 1978, 15 ♖ac1=.

C22
9 ♗f4   ♘b4
Other interesting ideas:
a) 9 ... ♗e6 (Keres) 10 ♘a3 ♘c5 11 cd ♕xd5 12 ♗b5 ♖fd8 ½-½ Haygarth - Clarke, Brighton 1972.

b) 9 ... ♘c5 and now:

b1) 10 cd ♘xd3! 11 ♕xd3 ♘b4 12 ♕g3 (12 ♕b3 ♘xd5 13 ♖d1 ♗e6) 12 ... ♗f5 13 ♗g5 ♕d7!=.

b2) Our interesting idea: 10 ♗xh7+!? ♔xh7 11 cd ♘b4 12 ♘c3∞.

10 ♘a3
Or:
a) 10 ♗xe4? de 11 ♘c3 ♕xd1 12 ♖fxd1 ♘d3∓ Haag - Dely, Pecs 1964.

b) 10 a3(?) ♘xd3 11 ♕xd3 ♘c5 12 ♕c2, Salov - Majorov, USSR 1979, 12 ... dc 13 ♕xc4 b6∓.

c) 10 ♗e2 dc 11 ♗xc4 ♕xd1 12 ♖xd1 ♗e6!=/∓ Arbakov – Mikenas, Vilnius 1967.

d) 10 cd ♕xd5 11 ♗e2 ♗f5! 12 ♘a3 ♖fd8 13 ♗c4 ♕xd1 14 ♖fxd1 c6 (preparing ... b5 and also ... ♘d5; 14 ... ♗e6 is also good) 15 ♗e3 (△ f3) 15 ... b5= 16 ♖xd8+! (after 16 ♗e2 ♘d5 Black is more active) 16 ... ♖xd8 17 ♗e2 ♘d5 and the two knights are very active in Ivanovic – Forintos, Bor 1980; 18 ♗xa7 can be met by 18 ... ♖d7 and Black has equal chances at least.

10 ... ♘c5

Other possibilities:

a) 10 ... ♘xd3? 11 ♕xd3 c6±.

b) 10 ... ♗f5 11 ♗b1 when:

b1) 11 ... ♕d7 12 ♗e3 b6 13 f3 ♘c5 14 ♗xc5 bc 15 cd ♗xb1 16 ♖xb1 ♘xd5 17 ♘c4±.

b2) 11 ... ♗g6 12 ♗e3! (△ f3) and now:

b21) 12 ... ♘c6?! 13 cd ♘e7 14 ♗xe4 ♗xe4, Barczay – Lukacs, Budapest 1973, 15 d6±.

b22) 12 ... ♕e7 13 f4 f5 14 cd ♖ad8 15 d6 cd 16 ♕b3+ d5 17 ♘b5!± van der Wiel – Zsu Polgar, Brussels 1985.

11 ♗b1 dc!

Weaker is 11 ... d4 12 ♘c2 ♘bd3 13 ♕d2 when:

a) 13 ... ♗f5(?) 14 ♗g3!± Schmid – Medina, Gstaad 1973.

b) 13 ... ♘xf4 14 ♕xf4 ♘e6 15 ♕e4±.

12 ♘xc4 ♗e6

With balanced chances.

C23

9 cd ♕xd5

White's e5 pawn is in extreme peril, but the position of Black's ♕d5 and ♘e4 are also uncertain.

White's choices include:

C231: 10 ♕f3
C232: 10 ♕c2

If 10 ♗xe4(?) ♕xe4 11 f4 ♗f5 12 ♘c3 ♕c4! Schrancz – Petran, Budapest 1972.

C231

10 ♕f3 ♗f5!

If 10 ... f5 11 ef ♘xf6 12 ♕xd5+ ♘xd5 13 ♗c4 ♗e6 14 ♖d1 ♖ae8 equalizes (15 ♖xd5? ♘b4∓). But we suggest 14 ♘c3.

11 ♕xf5

Better than either:

a) 11 ♖e1? ♖ad8! 12 ♗xe4 ♗xe4 13 ♕g3 ♗xb1 14 ♖xb1 ♘xe5!∓∓ Dückstein – Toth,

Lugano 1977.

b) **11 ♘c3?** ♘xc3 12 ♕xf5 g6 13 ♕g5 (13 ♕f6 ♕xe5∓∓) 13 ... ♕xd3 14 bc ♕xc3 15 ♗f4 ♘d4∓∓ Pangritz - Autenrieth, Bundesliga 1988/89.

11	**...**	**♕xd3**
12	**♘c3**	**♘c5**
13	**♕h5**	**♕g6**
14	**♕xg6**	

14 ♕e2? ♘d3! Zurla - Toth, Bologna 1977.

14	**...**	**hg**
15	**f4**	**♖fd8**

16 ♗e3 ♘d3! 17 b3 ♘cb4 18 ♖ad1 ♘c2 19 ♗c1 a6 20 ♖f3 ♘xc1 21 ♖xc1 ♘d4 22 ♖f2 ♘e6 23 g3 ♖d3∓ Lederman - Forintos, Budapest 1983.

C232

10	**♕c2!** *(42)*

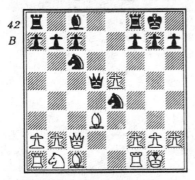

Black's choices are:

C2321: 10 ... ♘c5
C2322: 10 ... ♘b4

Or 10 ... ♗f5 11 ♘c3! ♘xc3 12 ♗xf5 ♘d4! 13 ♗xh7+ ♔h8 14 ♕d3 ♘ce2+ 15 ♔h1 ♕xe5 16 ♕h3 ♘f4 17 ♗xf4 (17 ♕h4±) ♕xf4 18 ♗e4+ (18 ♖ad1 ♕h6!±) 18 ... ♕h6, as in the game Knaak - Kostro, 1973 (E. Germany - Poland), 19 ♕xh6+!±.

C2321

10	**...**	**♘c5?!**
11	**♗xh7+**	**♔h8**
12	**♗e3**	**♘e6**
13	**f4**	

The tactical method of grasping the advantage. The other way is: 13 ♘c3 ♕xe5, Enders - Pacsay, Balatonbereny 1989, 14 ♗e4±.

13	**...**	**g6**

Or 13 ... ♘ed4 14 ♕e4 ♕d8 15 ♘c3 g6 16 ♗xg6 fg 17 ♖ad1 (17 ♕xg6? ♕h4!) 17 ... ♗f5 18 ♖xd4 ♘xd4 19 ♕xd4 ♕xd4 20 ♗xd4 leads to White's endgame advantage through his pawn majority on the kingside.

14	**♘c3**	**♕c4**
15	**♗xg6±**	

Keres' assessement, and it is borne out by:

a) **15 ... fg** 16 ♕xg6 ♘g7 17 ♘e4±.

b) **15 ... ♘ed4** 16 ♕d3 ♗e6 17 ♗e4 1-0 Petkevic - Kuzmichev, Riga 1967.

C2322

10	...	♘b4!

The only way.

11	♗xe4	♘xc2
12	♗xd5	*(43)*

A critical line.

12	...	♗f5

Covering the exit of the knight.

12 ... ♘xa1!? is also good, when:

a) 13 ♕e4 ♖e8!? 14 ♘c3 ♖xe5 15 ♕d2 ♖xe4 16 ♘xe4 ♘c2 17 ♖c1 ♗f5=.

b) After 13 e6 (Bellin) we suggest 13 ... ♘c2!, e.g. 15 ef+ ♖xf7 14 ♖d1 ♗f5=.

c) If 13 ♘a3 our analysis: 13 ... ♗f5 14 g4 ♗d3! 15 ♖d1 ♗e2 16 ♖e1 (16 ♖d2? ♗xg4∓) 16 ... ♖ad8! 17 ♕e4 ♖d1∓ and winning the a1-knight will cost a lot.

13	g4

If 13 e6 c6=.

13	...	♗xg4

Better than 13 ... ♗g6 14

f4 and now:

a) 14 ... ♗d3? 15 ♖d1! ♗a6 16 e6! fe 17 ♘xe6+ ♔h8 18 ♘a3 ♘xa1 19 ♕e3±± Popov - Riski, corr. 1968-69.

b) 14 ... c6! 15 ♗c4 b5 when:

b1) 16 ♗b3 ♘xa1 17 f5 ♘xb3 18 ab, Haskin - Popov, Riga 1967, 18 ... ♖ad8!= Popov.

b2) 16 f5! (16 ♘a3 ♘xa1 17 f5 is only a transposition) 16 ... ♘xa1 17 ♘a3 bc 18 ♗d2 ♖fd8 19 ♗c3 ♘b3 20 ab cb 21 ♘c4!± Ghinda - Witt, Galati 1973.

14	♗e4

The pawn was given up for this square. Other tries:

a) 14 ♘a3? ♘xa1 15 ♗e4 (15 ♗e3 ♖ad8! △ ... ♖d1∓) 15 ... ♗e2! 16 ♖e1 ♖ad8!∓ △ ... ♗d3, ... ♖d1 Damjanovic - Toth, Greece 1977.

b) For 14 ♗f4 ♘xa1 15 ♗e4 see 15 ♗f4. But 15 ♖c1! when:

b1) 15 ... ♖ad8 16 ♘c3 b5 17 ♗e4 b4 18 ♘d5± Sveshnikov - Belov, Moscow 1987.

b2) 15 ... c6 16 ♗e4 f5 17 ef ♖xf6 18 ♗e3 ♗e6 19 ♘d2 ♗xa2 20 ♖xa1, Sveshnikov - Tischbierek, Budapest 1988, 20 ... ♗f7±. Or 17 ♗g2 ♖ad8 18 ♘c3 h6 19 h4±, M Hansen - Almeida, European Junior

Ch. 1989.

14 ...   ♘xa1
15 ♗f4 *(44)*

The investigations of the last few years have focused on our suggestion above, dating from 1975. White keeps up the chance for various knight moves.

Others:

a) **15 ♘a3?** see 14 ♘a3? earlier.

b) **15 f3?** Though this stops counterplay by ... ♖d8 – d1, it loses a tempo:

b1) **15 ... ♗e6** 16 ♘c3 c6 17 ♗e3 ♘b3 18 ab ♗xb3=.

b2) **15 ... ♗h3** 16 ♖e1 f5 17 ef ♖ae8! 18 ♘a3 (18 fg? ♖xf3) 18 ... gf 19 ♗h6 f5! (△ 19 ♗xf8 ♔xf8∓) 20 ♗d5+ ♔h8 21 ♖xa1 ♖f6 22 ♗f4 ♖e2∓.

c) **15 ♗e3** f5 16 ♗d5+ ♔h8 17 ♘a3 ♖ad8 18 ♗c4 (Bellin) has not yet been tried.

d) **15 ♘c3** is the old main line. It seems as if Black has managed to achieve a balance. In fact it has been taken under excellent players' protection 15 ... ♗h3! 16 ♖e1 f5! (16 ... ♖fe8? 17 ♗f4 g5 18 ♗xg5 ♖xe5 19 ♗xh7+ ♔xh7 20 ♖xe5± Georgescu – Clarke, corr. 1972) 17 ef (17 ♗b1 ♖ae8 △ ... ♖e6∓) 17 ... ♖ae8! when:

d1) **18 fg(?)** ♖f7! (18 ... ♔xg7? 19 ♗d2 ♖xe4 20 ♘xe4 ♘c2 21 ♗c3+ and the knight is captive±) 19 ♗h6 (19 ♗xh7+? ♔xh7 20 ♖xe8 ♖xg7+ 21 ♔h1 ♗g2+ 22 ♔g1 ♗c6+) 19 ... ♗f5 or 19 ... ♖e6∓.

d2) **18 ♗e3** ♖xe4 19 ♘xe4 ♘c2 20 ♖c1 and now:

d21) **20 ... ♘xe3** 21 fe c6 (21 ... ♖c8 is also good: 22 f7+ ♔f8 23 ♘g5 ♗f5 24 ♖f1 h6 25 ♖xf5 hg= Psakhis – Makarichev, Vilnius 1981) 22 ♘g5 ♗f5 23 f7+ ♔h8 24 ♖f1 ♗g6 25 e4 h6 26 e5 hg 27 e6 ♔h7 27 ♖f3 g4 28 ♖f2 ♗xf7+ 29 ♖xf7 ♖e8 30 ♖xb7 ♖xe6 31 ♖xa7 ♖e2 ½-½ Tal – Timman, Reykjavik 1987; Gipslis' 21 ... ♗f5 is also interesting: 22 ♘g3 ♖xf6 23 ♖xc7 ♗h3! 24 ♖xb7 h5 25 ♖b4 g6 26 ♖f4 ♖c6=.

d22) **20 ... ♗f5** is the simplest: 21 ♖xc2 ♗xe4 22 ♖xc7

Rxf6 23 Bxa7 Rc6 ½-½ Makarichev - Karpov, Oslo 1984.

d3) **18 Bd2** Rxe4 19 Nxe4 Nc2 20 Rc1 Nd4 21 Rxc7 with three ways:

d31) **21 ... gf** (Porreca) 22 Bc3 (22 Bh6 Rf7=) 22 ... Ne2+ 23 Kh1 Bf5!=

d32) **21 ... Nf3+** 22 Kh1 Nxd2 (22 ... Qf5 23 Bb4 Bxe4 24 f7+!) 23 Rxg7+ Kh8 24 Ng5! Bf5! (Rxh7+ was threatened) 25 Nf7+ Rxf7 26 Rxf7 Be4+! (26 ... Kg8? 27 Rg7+ Kf8 28 f3! Nxf3 29 Rxb7±± Klovan - Levchenkov, Riga 1971) 27 f3 Bxf3+ 28 Kg1 Kg8! 29 Rg7+ Kf8 30 Rxh7 Bc6= (Gipslis).

d33) **21 ... Rf7!** 22 Rxf7 Nf3+! (the square g5 must be controlled) 23 Kh1 Kxf7 24 fg Kxg7 25 Be3 (25 Ng5+ Nxg5 and was drawn in a few moves in Razuvayev - Makarichev, Rostov/Don 1976) 25 ... b6 26 Nd2 (if 26 Nd6 White has to prevent the arrival of the black king on f1 and also deal with the threatened ... h5 - h4, ... Bf1 ... h3 threatening) 26 ... Nxd2 27 Bxd2 a5 28 f3 a4 29 Kg1 a3 ½-½ Tal - Karpov, Milan 1975.

15 ... f5!
a) **15 ... Bh3?** 16 Rc1!±

Trabattoni - Toth, Milan 1978.

b) **15 ... f6** when:

b1) **16 Nc3** fe 17 Bg3 (17 Be3!? - Smagin; 17 Bxe5 Rae8 18 f4 Rxe5 19 fe Rxf1+ 20 Kxf1 c6 21 Ke1 Kf7∞) 17 ... Rad8 18 Rxa1 Rd2! 19 b4 Bf3 20 a3!± Smagin-Schüssler, Copenhagen 1988.

b2) **16 Bxb7** Nc2 17 Bd5+ Kh8 18 Bxa8 Rxa8 19 ef gf 20 Bxc7 Nh3 21 Rc1 Re8! 22 Nc3 Nd4 with chances to equalize.

16 Bd5+!

Or 16 Bxb7 Nc2! 17 f3 Bh5 18 Bd5+ Kh8 19 Bxa8 Rxa8 20 Rd1 c5! with at least level chances in Romanishin - Kochiev, USSR Ch. 1978.

16 ... Kh8
17 Rc1! c6

17 ... Rad8? 18 Nc3 b5 19 e6! Rfe8 20 Bxc7±.

18 Bg2

Or 18 Be6 (18 Bc4 Rad8∓ Lysenko), 18 ... g5!? 19 Bxg5 Rae8 and now:

a) **20 Bh6** Rxe6 21 Bxf8 Bh3 22 Rc3 Rg6+ 23 Rg3 Kg8 24 Be7 f4 25 Rxg6+ hg 26 Na3 f3= Oll - Halifman, Vilnius 1988.

b) **20 Bc4(!)** b5 21 Bf1 and:
b1) **21 ... Rxe5?!** 22 Nd2 Re6 (22 ... Rg8 23 f3!) 23

♗c3+ ♔g8 24 ♘d2± van der Wiel - Mihalchishin, Lugano 1987.

b2) 21 ... f4! when:

b21) **22 ♗f6+** ♖xf6 23 ef ♗f5!= (Lysenko).

b22) **22 ♘d2** ♖xe5 (22 ... ♗f5? 23 ♗xf4!± Rosentalis - Ivanchuk, Minsk 1986) 23 ♗h4 ♖d5! - Lysenko.

18 ...   ♖fd8

A critical position, where Black threatens ... ♖d1. Feeble was 18 ... ♖ae8? 19 ♘c3 g5 20 ♗xg5 ♖xe5 21 ♗f4± (Lysenko).

19 f3

Or:

a) **19 ♘c3** ♖d4 20 ♗e3 ♖b4∞.

b) **19 ♘d2** with three ways:

b1) **19 ... h6** 20 h4 ♖d3 21 ♖xa1 g5 22 hg hg 23 ♗xg5 ♖g8, Rosentalis - Gelfand, Vilnius 1988, 24 ♗f6+! ♔h7 25 ♘f1± (Krasenkov).

b2) **19 ... ♖xd2** ♖d8 and now:

b21) **21 ♗e3** ♖d1+ 22 ♖xd1 ♗xd1 23 ♗xa7 ♘c2 24 e6 ♔g8 26 ♗c5 ♘e1 27 ♗f1 ♘f3+

28 ♔g2 ♘d2!= △ ... ♘xf1 or ♗f3+.

b22) **21 ♗c3!** ♖d1+ (21 ... ♘c2? 22 f3!) 22 ♖xd1 ♗xd1 23 ♗f1±.

b3) **19 ... ♖d4?!** 20 ♗e3 ♖b4 21 ♖xa1 f4 22 ♗c5 ♖xb2 23 ♘b3!± Nyman - Daw, corr. 1989.

19 ...   ♗h5
20 ♘a3

Now 20 ♘d2 is weaker than one move earlier, since after 20 ... h6 21 h4 ♖d3, ... g5 is much stronger, i.e. the f3-pawn is hanging at the end. See 19 ♘d2.

20 ...	♖d4
21 ♗e3	♖b4
22 ♘c4	♖a4
23 ♘a3	½-½

Sax - Yusupov, Thessaloniki (ol) 1988 and Dolmatov - Yusupov, Hastings 1989/90.

In our opinion 22 ♖xa1 would offer further chances for both parties, e.g. 22 ... f4 23 ♗d2 ♖xb2 24 ♗xf4 b5∞ (24 ... ♖f8?! 25 ♗g3±) or 22 ... ♖xb2∞.

14) 3 d4 d5 - Through the Looking Glass

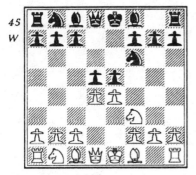

45
W

4   ed(!)

Other possibilities are:

a) **4 ♘xe5 ♘xe4** (4 ... de? 5 ♗c4) 5 ♗d3 etc. transposes into the lines discussed in Chapter 13.

b) **4 ♗e2** is poor. It is a difficult struggle to gain an advantage.

c) **4 ♗g5!?** (an interesting idea) 4 ... de 5 ♘xe5 ♗e7 and (5 ... ♗e6 can be considered; inferior is 5 ... ♗d6, e.g. 6 ♘c3! ♕e7? (6 ... ♗b4) 7 ♘d5 ♕d8 8 ♗c4 ♗e6 9 ♘xf6+ gf 10 ♗xe6 ♗xe5 11 de ♕xd1+ 12 ♖xd1 fg 13 ♗c8!± Basanta – Schwartzman, St.

John 1988) 6 ♗c4 0-0 7 0-0 (7 ♘c3 ♗f5) 7 ... ♘fd7!? 8 ♗f4 ♘xe5 9 de ♕xd1 10 ♖xd1 ♗e6! 11 ♘b3 ♗xb3 12 ab f5 13 ♘c3 ♔f7 14 ♘b5 (if 14 ♘d5 then ... ♗d8 is best) 14 ... ♘a6 15 e6+! ♔f6! (15 ... ♔xe6? 16 ♖xa6+ ba 17 ♘xc7+ ♔f7 18 ♘xa8 ♖xa8 19 ♖a1!±) 16 ♗d2 c5 17 ♗c3+ ♔xe6 18 ♗xg7 ♖fd8= Smirin – Akopyan, Vilnius 1988.

4   ...   ed

Or 4 ... e4 5 ♘e5 ♘xd5 6 ♗c4 (threatening ♘xf7) 6 ... ♗e6 when:

a) **7 0-0 ♘d7** to immediately exchange the e5 knight is the best.

b) **7 ♘d2** is a promising move in Horton's opinion. Black's possibilities are:

b1) **7 ... ♕g5?** 8 ♘xe4 ♕xg2 (accepting the pawn sacrifice, but Black's queen gets into trouble) 9 ♘g3! (now ♗f1 is threatened) 9 ... ♘f6 (9 ... ♕h3? 10 ♗g5! and the queen is captured) 10

♗xe6 fe 11 ♗g5±.

b2) **7 ... f6?!** 8 ♕h5+ g6 9 ♘xg6 ♗f7 10 ♕h3! ♗xg6 11 ♕e6+ ♘e7 12 ♕xf6 ♖g8 13 ♗xg8 ♘xg8 14 ♕e6+ ♘e7 15 ♘xe4 White has an advantage.

b3) **7 ... e3** 8 fe ♘xe3 (8 ... ♕g5? 9 ♘df3! ♕xg2 10 ♖g1 ♕h3 11 e4 ♘f6 12 ♖g3 ♕h5 13 ♖g5 ♕h6 14 ♖f5!±±) 9 ♗xe6!! ♘xd1 (9 ... fe 10 ♕f3!±) 10 ♗xf7+ ♔e7 11 ♘df3 White's development advantage compensates for the lost queen.

5 ♗b5+

Or:

a) **5 ♕xd4** ♕xd5 6 ♘c3 ♕xd4?! (6 ... ♕e6+ followed by ... ♘c6= is better) 7 ♘xd4± (Keres).

b) **5 ♗c4 ♗b4+** 6 c3 ♕e7+! Black would like to exchange queens.

b1) **7 ♗e2** dc 8 bc (8 ♘xc3=) 8 ... ♗c5 9 0-0 0-0 10 c4 ♖e8 11 ♗d3 ♗g4= (Polugayevsky).

b2) **7 ♔f1!?** dc 8 ♘xc3 0-0 9 ♗g5 h6 10 ♗h4 ♗f5 11 ♕d4 ♘bd7= Estrin - Vatnikov, Vilnius 1961.

5 ... c6

5 ... ♗d7? 6 ♘xd4 ♘xd5 7 0-0± - Keres. Moreover, Black would lose a pawn in the case of 6 ♗c4 ♗b4+ 7

♔f1.

6 dc (46)

6 ♕e2+ ♗e7 7 dc bc∞.

Now Black faces a choice:

A: 6 ... bc

B: 6 ... ♕a5+

A

6 ... bc
7 ♗e2

In Keres' opinion 7 ♗c4 is better, e.g.:

a) **7 ... ♗b4+** 8 c3! ♕e7+ 9 ♗e2 dc 10 ♘xc3 when White has an advantage, i.e. Black has isolated pawns on the queenside. While in the case of ... ♗xc3 White would get the bishop pair.

b) **7 ... ♕e7+** can be met by 8 ♗e2 c5 9 c3! and again White has the better position.

c) **7 ... ♗c5** 8 0-0 0-0 9 ♗g5 ♗g4 10 ♕d3 ♘bd7 11 ♘bd2 ♖e8 (△ 12 ♘xd4?

♘e5!). And now, in our opinion, White's strongest move is 12 ♖fe1 (♖xe8 threatens followed by ♘xd4).

7 ... ♗c5

7 ... ♗b4+ is wrong because of 8 ♘bd2 (or 8 c3).

8 c3 dc
9 ♕xd8+ ♔xd8
10 ♘xc3 ♔e7
11 0-0 ♖d8
12 ♖e1

Porreca considers 12 ♘a4 even better, as 12 ... ♗b6 can be met by 13 b3. Alternatively 12 b3 △ ♗b2, ♘a4 - Horton.

12 ... ♔f8
13 ♗f4

White had an advantage, for the isolated c-pawn in the game Stein - Bronstein, USSR Ch. 1966.

B

6 ... ♕a5+

In practice White's attacking chances are more than value for the piece.

7 ♘c3 bc
8 ♘xd4!

Not 8 ♕e2+? ♗e6 9 ♘xd4 cb 10 ♘xe6 fe 11 ♕xe6+ ♗e7 12 0-0 ♕a6∓∓ Makarov - Klochko, Habarovsk 1967.

8 ... cb
9 ♕f3

9 0-0 is also good - Keres.

9 ... ♕c7
10 ♗f4

Or:

a) If 10 ♕xa8? ♗b7 11 ♗f4 ♕e7+! or 11 ♕xa7 ♗c5∓.

b) 10 0-0 is suggested by Keres.

c) Znosko - Borovsky's idea: 10 ♘dxb5 ♕e7+ (10 ... ♕b7 11 ♕e2+!) 11 ♗e3 ♗b7 12 ♕f4! ♘h5 13 ♕c4±.

10 ... ♕b7
11 ♘cxb5 ♘a6

11 ... ♕xf3 is not quite clear, e.g. 12 ♘c7+ ♔d8 13 ♘xf3 (13 gf? ♘h5) 13 ... h5 14 0-0-0+ ♘d7! (14 ... ♗d7 15 ♘e5 f6 16 ♘xa8! ±) 15 ♗e5∞.

12 ♕e2+ ♕e4

If 12 ... ♕e7 then 13 ♗e5 planning 14 ♘d6+.

13 ♕xe4+ ♘xe4
14 0-0-0 ♗e6

The game Lepsenyi - Butler, corr. 1964-65, went 15 ♖he1 ♘ec5 16 b4 ♘xb4 17 ♘c7+♔e7 18 ♘dxe6 ♘xe6 19 ♗g5+ f6 20 ♖xe6+ ♔f7 21 ♖d7+♔g6 22 ♘xa8 ♔xg5 23 a3 ♔f5 24 ♘c7 1-0.

15) 3 ♘xe5: Introduction

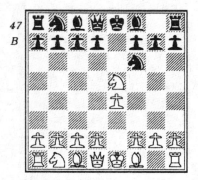

Now:

A: 3 ... ♕e7
B: 3 ... ♘xe4

The 3 ... ♘c6 gambit is even more unreal. Black has only two tricks after 4 ♘xc6 dc:

a) **5 e5 ♘e4 6 d3??** (⌒ 6 ♘c3, 6 d4 or 6 ♕e2) **6 ... ♗c5!** and White even resigned (0-1) in the game Lowens – Stafford, USA corr. 1950, for 7 dc ♗xf2+ is decisive.

b) **5 d3 ♗c5 6 ♗g5?** (6 ♗e2!±) **6 ... ♘xe4! 7 ♗xd8** ♗xf2+ 8 ♔e2 ♗g4 mate. 3 ... d6 is the only correct continuation and the different alternatives will be discussed in Chapters 16-33.

A

3   ...   ♕e7?

The Black queen might not stand well on the same file as its king.

4   **d4**

After 4 ♘f3 Black can try:

a) **4 ... ♕xe4+?** 5 ♗e2 d5 6 0-0 ♗g4 7 ♗b5+!± Anderssen – Goring, Leipzig 1871.

b) **4 ... ♘xe4** 5 ♗e2 ♕d8 6 0-0 ♗e7 7 d4! 0-0 8 c4 c6 9 ♕c2 d5 and White may transpose into Chapter 30 with 10 ♗d3 or 10 ♘c3±.

4   ...   **d6**

5   ♘f3   ♕xe4+

Or 5 ... ♘xe4 6 ♗e3 △ 7 ♗d3 – Polugayevsky.

6   **♗e2(!)**

Other moves are weaker:

a) **6 ♕e2 ♕xe2+ 7 ♗xe2**

♗e7 8 0-0 0-0 9 ♘bd2 ♗g4 10 ♘c4 ♘c6 11 c3 ♖fe8= Prajnfalk - Maric, Yugoslavia 1953.

b) 6 ♗e3 ♘d5 (6 ... ♘g4) 7 ♕d2 ♘xe3 8 fe c6! 9 ♗d3 ♕e7 10 0-0 g6 gives Black reasonable chances.

| 6 | ... | ♗f5 |
| 7 | c4 | ♗e7 |

8 0-0 0-0 (8 ... ♕c2±) 9 ♘c3 ♕c2 10 ♕xc2 ♗xc2 11 ♗f4 ♘bd7 12 ♖ac1 ♗g6 13 ♘h4± (Bardeleben and Mieses).

B

| 3 | ... | ♘xe4(?) |
| 4 | ♕e2 | |

Less promising is 4 ♕f3(?) ♘f6 5 d4 d6 6 ♘d3 ♘c6= Sozin.

| 4 | ... | ♕e7 |

4 ... d5? 5 d3 ♕e7 6 de ♕xe5 7 ed wins White a pawn.

| 5 | ♕xe4 | d6 |
| 6 | d4 | |

Or 6 f4 de (6 ... ♘c6 7 ♗b5 ♗d7 8 ♘c3!; for 6 ... f6 see note a to Black's next) 7 fe f6 and now:

a) 8 ♘c3 ♕xe5 9 ♕xe5 fe 10 ♗c4±.

b) 8 d4 ♘d7 9 ♗f4! fe 10 de g5 11 ♗g3 ♗g7 12 ♘c3 ♗xe5 13 ♗xe5 ♕xe5 14 0-0-0 0-0 15 ♗c4+ ♔h8 16 ♖hf1±.

| 6 | ... | de |

Other tries:

a) 6 ... f6 when:

a1) 7 ♘c3! de 8 ♘d5 ♕d6 9 de fe 10 ♗f4 c6 11 0-0-0± - Steinitz.

a2) Slightly weaker is: 7 f4 ♘d7 (7 ... ♘c6 8 ♗b5!) 8 ♘c3 fe 9 ♘d5 ♘f6 10 ♘xe7 ♘xe4 11 ♘d5 ♔d8 12 ♗d3 c6 13 ♗xe4 cd 14 ♗xd5 ed 15 ♗d2 △ 0-0-0±.

b) 6 ... ♘d7 7 ♘c3 de 8 ♘d5 ♘f6 9 ♘xf6+ gf 10 ♗b5+ when:

b1) 10 ... ♗d7 11 ♗xd7+ ♔xd7 12 0-0± - Sozin.

b2) 10 ... c6 11 ♗xc6+ ♔d8 12 ♗d2! a5 13 ♗d5± - Hooper.

c) 6 ... ♘c6 and now:

c1) 7 f4 de 8 de f6 9 ♘c3 fe 10 ♘d5 ♕d8 11 fe±.

c2) 7 ♗b5 ♗d7 8 0-0 (8 ♘c3 de 9 ♘d5? f5!) 8 ... de 9 d5 f5 10 ♕e2 ♘b8 11 ♖e1± Speelman - Keogh, Amsterdam 1978.

The pawn sacrifice of the main line was employed by USSR candidate master Jaroslavtsev successfully several times in the early seventies.

| 7 | de | |

The capture 7 ♕xe5 only helps develop Black's counterplay after the exchange of an active queen for an inferior one. Moreover, the advanced e5 pawn will be weaker, i.e. 7 ... ♕xe5+ 8 de ♗f5! (8 ... ♘c6? 9 ♗b5 ♗d7 10 ♗xc6 ♗xc6 11 0-0±) 9 ♘c3 ♘d7 (9 ... ♗xc2? 10 ♘d5±) 10 ♗f4 ♗c5 11 0-0-0 ♗xf2 12 ♘d5 ♗b6 13 ♘xb6 ♘xb6 14 ♗d3 ♗xd3 15 ♖xd3 0-0± Gemste-Zhemaitite, USSR 1979.

7 ... ♘c6

If 7 ... f6 8 ♘c3 (simplest) 8 ... ♕xe5 9 ♕xe5+ fe 10 ♗g5 △ 0-0-0±.

Now White faces a choice:

B1: 8 ♗b5
B2: 8 ♘c3

Or 8 ♗f4 g5! ∟ ... f5.

B1

8 ♗b5 ♗d7
9 ♘c3 0-0-0
10 ♗f4 g5

10 ... a6?! 11 ♗c4 ♗e6? 12 ♗xa6 ♔b8 (12 ... ♖d4 13 ♕xc6!) 13 ♗b5 ♖d4 14 ♕e3 ♘b4 15 ♗a4±± Sax - Hulak, Budapest 1975.

11 ♗g3

11 ♗xc6 ♗xc6 12 ♕f5+ ♔d7! 13 ♕xd7+ (13 ♕xg5 ♗e7!) 13 ... ♖xd7 14 ♗xg5 ♖g8 with even chances.

11 ... ♗g7

11 ... h5 12 h4 or 11 ... f5 12 ef ♕xf6 13 0-0±.

12 0-0-0

And it is not clear how Black can regain the pawn, e.g. 12 ... ♘xe5 13 ♗xd7+ ♖xd7 14 ♖xd7 ♕xd7 15 ♗xe5 ♖e8 16 ♖d1!±±; 12 ... f5 13 ef ♕xf6 14 ♗xc7! or 12 ... ♖he8 13 ♖he1 f5 14 ef ♕xf6 15 ♕a4±.

B2

8 ♘c3

This line avoids many of the complications and leaves White a slight positional advantage.

8 ... ♕xe5
9 ♕xe5+ ♘xe5

10 ♗f4 ♗d6 11 ♗g3! ♗d7 12 0-0-0 0-0-0 13 ♘e4 ♗c6 14 ♘xd6+ cd 15 f3 ♖he8 16 ♖d4± and, supported by the bishop pair, White successfully managed to advance his a-, b- and h-pawns in Vasyukov - Chehov, USSR 1975.

16) 3 ♘xe5 d6 4 ♘xf7
Cochrane Gambit

48
B

The Cochrane Gambit, named after the British master, dates from 1848. In his *200 Open Games* Bronstein says: "In reply to 3 ... d6 the knight retreats to f3, although no weaker, in the author's opinion, is the bold 4 ♘xf7!"

4 ... ♔xf7
5 d4

"White, with his two mobile pawns, has a long-lasting initiative in the centre" (Bronstein).

Other moves:

a) **5 ♗c4+?** and now:

a1) **5 ... ♔e8?** The short-coming of this move is that the king is not able to escape quickly on either wing, resulting in a lot of trouble for Black.

a2) **5 ... d5!** when:

a21) **6 ed ♗d6!∓** Bilguer.

a22) **6 ♗b3** and now:

a221) **6 ... ♘xe4 7 ♕h5+ ♔e6!** and Black defends himself – Steinitz.

a222) **6 ... ♗g4 7 f3 ♗e6! 8 e5 ♘h5∓**.

a223) **6 ... ♗e6 7 ♘c3** (7 e5 ♘e4 {△ ... ♘c5} 8 d4 c5∓) 7 ... de 8 ♗xe6+ ♔xe6 9 ♘xe4 ♘xe4 10 ♕g4+ ♔f7 11 ♕xe4 ♕e8∓.

a224) **6 ... ♕e8!** 7 d3 ♗e6 8 e5 ♗g4 (8 ... d4) 9 ♗xd5+ ♘xd5 10 ♕xg4 ♕xe5+∓ Osnos and Kalinichenko, 1990.

b) **5 ♘c3?!** ♕e7 6 d4 (6 ♗c4+ ♗e6 7 ♗xe6+ ♕xe6 8 0-0 c5!?) 6 ... g6 7 ♗d3 ♗g7 8 ♗g5 h6 9 ♗h4 g5 10 ♗g3 ♖f8 11 0-0 ♔g8 12 e5 ♘e8 13 ♕h5 ♗f3∞ Svenn – Mayarov, Hallsberg 1980.

After 5 d4 Black has tried:

A: 5 ... ♗e7
B: 5 ... c5
C: 5 ... g6

Or:

a) **5 ... ♘xe4?** 6 ♕h5+ ♔e7 7 ♕e2 △ ♗g5+±± (Bronstein).

b) **5 ... d5?** 6 e5 ♘e4 (6 ... ♘e8? 7 ♗d3 g6 8 h4± Osnos and Kalinichenko) 7 ♗d3 (7 ♕f3+ ♔g8 8 ♕xe4?? ♗b4+!) 7 ... ♕h4 8 0-0 g6 9 ♗xe4 de 10 f3! was dangerous for Black in Novoshilov - Orlov, corr. 1981-84.

c) **5 ... ♗e6?!** 6 ♘c3 (6 ♕f3 c6 7 e5? de 8 de ♕a5+∓) 6 ... ♗e7 7 f4 ♖e8 8 f5 ♗d7 9 ♗c4+ ♔f8 10 0-0± Drovalev - Kaliberdin, corr. 1981-84.

d) **5 ... ♕e7** 6 ♘c3 (△ 6 ... ♘xe4? 7 ♕h5+±±) 6 ... ♗e6?! (⌐ 6 ... g6 or 6 ... c6 7 f3∞) 7 ♕f3 ♔g8 8 e5 ♘fd7 (8 ... de) 9 ♘d5! ♕d8 10 ♗c4 ♗e7 11 ♘f6+!±± Rubin - Djakov, corr. 1981-84.

e) **5 ... ♗g4** 6 f3 ♗e6 7 ♘c3 ♗e7 8 ♗d3 ♖f8 9 0-0 ♔g8 10 ♔h1∞ Kurkin - Sablin, corr. 1981-84.

f) **5 ... ♘bd7** 6 ♗c4+! (6 e5 de 7 de ♕e7 8 ♗c4+ ♔e8∞) 6 ... d5 7 ♗xd5+ ♘xd5 8 ♕h5+ ∞/± Osnos and Kalinichenko.

g) **5 ... ♕e8** and now:

g1) **6 ♘c3** g6 see line C.

g2) **6 ♗c4+** ♗e6 (6 ... d5 7 ♗xd5+ ♘xd5 8 ♕h5+ g6 9 ♕xd5 ♕e6∞) 7 ♗d3 ♘c6 8 ♗e3 (8 c3 ♘xe4 9 ♗xe4 ♘f5∓) 8 ... ♘b4! 9 0-0 c5 10 ♘c3 ♘xd3∓ Shiryaev - Fedoseiev, corr. 1981-84.

g3) **6 ♗d3** (Pachman) 6 ... ♘c6 7 c3 and now we recommend 7 ... d5!? 8 0-0 (8 e5 ♘xe5∓) 8 ... de 9 ♗c4+ ♔g6 10 f3 ♗e6! △ 11 d5 ♘a5 with good play for Black.

h) **5 ... c6** when:

h1) **6 ♗d3** ♗e7 7 0-0 and now:

h11) **7 ... ♘a6** 8 ♘c3 ♗e6 9 f4 ♕c7? (⌐9 ... ♕b6) 10 e5 ♕b6 11 ♔h1! ♗g4 12 ♕e1 ♘d5 13 ♕g3 ♗c8 14 ♘xd5 cd 15 c3 ♕d8 16 f5± Vitolins - Aleksandrov, Riga 1990.

h12) **7 ... g6** 8 c4 ♔g7 9 ♘c3 ♘bd7 10 ♗e3∞ Vitolins - Butnoris, Vilnius 1985.

h13) **7 ... ♕a5!?** 8 c3 (8 ♘c3!) 8 ... ♖d8 9 f4 ♕h5 10 ♗e2 (⌐ 10 ♕b3+) 10 ... ♗g4 11 ♗xg4 ♕xg4 12 ♕b3+ d5 13 ♕xb7? (⌐13 e5! ♘e4 14 ♕xb7) 13 ... ♘xe4! 14 f5 (14 ♕xa8 ♕d7 △ ... ♘a6) 14 ... ♕e2! △ ... ♕a6∓ Visetti - Stanoievic, Dortmund Open

1987.

h2) **6 ♘c3** ♗e7 (6 ... ♕a5!?;
6 ... ♕e8!?) 7 ♗c4+ ♔e6! 8
♗xe6+ ♔xe6 9 f4 (9 ♕f3 ♕a5
10 g4! h6 ∞ or 9 ... ♘bd7 10
♕f5+ ♔f7 11 e5 de 12 de
♘xe5 13 ♕xe5 ♗d6 ∞) 9 ...
♖f8! 10 0-0 ♔f7 11 e5 ♘d5 12
♘xd5 cd 13 f5 ∞ Beckel -
Richter, corr. 1981.

A

5   ...   ♗e7 *(49)*

6   ♘c3
Or 6 ♗c4+ d5 7 ed ♗d6∓.
6   ...   ♖e8
Alternatives:
a) **6 ... ♗e6** 7 f4 ♖e8 8 f5
♗d7 9 ♗c4+ ♔f8 10 0-0⊥
Drovalev - Kaliberdin, corr.
1981-84.
b) **6 ... c6** 7 ♗c4+ (7 ♗d3!?)
and now:
b1) **7 ... ♗e6** 8 ♗xe6+ ♔xe6
9 ♕f3 (9 f4 ♕d7! 10 e5 ♘e6
11 ♕g4+ ♔c7 Lazarev - Prim-
akov, USSR corr. 1981; for 9

... ♖f8 10 0-0 ♔f7 see Beckel
- Richter, in h) 5 ... c6) 9 ...
♕a5 (for 9 ... ♘bd7 see h) 5
... c6) 10 g4 with a perilous
initiative — Osnos and Kalinichenko.
b2) **7 ... d5** 8 ed cd 9
♘xd5 ♗e6! (9 ... ♘xd5 10
♕h5+± R Markus - Klugert,
corr. 1987-88) 10 ♘e3 ♗xc4
11 ♘xc4 ♘c6∞/∓.
7   ♗c4+   ♔f8
Weaker are:
a) **7 ... d5?!** 8 ♘xd5 ♗e6 9
♘xf6! ♗xf6 10 ♗xe6+ ♖xe6
11 e5± Fedorov - Salnikov,
Leningrad 1977.
b) **7 ... ♗e6** 8 ♗xe6+! (8 d5
♗c8 9 e5 de 10 d6+ ♗e6—) 8
... ♔xe6 when:
b1) **9 ♕f3 ♔f7** (9 ... ♘bd7
10 g4±) 10 ♗e3 ♘c6 11 0-0-0
♕c8 12 h3 ♔g8 13 g4 with an
attack - Osnos and Kalinichenko.
b2) **9 g4** ♔f7 10 g5 ♘fd7
11 f4 ♘f8 12 f5 c5 13 0-0 ♔g8
14 ♕h5± Poleshuk - Pesh-
kov, USSR corr. 1981-84.
8   0-0
8 ♕f3 (Osnos) and now:
a) **8 ... c6?** 9 ♕f3 b5 10
♗b3 ♕c7 11 ♗f4 b4 12 ♘a4
♗g4 13 ♕g3± Polyakov -
Domuls, USSR 1982.
b) **8 ... ♗e4** 9 f3 ♗h6 10 g4
♗f7 11 ♗xf7 ♔xf7 12 f4 is
strong — Domuls.

c) **8 ... ♘c6** 9 f3! ♘a5 10 ♗d3 ♗d7? (△ 10 ... ♔g8) Ballon – Zimprich, corr. 1988-89.

B

5   ...   **c5!?** *(50)*

This move achieves its aim if met by 6 c3. But after 6 ♗c4+ there is a stereotyped solution: 6 ... d5 7 ed ♗d6! 8 0-0 ♕c7∓ Jandemirov – Plisetsky, Moscow 1983.

6   dc   ♘c6

Or:

a) **6 ... ♕a5+** 7 ♘c3 ♕xc5 8 ♗e3 ♕a5 (8 ... ♕c7; 8 ... ♕b4?! 9 a3! △ ... ♕xb2? 10 ♗d4±±) 9 ♗c4+ ♗e6 10 ♗xe6+ ♔xe6 11 0-0 ♘c6 12 f4 ♖d8 13 g4 (13 ♕d3!?) 13 ... d5 14 f5+ (14 g5 ♗c5!) 14 ... ♔f7 15 g5 ♗c5!∓ Novoshilov – Raetsky, corr. USSR 1981-84.

b) **6 ... d5** 7 e5 ♕e8 8 f4 ♗g4! (8 ... ♗xc5? 9 ♕e2) 9 ♕e2 ♗xe2 10 ♕xe2 ♗xc5!? 11 ef ♕c6! 12 ♔d1 g6 13 f5! (13 g4 ♕xf6∞ Vitolins – Halifman, Borzomi 1984; 13 ♘c3 ♘d7 △ ... ♘xf6) 13 ... ♘d7 14 ♕e6+ (14 ♖f1 ♖ae8 15 ♕g4 ♘e5 16 ♕g3 ♘c4∓) 14 ... ♕xe6 15 fe+ ♔xe6 16 ♖e1+ ♔xf6 17 ♘c3 ♘b6 18 ♗e3± Matsukevich.

c) **6 ... ♕e8** 7 ♘c3 d5?! (7 ... dc) 8 ♗g5! ♘bd7 9 ♗b5 ♗xc5? (9 ... ♕e6!=) 10 ♗xf6 gf 11 ♕xd5+ ♕e6 12 ♕h5+ ♔g7 13 ♗xd7± Vitolins – Viksma, Riga 1985.

d) **6 ... ♗g4** 7 ♗e2 (7 ♗c4+ d5) 7 ... ♗e6 8 0-0 ♘c6 9 f4 ♔g8 (9 ... d5?! 10 f5 ♗xc5+ 11 ♔h1 ♗c8 12 ed and the d5-pawn cannot be taken) 10 ♘c3 dc 11 e5 ♕d4+ 12 ♔h1 ♕xd1 13 ♖xd1 ♘g4 14 ♘e4, Vitolins – Kveinis, USSR 1987 and now, after 14 ... ♗e7! White's compensation is dubious; 8 ... ♘xe4 9 ♗f3 ♘xc5 10 b4 ♘c6 12 bc ♕f6 can also be considered.

7   ♗c4+   ♗e6
8   ♗xe6+   ♔xe6
9   0-0   d5

9 ... dc?! 10 ♕e2!

10   e5

If 10 ♘c3 d4! (10 ... de?! 11 ♕e2! ♔f7 12 ♗g5± Savko – Enin, Riga 1989) and neither

11 ⑤d5 nor 11 ♕e2 seems sufficient for White.

10 ... ⑤e4!
11 ♕g4+ ♔f7

a) 12 ♕f5+?! ♔e8 13 ⑤c3 ⑤d4 14 ♕h3 ♕d7 and White did not have enough compensation in Vitolins – Dautov, Minsk 1988.

b) 12 ⑤c3!? (Dautov):

b1) 12 ... ⑤xc3 13 ♕f5+ ♔e8 14 bc g6 (14 ... ♗xc5? 15 e6!) 15 ♕h3 ♗xc5 16 ♗h6⩲.

b2) 12 ... ⑤xe5 13 ♕h5+ ⑤g6 14 ⑤xe4 fe∞.

Besides the promising 5 ... c5 there is another defence which seems good for Black.

C

5 ... g6 *(51)*

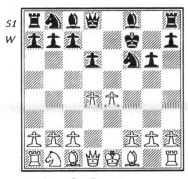

6 ⑤c3

6 ♗d3 must be met by ... c5 or ... ⑤c6 and not the stereotyped 6 ... ♗g7 7 0-0 ♖e8, e.g. 8 ⑤c3 ♔g8 9 h3

♗e6 10 f4 ⑤bd7 11 ♕f3 c6 12 ♗e3 ♕a5 13 g4 with a classical attack in Skotorenko – Per Bille Somod, corr. 1987-88.

Black's responses:

C1: 6 ... ♔g7
C2: 6 ... ♗g7
C3: 6 ... ♕e8

Others:

a) 6 ... ♗e6 7 ♗d3 ♗g7 8 0-0 (compare with the game Skotorenko – Per Bille Somod, after 6 ♗d3).

b) 6 ... c6 7 ♗c4+ (7 ♗d3 is more promising) 7 ... d5 8 ed (8 ♗b3 ♗b4) 8 ... cd 9 ⑤xd5 ♗e6!∓ Schulman – Ungurs, Riga 1986.

c) 6 ... ♗e7 7 ♗h6!? (Rodin) 7 ... ♖e8 8 ♗c4+ ♗e6 9 ♗xe6+ ♔xe6 10 ♕f3± (Osnos).

C1

6 ... ♔g7

a) 7 ♗g5 ♗e7 (7 ... h6!, Pachman) 8 ♕d2 h6! 9 ♗e3 ♗e6 10 h3 ⑤bd7 11 f4 d5 12 e5 ⑤h5∓ Amirov – Obuhov, USSR corr. 1981-84.

b) 7 ♗c4 c6 (7 ... ♗e7 8 f3 c5! 9 d5 ⑤bd7 10 ♗e3 ⑤e5 11 ♗e2 b5∓ Shetinin – Smirnov corr. 1982-83) 8 ♗g5 ♗e7 9 ♕d2 h6! 10 ♗xf6+ ♗xf6 11

0-0-0 ♖e8∓ Poletov - Kapustin, corr. 1982.

c) **7 f4** ♕e8 (7 ... d5 8 e5 ♘g4 9 ♕f3 ♗b4∞ Kaliberdin - Oleinik, USSR 1982) 8 e5 de 9 fe ♗b4 10 a3 (10 ♗d3 ♘d5 11 ♕d2 ♖f8) 10 ... ♗xc3+ 11 bc ♘c6 12 ♗e2 (12 ♗b5 — Nora) 12 ... ♘xe5 13 de ♕xe5 14 0-0 ♗f5∞ Vitolins - Kveinis, Jurmala 1981.

d) After **7 ♗e2**:

d1) **7 ... ♗e7** 8 ♗e3 ♗e6 9 ♕d2 h6 (9 ... ♖e8) 10 f3 ♘bd7 11 0-0-0 c6 12 g4, Schulman - Schmulders, Riga 1986, 12 ... b5∞.

d2) If **7 ... ♕e8** 8 f3.

d3) Feeble is **7 ... d5** 8 e5 ♘e4 9 ♘xe4 de 10 0-0 ♘c6 11 ♗e3, Vitolins - Meiers, Latvia 1989, 11 ... ♗e7 12 ♕d2 - Osnos.

C2

6	...	♗g7
7	♗c4+	♗e6
8	♗xe6+	♔xe6
9	f4!	♔f7
10	e5	

With two alternatives:

a) **10 ... ♘e8** 11 ♕f3 c6 12 f5 ♖f8 13 fg+ ♔g8 14 gh+ ♔h8 15 ♗f4± Rubin - Demidov, corr. 1981-84.

b) **10 ... ♖e8** 11 0-0 ♘c6 (11 ... ♘fd7 12 f5! de 13 fg+ ♔g8 14 ♕h5!±) when:

b1) **12 d5** de 13 dc ♕xd1= Vitolins - Anikayev, USSR Ch. 1979.

b2) **12 ef!** ♕xf6 13 ♘b5! (an important improvement) 13 ... ♖e7 14 c3± Vaiser - Visotzky, corr. 1981-84.

C3

6	...	♕e8
7	♗c4+	

Or:

a) **7 ♗d3** ♗g7 (7 ... c5!? 8 dc d5 Osnos and Kalinichenko) 8 0-0 and:

a1) **8 ... ♗g4?!** 9 f3 ♗e6 10 f4 (△ 11 f5) 10 ... ♔g8! (△ ... d5, ... ♗f7) 11 ♕f3 c6 12 h3 ♘a6 13 a3 ♘c7, Kahlert - Vogel, German League 1989, 14 g4∞.

a2) **8 ... ♖f8** 9 e5! ♘g4 (dubious: 9 ... de 10 de ♕xe5, e.g. 11 ♖e1 ♕c5 12 ♗e3 ♕c6, Florova - Lutzkane, Leningrad 1989, 13 ♗b5 ♕d6 14 ♗c4+ ♗e6 15 ♗c5!±) 10 h3 (In our opinion 10 ♗c4+ ♗e6 11 d5 ♗f5 12 e6+ ♔g8 13 ♗e2! △ ♘f6 13 g4 is better.) 10 ... ♘h6 11 ed ♔g8! (11 ... cd 12 ♖e1!±) 12 dc ♘c6 (12 ... ♘a6 — Domuls) 13 d5 ♘e5 14 ♗e4, Vitolins - Domuls, Riga 1983, 14 ... ♘hf7! △ ... ♘d6, ... ♘c4∞ Domuls.

b) **7 f3** (Osnos)

7	...	♗e6

8   d5
8 ♕e2 (Kärner)
 8   ...   ♗c8
8 ... ♗d7!? (Domuls).
 9   0-0   ♗g7
 10   ♖e1   ♖f8
With two ways:
a) **11 f4** ♔g8 12 e5 de 13 fe

♘g4 14 d6+ ♔h8 15 e6 ♘e5
16 d7 ♘bxd7 17 ed ♕xd7=
Popov - Grodsenski, corr.
1982-83.
 b) **11 e5** de 12 d6+ ♗e6 13
♖xe5 ♗xc4 14 ♖xe8 ♖xe8 15
dc ♘a6 16 ♗f4 ♖ec8∞ Vito-
lins - Anikayev, Riga 1982.

17) 3 ♘xe5 d6: Paulsen's 4 ♘c4

First played by Louis Paulsen in 1887, and then resuscitated by Yugoslav players in the 1950s.

4 ... ♘xe4 (52)

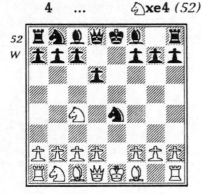

Now White can choose between:

A: 5 d3
B: 5 ♕e2
C: 5 d4
D: 5 ♘c3

A

5 d3 ♘f6
6 d4

If 6 ♗e2 then 6 ... d5 7 ♘e5 ♗d6.

6 ... d5

Also to be considered are:

a) 6 ... ♗f5 7 ♗d3 ♗xd3 8 ♕xd3 c6 9 0-0 ♗e7 10 ♗g5± Capello - Toth, Italy 1978.

b) 6 ... ♗e7 is playable.

7 ♘e3

7 ♘e5 transposes into a line of the Classical Attack (Chapter 26) but with colours reversed, i.e. Black may play the variations recommended for White.

7 ... c5!
8 ♗b5+ ♘c6

9 0-0 ♗e6! 10 b3 (10 f4 ♕b6) 10 ... ♗e7 11 ♗a3 cd 12 ♗xc6+ (12 ♗xe7? ♔xe7!) 12 ... bc 13 ♗xe7 ♕xe7 14 ♕xd4 0-0 15 ♘d2 a5= Tseshkovsky - Vladimirov, Moscow 1986.

B

5 ♕e2

Those who were dissatisfied with the part of the white knight in the alternative 4 ♘f3 ♘xe4 5 ♕e2 have tried this set-up. However, the knight does not find its right place here either.

    5   **...**   **♕e7**
    6   **♘e3** *(53)*

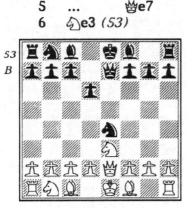

Others:

a) **6 b3**

a1) **6 ... ♘c6** 7 ♗b2?! (7 d3) 7 ... d5 8 ♘e3 ♗e6 9 g3 0-0-0 10 ♗g2 ♕d7 11 ♘c3 f5∓ Eolian - Haritonov, Sochi 1978.

a2) **6 ... d5** 7 ♘e3 c6 8 ♗b2 ♗e6 9 g3?! (⌐ 9 d3) 9 ... ♘d7 10 ♗g2 0-0-0 11 d3 ♘ef6 12 ♘d2 ♖e8∓ Vasyukov - Holmov, USSR 1990.

b) **6 d3** ♘f6 7 ♗g5 when:

b1) **7 ... ♕xe2+** 8 ♗xe2 and now:

b11) After **8 ... ♘bd7**:

b111) In the game Armas - Sariego, Cuba 1985, **9 ♘c3** was met by 9 ... c6 (we recommend 9 ... h6) 10 ♗f4 d5

11 ♘d6+ ♗xd6 12 ♗xd6 ♘f8! 13 0-0-0 ♗f5 14 ♖he1 ♘e6 15 d4?! (15 ♗f3) and with 15 ... ♘e4 Black gains equality.

b112) **9 0-0** h6! 10 ♗h4 d5 (10 ... ♗e7 can be considered first and if 11 ♗f3, then ... d5 12 ♘e3 ♘b6 with later ... ♗e6) 11 ♘e3 g6 12 ♗f3 gives White a slight advantage, Ljubojevic - Toth, Albufieri 1978.

b12) **8 ... ♗e7** 9 ♘c3 and:

b121) **9 ... a6** 10 0-0-0 ♘c6 11 d4 ♗d7 12 ♖he1 0-0-0 13 ♗f3 (13 d5 ♘e5 △ ... ♘xd5) 13 ... ♖de8! 14 h3 ♘d5= Dreev - Malaniuk, USSR Ch. 1989.

b122) **9 ... ♘c6** 10 ♘b5 ♔d8 11 ♘e3 (11 0-0-0 a6 12 ♘c3 ♘d4= Haag - Kolarov, Kecskemet 1962) 11 ... ♗e6 12 c3, Carlier - Hartoch, Wijk aan Zee 1987, 12 ... a6 13 ♘a3 ♘d5 14 ♗xe7+ ♘cxe7 15 ♘ac2 ♔d7=.

b123) **9 ... ♗d7** is also not bad, e.g. 10 0-0-0 h6 11 ♗xf6 (11 ♗h4 ♘c6 12 d4 0-0-0=) 11 ... ♗xf6 12 ♗f3 ♘c6 13 ♖he1+ ♔d8 14 ♗d5 ♖f8 15 ♘e4 ♗e7 16 c3 ♗e6!= Vitolins - Kochiev, USSR 1979.

b2) **7 ... ♗e6!?** 8 ♘c3 ♘c6 9 0-0-0 h6 10 ♗xf6 ♕xf6 11 ♘d5 ♕g5+ 12 ♘ce3 ½-½

Ljubojevic - Hort, Bugojno 1980.

| 6 | ... | ♘f6 |

6 ... c6 is also good, e.g. 7 c4!? (7 d3 ♘f6) 7 ... g6! 8 d3 ♘g5 9 ♗d2 ♗g7 10 ♗c3 ♗xc3+ 11 ♘xc3 ♘e6 12 ♘c2 c5! 13 ♘d5 ♕d8 14 h4 h5 15 0-0-0 ♘c6 16 d4 0-0∞ Cabrilo - Marjanovic, Pancevo 1987.

| 7 | g3 |

Or 7 d4 ♘c6 8 c3 g6 9 g3 ♗g7 10 ♗g2 0-0 11 h3 ♖e8 12 0-0 ♕d8 13 ♕d3 ♘e7 14 ♘d2 ♘f5 15 ♘dc4 c6 16 ♕d1 ♘xe3 17 ♘xe3 d5= Mnatsakanian - Butnoris, USSR 1979.

| 7 | ... | ♗d7 |

Both 7 ... ♘c6 (Janosevic) and also 7 ... g6 (Nikitin) would have led to similarly good set-ups.

8	♗g2	♗c6
9	f3!	g6
10	♘c3	♗g7?!

Black could have avoided cramp by 10 ... ♘bd7! 11 d4 ♘b6 - Minic.

| 11 | d4 | 0-0 |
| 12 | d5 | ♗d7 |

13 0-0 ♘h5 14 ♗d2 f5 15 f4 ♖e8 16 ♖ae1 (Planinc - Jones, Nice (ol) 1974) 16 ... a5±.

C

| 5 | d4 | d5 |

| 6 | ♘e3 |

If 6 ♕e2?! ♘c6 7 c3 ♗e7 8 ♗f4 0-0∓ 9 ♘e3?? ♘xd4!! 10 cd ♗b4+ 11 ♔d1 ♕f6 12 ♘e5 (better is 12 ♗g3 ♕xd4+ 13 ♔c1 - Toth) 12 ... ♘xf2+ 13 ♔c1 ♕c6+ 14 ♘c2 ♘xh1 15 ♕f3 ♖e8 16 ♗d3 ♗g4! 17 ♕xg4 ♖xe5! 18 de ♕h6+ 0-1 Cehl - Marshall, New Orleans 1913.

| 6 | ... | ♕f6!? | (54) |

A remarkable idea in this position. Other tries:

a) 6 ... ♘c6 This was considered to be the best move for a long time.

a1) 7 ♗b5 a6 8 ♗a4? (⌐ 8 ♗xc6+) 8 ... ♕h4 9 0-0 ♗d6 10 g3 ♕h3 11 ♘c3 h5! 12 ♘exd5 h4! ∓∓ Safonov - Gusev, Moscow 1960.

a2) 7 c3 ♗e7 (7 ... ♗e6 8 ♘d2 ♘xd2 9 ♗xd2 ♗d6 10 ♗d3 0-0 11 ♕c2 h6 12 0-0-0 ♘e7! van Houtte - Krukovsky, Brussels 1987, 13 g4∞)

8 ♘d2 0-0 9 ♗d3 ♘xd2 10 ♗xd2 ♗e6 11 ♕c2 h6 12 f4 ♕d6! 13 0-0-0 ♖ab8 14 f5 ♗d7 15 h4 b5 16 ♕b3 (△ 16 b4) 16 ... b4! 17 ♕xd5 bc 18 ♗xc3 ♘b4 19 ♗xb4 ♕xb4 20 ♖d2 ♗b5∞ Goldena – Vezzosi, Italian Ch. 1990.

a3) 7 ♘c3 ♗b4 8 ♗d2 ♗xc3 9 bc 0-0 10 ♗d3 ♗e6 11 0-0 ♕d7 12 f3 ♘xd2 13 ♕xd2 ♘e7= Heinrich – Weiler, Germany 1987.

b) 6 ... c6 7 ♘bd2 ♘xd2 8 ♗xd2.

b1) 8 ... ♗e7 9 ♗d3 0-0=.

b2) 8 ... ♘d7?! 9 ♕e2! ♕e7 10 0-0-0 ♘f6 11 ♗b4! ♕e6 12 ♗xf8 ♔xf8 13 f3± Smagin – Rosentalis, Barnaul 1984.

b3) 8 ... ♗e6 9 ♗d3 ♗e7?! (9 ... ♘d7 is better with a later ... ♘f6 – Pachman) 10 f4 ♘a6 11 0-0 ♕b6 12 c3 0-0-0 13 b4 ♘c7 14 a4 a6 15 ♕f3± Smagin – Arhipov, Moscow 1986.

c) 6 ... g6 7 ♘d2 ♗g7 (7 ... ♘xd2? 8 ♗xd2 ♗g7 9 ♗b4!±) 8 c3 0-0 (8 ... ♘xd2?! only helps White to develop) 9 ♘xe4 de 10 ♗c4 ♘d7 11 0-0 c5 12 dc ♘xc5 13 ♕c2 ♗e6! with balanced chances Smagin-Mihalchishin, USSR Ch. Riga 1985. If 14 ♖d1 then 14 ... ♕h4, while 14 ♗xe6 can be met by 14 ... fe 15

♕e2 ♕e7! 16 ♕c4 ♖ac8.

7   ♕e2

Or 7 ♗b5+ (an interesting and risky move) 7 ... c6 8 0-0 (8 ♕e2 ♗e6!) 8 ... cb! 9 ♘xd5 ♕d8 10 ♖e1 ♕xd5 11 ♘c3 ♕d8 12 ♖xe4+ (after 12 ♗g5 there follows 12 ... ♗e7 13 ♗xe7 ♔xe7 14 ♖xe4+ ♔f8∓) 12 ... ♗e7∓ Smagin – Makarichev, Moscow 1987; in the case of 13 ♗g5 there can follow: 13 ... ♘c6 14 ♕e2 (14 d5 0-0!∓) 14 ... b4 15 d5 0-0!

7   ...   ♗e6

Certainly not 7 ... ♕xd4? for 8 f3!

8   c3

8 ♘bd2!? Smagin.

8   ...   c6

8 ... ♘c6 is also possible, e.g. 9 ♘d2 0-0-0 10 g3 ♘xd2?! (better is 10 ... ♕g6 11 ♗g2 f5 with good prospects for Black) 11 ♗xd2 h5 12 h4 g6 13 ♗g2 ♗h6 14 0-0-0 ♖he8 15 ♖he1 ♖e7 16 ♕f1± Holmov – Nikolenko, Moscow 1987; or 10 ♘xd5!? ♗xd5 11 ♘xe4 ♕g6 12 ♘g3 ♗d6 13 ♕h5 ♖he8+ 14 ♔d1 ♗xg2! 15 ♗xg2 ♕d3+ 16 ♗d2 ♘xd4 17 ♕g4 (17 cd ♗xg3∞) 17 ... ♘e6 18 ♗f1 ♕d5 19 ♗c4 ♕c6 20 ♔c2 h5 21 ♕e4 ♘d4+∞.

9   g3   ♘d7

10 ♗g2   ♕g6

11 ♘d2 f5= 12 ♗f3 ♕f6
(12... 0-0-0 can be con-
sidered) 13 ♘xe4 (if 13 0-0,
then 13 ... ♘g5 14 ♗g2 f4 is
unpleasant) 13 ... fe 14 ♗g2
♗d6 15 0-0 0-0 16 f3! ef 17
♗xf3 ♕e7 (17 ... ♕g6) 18 ♘g2
½-½ T Horvath - Forintos,
Budapest 1986.

D

5   ♘c3 *(55)*

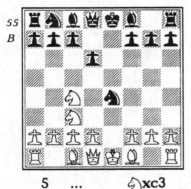

5   ...   ♘xc3

Or 5 ... ♘f6 6 d4 ♗e7
when:

a) 7 ♗d3 ♘c6 (7 ... ♗g4=)
8 d5 ♘b4 9 ♗e2± Matanovic
- Udovcic, Yugoslav Ch.
Sarajevo 1951.

b) 7 ♗e2 0-0 8 d5 (White
might be better advised to
play 8 0-0 and save this
advance for a more oppor-
tune moment) 8 ... ♘bd7 9
♗f4 ♘c5 10 ♗f3 ♗f5 11 0-0
♖e8 12 ♖e1 ♕d7= Suetin -

Malich, Berlin 1968.

6   bc

Or 6 dc (as in the Nimzo-
witsch variation except that
the knight stands on c4
instead of f3 but the difference favours Black. Some
examples:

a) 6 ... d5 B Toth con-
siders as a good move 7
♘e3 when:

a1) 7 ... c6 8 ♗d3 ♘d7 9
0-0 ♘f6 10 ♘f5 ♗xf5 11
♗xf5 ♗e7 12 ♖e1 0-0 13 ♗g5
♖e8 14 ♕f3 ♘d7 15 ♗xe7
♖xe7 16 ♖xe7 ♕xe7 17 ♗xd7
♕xd7 18 ♕e3 ½-½ Mariotti -
Toth, Italy 1974.

a2) 7 ... ♗e6 8 ♕h5 ♕d6 9
♗d2 ♘d7 10 0-0-0 0-0-0=
Benjamin - Law, London
1987.

b) 6 ... ♗e7

b1) 7 ♗d3 ♘c6 8 ♕h5 ♗e6
9 0-0 ♕d7 10 ♘e3 ♘e5 11 f4
♘xd3= Lehmann - Hooper,
Bognor 1955.

b2) 7 ♗f4 ♘c6 8 ♕d2 ♗e6
9 0-0-0 0-0 10 ♔b1 ♗f6 11
h3 ♖e8 12 ♘e3 ♗e5= Kara-
klaic - Bajec, Yugoslav Ch.
Sarajevo 1951.

b3) 7 ♕f3 ♗g5! 8 ♕e4+
♕e7 9 ♕xe7+ ♗xe7 10 ♘f4
♗f5= Malaniuk - Kochiev,
Tallinn 1987.

With 6 bc White attempts
to reinforce the centre, but

it's at the cost of a shattered pawn structure, which is difficult to mobilize, because the knight (c4) is in the way.

6 ... g6

a) 6 ... ♘c6 7 d4 d5 8 ♘e3 ♗e7 9 ♗d3 ♗e6 10 f4 f6 11 ♖b1 ♘a5 12 0-0 ♕d7 13 ♖b5 b6 14 ♕h5+ ♗f7 15 ♕e2 c6 16 ♖e1! g6 17 ♘xd5! cd 18 ♖xa5 0-0± Bertok - Andric, Yugoslav Ch. Sarajevo 1951.

b) 6 ... d5 7 ♘e3 ♗e6 8 ♖b1! b6 9 d4 ♗d6 10 ♕f3 c6 11 c4± Rossolimo - Alexander, Birmingham 1951.

c) 6 ... ♗e7 7 d4 and now:

c1) 7 ... 0-0 is weak because of 8 ♗d3, e.g. 8 ... ♘d7 9 0-0 ♘f6 10 ♖b1 b6 (10 ... c6 can be considered, planning a later ... ♕a5) 11 ♘e3 ♕d7 12 ♘f5 ♗d8 13 ♗h6!± (△ 13 ... gh 14 ♕f3!) Fedoseiev - Udalov, corr. 1985-86.

c2) 7 ... ♘d7! when:

c21) 8 ♗d3 ♘b6 (8 ... d5 9 ♘e3 ♘f6 10 ♘f5±) 9 ♘e3 0-0 (9 ... d5 10 0-0 0-0 11 f4 {11 ♘f5!?±} 11 ... f5= 12 ♕h5 g6 13 ♕f3 c6 14 g4 Fuderer - Kostic, Ljubljana 1951) 10 0-0 f5 11 f4 ♗e6 12 ♖e1, Puc - Milner-Barry, London 1951, 12 ... g6∓.

c22) In the case of 8 ♘e3

we recommend 8 ... ♘b6 and after 9 ♗d3 0-0 as above, or 9 ... g6 with level chances.

7 d4

Less effective are:

a) 7 h4?! ♗g7 8 h5 0-0 9 ♘e3 ♘d7 10 ♗c4 (10 hg= is better) 10 ... ♔h8 11 d4 ♘b6 12 ♗d3 ♔g8 13 ♕f3 c5∓ Bertok - Bajec, Yugoslav Ch. Sarajevo 1951.

b) 7 ♗e2 ♗g7 8 0-0 0-0 9 d4 ♘d7 10 ♘e3 ♘b6 11 c4 ♗e6! 12 c3 f5∓; Matanovic - Alexander, London 1951 continued 13 ♕b3 (13 f4) 13 ... ♕e7 14 ♗f3? ♕f7 15 ♗xb7? ♖ab8 16 ♗a6 f4 17 d5 ♗d7 18 ♘d1 ♘xd5 19 ♕a3 ♘b4!∓∓.

7 ... ♗g7

8 ♗d3

Or 8 h4 d5!? 9 ♘e3 0-0 10 ♕f3 c5! 11 ♘xd5 ♖e8+∓ Fedoseiev - Hrapin, corr. 1985-86.

8 ... 0-0

Hooper suggested 8 ... ♘d7 9 0-0 0-0 10 ♘e3 ♘b6 with level play.

9 0-0 ♘c6
10 ♖b1 ♖b8

11 f4 f5 12 ♕f3 ♘e7= Milic - Germek, Yugoslavia 1952.

Black obtains comfortable play in the 4 ♘c4 system.

18) 3 ♘xe5 d6: 5 d3

4	**♘f3**	**♘xe4**
5	**d3** *(56)*	

If 5 ♗e2, delaying the attack on the black knight and avoiding well-known variations, Black can consider:

a) **5 ... g6?!** (too slow) 6 0-0 ♗g7 7 ♗b5+! followed by ♖e1, or

b) **5 ... ♗e7** 6 0-0 0-0 7 c4 ♘c6 8 d3 ♘f6 9 ♘c3 b6? (9 ... d5 would have equalised) 10 d4 ♗b7 11 d5 ♘e5 12 ♘d4 ♘fd7 13 ♗e3 ♖e8 14 ♕d2 ♘g6 15 b4± Kuzmin - Segal, Nice (ol) 1974.

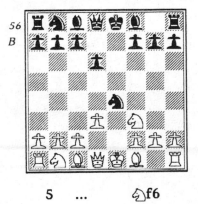

56
B

5	**...**	**♘f6**

The only move. Feeble is 5 ... ♘c5? 6 b4± (or 6 d4±).

6 d4

Alternatives:

a) **6 c4** will be discussed by transposition in Chapter 19.

b) **6 ♗e2** is a featureless move and can be strongly met by 6 ... d5 or even 6 ... g6 as 7 0-0 ♗g7 8 d4 0-0 9 ♖e1 ♘c6 10 c3 ♗f5 11 ♘bd2 a5 12 a4 ♘d7= Pfeiffer - Bronstein, Vienna, 1957.

c) **6 ♘c3** d5 7 ♗g5 ♗e7 8 ♗e2 (8 d4 Tarrasch) 8 ... 0-0 9 0-0 ♘c6 10 ♖e1 d4 11 ♘b1? ♘d5 12 ♗c1? ♗b4 13 ♘bd2 ♗f5∓ Janowski - Showalter, Nuremberg 1896.

d) **6 ♗g5** ♗e7 7 d4 ♗f5 8 ♗d3 ♗xd3 9 ♕xd3 0-0 10 0-0 ♘bd7 11 ♖e1 d5 12 ♘bd2 ♖e8 13 ♘e5 ♘f8 14 ♗xf6 (14 ♖e3) 14 ... ♗xf6 15 ♘df3 ♘e6 16 ♖ad1 c6 17 c3 g6 18 g3 ½-½ Cuijpers - van der Wiel, Hilversum 1984.

After 6 d4:

A: 6 ... ♗e7
B: 6 ... ♗g4
C: 6 ... ♗f5
D: 6 ... d5

Not 6 ... g6 for 8 ♕e2+ is unpleasant after 7 ♘c3 ♗g7.

A

6   ...   ♗e7

This is a clever adaptation! Black treats the opening in semi-closed fashion, compared with the 'closed' treatment (Chapter 24, var B) he gains a tempo which should suffice for equality

7   ♗d3

Or:

a) **7 c4** d5 (7 ... 0–0 8 ♘c3 c5?! {⊆ 8 ... d5} 9 d5 ♗f5 10 ♗d3 ♕d7 {10 ... ♗xd3} 11 0–0 ♘a6 12 ♗xf5 ♕xf5 13 ♘h4 ♕d7 14 ♕f3± Velimirovic – Miralles, Vrsac 1989) 8 ♘c3 0–0 9 ♗e3 ♘c6 10 h3 ♗b4 (10 ... ♗e6 or 10 ... ♗f5) 11 ♕c2 ♕e7 12 0–0–0 ♗xc3 13 bc ♗c6 14 c5 b6 15 ♗d3, Velimirovic – Mihalchishin, Palma de Mallorca 1989, 15 ... bc 16 dc ♘e4!?∞.

b) **7 h3** c6 8 c4 ♘a6 9 ♘c3 0–0 10 ♗e3 d5 11 c5 b6 12 ♕a4 (12 ♘e5!?) 12 ... ♘h8 13 ♗d3 bc 14 dc ♘fd7! 15 ♕c2 ♘xc5! 16 ♗xh7+ ♔h8 17 0–0–0 ♘ba6 18 a3 g6∓ Veli-

mirovic – Sisniega, Novi Sad (ol) 1990.

7   ...   ♗g4

Alternatives in the case of 7 ... 0–0 8 h3:

a) **8 ... ♖e8** 9 0–0 ♘bd7 10 ♖e1 ♘f8 11 c4 c6 12 ♘c3 ♘g6 13 ♗e3 ♗d7 Velimirovic – Chandler, Sarajevo 1985. In their opinion 14 b4!?+±/= can be considered here.

b) **8 ... c5!** 9 0–0 ♘c6 10 ♘c3 (10 c3 d5 11 dc ♗xc5 12 ♘bd2 h6 13 ♘b3 ♗b6=) 10 ... ♘b4 11 ♖e1 (11 ♗c4 ♗f5 12 ♗b3 ♘e4=) 11 ... h6 12 ♗f4 ♗e6 13 ♗f1 ♘bd5∓ Psakhis – Mihalchishin, Minsk 1986.

8   0–0

8 h3 ♗h5 9 ♘c3 ♘bd7 (⊆ ♘b6)= Zeliadinov – Butno-ris, Harkov 1967; 9 ... 0–0 is also good.

8   ...   0–0

9 h3 ♗h5 10 ♖e1 ♘c6 11 c3 ♕d7 12 ♘bd2 ♖fe8 13 ♘f1 ♗f8 14 ♖xe8 ♖xe8 15 ♗g5 ♘e4 16 ♗xe4 ♖xe4 17 ♘g3 ♗xf3 18 ♕xf3 ½–½ Kavalek – Tal, Tilburg 1980.

B

6   ...   ♗g4
7   ♗e2

White is afraid of ... ♕e7+, though 7 ♘c3 can be considered and then 8 ♗d3.

7   ...   ♗e7

8 ♘bd2

White followed quite a different opening plan in Pietzch - Mikenas, Leningrad 1960, viz. 8 0-0 0-0 9 c4 but Black was able to equalize with 9 ... d5! 10 c5 ♘c6 (10 ... b6 is also good) 11 h3 ♗h5 12 ♗e3 ♘e4.

	8	...	♘c6
	9	c3	0-0
	10	h3	♗d7(?)

10 ... ♗h5 is better.

11 0-0   ♕c8?

Instead a plan aiming at ... ♖e8, ... ♗f8, ... g6 and ... ♗g7 might be tried, or if Black seeks complications ... ♘d5 △ ... f5.

	12	♘c4	♘d5
	13	a4±	

Paoli - Trikaliotis, 1970. Now 13 ... a5 is correct.

C

	6	...	♗f5
	7	♗d3	♗xd3
	8	♕xd3	c6
	9	0-0	♗e7
	10	♕b3!?	♕c7

If 10 ... ♕b6 then 11 ♕e3. Now 11 ♗f4 ♘h5 12 ♗d2 d5(?) (△ 12 ... 0-0) 13 c4! dc 14 ♕xc4 0-0 15 ♘c3 ♘f6 16 ♖fe1 ♗d6 17 ♖ac1± was Georgadze - Schüssler, Dortmund 1979.

D

6 ...   d5 (57)

57
W

Theoretically Black cannot be criticized for transposing to the Exchange Variation of the French Defence, but in our opinion it is not necessary. On the other hand, ... ♗d6 may be achieved. Some of the following arose from the French Defence.

7 ♗d3

Harmless are:

a) **7 c4** and now:

a1) 7 ... ♘c6 (7 ... ♗b4+ is obviously also good) 8 ♘c3 ♗g4 9 ♗e3 ♗e7 10 h3 ♗h5 11 c5 (11 cd leads to more complications, see note a2) 11 ... 0-0 12 ♗b5 ♘e4= Alekhine - Bogoljubov, Salzburg 1942.

a2) 7 ... ♗e7 8 ♘c3 0-0 9 cd ♘xd5 10 ♗c4 ♘b6 11 ♗b3 ♗g4 12 0-0 ♘c6 13 ♗e3 ♗f6 14 h3 ♗h5 15 ♖c1 ♗xd4 16

♗xd4 ♗xf3 17 ♕xf3 Lombardy - Schüssler, Blue Lagoon 1984 (17 ... ♘xd4 18 ♕xb7=).

b) **7 ♗g5** ♗e7 8 ♗d3 ♗g4 9 ♘bd2 0-0 10 0-0 (10 ♘f1? ♘c6 11 c3 ♘e4=) 10 ... ♘bd7 11 c3 c6 12 ♕c2 ♗h5 13 ♖fe1 ♗g6±. In this symmetrical position White's slight advantage is harmless.

| 7 | ... | ♗d6 |

a) **7 ... ♗e7** is illogical and White even gained the advantage in the following two games:

8 0-0 ♗g4 (8 ... 0-0 Tarrasch) 9 ♖e1 0-0 10 c3 and now:

a1) **10 ... ♘bd7** 11 ♗f4 ♖e8 12 ♘bd2 ♘f8 13 ♕b3 b6 14 ♘e5 ♘e6 15 ♗g3± Tarrasch - Mason, Breslau 1889.

a2) **Slightly better is 10 ... ♘c6** 11 ♗f4 ♕d7 12 ♘bd2 ♘h5 Yanowsky - Suessman, Ventnor City 1942, 13 ♗e3±.

b) **7 ... ♘c6** (a logical move) 8 0-0 ♗g4 9 ♖e1 ♗e7 10 c3 0-0 11 ♘bd2 ♖e8 12 ♘f1 ♗d6 13 ♗g5 ♖xe1 14 ♕xe1 ♗xf3 15 gf h6 16 ♗h4 g5 17 ♗g3 ♕d7 18 ♘e3 ♖e8 19 ♕d2 ♘e7= A Rodriguez - Handoko, Dubai (ol) 1986.

| 8 | 0-0 | 0-0 |
| 9 | h3 | |

Other ideas to consider:

a) **9 ♗g5** ♗g4 10 ♘bd2 h6 (10 ... ♘bd7=) 11 ♗h4 ♗f4!? 12 ♖e1 g5 13 ♗g3 ♘h5 14 ♘f1 ♕f6 15 ♘e3= Puc - Nedeljkovic, Yugoslavia 1952.

b) **9 ♘e5?!** c5! Henkin - Geller, Leningrad 1971, and Black seized the initiative.

c) **9 c4** dc 10 ♗xc4 ♗g4!=.

d) After **9 ♘c3**:

d1) **9 ... ♖e8** 10 ♗g5 c6 11 ♖e1 ♖xe1+ 12 ♕xe1 ♘bd7 13 ♘e2 ♘f8 14 ♘g3 ♘e6 15 ♗h4 g6= Larsen - R Byrne, Havana (ol) 1966.

d2) **9 ... c6** is not bad either, only after 10 ♘e2 ♖e8 11 ♘g3 Larsen - Petrosian, Havana 1966, 11 ... ♘e4 is necessary - Maric.

d3) **9 ... ♘c6** is not bad either, viz. 10 ♗g5 ♗g4 transposing into the game of Zukertort - Mason.

d4) **9 ... h6** is a careful move for preventing the pin. If 10 ♖e1 ♘c6 11 ♘b5 then 11 ... ♘b4! is best, e.g. 12 ♘xd6 ♕xd6 △ 13 ♗f1 ♗f5.

d5) **9 ... ♗g4** 10 ♗g5 ♘c6 (10 ... c6 is also good, see note d2 above) 11 ♔h1 ♗e7, Zukertort - Mason, Vienna 1882, 12 ♗e2 or 12 ♗e3 equalise.

| 9 | ... | h6 |

9 ... c5 is leading to the common stereo position of

the French Defence, e.g. 10 dc ♗xc5 11 ♘bd2 ♗b6 12 ♘b3 ♘e4 13 ♘bd4 ♘c6 14 ♗e3 ♖e8 15 ♖e1 ♗c7 16 ♗f1 a6 = Malaniuk – Chuzman, Novosibirsk 1986.

After 9 ... h6:

a) 10 c4 c6 11 ♖e1 ♖e8 12 ♘c3 Shtirenkov – Kaidanov, USSR 1986. Now the right plan is 12 ... ♖xe1+ 13 ♕xe1 ♗e6 14 c5 ♗c7! in Kaidanov's mind; 10 ... dc 11 ♗xc4 ♘c6 (11 ... ♗f5) 12 ♖e1 ♘a5 13 ♗d3 c5 could also be considered.

b) 10 ♘c3 and now:

b1) 10 ... c6 11 ♘e5 ♘bd7 (here we recommend 11 ...

c5!?) 12 ♗f4 ♕c7 13 ♖e1 ♖e8 and now White can sacrifice a pawn by 14 ♖e3!± Kuzmin – Yusupov, USSR 1980.

b2) 10 ... ♖e8 11 ♘b5 ♗f8 12 ♗f4 ♘a6 13 a3 c6 14 ♘c3 ♘c7 is the simplest way of building a solid position, Kuzmin – Andrianov, USSR 1980.

c) 10 ♖e1 is also good, e.g. 10 ... ♘c6 11 a3 ♖e8 12 ♖xe8+ ♕xe8 13 ♘c3 a6 14 ♗e3 ♗d7 (14 ... ♗e6) 15 ♘h4 ♕e6?! 16 ♗f5 ♕e8 17 ♕f3 ♗xf5 18 ♘xf5 ♕e6 19 ♖e1± Chandler – Short, London 1986.

19) 3 ♘xe5 d6: 5 c4
Vienna/Kaufmann

4	♘f3	♘xe4
5	c4 *(58)*	

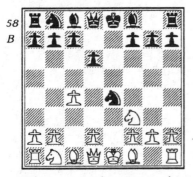

White, without rushing d3 – d4, slyly occupies the centre from the wing to try to make Black's development difficult.

A: 5 ... d5
B: 5 ... ♗e7
C: 5 ... ♘c6!

Or:

a) **5 ... c5?!** 6 d3 ♘f6 7 d4±, 6 ♘c3 is also good

b) **5 ... g6** and now:

b1) **6 d3** ♘f6 7 ♘c3 ♗g7 8 ♕e2+ ♕e7 9 ♕xe7+ ♔xe7 10 ♗g5 ♖e8 11 0-0-0 ♔f8 12 h3 a6, Keres – Rosetto, Buenos Aires 1964, and now 13 g4!? should have been played instead of 13 g3.

b2) **6 d4** ♗g7 7 ♗d3 ♘f6 8 0-0 (⌓ 8 ♕e2+) 8 ... 0-0 9 h3 ♖e8 10 ♘c3 ♘c6 11 ♗f4 d5= Kindermann – Knezevic, Budapest 1986.

b3) **6 ♘c3** when:

b31) **6 ... ♘f6** 7 d4 ♗g7 8 ♕e2+ ♕e7 9 ♕xe7+ ♔xe7 10 ♗g5 c6 11 0-0-0±.

b32) **6 ... ♘xc3** (6 ♗f5?? 7 ♕e2 ♕e7 8 ♘d5±±) 7 dc! ♗g7 8 ♕e2+ (8 ♗g5 *Schach Archiv*) 8 ... ♕e7 9 ♕xe7+ ♔xe7 10 ♗e3 b6 11 0-0-0 ♘c6 12 ♗d3 (12 ♖e1!?) 12 ... ♗b7 13 ♖he1 ♔d7 14 c5!? bc 15 ♗xc5 ♖he8 16 ♖xe8 ♖xe8 17 ♗e3 ♘e5= Kuzmin – Grember, Paris 1986.

A

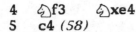

5	...	d5

It is not necessary to move the d-pawn again.

This only serves to benefit White.

6 ♞c3

6 cd ♛xd5 7 ♞c3 ♞xc3 8 bc c5= Polugayevsky.

6 ...   ♝c5

Black has also tried:

a) **6 ... ♞f6** 7 d4 ♝b4!? and not 7 ... ♝e7 8 ♝g5 Keres.

b) **6 ... ♞xc3** 7 dc c6 8 ♛d4 ♝e6 9 ♞g5± Keres – Ribeiro, Leipzig (ol) 1960.

c) **6 ... ♝e6** A strange move which may confuse the opponent, viz:

c1) **7 ♞d4?!** ♛f6!

c2) **7 ♞xd5** ♝xd5 8 cd ♛xd5 9 ♛a4+ ♞c6 10 ♝c4 ♛d7 11 ♝b5 ♞c5 12 ♛a3 0-0-0 13 0-0 ♞d3∓ Thomas – Alcock, England 1966.

c3) Gutman's **7 ♛c2** ♞xc3 8 dc dc 9 ♞d4 ♝d5 10 ♝e3 △ 0-0-0±. 8 ... ♞f6 is interesting, e.g. 9 ♞d4 ♝g4 10 cd ♝c5∞.

7 d4   ♝b4
8 ♛b3

Or:

a) **8 ♝d2** ♞xd2 9 ♛xd2 0-0 10 cd ♞d7 (10 ... ♝xc3 11 bc ♛xd5 12 ♝e2 c5!±, while if 10 ... ♝g4 one should expect 11 ♝c4) 11 a3! ♜e8+ 12 ♝e2, Keres – Keller, Zürich 1959, 12 ... ♝xc3 13 bc ♞b6 14 0-0 ♛xd5! controlling the white squares.

b) **8 ♛c2** ♛e7 9 ♝e3 ♞f5 10 ♛b3 0-0 △ ... ♜e8.

8 ...   c5?!

There have not been any examples of the pawn sacrifice 8 ... ♛e7 9 ♝e3 0-0 10 cd ♞f5. Here 10 ... ♜e8, threatening ... ♞xf2, is not effective because of 11 ♞e5!±.

9 ♝d3   ♛a5?
10 0-0!   ♞xc3

11 bc ♝xc3 12 ♝b2! ♝xb2 13 ♜ae1+ ♚f8 14 ♛xb2±± Evans – Bisguier, USA Ch New York 1958/59.

B

5 ...   ♝e7 *(59)*

White has three lines:

B1: 6 d4
B2: 6 ♞c3
B3: 6 ♝e2

B1

6 d4   0-0

Or:

a) **6 ... ♗g4** when:

a1) **7 h3** ♗h5 8 ♕b3 (more modest is: 8 ♗d3 ♘f6 9 ♘c3 0-0 10 ♗e3 c5! 11 d5 ♖e8 12 0-0 ♘bd7 13 ♗e2 ♗f8 14 ♖e1 ♘e4 15 ♘xe4 ♖xe4 16 ♘d2 ½-½ Ghinda - Tischbierek, Potsdam 1985) 8 ... ♘d7?! 9 ♕xb7 ♗xf3 10 gf ♘g5 11 ♗xg5 ♗xg5 12 ♕e4+ ♔f8 13 ♘c3 ♘f6 14 ♕f5 ♗h6 15 ♘e4 ♕b8 16 ♕b5 ♕xb5 17 cb ♖e8 18 ♗e2 ♘xe4= Tal - Smyslov, Moscow 1974.

a2) **7 ♕b3** ♘d7! c.f. note a1.

a3) **7 ♗e2** 0-0 8 0-0 ♖e8 (8 ... ♘c6 9 ♗e3 ♗f6 10 ♘bd2 ♘xd2 11 ♕xd2 d5=) 9 ♕c2! ♘f6 10 ♘c3 c6 (now 10 ... ♘c6 is not that strong because of 11 ♗e3 d5 12 ♖ad1! dc 13 ♘e5!± - Stoica) 11 h3 ♗h5 12 ♗f4 and White has slightly the freer position, Stoica - Lau, Lucerne 1985.

b) **6 ... d5!?**

b1) **7 ♘c3** ♘xc3 8 bc 0-0 9 ♗e2 (9 cd ♕xd5 10 ♗e2 ♗f5 11 0-0 ♘d7 {11 ... ♘c6!?} 12 ♘d2 ♘b6= Kupreichik - Agzamov, Frunze 1985) 9 ... ♘c6 10 0-0 ♗e6 11 ♖b1 ♘a5 12 cd ♗xd5 13 ♕a4 c6!? 14 c4 ♘xc4 15 ♖xb7 ♘b6 16 ♕a6 ♗d6 (△ ... ♗b8) 17 ♖xa7 ♖xa7 18 ♕xa7 ♖e8 19 ♗e3

♘c4 20 ♗xc4 ♗xc4 21 ♖c1 ♗d5 ∞ Ferreira - Miralles, Thessaloniki (ol) 1988.

b2) **7 ♗d3** ♘f6 (Polugayevsky thinks 7 ... ♗b4+ gives equality) 8 ♘c3 0-0 9 0-0 ♗g4 10 h3 (⌐ 10 cd) 10 ... dc 11 ♗xh7+ ♔xh7 12 hg ♘xg4 13 ♖e1 ½-½ G Hernandez - Schwartzman, St John 1988.

c) **6 ... ♘c6!?** 7 d5 ♘e5 8 ♘bd2 (8 ♘d4!?) 8 ... ♗f5 9 ♘d4 ♗g6 10 ♘xe4 ♗xe4 11 f3 ♗g6 12 f4 c5! 13 ♘c2 ♘d7!?∞.

7   ♗d3

Or 7 ♗e2 d5 8 0-0 c6 9 ♘c3 ♘f6 10 ♕b3 dc 11 ♗xc4 ♘bd7 12 ♘e5 ♕e8? (⌐ 12 ... ♘xe5±) 13 ♖e1 ♘b6 14 ♗xf7+! ♖xf7 15 ♘xf7 ♕f8 16 ♗g5 ♘fd5 17 ♘xd5 1-0, Kindermann - Radulov, Berlin 1986.

7   ...   ♘f6

a) **7 ... ♘g5** and now:

a1) **8 ♘c3** ♗g4 (8 ... ♘c6 9 ♗xg5 ♗xg5 10 ♕h5 ♖e8+! 11 ♘e2 h6) 9 ♗e2 ♘xf3+ 10 ♗xf3 ♗xf3 11 ♕xf3 ♘c6? (⌐ 11 ... c6!? 12 d5 c5 13 ♗f4 ♘d7 14 ♕g3 ♘f6 15 ♗h6 ♘h5 16 ♕g4 ♕e8! △ ... f5, ... ♗g5+∞) 12 ♗e3 ♗g5 13 0-0± Tseshkovsky - Makarichev, USSR Ch. 1979.

a2) **8 ♗e3** ♘c6?! (8 ... f5;

or 8 ... c6 △ ♖e8, ♘d7–f8∞)
9 ♘bd2 ♗g4 10 ♕b3 ♗xf3 11
gf d5 (⌷ 11 ... ♗f6) Mali-
shauskas – Sorokin, USSR
1987.

a3) **8 ♘xg5 ♗xg5 9 ♕h5**
♖e8+ 10 ♔d1 h6 11 ♗xg5
♕xg5 12 ♕xg5 hg 13 ♘c3
♗d7 14 ♔d2 ♘c6 15 ♘d5
♖ac8 16 ♔c3 ♘e7 17 ♘e3
♔f8! (17 ... a6 18 h4±) 18 g4
(18 h4 g4 19 g3 ♘g8 20 ♖he1
♘f6 21 ♘c2 c5 22 ♖xe8=
Kengis – Akopyan, USSR
1990) 18 ... g6! 19 h4 gh 20
♖xh4 ♔g7 = Kupreichik –
Akopyan, USSR 1990.

b) **7 ... d5** 8 0–0 transposing into line C, Chapter 30.
    8   ♘c3
Or 8 h3 ♘c6 9 ♘c3 d5 10
0–0 ♘b4 11 ♗e2 dc 12 ♗xc4
c6 13 ♖e1 ♘bd5 14 ♗g5 ♗e6±
Pühm – Nora, Strasbourg
1972. For further details see
Chapter 31.
    8   ...   ♗g4
    9   h3   ♗h5
a) **10 0–0** d5? (Overlook-
ing a pawn – one should
beware of this recurrent
motif. It is better to keep
the position closed by 10 ...
♘c6 or 10 ... ♗g6.) 11 cd
♘xd5 12 ♗xh7+ ♔xh7 13
♘g5+ ♔g8 14 ♕xh5±± Tseit-
lin – Karasev, USSR Ch.
1971.

b) **10 ♗e3** ♘bd7 11 g4 ♗g6
12 ♗xg6 hg 13 ♕e2 c6 Kup-
reichik – H Olafsson, Win-
nipeg 1986. 14 g5!? here, or
earlier 12 ♕e2 are Kupreichik's improvements.

B2

    6   ♘c3
Now Black has two main
methods:

B21: 6 ... ♘xc3
B22: 6 ... ♗f5

    Or:
    6 ... ♘g5 7 d4 0–0 8 ♗e2
♘c6 (8 ... ♗g4∞) when:
    a) **9 0–0** ♘xf3+ 10 ♗xf3
♗f6 11 ♘e2! ♗f5 12 ♗e3±
Kuzmin – Yusupov, Yere-
van Zonal 1982.
    b) **9 d5** ♘xf3+ 10 ♗xf3
♘e5 11 ♗e2 f5 12 f4 ♘g4 13
♗xg4± is Martinovic –
Kurajica, Sarajevo 1981.

B21

    6   ...   ♘xc3
    7   dc
Better then 7 bc when:
a) **7 ... 0–0** 8 d4 and now:
a1) **8 ... ♗f5!** 9 ♗d3 ♕d7 10
0–0 ♘c6 Michell – Hooper,
London 1922. Black has the
better pawn structure.
a2) **8 ... ♖e8** is also good
Marco – Maroczy, Monte

Carlo 1904.

b) Black obtained comfortable play with 7 ... ♘d7 in the game Blomdahl - Norberg, Stockholm 1975 after 8 d4 ♘f6 9 ♗e2 0-0 10 0-0 ♗f5 11 ♗f4 ♕d7 12 ♖e1 ♖fe8=.

$$7 \quad ... \quad ♘c6$$

Or 7 ... ♘d7 8 ♗e2 0-0 9 0-0 ♘c5 10 ♘d4 (10 ♗e3 ♗f6 11 ♕c2?! g6 12 ♖ad1 ♗f5= Ivanov - Rosentalis, Vilnius 1983; 10 ... f5!?) 10 ... ♗f6 11 ♗f3 ♗e5! 12 ♗e3 ♕f6 13 ♗d5 c6 14 f4 ♗xd4 15 ♗xd4 ♕g6 16 ♗f3 ♗f5= Dolmatov - Rosentalis, USSR 1983.

$$8 \quad ♗d3$$

This position is exactly the same as the one in line C1 after 8 ♗d3. See the details given there.

a) Developing the c1 bishop was premature and did not give anything in Teichmann - Marshall, San Sebastian 1911, viz. 8 ♗f4 ♗g4 9 ♗e2 ♕d7 10 ♕d2 0-0-0 11 0-0-0 h6 12 h3 ♗e6 13 ♘d4 ♘xd4 14 cd ♕a4=.

b) 8 ♗e3 ♗f5 9 ♗e2 0-0 10 0-0 ♖e8 11 a4 ♗f6= Sveshnikov - Plaskett, Hastings 1984/85.

$$8 \quad ... \quad ♘e5$$

Or 8 ... ♗g4 and now 9

♗e4! should not met by 9 ... 0-0?, e.g. 10 0-0 ♘e5 11 ♗xb7 ♖b8 12 ♗e4 ♔h8 13 h3 ♗xf3 14 ♗xf3 ♘xc4 15 ♗d5 ♘b6 16 ♕b3± Keres - Mikenas, Pärnu 1960 (White, with his bishop pair, is better). However 9 ... ♕d7! - See later in C1.

$$9 \quad ♘xe5 \quad de$$
$$10 \quad ♕c2 \quad ♗g5$$

11 0-0 ♗e6 12 ♖e1 ♗xc1 13 ♖axc1 ♕g5= Maroczy - Marshall, San Sebastian, 1911.

B22

$$6 \quad ... \quad ♗f5$$
$$7 \quad ♘d5$$

Or:

a) Black should not be afraid of 7 ♘d4, e.g. 7 ... ♗g6 8 ♕f3 ♘xc3 9 dc (9 ♕xb7 is met by 9 ... ♗e4) 9 ... ♕c8=.

b) 7 ♘xe4 ♗xe4 and now:

b1) 8 d4 d5= 9 ♕b3? ♘c6!∓ Ludolf - Maslov, USSR 1961.

b2) 8 ♗e2 ♘c6 9 0-0 0-0= Keres.

c) 7 d4 ♘xc3 8 bc 0-0 9 ♗d3 ♕d7= (Keres) 10 0-0 ♘c6 11 ♖b1 b6 12 ♖b5 ♗g6 13 ♗xg6 fg! 14 ♕d3 ♘a5∓ Ludolf - Vistanetsky, USSR 1961.

$$7 \quad ... \quad 0-0$$

| 8 | ♗e2 | ♖e8 |
| 9 | 0-0 | ♘c6 |

9 ... ♗f8 premature, e.g. 10 d3 ♘c5 11 ♗g5! ♕c8 12 ♗e3 c6 13 ♘c3 h6 14 b4 ♘ca6 15 a3 ♘d7 16 d4 was better for White, Tseshkovsky - Yusupov, USSR 1982.

| 10 | d4 | ♗f8 |

11 ♖e1 ♘e7 12 ♘e3 ♗g6 13 ♘h4 c6 14 f3 ♘f6 15 ♕d2 d5 16 c5 a5 17 a3 a4= Dolmatov - Barua, Frunze 1983.

B3

| 6 | ♗e2 |

In Kupreichik's method White is planning to castle first and only after that would he decide his further set-up. So Black must be prepared for different approaches.

| 6 | ... | 0-0 |
| 7 | 0-0 | d5 |

7 ... ♘c6 8 d4 ♗f6 - see line C.

| 8 | ♘c3 | ♘xc3 |

8 ... ♘f6 can also be considered.

| 9 | bc |

Or 9 dc dc 10 ♕xd8 ♖xd8 11 ♗xc4± (Kupreichik).

| 9 | ... | dc |

9 ... ♗f5 is not better, either, 10 cd ♕xd5 11 d4 ♘c6 12 ♖e1 ♗f6 13 ♗f4! ± Matulovic - Kapelan, Vrsac 1985.

However, 9 ... c5!? can be considered.

| 10 | ♗xc4 |

10 ♘e5!? (Kupreichik) 10 ... c5 (10 ... ♗g4 Kupreichik) 11 d4 ♘c6 12 d5 ♘a5 13 ♗d3 ♗f6, Kupreichik - Przewoznik, Lvov 1986, 14 ♖b1!, then c4± Kupreichik, (14 ... ♗xc3? 15 ♗xh7+!±).

C

| 5 | ... | ♘c6! *(60)* |

The latest and the most flexible treatment retaining the chance to transpose into the 5 d4 d5 6 ♗d3 ♘c6 7 0-0 ♗g4 8 c4 system, moreover into an even better alternative (see below).

C1: 6 ♘c3
C2: 6 ♗e2

C1

| 6 | ♘c3 |

Or 6 d4 d5 7 ♘c3 (After 7 ♗d3 Black will move the favourable 7 ... ♗b4+, or with 7 ... ♗g4 8 0-0 ♗e7 may transpose into Chapter 31) ♗b4 8 ♕c2 ♕e7! 9 ♗e3 (9 ♔d1 ♗xc3 10 bc∞, Mihalchishin) 9 ... ♗f5! 10 ♕c1? ♘xc3 11 bc ♗a3 12 ♕d2 ♘b4!∓ Kupreichik - Mihalchishin, Kuybishev 1986. Better is 10 a3 ♗xc3+ 11 bc ♘d6 (11 ... ♘g3 12 ♕b3 ♘xh1 13 ♕xb7 0-0 14 ♕xc6 is not clear either) 12 ♕b3 dc 13 ♗xc4 ♘xc4 14 ♕xc4 ♗e4 15 d5∞, Mihalchishin.

6   ...   ♘xc3

For 7 bc ♗e7 see above, line B21 7 bc.

7   dc   ♗e7

The struggle is simplified by 7 ... ♗f5, e.g. 8 ♘d4 ♘xd4 9 ♕xd4 ♕e7+! 10 ♗e2 ♕e4 ½-½ Chiburdanidze - Agzamov, Frunze 1985. 7 ... ♗g4 is also good, and then 8 h3 would be interesting. Whereas the game Marjanovic - Mihalchishin, Sarajevo 1985 went: 8 ♗e2 ♗e7 9 h3 ♗f5! 10 ♗f4 ♕d7 11 ♕d2 ♗f6! 12 0-0-0 0-0-0 13 g4 ♗g6 14 ♖he1 ♖he8 with equality.

8   ♗d3   ♗g4

8 ... ♘e5 is also good. See (with transposition)

line B21.

9   ♗e4!   ♕d7!

For 9 ... 0-0?! see Keres - Mikenas in B21.

10   ♗e3   ♗f5!

If 10 ... 0-0-0 11 ♕a4! with the initiative. Now 11 ♗xf5 ♕xf5 12 ♕d5! ♕xd5 13 cd ♘e5 14 ♘xe5 de 15 ♔e2 ♔d7! and in Timman's mind it's not easy to keep his slight advantage for White Timman - Yusupov, Hilversum (m) 1986.

C2

6   ♗e2   ♗e7
7   d4   ♗f6

7 ... d5?! 8 0-0 ♗e6 9 c5± Makarichev.

8   0-0   0-0
9   ♘c3

a) 9 d5 ♘e7 10 ♘a3 ♖e8(!) 11 ♘c2 h6 12 ♖e1 a5 13 ♖b1 ♗f5 14 ♗d3 ♕d7 (14 ... ♗h7=) 15 ♘fd4 ♗h7 16 ♗f4± Holmov - Raetsky 1988.

b) 9 ♗d3 ♗f5 10 ♖e1 ♖e8= Makarichev.

c) 9 h3 ♖e8 10 ♗f4 (10 ♖e1!, and not 10 ♘c3? because of 10 ... ♘xd4!; 10 ♗e3?! ♘g3!) 10 ... ♗f5 11 ♖e1 ♕d7 12 ♘a3? (12 ♗f1=) Chiburdanidze - Makarichev, Frunze 1985, and now 12 ... ♘b4! would have been advantageous to Black, according to Makarichev.

d) **9 ♗e3**

d1) **9 ... d5!?** 10 ♘c3 ♘xc3 11 bc dc 12 ♗xc4 ♗g4 13 h3 ♗h5 14 ♗e2 ♘a5 15 ♕a4 c6 16 c4 c5!?∞ Kindermann - Tischbierek, Budapest 1987.

d2) More solid **9 ... ♖e8** and now 10 ♕b3 can be met by ... ♘g5! Other alternatives:

d21) **10 ♘bd2 ♗f5!** 11 ♘b3!? d5! 12 ♖c1 dc 13 ♗xc4 ♘d6 14 ♗e2 ♘b4= Kupreichik - Makarichev, Frunze 1985.

d22) **10 ♘a3 ♗g4** 11 ♘c2 d5 12 c5 ♘g5 (12 ... a6=) 13 ♘xg5 ♗xe2 14 ♕xe2 ♗xg5 15 ♕b5 ♗xe3 16 fe ♕d7 17 ♖f4± King - Gruen, Bundesliga 1988.

| 9 | ... | ♘xc3 |
| 10 | bc | ♗f5 |

a) **10 ... ♖e8** 11 ♗e3 ♘e7?! (11 ... ♗f5 is better, transposing into the column) 12 ♕d2 ♗g4 (⌐ 12 ... b6) 13 h3 ♗xf3 14 ♗xf3 c6 15 ♖ab1 with an edge, Kupreichik - Schüssler, Malmö 1987/88.

b) **10 ... ♘a5** 11 ♗e3 c6 12 ♘d2 d5 13 ♗d3 ♖e8 14 c5 b6 15 cb ab 16 ♕c2 h6 17 ♖ab1 ♗a6 18 ♗xa6 ♖xa6 19 a4! ♖e7 20 ♖e1 ♘b7 21 ♗f4 ♖xe1+ 22 ♖xe1 c5! 23 ♕f5 g6 with equality, Kauschmann - Forintos, Stadthagen 1991.

| 11 | ♗e3 | ♖e8 |
| 12 | h3 | h6 |

12 ... ♕d7 was also to be considered.

| 13 | ♕d2 | ♗h7 |

14 ♖ad1 ♕d7 15 ♘h2 ♕f5 16 ♘g4 ♗g5 17 f4 (17 ♖b1) 17 ... ♗h4 18 ♖b1 ♕c2! 19 ♕xc2 ♗xc2 20 ♖b2 (20 ♖xb7? h5) 20 ... ♗e4 leads to a complicated position with good chances for Black in Kupreichik - Forintos, Budapest 1988. 14 ♖ae1 can also be considered.

20) 3 ♘xe5 d6: 5 ♘c3
Nimzowitsch Attack

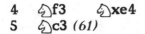

| 4 | ♘f3 | ♘xe4 |
| 5 | ♘c3 *(61)* | |

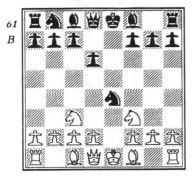

This is the attack popularised by Aron Nimzowitsch. It makes the least profit of the position of the e4-knight.

Now Black has tried:

A: 5 ... d5
B: 5 ... ♘f6
C: 5 ... ♘xc3

Not 5 ... ♗f5?? 6 ♕e2! 1-0 Zapata – Anand, Biel 1988.

A

| 5 | ... | d5? |

6	♕e2	♗e7
7	♘xe4	de
8	♕xe4	0-0
9	♗c4	

If 9 ♗d3 g6 10 ♕d4 ♗d6 11 ♕h4? (11 0-0∓) 11 ... ♖e8+ 12 ♗e2 ♕xh4! 13 ♘xh4 ♘c6 14 c3 g5 15 ♘f3 g4 16 ♘g1? (⊑ 16 ♘h4 ♗e7 17 g3) 16 ... ♘e5 17 d4 ♘d3+ 18 ♔f1 ♗f5∓ Gunsberg – Schlechter, Monte Carlo 1902.

Gunsberg was born in Hungary, in 1854, and as a chessplaying "child prodigy" paid a short visit to London and then to Paris when he was eight years old. Later he settled in England and amazed the public as a master secretly hidden in the chessplaying machine "Mephisto". His first places in Hamburg 1885 and London 1885 aroused attention and he became a professional chess master and journalist. He broke into the top level and

Steinitz found him worthy of playing a match for the World Championship title in 1890. Steinitz won a close fight +6 =9 −4 " ... a bit more strength in his attack and slightly more persistent defence and he would have succeeded " − wrote Dr Tarrasch at that time.

9 ... Bd6
10 0-0!

10 d4 is not the best, viz. 10 ... Re8 11 Ne5 Bxe5 12 de, Leonhardt − Schlechter, Barmen 1905, 12 ... Nc6!∞.

10 ... Re8

11 Qd3 Nc6 12 b3! Qf6 13 Bb2!! Qxb2 14 Ng5 Be6 15 Bxe6 fe 16 Qxh7+ Kf8, Alekhine − Rabinovitch, Moscow 1918, and now 17 c3!±± was needed (Alekhine).

B

5 ... Nf6
6 d4

When:

a) Gutman's recommendation **6 ... Bf5** can be met by the simple 7 Nh4 Bg4 8 Qd3 with good play for White, or 7 Bf4 Be7 8 Qd2 Ne4?! 9 Qd3! Ng3 10 Qb5+ c6 11 Qxb7 Nxh1 12 Qxa8 Qb6 13 Na4! Qc7 14 Ba6 0-0 15 Qb7 Qd8 16 Bd3± Blinov

− Tarsutin, corr. 1990.

b) **6 ... g6** 7 Qd3 (7 Qg5!?) 7 ... Bg7 8 Qe2+ Qe7 9 Qxe7+ Kxe7 10 Bg5 Re8 11 0-0-0 Kf8 12 h3 a6 13 Rhe1 Bd7 14 Ne4 Nxe4 15 Bxe4 Nc6 16 c3 ½-½ Plachetka − Knezevic, Vrnjacka Banja 1985.

c) **6 ... d5** 7 Qd3 White wins a couple of tempi this time instead of the usual one tempo. 7 ... Be7 8 Ne2 Ne4 9 c3± Panchenko − Knezevic, Dubna 1979

6 ... Be7

Now White may choose from:

a) **7 Be3** Bg4 8 h3 Bh5 9 Qd3 Nbd7 10 Ne4 Bxf3? (∆10 ... Nxe4 ∆ c6) 11 Qxf3 d5 12 Ng3± Persitzer − Mayer, Temesvar 1912.

b) **7 h3** (suggested by Tarrasch) 7 ... 0-0 8 Qd3 Nc6 9 a3 Re8 10 0-0 h6 11 Ne2 Bf8 12 Ng3 d5= Tseshkovsky − Smyslov, USSR 1974.

c) **7 Qd3** If Black wants to prevent the Ne2 − g3 manoeuvre, he may pin the knight.

c1) **7 ... Bg4** 8 h3 Bh5:

c11) **9 Bf4** 0-0 10 g4 Bg6 11 Qd2 Nc6 12 Bxg6 hg 13 d5 Na5 14 0-0-0 Qd7 15 Rhe1 Rfe8 16 Qd3 b6 17 Qb5 a6 18

♕xd7 ♘xd7= Tal - Smyslov, blitz game, Norway 1989.

c12) Tarrasch's witty sacrifice of a pawn deserves attention, viz. **9 0-0 0-0** (9 ... ♘c6 is more accurate with castling only after 10 ♗e3) 10 g4!? ♗g6 11 ♘h4!? ♗xd3 12 ♕xd3 ♘xg4 13 ♘f5 ♘f6 14 ♔h1 with good compensation for the pawn. 14 ♗h6 is even stronger in our opinion.

c2) **7 ... 0-0** and now:

c21) **8 0-0** ♗g4 9 h3 ♗h5 10 ♗e3 Gibaud - Skalicka, Paris 1924, or 10 g4!? transposing into note c12.

c22) **8 ♘e2** ♖e8 9 0-0 ♘c6! 10 c3 ♗f8 11 ♘g3 h6 (11 ... d5) 12 ♗c2 d5= Kochiev - Holmov, USSR 1978. 12 ♗f4 would have prevented d5 — Holmov.

c23) **8 h3** see the game Tseshkovsky - Smyslov in line b.

d) **7 ♗f4** 0-0 8 ♕d2 ♗f5 9 0-0-0 d5 (Black could have opened action on the queenside at once by 9 ... c6 and ... ♕a5 or ... b5) 10 ♘e5 c6 11 f3 ♕a5 12 g4 ♗e6 13 ♔b1 ♗b4 14 ♘d3, Chehov - Villareal, Yugoslavia 1975, 14 ... ♗xc3=.

e) **7 ♗g5** (Pachman's suggestion, planning 0-0-0).

Now:

e1) **7 ... ♗g4** 8 ♕d2±, Keres. The opening of the g-file would only help White's attack.

e2) Gutman's **7 ... ♗f5** is better △ 8 ♗d3 ♗g6.

e3) **7 ... 0-0** 8 ♕d2 d5 9 0-0-0 c6 10 h3? (10 ♘e5=) 10 ... b5 11 ♘e5? ♕a5 12 ♔b1 b4∓∓ Szavay - Barasz, Berlin 1912. This is Black's correct counterplay against 9 0-0-0 in any case.

f) **7 d5** is untested.

g) **7 ♕d3** 0-0 8 ♗g5 ♘c6 9 0-0-0 (9 a3) is unclear but 7 ... ♘c6 8 ♗g5 h6 seems sufficient.

C

5 ... ♘xc3 *(62)*

62
W

Bronstein's suggestion is best.

6 dc

6 bc has not become popular, the doubled pawn

being rather troublesome and there is no compensation for it, e.g.:

a) **6 ... ♗e7** 7 d4 0-0 8 ♗d3 ♗g4 9 0-0 ♘d7 10 ♖b1 b6= Bilguer.

b) **6 ... d5** 7 d4 ♗d6 8 ♗d3 0-0 9 ♗e3 and then ... ♘d7 is recommended (△ ... c5, ♘f6).

6   ...   ♗e7

a) **6 ... ♗e6?** is feeble, e.g. 7 ♘d4 ♕f6 8 ♘xe6 ♕xe6+ 9 ♗e2 ♗e7 10 0-0 ♘d7 11 ♖e1 ♕f6 12 ♗f3 c6 13 g3± Vecsey – Antal, Temesvar 1912.

b) **6 ... ♘d7?** 7 ♗g5! and either 7 ... ♘f6 or 7 ... ♗e7 can strongly met by 8 ♕e2.

c) **6 ... ♘c6** 7 ♗f4 mostly transposes into line C2.

Now White has tried:

C1: 7 ♗e3
C2: 7 ♗f4

Also:

a) **7 ♗c4** 0-0 8 0-0 ♗g4= Jaenisch.

b) **7 ♗d3** with three alternatives:

b1) **7 ... ♘d7** 8 ♗e3 ♗f6 and now the bishop is standing more confortably than the knight. 9 ♕e2 0-0 10 0-0-0 ♖e8 11 h3 ♘e5 12 ♘xe5 ½-½ in S Garcia – Vilela, Cuba 1983.

b2) **7 ... ♘c6** 8 ♗f4 ♗e6? (⌐ 8 ... ♗g4) 9 ♕e2 ♕d7 10 0-0-0 0-0-0 11 ♗b5! ♗f6 12 ♗e5 ♕e7 13 ♗xf6 ♕xf6 14 ♗xc6± Kasparian – Hachaturov, USSR 1968.

b3) **7 ... ♗g4** 8 h3 ♗h5 9 ♗e3 ♘c6 10 ♗e4! ♗g6 11 ♗xg6?! (11 ♗d5!) 11 ... hg 12 ♕e2 ♕d7= Skoularikis – Skalli, Thessaloniki (ol) 1988.

b4) **7 ... 0-0** is committal. 8 h3 ♘d7 9 0-0 ♘e5 Süchting – Rabinovich, Karlsbad 1911, 10 ♗f4±

As can already be seen, White has the option of castling either side with the various bishop moves he employs. No routine treatment can be recommended here – Black must react directly to White's individual set-up

C1

7   ♗e3 *(63)*

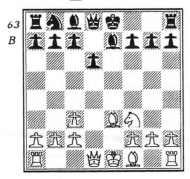

63
B

Black has three counters:

C11: 7 ... 0-0
C12: 7 ... ♘c6
C13: 7 ... ♘d7

7 ... d5? is inadvisable, 8 c4! dc 9 ♕xd8+ ♔xd8 10 ♗xc4 ♘f6 11 0-0-0 0-0 12 ♖he1± Nunn - Mascarinas, Thessaloniki (ol) 1984.

C11
> 7 ... 0-0
> 8 ♕d2

Consistent. 8 ♗d3 can also be recommended and for 8 ... ♘d7 see line C13.
> 8 ... ♘c6

8 ... ♗g4 is playable and Black may transpose into other lines if he wants to after 9 ♗e2 ♘c6 10 h3 with 10 ... ♗h5, or with 10 ... ♗e6
8 ... ♘d7 see line C13.
> 9 0-0-0

9 ... ♗g4 (9 ... ♘e5 see C12) 10 ♗e2 ♖e8 11 h3 ♗h5 12 ♖h2!? (△ g4, h4) 12 ... ♕c8 (12 ... ♗g6 △ ... ♘e5, ... ♗e4 is feasible) 13 g4 ♗g6 14 h4 (14 ♖g1) 14 ... ♕xg4 15 h5 ♗e4∞ van der Wiel - Stean, Leiden 1982.

C12
> 7 ... ♘c6
> 8 ♕d2

Other ideas are not bad, viz:

a) 8 ♗e2 ♘f6 9 ♕d2 ♘f5 10 0-0-0 ♕d7= Florian - Alexandrescu, Bucharest 1951.

b) 8 ♗d3 ♘e5!= is the simplest, exchanging an important White piece.

c) 8 h3 ♗f5 9 ♗d3 ♕d7 10 ♕d2 0-0 11 0-0-0 ♘e5 12 ♘xe5 de 13 ♗xf5 ♕xf5 14 ♕d5 b6= Michell - Scott, London 1920.

> 8 ... ♘e5

Some variations of lines 7 ... ♘d7 and 7 ... ♘c6 transpose here, so they haven't been distinguished in our earlier examples, they are discussed here.

Alternatives:

a) 8 ... ♗g4 9 ♗e2 ♕d7 and now:

a1) 10 0-0-0 0-0 11 ♖he1 ♖ae8 12 h3 ♗xf3 13 ♗xf3 ♗f6 14 ♗g4± is Nimzowitsch - Marshall, St. Petersburg 1914.

a2) White could consider the move order 10 h3 and if 10 ... ♗xf3?! 11 ♗xf3 ♗f6 12 0-0-0 0-0 immediately 13 ♗g4! ♕d8 and only then 14 ♖he1±/±.

b) 8 ... ♗f5 9 0-0-0 when:
b1) 9 ... ♕d7 10 ♘d4 (△ 10 h3 △ g4) 10 ... ♘xd4 11 ♗xd4 0-0 12 g4 ♗e4! 13 ♖g1 ♕a4!∓

(△ ... c5, ... d5) Losyev –
Pripis, USSR 1981.

b2) **9 ... 0-0** 10 ♘d4 ♘xd4
11 ♗xd4 ♕g5= Lloyd – Allen,
London 1961.

c) **8 ... 0-0** 9 0-0-0 ♗e6 10
♔b1 ♘e5! 11 ♘d4 ♗c4 12 b3
♗xf1 13 ♖hxf1 ♗f6 14 h3 ♕d7
15 g4 ♘c6 16 ♘f5 a5 17 h4
♘e7 18 ♘xe7+ ♗xe7 19 ♘d4
a4 20 ♖fe1 ½-½ Arnason –
Makarichev, Reykjavik 1990.

9   ♘d4

Or:

a) **9 ♗e2** 0-0 10 ♘d4 c5! 11
♘b3 ♗e6 12 ♖d1 ♕b6 13 0-0
a5∞ Sznapik – Borik, Dortmund 1981.

b) **9 ♗d4!? ♗f6** (9 ...
♘xf3+ is riskier due to the
opening of the g-file) 10
0-0-0 ♗e6! 11 ♕e3 (11 ♗xe5
winning a pawn does not
give an advantage, e.g. 11 ...
de 12 ♕e1 ♕e7 13 ♘xe5 ♗xa2
14 ♗b5+ c6! 15 ♘xc6 ♗g5+!)
11 ... ♘xf3 12 ♕xf3 ♗xd4 13
cd ♕g5+ with even chances
in Taulbut – Speelman,
Brighton 1980

c) **9 0-0-0** ♘xf3 10 gf ♗e6
11 ♔b1 ♗f6 12 ♘d3 c6 13 a3
♕a5 14 f4 0-0-0 15 c4 ½-½
van der Wiel – Barua, Novi
Sad (ol) 1990.

9   ...   0-0
10   0-0-0

10 f4 ♘g4 11 0-0-0 c5 12

♘f3 ♕e6 with counterplay
as in the game Short –
Condie, Brighton 1984.

10   ...   c5!?

10 ... a6 is also possible:
11 f4 ♘g4 12 ♗d3 (12 ♕g1 c5)
12 ... ♘xe3! 13 ♕xe3 ♗f6 14
♕f3 ♕d7 (14 ... c5 15 ♘f5!)
15 ♔b1 ♖b8 16 h3 g6 17 g4,
Howell – Zysk, Sharjah
1985, 17 ... b5! 18 ♗e4 b4
with mutual chances –
Schach Archiv.

11   ♘b5   ♗e6!

11 ... ♕a5?! 12 a3 a6? 13
♘xd6 ♖d8 14 ♘xc8!! ♖xd2
15 ♘xe7+ ♔f8 16 ♖xd2 ♔xe7
17 ♖d5! ♘d7 18 ♗e2 (△ ♗g4)
18 ... b6 19 ♗f3±± van der
Wiel – van der Sterren, Wijk
aan Zee 1984.

12   ♘xd6   ♕b6

13 b4 (13 ♗f4 f6) 13 ...
♗xd6 and after all the exchanges White has such a
slight advantage as in both
Nunn – Zsuzsa Polgar, Brussels 1985 and in Klinger –
Eisterer, Vienna 1986 which
led to only a draw. Instead,
13 ♘e4 can be met by 13 ...
♖ad8 and Black impercep-
tibly regains the offensive.

C13

7   ...   ♘d7
8   ♕d2

If **8 ♗d3** ♘e5= is the

simplest, compare with line C12.

8 ... 0-0
9 0-0-0

9 ♘d4 is met by ... ♘c5=, or 9 ... ♘f6. As for 9 ... ♘e5, it leads into C12 line by transposition.

9 ... ♘c5

With 9 ... ♘e5! Black may still transpose into C12.

10 h4

Or 10 ♘d4 ♘e4!? – Ciocaltea.

10 ... ♗g4

Instead, 10 ... ♖e8 11 ♘g5 (△ 12 ♘xf7, 13 ♗xc5) 11 ... ♗xg5 12 ♗xg5 (12 hg?! ♘e4) 12 ... f6 13 ♗e3 ♗e6 14 a3 Kupreichik – Szymczak, Polanica Zdroj 1981, and now 14 ... ♘e4!? △ ... ♗f7 is advisable.

11 ♗e2 ♕c8

12 ♘d4 ♗xe2 (12 ... ♘e4 13 ♗xg4!) 13 ♕xe2 ♖e8 14 ♕f3 ♗f6 15 h5± Pinal – Sieiro, Havana 1983.

C2

7 ♗f4

Apparently White's best chance, played specifically to prevent Black's exchanging manoeuvre ♘c6-e5. It does have shortcomings though ...

7 ... 0-0

The alternative is 7 ... ♘c6 when:

a) **8 ♗d3 ♗g4** 9 h3 ♗h5 10 g4?! (⌐ 10 ♗e4) 10 ... ♗g6 11 h4? ♕d7 12 ♖g1 0-0-0∓ Louma – Milner-Barry, London 1947.

b) **8 ♕d2** and now:

b1) **8 ... ♗f5**?! 9 0-0-0 ♕d7 10 h3 a6 11 g4 ♗e4 12 ♗g2 0-0-0 13 ♕e3! d5 14 ♘e5 ♕e6 15 ♗xe4 de 16 ♘xc6 ♕xc6 17 f3± Groszpeter – Halasz, Hungarian Ch. 1979.

b2) **8 ... ♗g4** 9 ♗e2 ♕d7 (9 ... 0-0?! 10 0-0-0 ♖b8, Michell – Tylor, Hastings 1935/36, White should play 11 h3±) when:

b21) **10 h3 ♗h5** (10 ... ♗xf3 see c by transposition. 10 ... ♗e6 can be considered, 11 0-0-0 0-0-0 and then transposing into b22, and 11 ♘g5 met by 11 ... ♗xg5 12 ♗xg5 f6 with an analogous idea. See b22 11 0-0-0 0-0-0 12 ♖he1 ♖he8 13 g4 ♗g6 15 ♗b5 a6! with even chances L Schmid – Alexander, Dublin 1957.

b22) **10 0-0-0** 0-0-0 11 h3 ♗e6!? 12 ♘g5 ♗xg5 13 ♗xg5 f6 14 ♗e3 h5!? ∞ Santo Roman – Miralleo, Lyon 1988.

b3) **Immediate 8 ... ♗e6** can be met by 9 ♘g5.

c) 8 ♗e2 ♗g4 9 ♕d2 ♕d7
10 h3 (10 0-0-0 see b22 by
transposition) 10 ... ♗xf3
(for 10 ... ♗h5 or 10 ... ♗e6
see note b21) 11 ♗xf3 ♕e6+
12 ♗e2 0-0 13 0-0 ½-½ Iv-
anovic - Smyslov, Bor 1980.

8 ♕d2   ♘d7

8 ... ♘c6 has been dem-
onstrably less effective
here:

a) 9 0-0-0 ♗f6 10 ♗d3
♘e5?! (10 ... ♖e8, ... ♗g4) 11
♗xe5! de 12 ♕e3! ♕e7 13 h4
♖e8, Holmov - Mayorov,
USSR 1979, 14 ♕e4± Hol-
mov.

b) 9 ♗e2 ♗g4 10 0-0-0
♗f6 11 h3 ♗xf3 12 ♗xf3
♘e5!? 13 ♗xb7 ♖b8 14 ♗d5
c5 Kupreichik - Schüssler,
Reykjavik 1980, 15 ♗xe5±.

9 0-0-0   ♘c5
10 ♘d4

Or 10 h3 ♖e8 when:

a) 11 g4 ♘e4 12 ♕e1 ♗f6 13
♗e3 c6?! (13 ... b6 △ ... ♗b7,
... c5; 13 ... ♗d7 △ ... ♗c6) 14
♗d3± Tseshkovsky - Zait-
sev, USSR 1975.

b) Nothing is given by 11
♗c4 ♗e6! 12 ♗xe6 ♘xe6 13
♗e3 a5 14 h4 a4 15 a3 ♕d7
with balanced chances, Savon - Kochiev, Lvov 1978.

10 ...   ♖e8
11 f3   ♘e6
12 ♗e3

White has nothing after
12 h4 ♘xf4 13 ♕xf4 d5 14
♘f5 ♗f6 15 ♗d3 ♗e5 16 ♕d2
½-½ Kupreichik - Makar-
ichev, USSR Ch. 1980/81.

12 ...   ♗g5

12 ... ♘xd4 13 cd ♗f6 14
♗d3 ♗e6 15 h4?! (15 ♔b1=)
15 ... c5! 16 ♗g5 (16 dc dc
just opens the diagonals
and files for Black's attack)
16 ... h6 17 d5 ♗d7∓ Sveshnikov - Kochiev and Koch-
iev - Holmov, Lvov 1978.

13 f4

13 ♗xg5 or 13 ♘xe6=.

13 ...   ♗f6
14 ♘f3   b6

Black, in Sveshnikov -
Kochiev, USSR Ch. 1977,
unnecessarily complicated
things by the sacrifice 14 ...
♘c5 15 ♗xc5 dc 16 ♕f2 ♕e7
17 ♖e1 ♕f8 18 ♖xe8 ♕xe8 19
♕xc5 ♕e4 but found him-
self without sufficient
compensation.

15 ♗c4

If 15 g4 Black gains con-
trol of e4 with 15 ... ♗b7.

15 ...   ♘c5
16 ♗d5   ♖b8

17 ♘d4 ♗xd4 18 cd ♘e4 19
♕d3 ♘f6 20 ♗f3 d5 and
Black has good prospects
on the white squares, Dolmatov - Yusupov, USSR Ch.
1980/81.

21) 3 ♘xe5 d6: 5 ♕e2
Introduction

4	**♘f3**	**♘xe4**
5	**♕e2** *(64)*	

Tarrasch established that this leads to early equality.

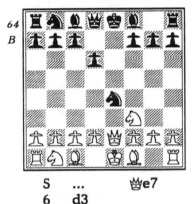

64
B

5	**...**	**♕e7**
6	**d3**	

Or:

a) **6 g3** ♗g4(!) 7 ♗g2 ♘c6∓.

b) **6 d4** ♗g4 (6 ... ♘c6 – Tartakower) 7 ♗e3 ♘c6 or 7 ... d5=.

c) **6 b3** ♗g4 7 ♗b2 ♘d7 8 d3 ♘ef6 or 8 ... ♗xf3=.

d) **6 h3** g6!=.

e) **6 ♘c3** ♘xc3 (6 ... ♘f6 is playable – Samaganov) 7 dc (7 ♕xe7+ ♗xe7 8 dc ♘c6 9 ♗e3 ♗f5 10 ♗d3 ♗xd3= Hort – Nunn, German League 1988) 7 ... ♕xe2+ (7 ... ♘c6 is also good, e.g. 8 ♗g5 ♕xe2+ 9 ♗xe2 ♗e7 10 ♗xe7 ♔xe7= Kochiev – Lein, Hastings 1978/79) 8 ♗xe2 and now:

e1) **8 ... ♘c6** 9 ♗e3 (9 ♗f4 ♗f5= Tringov – Suetin, 1967) 9 ... ♗e7 10 ♘d4 ♘xd4 11 cd ♗f5 12 0-0-0 0-0-0 ½-½ Korchnoi – L Stein, Riga 1970.

e2) **8 ... ♗e7** 9 ♗g5 (9 ♗f4 ♘c6 10 ♘d4 ♘xd4 11 cd c6 12 ♗d3 ♗e6= Prandstetter – Knezevic, Prague 1983) 9 ... ♗xg5 10 ♘xg5 0-0 11 0-0-0 ♘c6 12 ♖he1 h6 13 ♘f3 ♗g4= Lutikov – Suetin, USSR 1967.

6	**...**	**♘f6**

Or 6 ... ♘c5 7 ♘c3 ♗g4! 8 ♗e3 (8 ♘d5 suggested by Euwe would most probably have been met by 8 ... ♕xe2+ 9 ♗xe2 ♘e6, and later, ... c6) 8 ... c6 9 h3 ♗h5 10 g4 ♗g6 11 ♗g2 ♘bd7 12

♘d4 ♘e6 13 f4 ♘xd4 14 ♗xd4 f5 15 0-0-0 ♕xe2 16 ♘xe2 ♘f6± Hodgson - Barua, London 1986.

Now White has:

A: 7 ♘c3
B: 7 ♗g5

White may introduce other rational moves as well, e.g. 7 h3, 7 ♗e3, 7 c4, 7 b3 and 7 ♕xe7+.

Two examples of the latter: 7 ... ♗xe7 8 ♘c3 c6 9 ♗e2 0-0 10 0-0 ♖e8 11 ♖e1 ♗f8 (11 ... ♘bd7 12 ♗d2 ½-½ Ambroz - Knezevic, Prague 1985) 12 ♗f1 ♖xe1 13 ♘xe1 ♘bd7 14 ♘f3 d5 15 h3 ½-½ S Garcia - Knezevic, Bayamo 1985.

A
7 ♘c3

This knight move would be tried by those disappointed with 7 ♗g5. Now ♗g5 may be a threat.

7 ... ♘bd7

Probably the best, other tries:

a) 7 ... ♕xe2+ 8 ♗xe2 and now:

a1) 8 ... c6?! 9 ♘e4±.

a2) 8 ... g6 9 0-0 ♗g7 10 ♘b5 ♘a6 11 d4 0-0= Hazai - Petran, Hungarian Ch. 1979.

a3) 8 ... ♗e7 9 ♘b5 ♘a6 10 c4 c6 11 ♘c3 d5 12 ♗f4 ♗e6 13 0-0-0 0-0-0=. White may transpose to later variations with 9 ♗g5.

a4) 8 ... ♗g4 9 h3 ♗xf3 10 ♗xf3 ♘c6, Mnatsakanjan - Smyslov, USSR 1979, 11 ♘d5±.

b) 7 ... c6 8 ♘e4! ♘xe4 9 de ♘d7 10 ♗f4 ♘e5 11 0-0-0±.

c) For 7 ... ♘c6 8 ♗g5 see later Hennings - Bilek, by transposition.

If 8 ♘b5 Black has 8 ... ♗e6=.

d) 7 ... h6 8 ♘b5 ♘a6 9 c4 ♕xe2+ 10 ♗xe2 c6 13 ♘c3±.

e) After 7 ... ♗e6:

e1) For 8 ♗g5 see line B.

e2) 8 ♘d4 (Toth) ⌐ g3 and ♗g2.

f) 7 ... ♗g4 8 ♗e3 ♘c6 9 h3 when:

f1) Poor is 9 ... ♗xf3?! 10 ♕xf3 d5!? 11 ♘xd5 ♘xd5 12 ♕xd5 ♕b4+ 13 c3 ♕xb2 14 ♖c1± Haag - Dely, Budapest 1967.

f2) 9 ... ♗e6 and now:

f21) 10 ♘g5?! g6 11 ♘xe6 fe 12 d4 ♗g7 13 0-0-0, M Kovacs - Petran, Budapest 1972, 13 ... a6=.

f22) 10 d4! (planning ♕b5) 10 ... a6 11 0-0-0 (or 11 ♗g5) 11 ... ♘b4 12 a3 ♘bd5 13

♘xd5± (Dely).

g) **7 ... ♗d7** 8 ♗g5 ♕xe2+ see B, 7 ♗g5.

8 ♗e3

Or:

a) **8 g3** c6=.

b) **8 ♘b5** ♘e5! 9 ♘xe5 de= Dely – B Toth, Budapest 1968.

c) **8 ♗g5** transposes to line B.

8 ... ♘b6
9 0-0-0 ♘g4
10 g3 =

B

7 ♗g5 *(65)*

Black has to play very accurately to avoid any disadvantage.

65
B

Now Black has:

B1: 7 ... ♗g4
B2: 7 ... ♗e6

Or:

a) For **7 ... ♕xe2+** see Chapter 22.

b) For **7 ... ♘bd7** see Chapter 23.

c) **7 ... ♘c6** 8 ♘c3 ♕xe2+ (8 ... ♗e6 will be discussed by transposition in B32) 9 ♗xe2 ♗e7 10 ♘b5±.

B1

7 ... ♗g4

This move has also had its reputation tarnished.

8 ♘c3

Or 8 ♗xf6 when:

a) **8 ... gf** 9 ♕xe7+ ♔xe7 10 ♗e2, Suetin – Roizman, USSR 1953, 10 ... c6 △ ... ♗h6, ⌓ 9 ♘bd2.

b) **8 ... ♗xf3?** 9 ♕xe7+!±±.

8 ... ♕xe2+

The queens must be exchanged now or on the next move to avoid the following: 8 ... ♘bd7 9 0-0-0 0-0-0? (9 ... ♕xe2) 10 ♕d2! ♘b6 11 ♖e1 ♕d7 12 ♘d4 ♗e7 13 h3± Chistiakov – Samayev, Kiev 1938.

9 ♗xe2 ♗e7
10 0-0-0

Or 10 ♘d4 ♗xe2 11 ♘cxe2 ♘d5 12 ♗xe7 ♘xe7= Geller – Solmanis, USSR 1949.

10 ... h6
11 ♗h4 ♘bd7

Slightly better 11 ... ♘c6.

12 h3 ♗h5
13 g4 ♗g6

14 ♘d4! 0-0-0 15 f4±
Rabinovich - Khan, Moscow
1935.

B2

7 ... ♗e6

This move has nearly
disappeared from practice!
- Suetin.

8 ♘c3 *(66)*

After **8 d4** ♘bd7 is correct and not 8 ... d5? 9 ♘c3
c6 10 ♘e5± Duras - Marsh-
all, San Sebastian 1912.

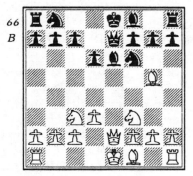

Black has three choices:

B21 8 ... ♘c6
B22: 8 ... h6
B23: 8 ... ♘bd7

Or 8 ... c6?! 9 ♘e4 ♘bd7
10 0-0-0± is passive.

B21

8 ... ♘c6?!
9 0-0-0

Or:

a) **9 ♘e4** is also good for
White, e.g. 9 ... d5 10 ♘xf6+
gf 11 ♗e3 0-0-0 12 d4 and
now:

a1) **12 ... ♗f5** 13 ♘h4±.

a2) **12 ... ♗g4!** 13 ♕d2 ♕e6
14 ♗e2 ♔b8 15 a3 ♘e7 16
0-0-0 ♘f5 17 ♗f4 ♘d6 (△ 18
... ♘e4) and Black has compensation for the doubled
pawn in Zhukov - Schiff-
man, corr. 1953.

b) **9 d4** forces 9 ... d5 and
10 0-0-0 0-0-0 transposes
to the column.

9 ... 0-0-0

9 ... h6? is premature, for
10 ♗xf6 is not properly met
by 10 ... ♕xf6 because of 11
d4±.

10 d4 d5
11 ♘e5!

11 ♕b5 means less
trouble for Black: 11 ... ♕b4
12 a3 ♕xb5 13 ♗xb5 ♘e7=
Gordon - Sharp, corr. 1932.

11 ... ♕e8
12 ♕e3!

Or:

a) **12 ♕f3** ♗e7 (12 ... ♘xe5
13 de ♗g4 is wrong because
of 14 ♕e3! ♗xd1 15 ♕xa7, in
Belyakov's opinion, 15 ...
♕xe5 can be met by 16 f4!
and then ♕a8+ is decisively
strong) 13 ♗b5 ♘xe5! 14 de
♘d7 15 ♗xd7+ ♕xd7 16 ♗xe7
♕xe7 17 ♘xd5 ♕c5 18 ♘c3

♕xe5= Lasker – Pillsbury, St. Petersburg 1895.

b) **12 ♕b5** a6! 13 ♕a4 ♘xe5 14 de ♕xa4 15 ♘xa4 h6 16 ef hg 17 fg ♗xg7= Kieninger – Kohler, Bad Oeynhausen 1940.

c) **12 ♘xc6** ♕xc6 13 ♗xf6 gf 14 ♕b5 ♕d6 15 g3 ♔b8 16 ♗g2 h5! 17 ♔b1 h4= Kieninger – Ahues, Bad Oeynhausen 1940.

12 ... ♗e7

Better is 12 ... a6, or 12 ... h6 13 ♗h4 a6.

13 ♗b5 ♗d7
14 ♘xd7 ♕xd7
15 ♗xc6±

Kieninger – Schuster, Essen 1948.

B22

8 ... h6

Avoiding the doubled f-pawn.

9 ♗xf6

More consistant than 9 ♗h4 when:

a) **9 ... g5** 10 ♗g3 ♗g7 11 d4 ♘c6 12 0-0-0 ♘d5 13 ♘xd5 (13 ♕b5 ♘xc3 14 ♕xb7 ♔d7∞) 13 ... ♗xd5 14 ♕b5 ♗xf3 15 gf 0-0-0∓ Kupchik – Marshall, New York 1915. Black may play 10 ... ♘d5∓, or 11 ... ♘d5∓ to avoid the complications of 13 ♕b5.

b) **9 ... ♘c6** is also good,

e.g. 10 0-0-0 0-0-0 11 d4 d5 12 ♘e5 ♘xe5 13 de ♕b4= Israel – Fazekas, England 1949.

9 ... ♕xf6

Or 9 ... gf 10 0-0-0 ♘c6 11 d4 d5 12 ♕b5 0-0-0 13 ♕a4 ♔b8 14 ♗b5 ♕d6 and the black bishops become strong (15 ♗xc6 bc!) Cullip – Barua, British Ch. 1989. We think 11 ♕e4!? is better : 11 ... 0-0-0 (11 ... f5? 12 ♕a4±) 12 ♘d5 ♗xd5 13 ♕xd5 ♕e6! 14 ♕b3±.

10 d4

Or 10 0-0-0 ♗e7 11 d4 0-0 transposes to column.

10 ... ♗e7

Weaker are:

a) **10 ... ♕e7** 11 0-0-0 d5 12 ♘e5 c6 13 f4 ♘d7 L Steiner – Kashdan, (m) 1930, when 14 g4± is best – Löwenfisch.

b) **10 ... c6** when not:

b1) **11 0-0-0?** d5 12 ♘e5 ♗b4! 13 ♘xd5?! ♗xd5 14 ♘g6! ♕e6 15 ♘xh8 ♕xe2 16 ♗xe2 ♔f8 17 a3 ♗d6 and now 18 f3 is the best, (Bilguer) although Black's endgame is more comfortable Morphy – Löwenthal, New Orleans 1850

J J Löwenthal was born in Hungary. Later he became a British subject when he was 40 years old and emigrated to America like a number of Hungarian revolutionists after the collapse of the War of Independence 1848-49. His brilliant opponent, Morphy, then 13 years old, won one game of the mini-match, while the other ended with the above mentioned draw. Later it was pointed out that

b2) **11 d5!?** cd 12 0-0-0 ♗e7 13 ♘xd5± gave White the advantage.

11   0-0-0

Or:

11 ♕b5+ ♘bd7 and now:

a) **12 ♕xb7** ♖b8 13 ♕xc7 0-0∞.

b) **12 ♘d5** ♗xd5 13 ♕xd5 c6 14 ♕b3 ♕e6+ with even chances Rossolimo - Tartakower, (m) 1948.

c) **12 ♗d3** g5 13 h3 0-0 14 ♕xb7 ♖ab8 15 ♕e4 ♕g7 16 b3 (16 0-0-0 is better, though more risky).

c1) **16 ... c5?** 17 0-0 cd 18 ♘d5± Capablanca - Marshall, St Petersburg 1914.

c2) Better **16 ... ♘c5** 17 ♕e3 ♗f6 - Tarrasch.

11	...	0-0
12	♕e4	c6
13	♗d3	g6
14	♕e3	

14 d5?! cd 15 ♘xd5 ♗xd5

16 ♕xd5 ♘c6 17 ♖he1 ♖fc8= Malevinsky - Gusev, USSR 1970.

14	...	♔h7

14 ... ♔g7? 15 ♘e4±±.

15   h4± (Yudovich)

B23

8	...	♘bd7
9	0-0-0	

9 d4 is answered not by:

a) **9 ... d5?** 10 0-0-0 c6 11 ♔b1 h6 12 ♗f4 0-0-0? (⌐ 12 ... ♕b4) 13 ♕a6!! ♘h5 14 ♕xc6+ bc 15 ♗a6 mate. Taube - Finotti, Hamburg 1939, but

b) **9 ... h6** 10 ♗h4 g5 11 ♗g3 ♘d5= or 10 ♗f4 ♘d5=.

9 ♘d4 is also good.

9	...	h6

9 ... 0-0-0 is feeble because of 10 d4 d5 11 ♘e5±.

10	♗h4	

10 ♗d2 also can be played, or 10 ♗e3, then the good c3-knight must be exchanged after 10 ... ♘d5 in order to make a place for the d7-knight.

10	...	0-0-0
11	d4	

Not 11 ♕e3? ♘b6 12 d4 g5 13 ♗g3 ♘h5 14 d5 ♗d7∓ Harris - Hooper, Hastings 1953.

11	...	g5
12	♗g3	♘d5!=

22) 3 ♘xe5 d6: 5 ♕e2 7 ... ♕xe2+

4	♘f3	♘xe4
5	♕e2	♕e7
6	d3	♘f6
7	♗g5	♕xe2+
8	♗xe2	(67)

Without queens and with no clear target one tempo has little importance.

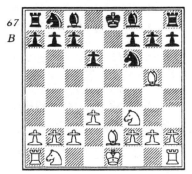

Or 8 ♔xe2 ♗e7 9 ♘c3 h6 10 ♗e3 c6 11 g3 ♘a6 12 ♗g2 0-0 13 ♖he1 ♖e8 14 ♔f1 ♗d7 15 ♖e2 ½-½ Ivkov - Petrosian, 1972.

8	...	♗e7

a) After 8 ... ♘d5?! (Developing a new piece is more practical) 9 c4 is strongest, and now:

a1) 9 ... ♘b6 10 ♔d2 h6 11 ♗e3 ♗e7 (better is 11 ... ♘c6) 12 ♘d4! 0-0 13 g4!± Mukhin - Voronov, USSR 1975.

a2) 9 ... ♘b4 10 ♔d2 ♗e7 11 ♗xe7 ♔xe7 12 ♘c3 h6 (12 ... f6) 13 a3 ♘4c6, Sahovic - Knezevic, Pancevo 1985, 14 ♖he1 ♔d8 15 b4±.

b) 8 ... ♘c6 9 ♘c3 ♗e6 (better is 9 ... ♗e7) 10 0-0-0 (the bishop pair compensate Black for the doubled pawn after 9 ♗xf6 or 10 ♗xf6) 10 ... ♗e7 11 d4 d5=.

c) 8 ... ♘bd7 The bishops develop later.

c1) 9 ♘c3 h6 10 ♗h4 (or 10 ♗f4 ♘b6 11 0-0-0 ♗d7 12 ♘d4 0-0-0 13 ♗g3 g6- Janssen - Yusupov, Graz 1981) 10 ... ♗e7 (10 ... g5 or 10 ... g6 are weaker) 11 0-0!? ♔d8 (11 ... a6 and 12 ... 0-0 seem more natural) 12 d4 ♘b6 13 a4 a5 14 ♗g3 ♗e6 15 ♘d2 c6 16 ♘d1 d5 17 ♘e3 ♘e8 18 ♗d3 g6 19 h3 ♗d6 20 ♗e5± Belyavsky - Benko, Hastings 1974/75.

c2) **9 0-0** ♗e7 10 ♖e1 h6 11
♗d2 0-0 12 ♘f1 ♖e8 13 ♘c3
c6 14 ♘e4 d5 15 ♘g3 ♘b6
½-½ Kurajica - Popovic,
Novi Sad 1982.

9   ♘c3 *(68)*

Alternatives:

a) **9 ♘bd2** ♘d5 10 ♗xe7
♔xe7 11 0-0-0 ♘f4 12 ♘f1 h6
13 ♖e1+ ♔d8 14 h4 ♖e8 15
♖xe8+ ♔xe8 16 g3 ♘e6 17 d4
♘d7 18 ♗d3 ♘f6 ½-½ Cioc-
altea - Karpov, Caracas
1970.

b) **9 c4** h6 10 ♗f4 ♘c6 11
♘c3 ♗f5 12 0-0-0 0-0-0 13
♖he1 g5 14 ♗e3 ♘g4 15
♘d5 ∞ Spassky - Karpov,
blitz TV World Cup 1982;
10 ... 0-0 11 ♘c3 ♖e8 12 0-0
♗f8 13 ♖fe1 ♘a6 14 a3 ♗d7
15 b4 c6 16 ♗f1 ♖xe1 17 ♖xe1
♘c7 18 ♘e4 ♘fe8 19 ♗d2
½-½ in Karpov - Smyslov,
Tilburg 1982.

Now Black has:

A: 9 ... ♗d7
B: 9 ... h6
C: 9 ... c6

Or:

a) **9 ... 0-0** 10 0-0-0 c6
(to prevent 11 ♘b5 ♗d8 12
♗xf6) 11 ♖he1 d5 12 d4 ♗d6?
(⌐ 12 ... ♗e6) 13 ♗xf6 gf 14
g3! ♘a6 15 ♘h4 ♘c7 16 ♗d3
♘e8 17 ♗f5!± R Byrne -
Burger, USA 1968.

b) **9 ... ♗g4** when:

b1) **10 h3** ♗h5 11 ♘d4 ♗xe2
12 ♔xe2 h6 13 ♗h4 (13 ♗e3!?)
13 ... ♘c6 14 ♘f5 ♘h5! 15
♘xe7 ♘xe7 (△ 16 ... ♘g6) 16
♗xe7 ♔xe7 17 ♘d5+ ♔d7=
Smyslov - Kogan, Moscow
1938.

b2) **10 ♘d4** ♗xe2 11 ♔xe2±
(Keres).

c) **9 ... ♘c6** 10 ♘b5 is a
typical move for gaining
the advantage, e.g. 10 ...
♔d8 and now:

c1) **11 0-0-0** a6 12 ♘c3 o r
12 ♘bd4± (Keres).

c2) Weaker is **11 0-0** a6 12
♘bd4 (Kashdan - Mikenas,
Folkestone 1933) 12 ... ♘xd4
13 ♘xd4 ♘d5 = .

A

9   ...   ♗d7
10   0-0

Or:

a) **10 d4** ♘c6 11 d5 ♘e5 12
♘d4! 0-0-0 13 ♗e3 g6?! (⌐

13 ... ♘fg4) 14 h3 ♘e8 15 0-0-0± Pribyl - Kostro, Polanica Zdroj 1973.

b) **10 0-0-0** ♘c6 and now:

b1) **11 ♖he1** 0-0-0 (the c7 pawn must be defended) 12 d4 ♖he8=.

b2) **11 d4** h6 (11 ... 0-0-0 12 ♗c4 ♖hf8 13 ♖he1 ♖de8 14 d5 ♘b8 15 h3 a6 16 ♗d3 h6 17 ♗e3± Georgiev - Below, Moscow 1985) 12 ♗h4 0-0-0 13 ♗c4! Fine - Alexander, Hastings 1935/36 - see line B.

b3) **11 ♘e4** ♘xe4 12 de ♗xg5+ 13 ♘xg5 h6 14 ♘f3 0-0-0= Velimirovic - Ivanovic, Novi Sad 1984.

b4) **11 ♘b5** 0-0-0 12 ♖he1 ♖de8! 13 ♘fd4 ♘xd4 14 ♘xd4 ♘d5= Spiridonov - Malich, Debrecen 1969.

10 ...   0-0

More secure: 10 ... ♘c6 11 ♖fe1 0-0-0.

11   ♖fe1   ♘c6
12   d4   ♖fe8
13   ♗b5!   a6
14   ♗a4±

Black would conclude that it is better to insert 9 ... h6 in order to force the dark-squared bishop to commit itself.

B

9   ...   h6

10   ♗h4

Other ideas:

a) **10 ♗f4** ♘c6 (10 ... ♗g4 11 h3 ♗h5 12 0-0-0 {12 ♘d4!?} 12 ... ♘bd7 13 ♖he1 0-0-0 14 ♘d4 ♗xe2= Kavalek - Smyslov, Tilburg 1977) 11 0-0-0 ♗f5 12 h3 0-0-0 13 ♖he1 d5 14 d4 ♗b4= Grechkin - Lilienthal, USSR 1938. 13 g4 or 12 ♖he1 or 11 ... ♗d7 are better alternatives.

b) **10 ♗e3** ♘c6 11 0-0 ♗d7 12 a3 0-0 13 d4 a6= Gligoric - Rossetto, Amsterdam 1954.

c) **10 ♗d2** c6 (10 ... ♗d7=) 11 0-0 0-0 12 ♖fe1 d5 13 h3 ♗d6 14 ♗f1 ♘a6 15 a3 ♗f5 ½-½ Ciocaltea - Malich, East Germany 1960.

10   ...   ♗d7 *(69)*

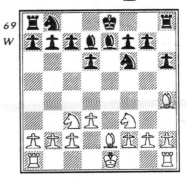

This resembles line A with ... h6/♗h4 interpolated.

Other ideas:

a) **10 ... a6?** 11 0-0 ♘c6 12

d4 ♗g4 13 h3 ♗h5 14 g4!± L
Steiner - Mattison, Debrecen 1925.

b) **10 ... ♘c6 11 ♘b5 ♔d8
12 c4±**.

c) **10 ... c6 11 0-0-0 ♗f5!**
12 ♘d4 ♗h7 13 f4 ♘bd7 14
♘f3 0-0 15 ♖de1 ♖fe8 ½-½
Ciocaltea - Suba, Romania
1982.

d) **10 ... ♗e6 11 0-0-0** (11
♘d4 ♗d7 12 ♘cb5 ♔d8 13 c4
is our suggestion) **11 ... ♘c6
12 ♖he1** (12 d4 and if 12 ...
d5, 13 ♗b5 is more accurate
- Capablanca) **12 ... 0-0-0 13
d4 d5 14 ♗b5 ♘b8 15 ♘e5
♗b4 16 ♘g6±** Capablanca -
Marshall, New York 1915.

11	**0-0-0**	**♘c6**
12	**d4**	**0-0-0**
13	**♗c4!**	**♖hf8**
14	**♖he1**	

In our opinion Steiner's
14 h3 planning ♗g3, d5 and
♘d4, is White's only real
try for the initiative.

14	**...**	**♖de8**
15	**d5**	**♘b8**
16	**♗b5**	

16 ♘b5 a6 17 ♘bd4 ♗d8
gave only a fruitless space
advantage in Katalimov -
Baranov, Sochi 1952.

16	**...**	**a6**

17 ♗xd7+ ♘bxd7 18 h3
♗d8= Tan - Fried, Leipzig
(ol) 1960.

C

9 ... c6 *(70)*
Currently the most pop-
ular alternative.

70
W

10	**0-0-0**

Others:

a) **10 b4 ♘bd7 11 0-0
♘f8!? 12 b5 ♘e6 13 bc bc 14
♗h4** (14 ♗d2!?) **14 ... h6 15
♖ab1 g5 16 ♗g3 ♘h5 17 ♖fe1
0-0 18 ♘d2 ♘xg3 19 hg d5=**
Spassky - Karpov, Linares
1981.

b) **10 ♘e4 ♘xe4** (10 ...
♘bd7 11 0-0-0 ♘xe4 12 de
♘c5= Dreev - Arhipov, Moscow 1985 or 11 ... d5 12
♘xf6+ ♘xf6 13 h3 0-0 14
♖he1 ♖e8 15 ♗f1 ♗e6 16 ♘e5
½-½ Radulov - Popovic,
Polanica Zdroj 1982) **11 de
♗xg5 12 ♘xg5 h6 13 ♘f3
♔e7 14 0-0 ♘d7 15 ♖fe1
♘e5=** Kurajica - Knezevic,
Sarajevo 1981.

c) **10 h3 ♘a6 11 0-0-0 ♘c7
12 ♘e4 ♘xe4 13 de ♗xg5+ 14**

♘xg5 ♔e7 15 ♖he1 ♘e6=
Matanovic - Zsuzsa Polgar,
Vienna 1986 and Black has
gained an important tempo
to organize the defence
compared to the column.

d) **10 d4** ♗c6 (10 ... ♗g4 11
0-0-0 ♘bd7 ½-½ Timman -
Hort, Amsterdam 1978).

d1) **11 0-0-0** ♘bd7 12 ♖he1
h6 13 ♗h4 0-0-0 14 ♗d3 (14
♗f1!?) 14 ... ♖he8 15 h3 ♘b6
16 a3 ♘bd5= Spassky -
Hawksworth, London 1984.

d2) **11 h3** ♘bd7 12 0-0-0
h6 13 ♗h4 ♘b6 14 ♖he1 ♔d7
15 ♗d3 ½-½ Short - Karpov
Tilburg 1988.

e) **10 0-0** ♘a6 (If 10 ... h6
11 ♗d2!± Hennings - Nefra-
kis, Sofia 1967) 11 ♖fe1 ♘c7
when:

e1) **12 ♗f1** (12 ♘d4 ♘e6=)
12 ... ♘e6 13 ♗d2 0-0 14 d4
d5 (if 14 ... ♖e8 15 d5 ♘xd5
16 ♘xd5 cd 17 ♗b5 ♖d8=
Spassky - Karpov, Turin
1982) 15 ♘e5 ♘d7 16 ♘d3
♗f6= Spassky - Timman,
London 1982.

e2) **12 d4** d5 13 ♗d3 (13
♗f1!? Yusupov) 13 ... ♘e6 14
♗e3 0-0 15 ♖ad1 ♗d6 16 ♘e5
♘e8 17 ♘e2 f6 18 ♘f3
♘8c7= Spassky - Yusupov,
Toluca 1982.

10 ...   ♘a6
Alternatives:

a) **10 ... ♘bd7?!** 11 ♖he1
♘c5, Pavlov - Ciocaltea,
Netanya 1983, 12 d4±.

b) After **10 ... h6** we recommend 11 ♗d2.

Or:

b1) **11 ♗h4** ♘a6 12 ♘e4
♘xe4 13 de ♘c5 14 ♗xe7 led
to even chances in Gulko -
Razuvayev, USSR 1985.

b2) **11 ♗f4** g5!? 12 ♗g3
♘h5 13 d4 f5! 14 ♘d2 ♘xg3
15 hg ♘d7 16 ♘f3 ♘b6! 17
♗d3 ♗d7 18 ♖de1 ♔f7 19
♘d1= Apicella - Forintos,
Val Maubuee 1988. And
now 19 ... ♔f6 was necessary planning ♗f8 - g7. Earlier 16 d5∞ could also be
considered.

c) **10 ... 0-0** 11 ♖he1 ♖e8
(11 ... ♘a6? 12 ♗f1 ♗e6 13
♘d4 ♘c7 14 ♘f5!±). After
12 ♗f1 ♔f8 13 h3 ♘a6 14 ♘e4
d5!? 15 ♘xf6 ♗xf6 16 ♗xf6
gf 17 d4 ♘c7 18 ♗d3 ♔g7,
Black did not manage to
benefit from the doubled
f-pawn in Hazai - Malich,
Halle 1981.

11   ♖he1
Others:

a) **11 h3** ♘c7 (11 ... d5 12 d4
♘c7 13 ♘e5 0-0 14 ♖he1 ♖e8
15 ♗f4 ♘e6 16 ♗h2 ♗b4 17 f3
♗a5 18 a3 ♗b6 19 ♗g1
♘xd4!∓ Riedel - Autenrieth,
German League 1988/89, 14

g4!? and 15 a3!? can also be considered) and now:

a1) **12 ♖he1** ♘e6 13 ♗d2 0-0= Plachetka - Knezevic, Keszthely 1981.

a2) **12 d4** ♘e6?! (12 ... ♘d5) 13 ♗e3 d5 14 ♖he1 ♗b4!? 15 a3 ♗a5 16 ♘e5± Pribyl - Knezevic, Olomouc 1975.

b) **11 ♘e4** ♘xe4 12 de ♘c5 when:

b1) **13 ♗xe7** ♔xe7 14 ♖he1 (14 ♘d2 ½-½ in Addison - Karpov, Caracas 1970) 14 ... ♗e6 (14 ... ♖e8 15 ♘d4 ♔f8 ½-½ Spassky - Salov, Barcelona 1989) 15 e5 (15 ♘d4 ½-½ Spassky - Korchnoi, Brussels 1985) 15 ... de 16 ♘xe5 ♖hd8 led to an equal position in Imanaliev - Gipslis, Riga 1981.

b2) **13 ♖he1** ♗xg5+! 14 ♘xg5 ♔e7 15 ♘f3 ♖d8 16 ♘d4 g6 17 ♗f1 ♔f8 18 b4 ♘e6 19 ♘b3 b6 (△ ♗b7)= in Spassky - Petrosian, (m/13) 1969.

c) **11 ♘d4 ♘d5!?** Smyslov's improvement. (After both 11 ... ♘c7 12 ♖de1 and 12 ♗h4, 12 ... ♘fd5! is best to even things up. There is not any contradiction in Hort - Seirawan, Lucerne 1982: 11 ... ♘c7 12 ♖he1 ♘e6 13 ♘xe6 ♗xe6 ½-½) 12 ♘e4 f5! 13

♗xe7 ♔xe7 14 ♘d2 ♘b6 15 ♖de1 ♔f6= Karpov - Smyslov, Moscow 1981.

11   ...   ♘c7

11 ... h6 12 ♗h4 ♗e6= is Wockenfuss - Schussler, German League 1981/82. 12 ♗f4 or 12 ♗d2 can also be considered.

12   ♘e4

Alternatively:

a) **12 ♗f1** ♘e6 13 ♗d2 (13 ♗h4 d5 14 d4 ♗d7 15 h3 ♖d8 16 ♘e5 ♗c8 17 f3 ♘d7 and Black equalized slowly in Ernst - Schüssler, Gausdal 1985. Also not bad is 13 ... ♘h5) 13 ... ♗d7 14 d4 h6= 15 ♗d3 d5 16 h3 ♖d8 17 a3 0-0 18 ♗e3 ♗c8 19 ♘h4 ♖fe8 ½-½ Spassky - Petrosian, (m/15) 1969.

b) **12 ♘d4** ♘e6 (12 ... h6 is dubious, because after 13 ♗h4 ♘e6 the move 14 ♘f5 is strong though the direct action led only to draw in Martinovic - Knezevic, Sarajevo 1981: 13 ♗xf6 ♗xf6! 14 ♗g4+ ♔f8 15 ♗xc8 ♖xc8 16 ♘f5) 13 ♘xe6 ♗xe6 14 ♗f3 ♔d7 (14 ... d5 ½-½ Charitonov - Vladimirov, USSR 1981) 15 ♘e2 h6 ½-½ Spassky - Karpov USSR 1979.

c) **12 h3** h6?! (12 ... ♘e6 seems better) 13 ♗f4! ♘e6 14 ♗h2 0-0 15 d4 Spassky

– Larsen, Reykjavik 1985. Black has not completely equalized yet.

12	...	♘xe4
13	de	♗xg5+
14	♘xg5	♔e7

Weaker are:

a) 14 ... h6 15 ♘f3 ♔e7 16 ♘d4! ♖d8 17 f4 c5 18 ♘f3 b6 19 c3 ♗b7 20 e5± Hazai – B Toth, Budapest 1972.

b) 14 ... f6 15 ♘f3 ♔e7 16 ♘d4 ♗e6 17 h4 ♖ad8 18 h5 h6 19 b3 ♖he8 20 ♗c4 ♗c8 21 f3 ♔f8 22 g4±, Spassky – Almada, Thessaloniki (ol) 1988.

15 f4

Less powerful continuations are:

a) 15 ♘f3 ♘e6= Yrjölä –

Kochiev, Tallinn 1987.

b) 15 ♗c4 ♘e6 16 ♗xe6 ♗xe6 ½-½ Gipslis – Tal, Jurmala 1985.

c) 15 h3 ♘e6 see above c 10 h3 Matanovic – Zsuzsa Polgar with transposition.

| 15 | ... | ♘e6 |
| 16 | ♘h3 | ♘c5± |

17 ♘f2 ♖d8 18 ♗f3 Spassky – Hort, (m/5) 1977. White has already achieved something with this set-up: he has a small advantage in space, the opportunity to advance on the kingside, and, moreover he may attack the weak d-pawn.

Conclusion: with 7 ... ♕xe2+ Black has only slight difficulties.

23) 3 ♘xe5 d6: 5 ♕e2 Milner-Barry's 7 ... ♘bd7

4	♘f3	♘e4
5	♕e2	♕e7
6	d3	♘f6
7	♗g5	♘bd7 *(71)*

Milner-Barry's Defence, which was further developed by Bronstein.

71 W

8   ♘c3

8 c4 is a logical move, though in Kurajica - Hulak, Banja Luka 1983 Black equalised easily: 8 ... h6 9 ♗d2 ♘c5! 10 ♕xe7+ ♗xe7 11 b4 (11 ♘c3 ♗f5!) 11 ... ♘a4! 12 ♘c3 ♘xc3 13 ♗xc3 0-0 14 ♗e2 ♘h5 15 g3 ½-½.

Now:

A: 8 ... h6
B: 8 ... ♕xe2+

A

8	...	h6
9	♗e3!	

White can try to utilize the fact that Black has not taken the opportunity to exchange queens.

9 ♗h4 is also playable:

a) 9 ... ♕xe2+ 10 ♗xe2 ♗e7 11 0-0-0 a6 12 ♖he1 0-0 13 ♗f1 ♖e8= Zara - Karpov, European Junior Ch.1967/68; 10 ... c6 and 10 ... g5 transposing to the subsequent line of this chapter.

b) 9 ... g5 10 ♗g3 ♘b6 11 0-0-0 ♕xe2 12 ♗xe2 ♗d7 13 ♘d2 ½-½ Hübner - Yusupov, Munich 1988.

9	...	♘b6

If 9 ... c6 White might threaten with ♕d2, and ♖e1 after 10 0-0-0.

10	0-0-0	♗e6

Other ideas:

a) **10 ... ♗d7** (Keres' suggestion) is met by 11 ♕d2 0-0-0 12 ♖e1±.

b) **10 ... ♘fd5** 11 ♘xd5 ♘xd5 12 ♕d2! ♘xe3 13 ♖e1 ♗e6 14 ♖xe3 0-0-0 (14 ... ♕f6 △ ... 0-0 is better) 15 d4 d5 16 ♕a5± (Gutman).

11 ♘d4!

Or 11 ♖e1 ♘bd5? (11 ... 0-0-0=) 12 ♗d2 ♘xc3 13 ♗xc3 ♘d5 14 ♘d4 ♘xc3 15 bc ♔d7 16 g3 ♖e8 17 ♘xe6 fe 18 ♗h3 d5 19 ♕f3± Mukhin - Vistanetsky, USSR 1963.

11 ... 0-0-0

It's more advisable for Black to play 11 ... ♘bd5, e.g. 12 ♘xe6 ♕xe6 13 ♘xd5 ♘xd5 14 g3 and now: 14 ... ♘xe3 15 ♕xe3 (otherwise 15 ... ♕xa2) ♕xe3+ 16 fe d5 is a tenable position with opposite-coloured bishops.

12 ♘xe6 ♕xe6

13 g3 ♘bd5 14 ♗d2 ♘xc3 15 ♕xe6+ fe 16 ♗xc3 e5 17 ♗h3+ ♔b8 18 ♗e6 ♗e7 19 f4± Gufeld - Lein, Tbilisi 1966.

B

8 ... ♕xe2+!
9 ♗xe2 h6 *(72)*

Or:

a) **9 ... g6** when:

a1) **10 0-0-0?!** ♗g7 11 ♖he1 0-0! 12 ♘b5 ♘d5 13 c4 a6 14

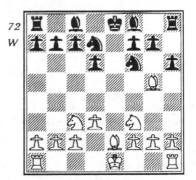

♘xd6 cd 15 cd ♘f6∓ Suetin - Petran, Olomouc 1975.

a2) In our opinion **10 ♘b5 ♔d8 11 c4±** is the proper play for White.

b) After **9 ... ♗e7**:

b1) **10 0-0-0?!** (10 ♘b5 c4 gaining space or 10 ♘d4 are recommended) 10 ... h6 11 ♗h4 and:

b11) **11 ... ♘b6** 12 ♖he1 ♘fd5= Dely - Hennings, Debrecen 1969.

b12) **11 ... 0-0** 12 ♖de1 ♖e8 13 ♗xf6 ♘xf6 14 h3 ♗d7= Kirov - Minic, Pamporovo 1982.

b2) **10 0-0** h6 11 ♗h4 0-0 12 ♖ae1 c6 (12 ... ♖e8, 12 ... a6) 13 ♗d1 ♖e8 14 ♘d4± Steil - Brand, Dortmund Open 1987.

c) **9 ... c6** 10 0-0-0 ♗e7 and

c1) **11 ♘e4** d5 12 ♘xf6+ ♗xf6 13 d4 ♗g5+ 14 ♘xg5 0-0 = Kiprichnikov - Klovan, Jurmala 1978.

c2) **11 ♖he1** d5 12 ♘d4 ♘c5! △ ... ♘e6= Moors - Zysk, Munich 1985.

d) Black's attempts to gain space are improved by **9 ... h6**.

Now White has tried:

B1: 10 ♗d2
B2: 10 ♗h4

Or:

a) **10 ♗e3** has not appeared in play; the idea of blocking the e-file would not compensate for the tempo lost after ... ♘b6 and ... ♘b(f)d5.

b1) **10 ♗f4?!** reveals the drawback of the ♘b6 - d5 manoeuvre.

b1) **10 ... g6**

b11) **11 0-0-0** ♗g7 12 h3 (12 ♘b5? ♘d5! 13 ♗d2 a6 Majer - Toth, Hungary 1969) 12 ... ♘b6 13 ♘d2 ♘fd5 14 ♘xd5 ♘xd5 15 ♗h2?! 0-0∓ (three minor mistakes probably equal one full mistake - Bronstein) Trifunovic - Bronstein, Leningrad 1957.

b12) **11 ♘d4** and here things look badly for the knight, e.g. 11 ... a6 12 0-0 ♗g7 13 ♖fe1 0-0 14 ♗f3 g5 15 ♗d2 ♘e5 16 ♗d1 c5!= Kr Georgiev - Plaskett, Plovdiv

1984.

b2) **10 ... ♘b6!** 11 0-0-0 ♗d7 12 ♘d4 0-0-0 13 ♗g3 g6=, Janssen - Yusupov, Graz 1981.

B1

10 ♗d2

The bishop is innocuous here, but at least it is not exposed to attack by ... ♘d5.

10 ... g6

Or:

a) **10 ... ♘b6?!** and now:

a1) **11 ♘b5** when:

a11) **11 ... ♘bd5?** 12 c4 a6 (Black achieved equality after 12 ... ♗d7 13 a4 c6 14 ♘bd4 ♘c7 15 0-0 ♗e7 16 b4 0-0 17 ♘b3 ♖fe8 18 ♖fe1 ♘h7 19 ♘fd4 ♗f6 20 ♖ab1 ♖ad8 21 ♗e3 ♗g5 in Spassky - Yusupov, Moscow 1981) 13 ♘bd4 ♘b6 14 0-0 g6 15 ♖fe1 ♗g7 16 ♗d1+! ♔d8 17 b4± Taimanov - Suetin, Leningrad 1967.

a12) **11 ... ♔d8** is somewhat better, viz. 12 0-0 ♗d7 13 d4 a6? (13 ... ♘e4 was required) 14 ♘c3 ♗f5 15 ♖fc1 g5 16 a4 ♗g7 17 h4 g4 18 ♘h2 ♖e8 19 ♘f1 ♘fd5 20 ♘g3± Holmov - Mikenas, Harkov, 1967.

a2) **11 a4** can also be considered, e.g. 11 ... ♗e6 12 a5

♘bd5 13 ♘e4±.

a3) **11 0-0-0** (feeble) 11 ...
♗d7 (11 ... d5 12 ♖de1 ½-½
Lein - Lombardy, 1985) 12
♘d4 (12 ♘e4 ♗e7 13 ♖he1
0-0-0 14 h3 ♖de8= Pan-
chenko - Makarichev, Sochi
1983) 0-0-0 13 ♗f3 ♗e7 14
♖de1 ♖he8 15 ♘b3 ♗e6 16
♘d4 ♗d7 (½-½, 19) Mali-
shauskas - Rosentalis, Vilnius 1988.

b) **10 ... ♘c5** 11 0-0-0
(playing 11 b4 ♘e6 12 ♘e4 is
more advisable) 11 ... ♗d7 12
♖de1 0-0-0 13 ♗d1 g6 14 d4
♘a4= Ritov - Vistanetsky,
Riga 1971.

c) **10 ... c6** 11 0-0 ♗e7 12
♖fe1 0-0 13 d4 ♘b6 14 ♗d3
♖e8 15 h3 ♗e6 with a solid
position for Black.

d) **10 ... a6** suggested by
Barcza; in that case White
should seek to make some-
thing of 11 0-0 ♗e7 12 ♖fe1
0-0 13 d4 ♖e8 14 ♗c4.
Black's equalizing is more a
question of patience than a
task demanding professional care.

11   ♘b5

11 0-0-0 is not better, e.g.
♗g7 when:

a) **12 d4** ♘b6 13 ♘b5 ♔d8
14 c4 ♖e8 15 ♖he1 ♗d7,
Westerinen - Butnoris, Vilnius 1964, 16 ♘c3=.

b) **12 ♖de1** 0-0 13 ♘h4?!
♘b6 14 f4 ♗d7 15 ♗f3 d5
Nagy - Toth, Budapest 1969
(16 h3 c5∓ Toth).

11   ...   ♔d8
12   c4   ♗g7

13 0-0 a6 14 ♘c3 ♖e8 15
♖fe1 ♘f8 16 ♘d4(?) (16 b4,
to aim for a slight, but
promising, initiative) 16 ...
♗g4 17 ♗f1 ♖xe1 18 ♖xe1
♗d7= Passerotti - Toth,
Rome 1979.

B2

10   ♗h4

Now Black has a choice:

B21: 10 ... g5
B22: 10 ... g6

Or:

a) **10 ... c6** 11 ♘e4! ♗e7 12
0-0-0 (12 ♗g3±, e.g. 12 ...
♘xe4 13 de ♘c5 14 ♘d2) 12
... d5 13 ♘xf6+ ♗xf6, Gufeld
- Savon, Moscow 1970, 14
♗g3±.

b) **10 ... a6** 11 0-0 g6 12 d4
♗g7 13 ♗c4 ♘b6!? 14 ♖fe1+
♔f8 Black can take the risk
of missing the castling
even this time, Hecht -
Vladimirov, Munich 1988.

c) **10 ... ♗e7** and now.

c1) **11 0-0-0** ♘b6 12 h3 (12
♖he1!) 12 ... ♘bd5 13 ♘xd5
♘xd5 14 ♗xe7 ♔xe7 15 ♖he1

♖e8 16 ♕f1+ ♔f8 17 ♖xe8+ ♔xe8 ½–½ I Zaitsev – Holmov, Riga 1968.

c2) better 11 ♘b5 ♔d8 12 c4.

B21

10 ... g5

A critical alternative; Black gains a tempo for completing his development and, moreover puts the opponent's bishop into 'cold storage'. But the f5 square and the g5 pawn itself become weak.

11 ♗g3 ♘b6

Alternatively:

a) 11 ... ♘h5(?) Minic – Trifunovic, Belgrade 1961 and now 12 ♘d5 ♔d8 13 d4± (Mikenas). White's knight may retreat to e3 to gain the f5 square, especially in the case of ... ♘xg3, hg.

b) 11 ... ♗g7 and now:

b1) 12 ♘d4 ♘b6 13 ♘db5 ♘bd5 (Black may equalize with 13 ... ♔d8 as White's b5 knight has no good square after ... ♖e8 and ... a6) 14 ♘xd5 ♘xd5 15 ♕f3 a6 16 ♘xd6+ cd 17 ♗xd5 ♗xb2 18 ♖b1 ♗c3+ (Alexander – Milner–Barry, Margate 1938) and now 19 ♔d1! △h4±, the d6 and b7 pawns are weak.

b2) Weaker is 12 h4 g4 13 ♘d2? 0-0 14 0-0-0 ♘b6 15 h5 ♗d7∓ Kramer – Milner–Barry, London 1948.

12 0-0-0

12 h4?! is not advisable, e.g. 12 ... g4 13 ♘d2 ♘h5 14 ♗h2 ♗d7 15 0-0-0 0-0-0∓ A Sherzer – Wolff, USA 1987, but 12 ♘d4 can be considered.

12 ... ♗d7

13 h4?

White should have played 13 ♖de1 0-0-0 14 ♘d4 preparing f4.

13 ... g4

14 ♘d2 ♗g7

15 f3 0-0-0∓ Arulaid – Vistanetsky, Tallinn 1964.

10 ... g5 cannot be considered as giving perfect equality. Better protection of the f5 square, offering less of a provocative target, can be achieved by the next defence.

B22

10 ... g6

Bronstein's fine discovery.

11 0-0-0

Or:

a) 11 ♘b5?! ♘d5 12 c4 c6 13 cd? (◻13 ♘bd4 ♘f4 14 ♗g3 ♘h5∓, B,Toth) 13 ... cb 14 d4 a6 15 0-0 f5∓∓ Koszorus – Toth, Budapest 1968.

b) 11 d4 a6 12 0-0-0 ♗g7

13 ♖he1 0-0 14 ♗c4 b5 15 ♗d5 ♖b8 16 ♗c6 ♘b6 17 a3 ♗b7 18 ♗xb7 ♖xb7 19 ♗xf6 ½-½ Kasparov - Cramling, Wattignies 1976.

11 ... ♗g7
12 ♘b5

No other move can be seen as searching for the advantage in the opening:

a) if **12 d4** then 12 ... a6

b) **12 ♖he1** and now:

b1) **12 ... a6** 13 ♗f1+ (13 d4 0-0) 13 ... ♔d8 14 h3 and now:

b11) **14 ... ♖e8**, or

b12) **14 ... g5** 15 ♗g3 ♘b6=,

Keres.

b2) **12 ... 0-0!?** 13 ♘b5 ♘d5 14 c4 is a critical position where Black gets compensation for the pawn after 14 ... a6 15 ♘xd6 (15 ♘bd4 ♘f4 was better) 15 ... cd 16 cd ♘f6 as could be seen in Suetin - Petran, 1975 (note a to Black's ninth).

12 ... ♔d8

The game Holmov - Bronstein, USSR Ch 1961 went 13 ♖he1 ♖e8 14 ♘fd4 ♘f8=; 13 ♘d2 can be considered, intending f2 - f4.

24) 3 ♘xe5 d6: 5 d4 Introduction

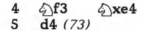

4	♘f3	♘xe4
5	d4 *(73)*	

First analysed by Petroff and Jaenisch. The attack against Black's e4-knight can wait one move Black's main move, 5 ... d5, is discussed in Chapters 26-33.

Black also has:

A: 5 ... ♗g4
B: 5 ... ♗e7

Other ideas:

a) 5 ... ♘d7 6 ♗d3 ♘df6 (the only way to give meaning to 5 ... ♘d7 but it does not solve the prob-

lems) 7 0-0 ♗e7 8 ♖e1 d5 9 c4 (9 ♘e5 promises less than normal development) and now:

a1) 9 ... ♗e6 10 cd ♗xd5 11 ♕c2 ♘d6 12 ♘e5 0-0 13 ♘c3 c6 (⌒ 13 ... ♗e6) 14 ♗g5!±; Honfi - Toth, Budapest 1972 went 14 ... h6 15 ♗xf6 ♗xf6 16 ♘xd5 cd 17 ♕b3! 1-0.

a2) 9 ... c6 10 ♘c3 ♘xc3 11 bc 0-0 12 ♘e5± — Gutman.

b) 5 ... ♘f6 and now:

b1) 6 ♗d3 would be met by 6 ... ♗g4 nearly equalizing, see line B2 by transposition.

b2) We consider 6 c4 by transposition as well - see var. B, except for Velimirovic - Reshevsky, Skopje 1976, which went 6 ... ♗e7 7 ♘c3 0-0 8 h3 ♖e8 9 ♗e3 ♗f5?! 10 g4 ♗g6 11 ♘h4 ♗e4? 12 ♖g1! ♘d5 13 cd ♗xh4 14 ♘xe4 ♖xe4 15 ♕f3±.

b3) 6 h3 g6 (6 ... ♗e7 transposing to lots of

lines. The fianchetto is perfect here because White cannot give a rook check on e1) 7 ♗d3 ♗g7 8 0-0 0-0 9 c4 when:

b31) **9** ... **♘c6 (?)** 10 ♘c3 ♖e8 (10 ... d5!?) 11 ♗f4 ♘h5 12 ♗g5 f6 13 ♗d2 f5 14 ♗g5!± Sax – Petran, Hungarian Ch. 1975.

b32) **9** ... **c5** tries to open the diagonal of the g7-bishop.

b321) **10** ♘c3 ♘c6 11 d5 ♘b4 12 ♗b1 ♘e8 13 ♗d2 f5 14 a3 ♘a6 transposes into a main line of the King's Indian Defence!

b322) **10 d5** b5! 11 cb ♗b7∞.

b4) **6** ♘c3 d5(?) losing a tempo, e.g. 7 ♘e5 ♗e7 8 ♗d3 0-0 9 0-0 ♖e8 10 ♖e1± ♘bd7? 11 ♘xd5! ♘xd5 12 ♗xh7+ ♔f8 13 ♘xf7!±± as in Shlekis – Maslov, corr. USSR 1982.

A

   5 ... **♗g4(?)**
   6 h3

For 6 ♗d3 ♘f6 7 0-0 ♗e7 8 ♖e1 see line B2, by transposition. Now the game Tarrasch – Marshall, Nuremberg 1905 is recalled which went 8 ... 0-0 9 ♘bd2 ♘c6 10 c3 d5?! (⌓ 10 ... ♖e8)

11 ♘f1 ♕d7 12 ♘g3 ♗d6 13 h3 ♗xf3 14 ♕xf3 ♗xg3 15 fg! ♖ae8 16 ♗g5± with the advantage of the bishop pair.

   6 ... **♗h5**
   7 ♕e2!

Or 7 ♕d3?! ♕e7! △ ... ♗g6=. If 8 ♕b5+ c6 9 ♕xh5? ♘f6+!

   7 ... **♕e7**
   8 ♗e3

Planning g4, ♗g2± (Polugayevsky).

Any capture on f3 only aids White so the bishop sortie ... ♗g4 should be delayed.

B

   5 ... **♗e7** *(74)*

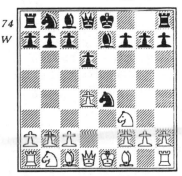

74
W

Alapin's treatment. Black makes an effort to finish his development quickly and to post his pieces according to White's set-up. However, his possibilities are modest because he has refrained from d6 - d5. However, White cannot utilize his slightly better position easily, which is why many games in this line end in a draw.

6 ♗d3

Or:

a) **6 c4** and for 6 ... 0-0, 6 ... ♗g4, 6 ... d5 or 6 ... ♘c6 see line B1 in Chapter 19, by transposition.

b) After **6 d5** ♗g4 is good.

6 ... ♘f6

Others:

a) **6 ... d5** transposes to lines discussed in Chapters 29-33.

b) **6 ... ♘g5** and now:

b1) **7 ♘xg5** ♗xg5 8 ♕e2+ ♗e7 9 0-0 0-0 10 ♕e4 f5 11 ♕f3 ♘c6 12 c3 Makarichev - Bronstein, USSR 1978, 12 ... ♔h8 with mutual chances.

b2) **7 0-0** (7 h3 0-0) 7 ... ♘xf3+ (not 7 ... ♗g4? 8 ♗xg5 ♗xg5 9 ♕e1+!) 8 ♕xf3 ♘c6 9 c3 0-0 10 ♘d2 (10 ♘a3 △ ♘c2-♘e3) 10 ... d5 11 ♖e1, Klovan - Arhipkin, Riga 1980, 11 ... ♗e6 with even chances.

7 0-0

Or:

a) **7 h3** is discussed in Chapter 25.

b) **7 ♘c3** ♗g4 8 h3 ♗h5 9 g4 ♗g6 10 ♗e3, Schiffers - Caro, Vienna 1889, 10 ... c6 △11 ♕d2 b5 with mutual chances.

c) **7 ♘bd2** 0-0 8 ♘f1 ♖e8 9 ♘g3 ♗f8+ evens things up. The ♘bd2 move is better postponed, e.g. Hübner - Petrosian, 1981 - see line B2.

White might make some more other reasonable moves (7 b3, 7 c3, 7 c4, 7 ♗g5) which transpose into other lines.

Now Black has a choice:

B1: 7 ... 0-0
B2: 7 ... ♗g4

Inadequate is 7 ... d5? viz. 8 ♘e5! 0-0 9 ♖e1± Gaprindashvili - de Caro, Medellin (ol) 1974.

B1

7 ... 0-0
8 h3

Though Black appears uninterested in pinning the ♘(f3) this move seems best.

Other tries:

a) **8 ♘c3(?)** ♗g4 9 h3 ♗h5 10 g4 ♗g6 11 ♘h4!? ♗xd3? (⌐ 11 ... ♘c6) 12 ♕xd3 ♘xg4? 13 ♘f5! ♘f6 14 ♔h1 ♘c6 15 ♖g1 with the attack, Tarrasch - Mannheimer, Breslau 1864. And the only defence is 15 ... g6 (Tarrasch) and not 15 ... ⟳e8? 16 ⟳xg7!

b) 8 ♗g5 ♗g4 9 ⟳bd2 ⟳c6 10 c3 h6 11 ♗h4 ⟳h5! 12 ♗xe7 ⟳xe7= Keres – Bronstein, USSR Ch. 1961.

c) 8 ♖e1 and now:

c1) 8 ... ♖e8 9 h3 ⟳bd7 10 c4 ⟳f8 11 ⟳c3 ⟳g6 12 ♕c2 c6 13 ♗g5 ♗d7 with a solid position for Black, Prasad – Barua, Calcutta 1986.

c2) 8 ... ♗g4 9 ⟳bd2 when:

c21) 9 ... ⟳bd7 10 ⟳f1 ♖e8 11 ⟳g3 Schlechter – Mason, London 1899 (11 ... ♗f8±).

c22) 9 ... c5 10 h3 (10 dc see B2 line at 9 ... c5) 10 ... ♗h5 11 ⟳f1 ⟳c6 12 ⟳g3! ♗g6 (12 ... ♗xf3 13 ♕xf3 ⟳xd4 14 ♕xb7 ♖e8 15 ⟳f5± Ljubojevic – Smyslov, London 1984) 13 c3 cd?! (△ 13 ... ♖e8) 14 ⟳xd4 ⟳xd4 15 ♗xg6! hg 16 ♕xd4 d5 17 ♗g5 ♕d6 18 ♖e5± and the d-pawn is too feeble, Belyavsky – Barua, London 1985.

d) 8 c4 ♗g4(!) is discussed by transposition in var. b2, line B2.

8 ... ♗e6?

Other moves are discussed by transposition in Chapter 25.

a) 9 ⟳c3?! ⟳c6 10 d5 (10 ⟳e2 ⟳b4=) 10 ... ⟳xd5 11 ⟳xd5 ♗xd5 12 ♗xh7+ ♔xh7 13 ♕xd5 ♕d7= – Bilguer.

b) 9 c4! c6 10 ⟳g5 ⟳a6 11 ⟳c3 ⟳c7 12 f4 h6 13 ⟳f3 ♕c8 14 ♕c2 ♖b8 15 f5 ♗d7 16 ♗f4± Tarrasch – Marco, Vienna 1898.

Black might deduce ♗g4 should be played as soon as possible.

B2

7 ... ♗g4(!) (75)

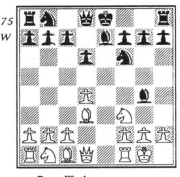

75
W

8 ♖e1

Or:

a) 8 h3 ♗h5 9 ♖e1 0-0 10 ⟳bd2 and now Gutman's suggestion, 10 ... ♖e8 is best.

b) 8 c4 when:

b1) 8 ... ⟳c6 9 ♗e3 0-0 10 ⟳c3 ♖e8 11 h3 ♗h5 12 ♗e2 h6 13 ♕b3 ♕c8 14 ♖ae1 Pinter – Petran, Salgotarjan 1974. Here 14 ... ♗f8 was necessary with tenable position.

b2) **8 ... 0-0** 9 h3 ♗h5 10 ♘c3 d5? (⌐ 10 ... ♘c6 11 ♗e3 d5) 11 cd ♘xd5 12 ♗xh7+ ♔xh7 13 ♘g5+ ♔g8 14 ♕xh5± Tseitlin - Karasev, USSR Ch. 1971.

8 ... 0-0
9 ♘bd2 ♖e8

Others:

a) **9 ... ♕d7** 10 ♘f1 ♘c6 11 c3 Stein - Nezhmetdinov, Kislovodsk 1972, 11 ... ♖ae8! 12 ♘g3 ♗d8± - Polugayevsky.

b) **9 ... ♘bd7** 10 ♘f1 ♖e8 (10 ... ♗h5 △ ... ♗g6) 11 ♘g3 ♘f8 (⌐ 11 ... ♗f8±) 12 h3± Schlechter - Mason, London 1899.

c) **9 ... c5?!** 10 dc! (10 h3 see line B1 var. c22) 10 ... dc 11 ♘c4 ♘c6 12 ♘e3 ♗d7 13 c3 g6 14 ♕c2± Honfi - Petran, Budapest, 1974.

d) **9 ... d5** 10 ♘f1 ♖e8 11 ♘g3 ♘bd7 12 h3± - Euwe.

e) **9 ... ♘c6** 10 c3, Tarrasch - Marshall, Nuremberg 1905, 10 ... ♖e8 followed by ... ♗f8 with balanced play.

10 ♘f1 ♗f8

11 ♖xe8 ♕xe8 12 ♗g5 ♘bd7 13 ♘g3 g6! 14 h3 ♗e6 15 ♕d2 ♗g7 16 ♗h6 ♘f8 17 ♗xg7 ♔xg7 18 ♘g5 h6 19 ♘xe6+ ♕xe6 20 ♕a5 c5 ½-½. Hübner - Petrosian, Tilburg 1981.

25) 3 ♞xe5 d6: 5 d4 ♝e7

4	♞f3	♞xe4
5	d4	♝e7
6	♝d3	♞f6
7	h3	0-0

a) 7 ... **c5** 8 ♞c3 ♞c6 9 0-0 0-0 see line B. If 8 d5! 0-0 9 c4 b5 10 cb ♝b7 ∞.

b) 7 ... **c6** 8 c4 ♝f5! 9 0-0, Westerinen – Castro, Calella 1981, 9 ... ♝xd3 10 ♛xd3 0-0 11 ♞c3 d5= Westerinen; ⌐ 9 ♝xf5.

8 0-0 (76)

Other moves, e.g. 8 c4, usually transpose.

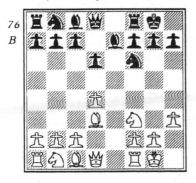

A: 8 c6
B: 8 ... ♖e8
C: 8 ... ♞c6

Or:

a) **8 ... ♝e6?** – see line B1, Chapter 24.

b) **8 ... c5** (Smyslov's experiment) 9 ♞c3 (9 b3) 9 ... ♞c6 and now:

b1) **10 ♖e1** a6 (or 10 ... ♞b4, e.g. 11 ♝f1 ♝f5 12 ♖e2 ♖e8 planning ... ♝f8 with about level chances) 11 d5 ♞a7 (11 ... ♞b4 12 ♝e4!? or 12 ♝f1 ♝f5 13 ♖e2± Karpov) 12 a4 ♝d7 13 a5 ♖e8 14 ♝f1, Karpov – Smyslov, Moscow 1972, 14 ... ♞b5 with balanced chances.

b2) An interesting idea: **10 a3** cd 11 ♞e2 ♞e5 (⌐ 11 ... d5 12 ♞exd4 ♝c5) 12 ♞exd4 ♞xd3 13 ♛xd3 ♛a5 14 ♖e1 ♖e8 15 ♝g5 ♝d7 16 ♖e2 h6 17 ♝h4 ♝d8 18 ♖xe8+ ♞xe8 19 ♝xd8 ♛xd8 20 ♖e1 and Black failed to even things up, Short – Asmundsson, Iceland 1985.

A

8	...	c6
9	♖e1	

Or 9 c4 and now:

a) **9 ... ♘bd7** 10 ♘c3 ♖e8 11 ♕c2 ♘f8 12 ♗e3!?± Haag – Koszorus, Pecs 1974.

b) **9 ... ♖e8** 10 ♘c3 a6 11 b4 (11 a4? a5!) 11 ... ♘bd7 12 ♗e3 ♘f8 13 a4 a5 14 b5 ♘g6 15 ♖e1 ♘h5 16 ♕d2 ♗d7 17 ♖ab1± as seen in the encounter Tukmakov – Bronstein, Moscow 1971.

9 ... ♘bd7
10 ♗f4

Or 10 c4, e.g. 10 ... ♖e8 11 ♘c3 ♘f8 when:

a) **12 ♗f4** transposes into the column.

b) **12 ♗e3** a6 13 a4! a5 14 d5 c5 15 ♕c2 ♘g6 16 ♖e2 ♗f8 17 ♖ae1 ♗d7 18 ♘g5!± Pilnik – Smetan, Buenos Aires 1972.

c) **12 ♕c2** ♘g6 13 ♗g5 ♗d7 14 ♖e2 ♘h5! 15 ♗d2! ♗f8 16 ♖ae1± Timman – Radulov, Wijk aan Zee 1974.

10 ... ♖e8
11 c4 ♘f8
12 ♘c3 a6

a) **13 ♕b3?!** ♘e6 14 ♗h2 ♗f8 15 ♖e2 b5 16 ♖ae1 ♗b7 17 ♕c2 g6= Fischer – Petrosian, (m) Buenos Aires 1971.

b) **13 b4** ♘e6 14 ♗h2 ♗f8 15 ♕b3 b5 16 d5!± I Polgar – B Toth, Hungary 1971.

c) **13 ♕d2** △ ♖e2, ♖ae1± (Spassky).

B

8 ... ♖e8
9 c4

a) **9 ♖e1** ♘bd7 10 c4 c6 11 ♘c3 ♘f8** and now:

a1) **12 ♗e3!?** see game Pilnik – Smetan in line A.

a2) **12 ♗f4** a6 transposes to White 12th in line A.

b) **9 c3** ♘c6 see line C.

9 ... ♘c6

Other ideas:

a) **9 ... c6** 10 ♘c3 a6 (10 ... ♘bd7 transposes to the above mentioned line) and now:

a1) **11 b4** ♘bd7 12 ♗e3 ♘f8 13 a4± Tukmakov – Bronstein, Moscow 1971.

a2) **11 ♕c2** can be considered.

a3) **11 a4?** a5! 12 ♖e1 ♘a6 13 d5 ♘b4∓ Walter – Eperjesi, corr. 1973–75.

b) **9 ... ♘bd7** 10 ♘c3 ♘f8 (10 ... c6 11 b4 see note a1; or 11 ♖e1 ♘f8 12 ♗f4 a6 13 b4!± – Petrosian) and now:

b1) **11 d5!** ♘g6 12 ♖e1 ♗d7 (12 ... ♘d7 13 ♘d4 ♘de5 14 ♗f1±) Tal – Smyslov, USSR 1971, 13 ♘d4± (Korchnoi).

b2) **11 ♗f4** is also good, e.g. 11 ... ♘g6 12 ♗h2 c6 (12 ... ♗d7 13 ♕c2 a5) 13 b4 a5?! (13 ... a6) 14 b5 ♗d7 15 ♖b1± Kurajica – Hammer, Biel 1981.

b3) **11 ♖e1 ♘g6** (11 ... ♘e6
12 b4 g6 13 ♖b1 c6 14 ♖b2!?
♗f8 15 ♖be2± Vasyukov –
Rosetto, Camaguey 1974) 12
♕c2 ♗d7 13 ♗g5 ♗c6 14 d5
♗d7 15 ♖ad1 a6 16 ♗e3 ½–½
Arnason – Karpov, Oslo
1984.

c) **9 ... c5** 10 d5 ♗f8 (10 ...
b5 11 cb ♗b7∞) 11 ♘c3 a6 12
a4± Fedorowicz – Smyslov,
Dortmund 1986.

10	**♘c3**	**h6**
11	**♖e1**	**♗f8**
12	**♖xe8(!)**	**♕xe8**
13	**♗f4**	**♗d7?!**

13 ... g5 should have been
tried.

14 ♕d2±
Fischer – Gheorghiu, Bu-
enos Aires 1970.

C

8	**...**	**♘c6**
9	**c3**	

For 9 c4 d5 10 ♘c3 ♘b4
see line C22 in Chapter 31,
by transposition.

9	**...**	**♖e8**

9 ... h6 see with trans
position, at 10 ... h6, King –
Barua.

10	**♖e1**	

Or:

a) **10 ♕c2 h6** 11 ♘bd2 ♗f8
13 ♘c4 ♗d5!? 13 ♘e3 ♘f4=
Rlumin – Goglidze, Moscow
1935. If 13 a4 a5 △ ... ♕f6
equalizes.

b) **10 ♗f4** (the bishop is
developed first, ♘d2 or ♖e1
only after that) 10 ... ♘h5 11
♗h2 g6 12 ♖e1 and now:

b1) **12 ... ♗f8** 13 ♖xe8
♕xe8 14 ♘bd2 ♗g7 15 ♕b3±
Kavalek – Smyslov, Tilburg
1979.

b2) **12 ... ♗e6** 13 ♘bd2 (13
c4 d5) 13 ... a6 14 ♘c4 ♗f8
15 ♘c3 d5 deserves con-
sideration.

10	**...**	**♗d7**

Or 10 ... h6 11 ♘bd2 ♗f8
12 ♘f1 d5? (the e5 square
has weakened, better 12 ...
♖xe1 13 ♕xe1 g6) 13 ♘e5 ♗d6
14 ♗f4 ♗xe5 15 de ♘d7 16
♕h5 ♘c5 17 ♗c2 ♖e6 18
♖ad1± King – Barua, Lon-
don 1982.

11	**♘bd2**	

Or:

a) **11 ♘a3 h6** 12 ♘c4 ♗f8
13 ♘e3 a6?! (13 ... ♕c8) 14 a4
a5 15 ♕b3 ♕c8 16 ♗d2±/±
Matulovic – Toth, (m) Bu-
dapest 1972.

b) **11 ♗f4 h6(?)** (better
first 11 ... ♗f8 △ ... g6) 12
♘bd2 ♗f8 13 ♕c2 ♖xe1+ 14
♖xe1 ♕c8, I Polgar – B Toth,
Kecskemet 1972, 15 ♘e4±.

11	**...**	**♗f8**
12	**♘c4(!)**	**d5**

13 ♘g3 ♗d6 14 ♖xe8+
♕xe8 15 ♕c2 h6 16 ♗d2 ♕f8
17 ♘f5 ♗xf5 18 ♗xf5 ♖e8 19

♗d3 ♘d8 20 c4! c6 Bron-
stein - Smyslov, USSR Ch.
Leningrad 1971. White

would have retained his
slightly better prospects
with 21 c5 - Korchnoi.

26) 3 ♘xe5 d6: 5 d4 d5 Introduction

	4	♘f3	♘xe4
	5	d4	d5 *(77)*

The main line.

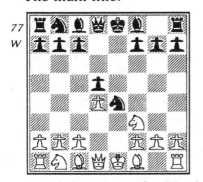

It seems as if Black has moved once more than White. Actually while White lost two tempi by ♘f3 - e5 - f3, Black only lost one tempo by d6 - d5. Let us compare with the French Defence line 1 e4 e6 2 d4 d5 3 ed ed 4 ♘f3 ♘f6 and if Black moved again then exactly the diagram position would come out by ... ♘f6 - e4. Nevertheless:

a) the e4-knight is a target that may need to be defended;

b) the d5 pawn is not defended by the f6-knight;

c) Black might have difficulty counter-attacking against the d-pawn as it is defended satisfactorily.

6   ♗d3

Aiming to exploit the exposed position of the e4-knight.

Other ideas:

a) **6 c4?** ♗b4+! 7 ♘bd2 0-0 8 ♗e2 ♘c6 9 0-0 ♗xd2 10 ♗xd2 dc 11 ♗e1 ♕d5 (10 ... ♗e6) 12 ♖c1, Sommerfeld - Mende, German League 1987, 12 ... ♘d6∓.

b) **6 ♘e5?!** spontaneously takes Black's function, 6 ... ♗d6 7 ♘d2 0-0 (see line B 6 0-0 in Chapter 10 with reversed colours) 8 ♘xe4 de 9 ♘c4 ♘c6 10 ♘xd6 cd 11 ♗e3 d5 12 ♕d2 a5 13 0-0-0 b3!? with good play for Black in Wolff - Kogan, USA Ch. 1985.

c) **6 h3** ♗d6 (6 ... ♗e7 7

♗d3 0–0 8 0–0 see Chapter 30) 7 ♘d3 0–0 8 c4 (◿ 8 0–0 ♖e8 9 c4 c6 see Chapter 28) 8 ... ♗b4+ 9 ♔f1 c6= Kurajica – Pavcic, Yugoslav Ch. 1977.

d) **6 ♗e2 ♘d6** 7 0–0 0–0 when:

d1) **8 b3?!** ♕f6 9 ♗b2 ♘c6∓.

d2) **8 ♘bd2 ♗f5** 9 ♘xe4 ♗xe4 10 ♗g5 ♕d7 11 ♕d2 ♘c6 13 c3 h6 14 ♗f4 ♖fe8 15 ♗xd6 ♕xd6 ½–½ Am Rodriguez – Garcia Gonzales, Cuba 1987.

d3) Nor does Chehov's **8 c4** lead to any advantage. After 6 ♗d3:

A: 6 ... ♗g4
B: 6 ... ♘c6

Or:
a) **6 ... ♗d6** – see Chapters 27–28.

b) **6 ... ♗e7** – see Chapters 29–34.

c) **6 ... ♗f5** 7 0–0 ♗e7. This position (except the trappy 7 c4? ♗b4+) is usually reached by 6 ... ♗e7 7 0–0 ♗f5 or via 7 ... 0–0 8 ♖e1 ♗f5. See Chapters 29–34.

d) **6 ... ♘d6** partly prevents c2-c4, partly prepares ... ♗f5 and usually transposes into 6 ... ♗e7

7 0–0 ♘d6. See line B Chapter 29.

e) **6 ... ♘f6** 7 0–0 ♗e7 8 ♘e5 (8 ♖e1 0–0 9 ♘bd2 b6 10 ♘f1 c5 11 c3= Kuzmin – Falcon, Nice (ol) 1974) 8 ... 0–0 9 c3 b6 (◿ 9 ... c5 △ ... ♘c6) 10 ♗g5 ♗b7 11 f4± Capablanca – Tenerwurzel, New York 1911. Most probably the strongest move is 8 c4 see line D Chapter 30.

A

6 ... ♗g4
Marshall's early defence. Since Lilienthal found an important improvement for White, it has been postponed until later.

7 ♕e2!
Or:
a) All the games with 7 **0–0 ♗e7** or 7 ... ♗d6 are to be found as transposition in the next Chapters, while 7 ... c6 transposes into line B. Weaker is 7 ... f5? 8 c4 ♘c6 9 ♘c3 ♗xf3 (◿ 9 ... ♘xc3±) 10 gf!± Sir G Thomas – A R B Thomas, Hastings 1937/38.

b) **7 h3 ♗h5** 8 ♕e2 f5? (◿ 8 ... ♕e7±) 9 g4! fg 10 ♘e5±.

7 ... ♕e7!
7 ... f5? 8 h3 ♗h5 9 g4! ♗g6 (9 ... fg 10 ♘e5±) 10 ♘e5 ♗e7 11 ♘c3± Z Varga –

E Kahn, Budapest 1987, better is 11 ♘bd2 △ ♘c6 12 ♘df3±.

8 0-0 ♘c6
9 ♗b5!

9 c3 f5 (9 ... 0-0-0=) 10 h3 ♗h5 11 ♖e1 0-0-0 12 ♗f4?! ♖g8∞ Desler – Anderssen, Copenhagen 1929.

9 ... a6
10 ♗xc6+ bc
11 ♖e1±

White has an edge.

B

6 ... ♘c6 (78)

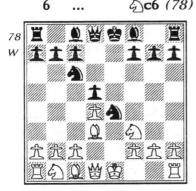

Marshall's second defence often put into practice even nowadays.

7 0-0

Or:

a) **7 ♕e2 ♗f5** (7 ... ♕e7(?) 8 0-0 ♗g4 9 ♗b5! transposes into line A) 8 ♘bd2 ♕e7 9 0-0 when:

a1) **9 ... ♘xd2** 10 ♕xd2 ♗xd3 11 ♕xd3 0-0-0 and

now:

a11) **12 ♗e3?!** f6! 13 a3 ♕e4 14 ♕d1 g5 15 ♖c1 ♗d6 Kupreichik – G Agzamov, Riga 1985.

a12) **12 ♖e1 ♕d6** 13 ♗d2 (13 ♘e5 ♘xe5 14 de ♕g6=) 13 ... f6 14 a3 (14 ♖eb1 ♘b4!) 14 ... ♕d7 15 b4, Kupreichik – Mihalchishin, USSR Ch. 1985, and now 15 ... ♗d6 can be recommended.

a2) **9 ... ♘d6** simply equalizes.

a3) **9 ... 0-0-0** is also playable.

b) **7 ♘bd2 ♘d6** (7 ... ♗f5 8 ♕e2 ♕e7 see var. a) 8 0-0=.

7 ... ♗g4

7 ... ♗e7 leads to Chapters 29-34.

8 c4

Or:

a) **8 ♘c3** f5 and now:

a1) **9 ♖e1** (9 ♕e1 ♗e7, and not 9 ... ♗xf3? 10 gf ♘xd4 11 ♕e3±±) 9 ... ♗e7 10 h3 ♗xf3 11 gf ♘xc3 12 bc 0-0 13 ♔h1 ♗d6 14 ♖g1 ♕h4 15 ♕f1 ♗f4∓ Ghinda – Forintos, Berlin 1987.

a2) **9 h3 ♗xf3** 10 gf ♘xc3 11 bc ♕f6 12 ♖e1+ ♗e7 13 c4 dc 14 ♗xc4 0-0-0 (not 14 ... ♕xd4? 15 ♕xd4 ♘xd4 16 ♗a3!±) 15 c3 ♗d6 16 f4 ♖de8 17 ♗e3 h6 18 ♕f3 ♘d8 19 ♖ad1 c6 20 ♗d3 ♖hf8 21 ♗d2

♖xe1+ 22 ♖xe1 g5 23 ♔f1
♔b8 24 ♗c4 ♕g7 25 fg hg 26
♕h5 f4 27 ♖e8 ½-½ Speel-
man – Seirawan, Reykjavik
1990.

b) **8 c3** when:

b1) **8 ... ♗d6?** 9 ♖e1 f5 10
h3 ♗h5 11 ♕b3! ♕f6, Sprag-
gett – Sieiro Gonzalez, Havana 1986, 12 ♕xd5!±.

b2) **8 ... ♗e7** 9 ♘bd2 (9
♖e1 f5 see Chapter 34) 9 ...
♘xd2 (9 ... f5?! 10 ♕b3!) 10
♗xd2 ♕d6 11 ♖e1, Valda –
A Fayard, Cap'd Agde 1986,
11 ... 0-0-0=.

c) **8 ♖e1 ♗e7!** transposes
into Chapter 33.

Feeble is 8 ... f5?! 9 c4
and now:

c1) **9 ... ♗e7** 10 cd ♕xd5 11
♘c3 ♘xc3 12 bc 0-0 13 ♖b1±
Bilguer.

c2) **9 ... ♗b4** 10 ♘c3 0-0 11
cd ♗xf3 12 gf! ♘xf2 (12 ...
♘xc3 13 bc ♗xc3 14 dc±) 13
♔xf2 ♕h4+ 14 ♔g2 ♗d6 15
f4 ♘xd4 16 ♖e3 ♖f6 17 ♖h3
♖g6+ 18 ♖g3 ♖e8 19 ♕g1?!
♗xf4∞ Doncevic – Haubt,
German League 1989/90;
better is 19 ♕f1!±±.

8   ...   ♘f6

a) In Yusupov's view the
knight may as well stay on
e4, e.g. **8 ... ♗e7** 9 cd (9 ♖e1
transposes into Chapter
33) 9 ... ♕xd5 10 ♘c3 ♘xc3

11 bc 0-0 12 ♖e1 ♗xf3 13
♕xf3 ♕xf3 14 gf ♗d6 15 ♗e3
♖ad8 (15 ... ♘e7 16 c4 c6 17
♖ab1 b6 18 a4 ♖ab8 19 ♖b3
h6 20 ♖eb1 ♖fd8 21 ♗c2
♗c7= Timman – Yusupov,
Belfort 1988) 16 ♖ad1 b6 17
♗g5 f6 18 ♗e3 ♘e7= Ehl-
vest – Yusupov, St. John
(m) 1988; 15 ♖b1!?

b) Not **8 ... ♘b4?** 9 cd
♘xd3 10 ♕xd3 ♕xd5 11 ♖e1±.

After 8 ... ♘f6:

B1: 9 cd
B2: 9 ♘c3

Alternatively 9 ♖e1+ ♗e7
transposes into Chapter 33.

B1

9   cd   ♗xf3 *(79)*

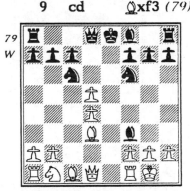

9 ... ♘xd5?! when:

a) **10 ♖e1+ ♗e7** transposes
to line B Chapter 33.

b) **10 h3 ♗xf3** (10 ... ♗h5 11
♗e4 or 11 ♖e1+ with a slight

advantage to White) 11 ♕xf3 ♘xd4 12 ♕e4+ ♘e6 13 ♖d1 with rich compensation for the pawn.

10 ♕xf3 ♕xd5

10 ... ♘xd5? 11 ♖e1+ ♗e7 12 ♗c4±.

11 ♕e2+

Or:

a) For 11 ♖e1+ ♗e7 see Chapter 33.

b) 11 ♕xd5 ♘xd5 12 ♘c3 0-0-0 13 ♗e3 (13 ♗e4 ♘ce7 △ ... ♘f6) 13 ... g6= Feher – Forintos, Budapest 1990.

11 ... ♗e7

11 ... ♕e6! 12 ♕xe6+ fe 13 ♗b5 0-0-0 14 ♗xc6 bc 15 ♗e3 ♘d5 16 ♖c1 c5!= Kasparov.

12 ♗b5! ♕d6

12 ... ♕xd4 13 ♘c3± Timman.

13 ♘c3

13 ♖e1 0-0! 14 ♗xc6 bc=, but not 15 ♕xe7?? ♖fe8.

13 ... 0-0

14 ♗xc6 bc

a) 15 ♗e3 ♘d5! 16 ♖ac1± Kasparov, (if 16 ♖fc1 ♘xe3! 17 fe ♖fe8∞ – Timman) and now:

a1) 16 ... ♖ab8 17 b3 ♘xe3 18 ♕xe3 ♖fd8 19 ♖fd1 c5? 20 d5 ♗f8 21 ♘e4± Short – Plaskett, London 1986; or 19 ... ♗f8 20 g3± Mestel – Plaskett, British Ch. 1986.

a2) 16 ... ♖fe8 17 ♘xd5 ♕xd5 (⌐ 17 ... cd 18 ♕c2± Timman) 18 ♕c4 ♗d6 19 b3 ♖e6, Timman – Yusupov, Tilburg (m) 1986, 20 g3±.

b) 15 ♖d1 ♖fe8 16 ♕f3 when:

b1) 16 ... ♖ab8 17 b3 ♕d7 18 d5!± Lobron – Kir Georgiev, San Bernardino 1987, or 17 ♗f4 ♕d7 18 d5!± (Kir Georgiev).

b2) 16 ... ♘d5 17 ♘xd5 ♕xd5 18 ♕xd5 cd 19 ♗f4 c6 20 ♖ac1 ♖ac8 21 ♔f1± Short – H Olafsson, Reykjavik 1987.

B2

9 ♘c3 ♗xf3

Other possibilities:

a) 9 ... ♘b4? 10 ♖e1+±.

b) 9 ... ♘xd4? 10 ♕e1+ ♘e6 11 ♘e5± (Yusupov).

c) 9 ... ♗e7 10 cd ♘xd5 11 h3 ♗e6 12 ♖e1 0-0 see line B2 Chapter 33.

10 ♕xf3 ♘xd4

With two lines:

B21: 11 ♕e3+
B22: 11 ♕h3

Or:

a) 11 ♕g3 which has not been tried yet.

b) 11 ♖e1+ gives enough compensation without any

real advantage. After 11 ...
♗e7 see Chapter 33.

B21

11	♕e3+	♘e6
12	cd	♘xd5

If 12 ... ♗c5? 13 ♕f3 ♘d4
14 ♖e1+ ♔f8 15 ♕f4 ♘xd5 16
♘xd5 ♕xd5 17 ♕xc7 ♘e6 18
♕g3±.

13	♘xd5	♕xd5
14	♗e4!	♕b5
15	a4	♕a6!

15 ... ♕c5? (15 ... ♕b6? 16
a5!±) 16 ♗xb7 ♖b8 17 b4!±
and soon ♗c6+ came in the
game Ivanchuk – Serper,
Sochi 1986.

16 ♖d1

16 ♕f3? ♘d4! 17 ♕e3
0-0-0∓ or 17 ... ♘e2+?! 18
♔h1 ♘g3+ 19 hg ♕xf1+ 20
♔h2∞ (Kasparov).

16 ... ♗e7

16 ... ♗d6!? can be con-
sidered (Makarichev and
Nunn).

Feeble is 16 ... ♗c5?! 17
♕f3 when:

a) **17 ... c6?!** 18 ♖d7!! 0-0
(18 ... ♔xd7? 19 ♕xf7+ ♗e7
20 ♗f5 ♕c4 21 ♗f4!±± or 19
... ♔d6 20 ♗f4+ ♘xf4 21
♕xf4+ ♔e7 22 ♕e5+ ♔f7 23
♕f5+ ♔e8 24 ♕xc5±) 19 ♗d3
♕b6 20 a5 ♕b4 21 ♗d2! ♕h4
22 ♖xb7 ♖ad8 23 ♗c3±
(Kasparov).

b) **17 ... ♖d8** 18 ♖xd8+
♘xd8 19 ♗f4±, e.g. 19 ... 0-0
20 ♕h5±; 19 ... ♘e6 20 ♗e5!
and if 20 ... 0-0 or 20 ...
♘g5 21 ♕f5! wins.

17 b4

Or:

a) **17 b3 ♗f6!** 18 ♖a2 0-0∞̄.

b) **17 ♕h3 ♖d8** 18 ♖xd8+
♘xd8 19 ♗e3 ♗f6!= (Kas-
parov).

c) **17 ♕f3** and now:

c1) **17 ... ♖d8** 18 ♗d3 when:

c11) **18 ... ♕b6!?** 19 ♗e3
♕xb2 20 ♖ab1 ♕c3∞ (Yu-
supov).

c12) **18 ... ♕a5!** 19 ♗d2 ♗b4
20 ♗e3 0-0 (20 ... c6 21 ♕e4
△ ♗c4±) 21 ♕xb7 ♘c5 22
♗xc5 ♗xc5 23 ♕b5 ½-½
Timman – Yusupov, Hilver-
sum (m) 1986.

c2) **17 ... ♖b8** 18 b4 0-0 19
♖d7 ♖bd8! 20 ♗xb7 (20
♖xe7? ♕d6 21 ♗a3 ♕xe7 22
b5 ♘c5 23 ♗xh7+ ♔xh7 24
♕h5+ ♔g8 25 ♗xc5 ♕f6!∓)
20 ... ♕c4∓ Howell – Ivanchuk, Groningen 1986/87; 18
♕h5!? is Rosendaal's sug-
gestion, but has not been
tried yet.

17 ... 0-0

a) **17 ... ♗xb4?** 18 ♕f3 c6
19 ♖d7! 0-0! (19 ... ♔xd7? 20
♕xf7+ ♔d6 21 ♗g5! – Kas-
parov) 20 ♕h3 g6 21 ♗xg6!
hg 22 ♗b2 ♘g7 23 ♕h6±

(Dlugy).

b) **17 ... ♗f6?** 18 b5 ♕b6 19 ♕xb6 ab 20 ♗xb7 ♗xa1 21 ♗xa8 0-0 22 ♗c6 ♖d8 23 ♖xd8+ ♘xd8 14 ♗d5± (Kasparov).

18 ♕h3!   g6!

and White can choose:

a) **19 ♗b2 ♕c4!** 20 ♖d7 ♖ae8!∓ Kasparov - Karpov, (m) London 1986, better is 20 ♗d5 ♕c2 21 ♖ab1! ♖ad8 22 ♖dc1= (Makarichev).

b) **19 ♕c3!** (Judovich) when:

b1) **19 ... c5?!** 20 ♗b2 ♘d4 21 ♗d3 ♕b6 22 a5 ♕c7 23 bc ♗xc5 24 ♗f1 25 ♖a4± Aseev - Ivanchuk, Irkutsk 1986.

b2) **19 ... ♘g5!** 20 ♗xg5 ♗xg5 21 ♕xc7 ♖ad8! is enough for maintaining his position — Kasparov. The World Champion must have counted on 22 ♖xd8 ♖xd8 23 ♗xb7, a pawn up.

B22

11   ♕h3   dc!

This is best, hunting the bishop from the h7 square. Others:

a) **11 ... c6?** 12 ♖e1+ ♗e7 13 ♗g5 dc (13 ... ♘e6 14 ♗xf6 ♗xf6 15 cd cd 16 ♗f5+) 14 ♗xf6 gf 15 ♗xc4 with a powerful attack.

b) **11 ... ♘e6?** 12 cd ♘xd5

c) **11 ... ♗e7** 12 cd! ♘xd5 13 ♖e1 c6 14 ♗g5 ♘e6 15 ♗xe7 ♕xe7 16 ♘xd5 cd 17 ♗f5 0-0-0 18 ♕g3 ♕d6! 19 ♕xg7 ♔b8 20 ♕xf7 ♘d4 21 ♖e7, J Horvath - Forintos, Budapest 1987, 21 ... ♕b6 22 ♗d3±.

12   ♗xc4

12 ♖e1+ ♗e7! and not 12 ... ♘e6? 13 ♗g6!

12   ...   ♗e7

12 ... ♕d7? 13 ♖e1+ ♗e7 14 ♕xd7+ ♔xd7 15 ♗xf7±.

13   ♗g5   ♕c8

Feeble are:

a) **13 ... ♕d7?!** 14 ♕xd7+ ♔xd7 15 ♖ad1 c5 16 ♘b5±.

b) **13 ... 0-0?** 14 ♖ad1 c5 15 ♖fe1 and White has a decisive attack, e.g. 15 ... h6 (15 ... ♖e8 16 ♗b5) 16 ♗xh6 (16 ♖xe7 is also good) 16 ... gh 17 ♕xh6 ♘h7 18 ♖d3 ♗g5 19 ♕h5 ♕f6 20 ♖h3! (after 20 ♖g3 in Kupreichik - Yusupov, Minsk 1987 Black could have kept his position) 20 ... ♕g7 21 f4! ♗xf4 22 ♘d5 and now:

b1) **22 ... ♗d6** 23 ♖e4 ♘e6 24 ♖g4 ♘eg5 25 ♖xg5! ♘xg5 26 ♖g3! wins — Meleghegyi.

b2) **22 ... ♗g5** 23 ♘e7+ ♗xe7 24 ♖xe7 ♘f6 25 ♕xc5± Thesing - Autenrieth, Budapest 1987.

14 ♕d3   ♘e6

Or 14 ... ♕g4!?

15 ♗xe6   fe

16 ♖fe1 ♕d7 17 ♕c4 0-0-0 when:

a) **18 ♖ad1** ♕c6 19 ♕xc6 bc 20 ♖xd8+ ♔xd8 21 ♖xe6 ♔d7 22 ♖e2 ♖b8 23 g3 ♖b4 with a tenable position in Vehi – Forintos, Barcelona 1987.

b) **18 ♖xe6** ♘d5! 19 ♗xe7 ♕xe6 20 ♗xd8 ♖xd8 21 ♖d1 c6 22 ♘xd5 b5! 23 ♕f4 (23 ♘b6+ ♔b7!) 23 ... ♖xd5 24 ♕f8+ ♔b7 25 ♕xg7+ ♔b6 with level chances in J Horvath – Forintos, Kecskemet 1987.

White seems to have sufficient play for the pawn after 11 ♕h3, but no more.

27) 3 ♘xe5 d6: 6 ♗d3 ♗d6
(Staunton's Defence)
Introduction

4	♘f3	♘xe4
5	d4	d5
6	♗d3	♗d6 *(80)*

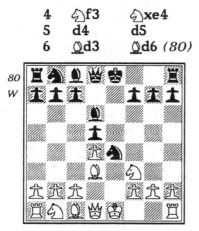

The disadvantage of this seemingly most active move is that Black's feeble d5-pawn becomes weaker. Marshall often sacrificed it, though this would rather be postponed in our days. Staunton used it against Williams in the first International Tournament in London, 1851.

White can choose from:

A: 7 c4
B: 7 0-0

A

7 c4
Premature.

7 ... ♗b4+
This takes away c3 from White's b1 - knight, and leads to equality.

Or 7 ... 0-0 8 cd? (8 0-0 transposes into Chapter 28) 8 ... ♗b4+ 9 ♘bd2 ♘xd2 10 ♗xd2 ♖e8+ and Black has at least equal chances.

8 ♘bd2
Or 8 ♔f1?! 0-0 9 cd (⌐ 9 ♕b3) 9 ... ♕xd5∓ 10 ♕c2 ♖e8 11 ♘c3? ♘xc3 12 bc ♕xf3!! Janowski - Marshall, (m) Biarritz 1912.

8 ... 0-0
Or:
a) 8 ... ♗xd2+ 9 ♗xd2 0-0 10 0-0 transposes to the main line.
b) 8 ... ♘xd2 9 ♗xd2 when:
b1) 9 ... ♗xd2+ 10 ♕xd2 0-0 11 0-0 ♘c6 12 ♖fe1 ♗g4 13 ♘e5 ♘xe5 14 ♖xe5 dc 15 ♗xc4 ♕f6 16 ♖ae1± Capa-

blanca - Marshall, St. Petersburg 1914.

b2) **9 ... ♕e7+!** 10 ♕e2 (10 ♔f1 dc 11 ♗xb4 ♕xb4 12 ♕e1+ ♕xe1 13 ♖xe1+ ♔d8! 14 ♗xc4 f6 15 d5 ♘d7 16 ♘d4 ♘b6 17 ♗b3 ♗d7 18 f4 ½–½ Palac - Forintos, Novi Sad 1990, 18 ... a5=) and now:

b21) **10 ... ♕xe2+** 11 ♔xe2 ♗xd2 12 ♔xd2 ♗e6 (12 ... dc 13 ♖he1+±) 13 cd ♗xd5 14 ♖he1+ ♔d8 15 ♗e4!± Alekhine - Marshall, St. Petersburg 1914.

b22) **10 ... ♗xd2+** 11 ♔xd2 ♕xe2+ 12 ♗xe2 dc 13 ♗xc4 0–0 14 ♖he1 ♘c6± Janowski - Marshall, New York 1913.

9	0–0	♗xd2
10	♗xd2	♗g4!
11	♗f4	♘c6
12	♖e1	♘xd4

12 ... ♗xf3? 13 ♕xf3 ♘xd4 14 ♕e3 ♘f5 15 ♕h3± (Tarrasch).

13	♗xe4	de=

14 ♕xd4 ef 15 ♕xd8 ♖fxd8 16 ♗xc7 ♖d2 with level chances in Tarrasch - Marshall, St. Petersburg 1914.

B

7	0–0	♗g4

Alternatives:

a) For **7 ... 0–0** see Chapter 28.

b) **7 ... ♗f5** and now:

b1) **8 ♖e1** 0–0 9 c4 c6 10 ♘c3 ♖e8?! (∟ 10 ... ♘xc3±) 11 ♕c2 ♗b4 12 ♗g5! f6 13 ♘h4 ♘xc3 14 ♖xe8+ ♕xe8 15 ♘xf5 ♘e4 16 ♗f4± Poppenheimer - Bauer, Frankfurt 1887.

b2) **8 c4** dc 9 ♗xe4 ♗xe4 10 ♖e1 f5 11 ♘c3 0–0 12 ♘xe4 fe 13 ♖xe4±.

8	♖e1

Or:

a) **8 ♗xe4** de 9 ♕e1, Hennig-Rotenstein, Berlin 1921, 9 ... ♕e7 10 ♘g5 ♘c6!=.

b) **8 ♕e2** f5 and now:

b1) **9 c4?** ♘c6! 10 cd ♘xd4 11 ♕e3 ♘xf3+ 12 gf ♕h4∓ Michelsen - Marshall, New York 1915.

b2) **9 h3** ♗h5 10 g4 fg!∞.

c) **8 ♘c3** ♘xc3 9 bc 0–0 10 h3 (10 c4? dc 11 ♗xc4 ♗xf3 12 ♕xf3 ♕h4∓ Bäuerle - Frank, Germany, 1976) 10 ... ♗h5 11 c4 dc 12 ♗xc4 ♘c6 (12 ... ♘d7 13 ♖b1 ♘b6 with equality Teichmann - Marshall, Carlsbad 1911) 13 c3 ♖e8 14 ♖b1 ♘a5 15 ♗d3, Teichmann - Marshall, Bad Pistyan 1912, 15 ... c5!=.

d) **8 c4!** when:

d1) **8 ... c6?** and now:

d11) Also **9 ♖e1** when 9 ... 0–0 does not give Black enough compensation.

d12) If **9 ♘bd2!?** f5 (9 ... ♘xd2? 10 ♖e1+!) 10 cd cd 11 ♕a4+ ♕d7 12 ♗b5 ♘c6 13 ♘e5 ♗xe5 14 de± Knowe – Hoing 1865.

d13) **9 h3 ♗h5** 10 ♖e1 0-0 11 ♗xe4 de 12 ♖xe4 and the bishop pair was not enough compensation for the pawn in Krause – Nielsen, Copenhagen 1896.

d2) Correct is **8 ... 0-0** transposing to Chapter 28.

8	**...**		**f5**
9	**c4**		**0-0**

Better than either:

a) **9 ... ♘d7** 10 cd?! 0-0 11 ♘c3 ♘df6, Ruck – Tarrasch, Nuremberg 1906, 12 ♗e2 or 12 h3 ♗h5 13 ♗e2±/=; we suggest 10 c5 ♗e7 11 ♕b3±.

b) **9 ... c6** 10 ♘c3 0-0 11 cd? (11 h3± Bilguer) 11 ... ♗xh2+! (a stereotyped sacrifice) 12 ♔xh2 ♘xf2 13 ♕e2 ♘xd3 14 ♕xd3 ♗xf3 15 g5! (15 ♕xd3 ♕h4+ △ ... ♕xe1) 15 ... ♕xg5 16 ♕xf3, Capablanca – Wolbrecht, St. Louis 1909, 16 ... ♘d7∓.

10	**♘c3?**

10 cd? ♗xh2+! Janowsky – Marshall, Biarritz 1912.

Best is Bilguer's 10 h3!

10	**...**	**♗xh2+**
11	**♔f1**	**♘c6**

12 ♘xd5 ♗xf3 13 ♕xf3, Leonhardt – Marshall, Hamburg 1911, 13 ... ♘xd4 14 ♕h3 ♗d6∓.

28) 3 ♞xe5 d6: 6 ♗d3 ♗d6 7 0-0 0-0

4	♞f3	♞xe4
5	d4	d5
6	♗d3	♗d6
7	0-0	0-0
8	c4! *(81)*	

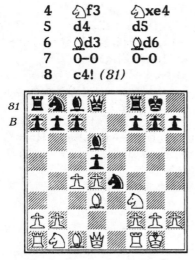

81
B

Black has no time for ... ♗f5.

Other ideas for White:

a) **8 ♞bd2 ♗f5 9 ♖e1 ♖e8 10 ♞f1 ♗g6 11 c3 ♞d7=** Rossetto - Pilnik, (m) 1946.

b) **8 ♞c3 ♞xc3 9 bc c5!** (△ ... c5-c4) if **10 c4? dc 11 ♗xc4 cd∓** (Kmoch); or **9 ... ♞d7 10 ♖e1 c5=** Garcia Martinez – Knezevic, Camaguey 1987.

c) **8 ♖e1** and now:

c1) **8 ... ♞c6?! 9 c4!±**.

c2) **8 ... ♞f6** is met by **9 ♗g5±**.

c3) **8 ... f5 9 c4 dc 10 ♗xc4+ ♔h8 11 ♞c3 ♞xc3 12 bc f4 13 ♞e5±** Glass - Drosd, Vienna 1961.

c4) **8 ... ♗f5** can be considered, e.g. **9 ♞bd2 ♖e8=** see note a; for **9 c4 c6** see var. b. in D1.

c5) For **8 ... ♖e8 9 c4** see line D1 9 ... ♖e8.

Now Black has tried:

A: 8 ... ♞f6
B: 8 ... ♗e6
C: 8 ... ♗g4
D: 8 ... c6

Or **8 ... f5? 9 cd ♞d7 10 ♞c3 ♞df6 11 ♕b3±** Quinteros – Bartrina, Olot 1974.

A

8	...	♞f6

A modest reply.

9	♕b3

± – Polugayevsky.

Others:

a) **9 ♘c3** dc 10 ♗xc4 when:

a1) **10 ... ♗g4** 11 h3 ♗h5 12 ♖e1± (Polugayevsky).

a2) **10 ... ♘c6** 11 h3 (11 ♗g5 h6 12 ♗h4 ♗g4= Hooper) 11 ... h6 12 ♗e3 ♗f5= Harrwitz – Löwenthal, London 1854 and Wolf – Pillsbury, Hannover 1902. After 12 ♕c2 White has slightly better chances.

b) **9 ♗g5** dc 10 ♗xc4 ♗g4 (10 ... h6) 11 h3 ♗xf3 12 ♕xf3 ♘c6, O'Kelly – Radulescu, Bucharest 1953, 13 ♖d1!±.

c) **9 h3** can be considered.

d) **9 c5 ♗e7** and now:

d1) **10 h3** b6!

d2) **10 ♘e5** c6 (10 ... b6 11 c6!? △ ♕c2, ♗g5) 11 ♗g5 h6 12 ♗h4 ♘fd7= Weiner – Treppner, 1977; 12 ... b6 is also good.

B

8 ...   ♗e6 *(82)*

Black is planning to put a bishop on d5, but here the benefits are illusory.

9   cd

Or:

a) **9 ♕b3** dc 10 ♗xc4 ♗xc4 11 ♕xc4 c6 12 ♘c3 ♘f6= Bilguer.

b) **9 ♕c2** f5 (9 ... c6 10 cd cd 11 ♗xe4 de 12 ♕xe4 ♗d5!∞ Hildkrog – Chris-

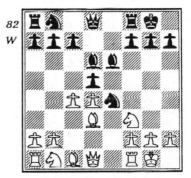

tensen, corr. 1985) 10 c5! (10 ♕b3∞) ♗e7 11 ♘e5± Steinitz.

c) **9 ♘c3 ♗xc3** 10 bc dc 11 ♗e4 (11 ♗xh7+ ♔xh7 12 ♘g5+ ♔g6!∞) 11 ... ♗c8!∞ Haag – Pacsay, Budapest 1965.

d) **9 ♖e1 ♖e8!** 10 ♕b3 (10 c5 ♗e7=) 10 ... dc 11 ♗xc4 ♗xc4 12 ♕xc4 ♘d7 13 ♘c3 ♘df6= (Bilguer).

e) **9 c5 ♗e7** 10 ♘bd2 f5=.

9	...	♗xd5
10	♘c3	♘xc3
11	bc	♘d7

Planning 12 ... c5. Other tries:

a) **11 ... c5?!** 12 dc ♗xc5? (12 ... ♗e7 sacrificing a pawn is better) 13 ♗xh7+!± or 13 ♘g5.

b) **11 ... ♘c6** 12 ♘g5!? h6 13 ♕h5±.

C

8 ...   ♗g4 *(83)*

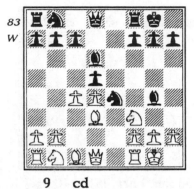

83
W

9   cd

Also good: 9 ♞c3 ♞xc3 10 bc dc 11 ♗xc4 ♞d7 (11 ... ♕f6) 12 ♕d3 (12 h3 ♗h5 13 g4 Maroczy - Milner-Barry, London 1932 and then 13 ... ♞b6 is necessary — Alekhine) 12 ... c5 13 ♞g5 ♞f6 14 h3 ♗h5 15 f4! h6 16 g4 b5 17 ♗d5± Corso - Marshall, Havana 1913.

	9	...	f5
	10	♞c3	♞d7
	11	h3	♗h5
	12	♞xe4	fe
	13	♗xe4	♞f6
	14	♗f5	♔h8

14 ... ♞xd5? 15 ♗e6+ ♗f7 16 ♞g5!±.

	15	g4!	♞xd5
	16	♗e6!	♗f7
	17	♞g5	♗xe6

18 ♞xe6 ♕h4 19 ♕b3! (△ 10 ♗g5)±± Alexander - Mallison, Brighton 1938.

The 8 ... ♗g4 gambit can be considered rejected.

D

8   ...   c6 *(84)*

Black supports his centre before launching any action on the kingside.

84
W

White has a considerable choice:

D1: 9 ♖e1
D2: 9 ♞c3
D3: 9 ♕b3
D4: 9 ♕c2
D5: 9 cd

Or:

a) 9 ♗xe4 de 10 ♞g5 and now:

a1) **10 ... ♗f5** 11 ♞c3 h6 12 ♞gxe4 ♗xe4 13 ♞xe4 ♗xh2+ 14 ♔xh2 ♕h4+ 15 ♔g1 ♕xe4 16 ♖e1 ♕h4 is slightly advantageous for White.

a2 **10 ... f5** can also be considered, e.g. 11 c5 ♗e7 12 ♕b3+ ♕d5 14 ♕xd5 cd 15 ♞c3 ♖d8.

b) **9 h3** is slow:

b1) **9 ... ♖e8** 10 cd cd 11 ♘bd2 (⌑ 11 ♘c3) 11 ... ♘c6 12 ♖e1 ♘xd2 13 ♗xd2 ♖xe1+ 14 ♕xe1 h6= Yanovsky – Kiseljov, Moscow 1986.

b2) **9 ... ♘d7** 10 ♘c3 ♘xc3 11 bc dc 12 ♗xc4 ♕a5 (12 ... ♘f6 or 12 ... ♘b6), Aseev – Rosentalis, Vilnius 1984, 13 ♕c2 ♘f6 14 ♗d3± Tukmakov.

D1

9   ♖e1   ♖e8

a) **9 ... ♘f6(?)** (passive) 10 ♘c3 (10 ♗g5 is also good) 10 ... dc 11 ♗xc4± Klovan – Levchenkov, Riga 1971.

b) **9 ... ♗f5** and now:

b1) If **10 c5 ♗c7** 11 ♕c2 ♗g6 with balanced chances, but tactical possibilities are hidden in the position, e.g. 12 ♘e5 ♘xf2!? 13 ♕xf2 ♗xe5 14 ♗xg6 fg∓ – analysis.

b2) **10 ♘c3 ♘xc3** 11 bc ♗xd3 12 ♕xd3 dc 14 ♕xc4 ♘d7 de Firmian – P Wolff, Philadelphia 1987, with chances to equalize.

b3) **10 ♕c2 ♘a6** (10 ... ♗g6 11 c5 ♗c7 12 ♘c3 ♘xc3 13 ♗xg6 hg 14 bc ♘d7 15 ♗g5 ½-½ Yudasin – Rosentalis, USSR Ch. Leningrad 1990) 11 a3 ♗g6 12 c5 ♗c7(!) 13 ♘c3 (13 ♘bd2 f5 14 b4 ♕f6=

Manca – Savva, Groningen, 1986) 13 ... ♖e8 (13... f5) 14 b4 ♕f6? (⌑ 14 ... ♘xc3) 15 ♘xe4± Yudasin – Rosentalis, Lvov 1990.

b4) **10 ♕b3 ♘a6** (10 ... ♕d7 11 cd cd 12 ♘c3 ♗e6 13 ♗xe4 de 14 d5 ♗xd5 15 ♘xd5 ½-½ in Mihalchishin – Ionow, Klaipeda 1988) 11 ♘c3! (11 cd ♘ec5! 12 dc ♘xc5 13 ♗xf5 ♘xb3 14 ab cd= Mardle – Milner-Barry, Bognor 1964) when:

b41) **11 ... ♘ac5?!** 12 dc ♘xc5 13 ♗xf5± Halifman – Rosentalis, Vilnius 1988.

b42) **11 ... dc** 12 ♗xc4 ♘xc3 13 bc b5 14 ♗f1 ♘c7 15 a4 (15 ♗a3 ♗e6 16 ♕b2 ♗d5 17 ♘e5 ♖e8 18 ♗xd6 ½-½ Serper – Akopyan, Adelaide 1988) 15 ... a5!? (15 ... a6) 16 ♗g5 ♕d7 17 ♘e5 ♗xe5 18 de ♗e6 19 ♖ed1 ♗xb3 20 ♖xd7 ♖fc8∞ Oll – Rosentalis, Klaipeda 1988.

c) **9 ... ♘a6!?** (sacrificing a pawn) and then:

c1) **10 ♗xe4** de 11 ♖xe4 ♗f5∞.

c2) **10 ♘c3(!) ♘xc3** 11 bc dc 12 ♗xc4 ♕a5 13 ♕b3 ♘c7 14 ♘e5 ♘d5 15 ♗d2± Renet – Miralles, Marseille 1988.

d) **9 ... ♗g4** 10 ♗xe4 (10 ♘c3; 10 cd) 10 ... dc 11 ♖xe4 f5 12 ♖e1 (12 ♖e3 ♗f4=) 12 ...

♗xf3 13 ♕xf3 ♕h4 14 h3 ♕xd4 15 ♕b3 (15 c5? ♗xc5 16 ♕b3+ ♔h8 17 ♗e3 ♕b4!∓∓) 15 ... ♕b6= Hjartarson - Ye Rongguang, Novi Sad (ol) 1990: we suggest 12 ♖e6.

10 ♘c3

Or:

a) 10 ♘bd2 ♗f5! 11 c5 ♗f8 12 ♕c2 ♘d7!= Halifman - Rosentalis, USSR 1985.

b) 10 h3 (slow) 10 ... ♗f5 (also 10 ... ♘d7 △ ... ♘df6 can be mentioned) 11 ♕b3 ♘a6! 12 cd and now:

b1) 12 ... ♘ac5? 13 dc ♘xc5 14 ♖xe8+ ♕xe8 15 ♕a3 ♘xd3 16 ♕xd6 ♘xc1 17 ♘c3±.

b2) 12 ... cd 13 ♘c3 ♘b4 then:

b21) 14 ♗xe4 ♗xe4 15 ♘xe4 de 16 ♘g5 ♕c7 17 ♗d2 ♘c2 18 ♘xf7! ♘xa1 19 ♘h6+ ♔h8 20 ♘f7+ equalizes (Mihalchishin).

b22) 14 ♗b1 ♗d7 15 ♘e5 (15 a3? ♗xh3!) 15 ... ♘xc3! 16 bc ♗xe5 17 ♖xe5 ♘d3 18 ♖xe8+?! (18 ♗xd3=) 18 ... ♖xe8 19 ♗e3 ♕c6! 20 ♗c2 ♗e4 △ ... ♕g6∓ Yudasin - Mihalchishin, Lvov 1987.

c) 10 ♕c2 ♗g4! 11 ♗xe4 de 12 ♖xe4 ♗xf3 13 gf ♘d7⊚ Petrushin - Rosentalis, USSR 1984.

d) 10 ♕b3 ♘a6 11 cd cd 12 ♘c3 ♗e6!= Makarichev - Nikolenko, Moscow 1987.

10 ... ♘xc3

11 bc

Or 11 ♖xe8+ ♕xe8 12 bc and now:

a) 12 ... ♗g4 13 ♗d2 (planning 14 ♗xh7+. We suggest first 13 cd cd and then 14 ♗d2; if 13 ... ♗xf3, then 14 ♕xf3 ♕e1+ 15 ♗f1 ♗xh2+ 16 ♔xh2 ♕xf1 17 ♗h6! △ ♕g4±) 13 ... ♕d8 and now:

a1) 14 ♗xh7+? ♔xh7 15 ♕b1+ ♔g8 16 ♘g5 g6 17 ♕xb7 ♘d7 18 ♕xc6 ♘f6 19 ♕b7 ♗e6 20 c5 was Weinkauf - Werner, corr. 1966, and now 20 ... ♗c7∓.

a2) 14 ♖b1 dc 15 ♗xc4 ♕c7 16 h3 ♗f5 17 ♘g5!? ♕g6 18 ♕e2 ♘d7= Burn - Marshall, Carlsbad 1911.

a3) 14 cd cd 15 h3 ♗h5 16 ♖b1! (Polugayevsky) or 16 ♕b3⊚ (Jonsson) also deserves attention.

b) 12 ... dc 13 ♗xc4 ♗g4 14 ♗g5! (14 ♗e3 ♘d7 15 ♗e2 b5= Korzubov - Rosentalis, Lvov 1985) 14 ... ♘d7?! 15 ♕d3!± (△ 16 ♖e1, 17 ♘e5) L A Schneider - Valkesalmi, Torshavn 1987; better is 14 ... h6 15 ♗h4 ♕e4∞.

11 ... ♗g4

a) 11 ... dc?! 12 ♗g5! ♖xe1+ 13 ♕xe1 ♕f8 14 ♗xc4 ♘d7 15

♗d3± Halifman - Rosentalis, Minsk 1986.

b) Playable is **11 ... ♖xe1+ 12 ♕xe1 h6! 13 h3 ♗e6** Hawelko - Garcia Gonzalez, Polanica Zdroj 1987.

**12 ♗g5   ♖xe1+
13 ♕xe1   ♕d7!
14 ♕e3   ♕e6!** =

15 ♖b1 b6 (15 ... dc 16 ♗xc4!) 16 cd cd 17 c4 when:

a) **17 ... ♘d7?!** 18 cd ♕xd5 19 ♖b5!∞ Timman; 19 ♗e4?! ♕xa2 20 ♕d3 ♖e8 21 ♗xh7+ ♔f8∓ (Hübner).

b) **17 ... ♕xe3** 18 fe (18 ♗xe3 ♗xf3 19 gf ♘c6 20 cd ♘e7= Timman) 18 ... ♘c6! 19 cd ♘b4 20 ♗c4 ♗f5 21 ♖b2 ♖c8 22 ♘d2 ♗d3 with sufficient compensation for the pawn in Hübner - Timman, Rotterdam 1988.

D2

9   ♘c3   ♘xc3

Inferior are:

a) **9 ... f5?** 10 ♕c2!± or 10 ♕b3±.

b) **9 ... ♘f6** 10 ♗g5 dc±.

10 bc

With two alternatives:

D21: 10 ... dc
D22: 10 ... ♗g4

Or 10 ... ♘d7, Puc - Kindij, Sarajevo 1951, 11 ♗g5±.

D21

10   ...   dc *(85)*

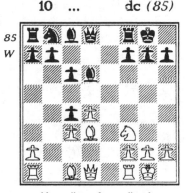

85
W

11 ♗xc4   ♗g4

a) **11 ... b5?** 12 ♗b3 ♗f5 13 ♘e5 ♗xe5 14 de ♕xd1 15 ♖xd1 a5 16 a4!± Tal - Mephisto, DAM 1985.

b) **11 ... ♗f5?!** 12 ♘e5± Slimani - Murillo, Thessaloniki (ol) 1988.

12 ♕d3!

Or:

a) **12 h3 ♗h5 13 ♖e1 ♘d7 14 g4?! ♗g6 15 ♘e5? ♗xe5!** 16 de ♘xe5! 17 ♕xd8 ♘f3+∓ Stefansson - P Wolff, Baguio 1987.

b) **12 ♖b1 b5!** (for 12 ... ♘d7 see var. a1 12 ... ♘d7 in D22; 12 ... ♕c7!?) when:

b1) **13 ♗d3 ♘d7** and now:

b11) **14 ♖e1 ♘b6 15 ♗c2 ♖e8 16 ♗g5! ♕c7! 17 ♕d3 g6 18 h3 ♗f5 19 ♕d1 ♖xe1+ 20 ♘xe1 ♗xc2 21 ♘xc2** was Short - Makarichev, Rotterdam 1988, 21 ... ♘d5!∓.

b12) **14 a4** a6 15 ♗e4 ♖c8 (for 15 ... ♕c7 see the following variation) 16 ab ab 17 h3 ♗h5 18 ♕d3 ♗g6 19 ♗xg6 hg 20 ♘g5 ♗e7 21 h4 ♘b6 with counterplay in Fedorov - Nikolenko, Moscow 1986.

b13) **14 h3** ♗h5 15 ♗e4 and then:

b131) **15 ... ♕c7?!** 16 ♗xh7+ ♔h8 17 ♗d3 f5 with not enough compensation for the pawn in de Firmian - Shirazi, USA Ch. 1986.

b132) **15 ... ♖c8** 16 ♕d3 ♗g6 17 ♗xg6 hg 18 c4 a6 19 ♖d1 (19 a4? ♘c5!∓) 19 ... ♕a5 20 ♗e3?! (20 a3=) 20 ... ♕xa2 21 ♘d2 ♕a5 22 ♖a1 ♕d8 23 ♖xa6 ♘c5! 0-1 Dvoiris - Kochiev, Volgograd 1985.

b2) **13 ♗e2** ♘d7 (13 ... a6 14 h3 ♗h5 15 c4 bc 16 ♗e3 ♘d7 17 ♘d2 ♗g6= Kupreichik - Halifman, Minsk 1985) 14 a4 (14 d5!?) 14 ... a6 15 c4 bc 16 ♕c2 ♗xf3 17 ♗xf3 ♕h4 18 g3 ♕xd4, Ivanovic - Halifman, Plovdiv 1986, 19 ♖d1 ♕f6 20 ♗xc6 ♖ad8 21 ♗xd7 ♖xd7 22 ♗f4=.

c) **12 ♖e1** ♘d7 13 ♗d3 ♕f6= Puskas - Polacek, Trnava 1980; 13 ♖b1 Pieper - Schuster, German League 1989/90, 13 ... b5=, compare var. b. 12 ♖b1 b5!

d) **12 ♗e2** ♘d7 13 ♖b1 ♕c7 14 h3 ♗f5 15 ♗d3 ♗xd3 16 ♕xd3 ♖e8 (16 ... b5) 17 c4± Belyavsky - Christiansen, Szirak 1987.

12 ...   ♘d7

Or 12 ... ♗h5 and now:

a) **13 ♖e1** ♗g6 (13 ... ♘d7 is also good: 14 ♗g5 ♗g6 15 ♕d2 ♕c7 16 ♗b3 ♖ae8 17 ♖xe8 ♖xe8 18 ♖e1 ♕b8= Kapengut - Kochiev, Ashabad 1978) 14 ♕e2 ♘d7 15 ♗g5 ♕a5 16 ♕d2 ♘b6 (16 ... ♕c7) 17 ♗b3 ♘d5 18 ♗xd5 ♕xd5 19 ♗e7= Armas - Ye Rongguang, Thessaloniki (ol) 1988.

b) **13 ♘g5** ♗g6 14 ♕h3, Schlosser - Kaspret, Bad Schallerbach 1989, 14 ... h6 15 ♘f3 ♕f6=.

c) **13 ♗g5!** ♕c7 (13 ... ♗g6 14 ♕xg6! hg 15 ♗xd8 ♖xd8 16 ♘g5±) 14 ♖ae1!? ♘d7 (14 ... ♗xf3 15 ♕xf3 ♗xh2+ 16 ♔h1 ♗d6 17 ♖e4 with an attack. Better is 14 ... ♗g6) 15 ♗e7 ♗xe7 (15 ... ♖fe8? 16 ♘g5 ♗g6 17 ♗xf7+!±; 15 ... ♗g6 16 ♕e2±) 16 ♖xe7 ♕d6 (16 ... ♖ae8? 17 ♘g5 ♗g6 18 ♗xf7+!) 17 ♖fe1 b5 18 ♗b3 ♗g6 (18 ... ♘c5 19 ♕f5 ♘xb3 20 ♕xh5±) 19 ♕e2 a5 20 c4± Chandler - Barua, Thessaloniki (ol) 1988.

13 ♘g5

Or:

a) **13 ♗g5 ♕c7 14 h3 ♗h5** △ ... ♗g6=.

b) **13 ♖e1 ♕c7 14 h3 ♗h5 15 ♘h4 ♔h8 16 ♗g5**, Rotlewi – Davidson, Cologne 1911, 16 ... ♘b6 17 ♗b3 c5=.

c) **13 ♗b3 ♘c5!=** Mainka – Finegold, Dortmund 1990.

13 ... ♘f6

Or 13 ... g6 14 ♘e4±.

14 h3   ♗h5
15 f4   h6

16 g4 (16 ♘f3 ♗xf3 {⌒ 16 ... ♗g6, △ ... ♕c7} 17 ♕xf3 ♕e7 18 ♗d3 Plaskett – Finegold, Hastings 1988/89) 16 ... hg (16 ... ♗xg4? 17 ♘xf7 ♖xf7 18 ♗xf7+ ♔xf7 19 hg ♘xg4 20 ♕f5+± Nunn) 17 fg:

a) **17 ... ♘xg4** 18 hg and now:

a1) **18 ... ♗xg4?** 19 ♕e4± Capablanca – Northrop, New York 1909 or 19 g6 ♗e6 20 ♖xf7! 1-0 Ghizdavu – Stanciu, Romania 1972.

a2) **18 ... ♕d7!** 19 gh (19 ♕f5 ♗xg4 – see below Nunn – Salov) 19 ... ♕g4+ 20 ♔f2 ♖ae8! and now:

a21) **21 ♖h1** b5 22 ♕f3! ♕xf3+ 23 ♔xf3 bc 24 ♗f4 ♗xf4+ 25 ♔xf4 c5=.

a22) **21 ♖g1 ♕h4+ 22 ♔g2** b5 23 ♗b3 c5? 24 ♖h1! 1-0 Short – Hübner, Tilburg

1988, and wins after 24 ... ♕g4+ 25 ♔f1 c4 26 ♗d1! Better is 23 ... ♖e4 transposing into the next variation.

b) **17 ... b5!** 18 ♗b3 ♘xg4 19 hg ♕d7! (19 ... ♗xg4 20 g6 ♗e6 21 ♖xf7!) and now:

b1) **20 ♕f5?!** ♗xg4 21 ♕xd7 ♗xd7 22 ♖xf7! (22 g6? ♗e6∓) 22 ... ♖xf7 23 g6 ♗e8, Nunn – Salov, Brussels 1988, 24 ♗g5! a5 25 ♖f1 ♖a7 26 ♖f3!= (Salov).

b2) **20 gh ♕g4+ 21 ♔f2** ♖ae8 22 ♖g1 ♕h4+ 23 ♔g2 when:

b21) **23 ... ♖e4?!** 24 ♕f3 ♗h2 and now:

b211) **25 ♖h1?** ♖g4+ 26 ♔f1 ♖g3 27 ♕xc6 ♕h3+ 28 ♔f2 ♕f5+ 29 ♔e1 (29 ♔e2 ♕d3+ 30 ♔e1 ♖h3!∓) 29 ... ♖c8?? (29 ... ♗g1!∓) 30 ♗e6! 1-0 Psakhis – Mihalchishin, Klaipeda 1988.

b212) **25 ♗d2!** ♖g4+ 26 ♕xg4 ♕xg4+ 27 ♔h2 ♕h4+ 28 ♔g2 ♕e4+ (28 ... ♖e8 29 ♗d1!) 29 ♔f2 ♕f5+ 30 ♔e2 ♖e8+ 31 ♔d1± (Short).

b22) **23 ... ♕h2+!** 24 ♔f1 ♗f4 25 ♕f3 (25 ♗d1 ♖e1+!∓; 25 ♗xf4 ♕xf4+ 26 ♔g2 ♖e3∓) 25 ... ♖e1+ 26 ♔xe1 ♕xg1 27 ♔e2 ♗xc1 28 ♖xc1! (28 ♔d3 ♕xg5∓) 28 ... ♕xc1 29 g6 ♖e8+ 30 ♔d3 ♕b1+ 31 ♔d2 (31 ♗c2? ♕xa2∓) 31 ...

♕e1+ with perpetual check in A Sokolov - Oll, USSR Ch. 1989.

D22

10 ...   ♗g4 *(86)*

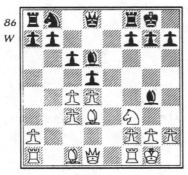

11 cd

Or:

a) **11 ♖b1** dc! 12 ♗xc4 and now:

a1) **12 ... ♘d7** 13 h3 ♗h5 14 ♖xb7!? ♘b6 15 ♗a6 ♕f6 16 c4! ♗xf3 17 ♕xf3 ♕xd4 18 ♕xc6 ♖ac8 19 ♕b5, A Sokolov - Rosentalis, Sochi 1982, 19 ... ♖c5±.

a2) For **12 ... b5!** see var. b. 12 ♖b1 b5! in D21.

b) **11 ♗e2** (loss of tempo) 11 ... dc 12 ♗xc4 ♘d7 13 ♕d3 ♗h5 14 ♘g5, Peters - Kochiev, Hastings 1978-79, 14 ... ♗g6∞.

c) **11 h3** ♗h5 and now:

c1) **12 ♖e1** dc 13 ♗xc4 ♘d7 = .

c2) **12 ♖b1** dc 13 ♗xc4 ♘d7

(for 13 ... b5! see var. b. 12 ♖b1 b5! in D21) 14 ♗e2 ♖e8 15 ♗e3 ♕c7 16 c4 ♘f6= Schallopp - Fritz, Coburg 1911.

c3) **12 cd** cd when:

c31) **13 ♕b3?!** ♗xf3 14 ♕xb7 ♘d7 15 gf ♘b6 16 ♖b1 ♕f6 17 ♔g2 ♖ac8 18 ♕xa7 ♖xc3 19 ♖xb6 ♖xd3 20 ♗e3 ♕g6+ 21 ♔h1 ♕e6 22 ♔g2 ♕g6+ ½-½ Capablanca - Marshall, (m) New York 1909.

c32) **13 ♖b1** b6 (c.f. line D52) 14 c4 ♘c6 15 ♖b5! ♕f6 (15 ... ♘xd4? 16 ♖xd5± or 15 ... ♗xf3 16 ♕xf3 ♘xd4 17 ♗xh7+!±; ⌐ 15 ... ♘e7!?) 16 g4 ♗xg4 17 hg ♘xd4 18 ♘xd4 ♕h4 19 ♔g2 ♕h2+ 20 ♔f3 ♕h3+ 21 ♔e2 ♕xg4+ 22 ♘f3 dc 23 ♗xh7+!±± Pirisi - Michaelsen, Balatonbereny 1989.

d) **11 c5** ♗c7?! (⌐ 11 ... ♗e7 12 h3 ♗xf3) 12 ♗g5! ♕c8 (⌐ 12 ... ♕xg5±) 13 ♖e1 h6 (⌐ 13 ... ♗f5) 14 ♗e7 ♖e8 15 ♕c2!± (15 ... ♗xf3 16 gf △ ♗f5) Shiatdinov - Galachov, USSR 1986.

e) **11 ♖e1** ♘d7 (11 ... dc!) 12 c5 ♗c7 13 ♗g5 f6 (13 ... ♕xg5 14 ♗xh7+±; better is 13 ... ♘f6 14 ♕d2 ♗xf3 15 gf h6 16 ♗xh6 ♘h5!∞) 14 ♗h4 ♖f7 15 ♕c2± Shiatdinov - Zagrebelny, USSR 1985.

f) **11 a4** dc 12 ♗xc4 ♘d7 13
♖b1 ♖b8! 14 h3 ♗h5 15 ♕e2
♖e8 16 ♗e3 ♘f6 17 c4 ♘e4
(△ ... ♘g3) 18 ♕b3 c5= Popovic - H Olafsson, Dort-
mund 1988.

    11   ...   cd
    12   ♖b1

This set-up entirely corr-
esponds to the one after 12
♖b1 (or 12 h3 ♗h5 13 ♖b1) in
line D5. See the complete
material there.

D3

    9   ♕b3   ♗g4
If 10 ♕xb7? ♗xf3! 11 gf
♕h4!∓.

    10   ♗xe4
Keres' 10 ♘bd2 is a posi-
tional way.

    10   ...   de
    11   ♘g5   ♗e7!
11 ... ♗c7 12 d5!±.

    12   ♘xe4   ♕xd4
    13   ♕xb7   ♕xe4

14 ♕xa8 ♗d6! 15 ♕xa7
♗h3! 16 gh ♕e5 17 ♖d1!
♕xh2+ 18 ♔f1 ♕xh3+ 19 ♔e1!
(19 ♔e2? ♕h5+ △ ... ♗c5∓)
19 ... ♗b4+! 20 ♘c3 ♗xc3+ 21
bc ♕xc3+ 22 ♗d2 ♖e8+ 23
♔f1 ♕h3+ 24 ♔g1 ♕g4+ ½-½
Dührssen - Batik, corr. 1928.

D4

    9   ♕c2

Now Black has a choice:

D41: 9 ... f5
D42: 9 ... ♘a6

Or:

a) **9 ... ♗f5?** 10 ♘c3± (Keres).

b) **9 ... ♘f6** 10 ♗g5 h6 (⌐
10 ... dc — Steinitz) 11 ♗h4
dc 12 ♗xc4 ♘bd7 13 ♘c3 and
now:

b1) **13 ... ♕a5?!** 14 ♖fe1
♕h5 15 ♘e2± Ilyin Zhenev-
sky - Poljak, Leningrad 1938.

b2) **13 ... ♕c7?!** (13 ... ♘b6)
14 ♖fe1 ♘b6? (14 ... b5) 15
♗xf6 ♘xc4 16 ♘e4!± Kadar
- Koszorus, Hungary 1970.

c) **9 ... ♖e8** 10 ♘c3 ♘f6 11
♗g5 - compare var. b 9 ...
♘f6.

d) **9 ... ♗e6** 10 cd cd 11
♗xe4 de 12 ♕xe4 ♗d5 13 ♕f5
♗e6 14 ♕h5 ♘c6 15 ♘c3
♘b4∞ Hildkrog - Christen-
sen, corr. 1985. Or: 10 ♗xe4
de 11 ♘g5 ♗f5 12 ♘xe4 (12
♘c3 ♗e7!) 12 ... ♗xh2+ 13
♔xh2 ♕h4+ 14 ♔g1 ♗xe4 15
♕c3 (△ f3, ♗e3)=.

D41

    9   ...   f5
    10   ♘c3
Or:

a) After **10 cd** cd 11 ♘e5
we suggest 11 ... ♗e6!? △ 12

f3 ♕b6!

b) **10 c5** ♗c7 11 ♘c3 ♘d7 12 ♘e2! ♕e8 13 ♗f4± Geiser – Kotschil, corr. 1987; better 10 ... ♗e7 △ ... ♗f6.

c) **10 ♕b3!?** ♔h8! 11 ♘c3 ♘a6! 12 cd cd and now:

c1) **13 ♗xa6** ba 14 ♕xd5 ♖b8 15 ♘e5 (15 ♕c4 ♖b4 16 ♕e2 ♗b7 17 ♗e3 ♖e8∓ Madsen – Christiansen, 1986) ♗b7 16 ♕e6 ♕h4 17 f4 ♗xe5 18 fe! (18 de? ♘xc3 19 bc ♗e4 △ ♖b6 – f6) 18 ... ♘xc3 19 bc ♕e4= Rodriguez – Sieiro, Cuban Ch. 1982.

c2) **13 ♘xd5** ♗e6 14 ♕xb7 ♘ac5! 15 dc ♘xc5 16 ♗g5! ♗xd5 17 ♕b5 ♕c7! 18 ♗e2 ♘b3 19 ♕b5 ♗xf3= Zagorovsky – P Viner, corr. 1984-85.

c3) **13 ♘b5** ♗b8 14 ♖e1 ♗e6 15 a3 ♗g8 16 ♘c3 ♗d6 17 ♗f1 Volchok – Borisov, corr. 1984-85, and now 17 ... ♘ac5!? 18 dc ♗xc5 △ ... d4 can be considered.

c4) **13 ♘e2** ♘b4 14 ♗f4 a5 15 ♗b5 ♗xf4 16 ♘xf4 g5∞ has been played in several games; or 14 ... ♗xf4 15 ♘xf4 ♕d6 16 g3 ♘xd3 17 ♕xd3 g5 18 ♘g2 f4 19 ♘e5 ♕h6= Poulsen – Christiansen, corr. 1984.

10 ... ♘a6!
10 ... ♗e6? 11 ♕b3!±.

11 a3

11 ♕b3 ♔h8! transposes into the above note c 10 ♕b3. Or 11 cd ♘b4 12 ♕d1 Ernst – Machado, Malmö 1987, 12 ... cd is equal.

11 ... ♘c7
12 ♘e2!?

Or 12 ♖e1 (12 b4) 12 ... ♔h8 13 b4 (13 c5) 13 ... ♗d7! 14 ♗b2 (14 ♘e5 ♘e6!) 14 ... ♗e8! 15 c5 ♗e7 16 ♘e5 ♕h4! with good play for Black in Gufeld – Kochiev, USSR 1980.

12 ... ♘e6

13 b4 ♗d7 (for 13 ... ♔h8 see 13 ... ♔h8 in D42) 14 ♗b2 ♖f6 (⌓ 14 ... ♘f4) 15 ♖ae1 ♖h6 16 ♗c1 ♘4g5 17 ♘e5 ♗xe5 18 de ♘f3+!? 19 gf f4 20 ♗f5, Chandler – Dive, Wellington 1988, and now 20 ... ♕h4 21 h3 ♘g5! is still dangerous, though it is not correct.

D42

9 ... ♘a6
Krause's Gambit. After 10 ♗xe4 de 11 ♕xe4:

a) **11 ... ♖e8** 12 ♕d3 (12 ♕h4? ♕xh4 13 ♘xh4 ♘b4 14 ♘a3 ♖e4 15 ♘f3 ♗g4 16 ♗e3 ♗xf3 17 gf ♖h4∓ Keres) and now:

a1) **12 ... ♘b4?** 13 ♕b3 ♗f5 14 ♗g5!± Keres.

a2) **12 ... c5!?** Borisov and Rodin.

a3) **12 ... ♗g4!** 13 ♘g5 (13 ♘g5 g6 14 ♘c3 {14 ♘e4? ♗f5 15 ♘bc3 ♘c5!∓∓} 14 ... ♘b4 15 ♕d2 ♗f5 with compensation) 13 ... ♕d7 (13 ... f6 14 ♗h4±) 14 ♘bd2 h6 15 ♗e3 f5 with compensation in Kruppa - Rosentalis, Lvov 1985.

b) **11 ... ♘b4** 12 ♘g5 f5 13 ♕e2 f4! 14 ♘e4 (14 ♘f3 ♗f5! 15 ♘e1 f3!∞) 14 ... f3 15 gf ♗h3 16 ♖e1 ♕c7 17 a3 ♗xh2+ 18 ♔h1 ♘a6= Hramov - Raetsky, corr. 1986; or 12 ♘a3 ♖e8 13 ♕h4 ♕xh4 see var. a.

    10 a3   f5

This resembles 9 ... f5 very clearly. However, it happens at a more favourable moment. Or:

a) **10 ... ♖e8** 11 ♘c3 (after 11 ♘bd2 or 11 h3 ♗f5=) 11 ... ♗g4! and now:

a1) **12 c5?!** ♗c7 13 ♘xe4 de 14 ♗xe4 ♗xf3 15 ♗xf3 ♕xd4 16 ♗e3 ♖xe3!∓ Ehlvest - Dokhoian, USSR 1986.

a2) **12 ♘xe4** de 13 ♗xe4 f5! 14 ♗xf5 ♗xf3 15 gf ♕h4 with sharp play (Dokhoian).

b) After the gambit **10 ... ♗g4!?**:

b1) **11 ♗xe4?!** de 12 ♘g5?! (⌐ 12 ♕xe4 ♗xf3 13 ♕xf3

♕h4∓) 12 ... ♗f5 13 ♘c3 ♖e8 14 ♖e1 ♗c7, Ljubojevic - Timman, Linares 1988, 15 ♗e3 ♕d6 16 g3 ♕g6∓ (Timman).

b2) **11 ♘bd2** ♘xd2 12 ♗xd2 ♕h4 13 f4 ♖ae8 14 c5 ♗b8 (14 ... ♗c7!?) 15 ♘b3 ♖e7 16 ♗d2 ♖fe8 17 ♖f2 ♘c7 (17 ... ♗c7 △ ... ♘b8) 18 g3 ♕h5 19 f5 f6 20 a4 Short - Hort, German League 1988, 20 ... ♘a6! 21 ♖af1 ♗h3=.

b3) **11 c5 ♗c7** 12 ♘e5 ♗xe5 13 de and:

b31) **13 ... ♘axc5** 14 f3! (14 ♗xe4? ♘xe4 15 f3 ♕b6+ 16 ♔h1 f5! with attack) 14 ... ♕b6 15 ♗e3 d4 16 ♗xd4 ♖fd8! 17 ♗xe4! ♖xd4 18 ♗xh7+ ♔h8 19 fg ♘b3 20 ♔h1 ♘xa1 21 ♕f5 c5 22 ♕xf7! ♔xh7 23 e6 ♖d5? (23 ... ♕xb2±) 24 ♘c3! ♖e5 25 ♘e4! ♔h8 26 ♘g5!! (△ ♖xg5 27 ♖f3) 1-0 Shakarov - Rosentalis, corr. USSR 1986.

b32) **13 ... ♘exc5!** 14 ♗xh7+ ♔h8 15 b4!? ♕h4! 16 ♗d3 (16 bc ♕xh7=) 16 ... ♘xd3 17 ♕xd3 ♘c7 (17 ... ♕h7 18 ♕g3 ♗e2 19 ♖e1 ♗d3= *Schach Archiv*) 18 h3! ♗h5 19 f4 f5∞ Timman - Salov, St. John (m/4) 1988.

b4) **11 ♘e5!? ♗xe5** (11 ... ♗h5!? 12 cd cd 13 ♗xe4 de 14 ♕xe4 ♖e8⯑ Timoshenko -

Makarichev, Moscow 1990)
12 de ♘ac5 and now:

b41) **13 f3** ♘xd3 **14** ♕xd3
♘c5 **15** ♕d4 ♘b3 **16** ♕xg4
♘xa1 **17** ♗h6, Ljubojevic –
Hort, Amsterdam 1988, 17
... ♕b6+ **18** ♔h1 g6∞ Hort.

b42) **13 b4** ♘xd3 **14** ♕xd3
♗f5 **15** cd cd **16** ♕d4 ♖c8 **17**
f3 ♘g5 **18** ♗xg5 ♕xg5 **19**
♘d2 h5! **20** ♖ac1 h4 with
balanced chances in Hazai –
Vladimirov, Rotterdam 1988.

11 ♘c3

Or **11** c5?! ♗e7 **12** ♘e5 ♘c7
13 f3 ♘e6 **14** ♗e3 ♗g5!? **15** f4
♗f6! (15 ... ♗h6? **16** ♘c3 ♗d7
17 b4 ♗e8 **18** g4 g6± de Firmian – Kogan, USA Ch. 1986)
16 b4 g5 **17** g3 gf **18** gf, Ru-
sakov – Glek, corr. 1988, 18
... ♗xe5!? **19** de d4 **20** ♗c1
♔h8∓ Glek.

11 ... ♘c7
12 ♘e2

Or:

a) **12** ♕b3 ♔h8 **13** cd cd=
Sevillano – Wolff, Baguio
1987. If **14** ♔h1 ♕f6 △ **15**
♘xd5 ♕f7!

b) **12** ♖e1 ♔h8 **13** b4 ♗d7
14 ♗b2 ♗e8! △ ... ♗h5∞ Gufeld – Kochiev, USSR 1980.

c) **12 b4** ♘xc3?! (⌐ 12 ...
♔h8) **13** ♕xc3 dc **14** ♗xc4+
♘d5 **15** ♕b3 ♔h8 **16** ♗g5±
Gaprindashvili – Sternina,
USSR 1974.

d) **12 c5** ♗e7 **13** ♗f4 ♗e6 **14**
♗e5 ♗f6 **15** ♘e2 ♕e8 ⌐
♘xd4= H Franke – Demp-
ster, corr. 1990.

12 ... ♘e6
13 b4 ♔h8

13 ... ♗d7 **14** ♗b2 ♖f6 (⌐
14 ... ♘f4) Chandler – Dive,
Wellington 1988, see 12 ...
♘e6 in line D41.

14 ♗b2 ♕e8
15 ♖ae1 ♕h5
16 ♘e5 f4

17 f3 ♘4g5 **18** cd cd **19**
♗c1! (△ ♕b3)± Timman –
Salov, St. John 1988 (m/2).

D5
9 cd *(87)*

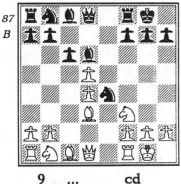

9 ... cd
10 ♘c3 ♘xc3

10 ... ♖e8!? – Suetin.

11 bc ♗g4

11 ... ♘c6 is an untested
possibility.

12 ♖b1

The same position may

occur by transposition as well: 9 ♘c3 ♘xc3 10 bc ♗g4 11 cd cd 12 ♖b1 (line D2). White's other tries:

a) The sly **12 ♗b1** must be met by 12 ... ♘c6! and not 12 ... ♗h5 13 ♕c2 ♗g6 14 ♕b3 b6 15 ♗xg6 hg 16 ♔h1 ♘c7 17 ♗a3 ♖e8 18 ♖ae1 ♖xe1 19 ♖xe1 a6 20 ♘e5± Tseshkovsky - Vladimirov, Tashkent 1987

b) **12 ♗c2** is best met by 12 ... ♗h5.

c) **12 h3** ♗h5 13 ♖b1 ♘d7 leads to the column.

Now Black has a choice:

D51: 12 ... ♘d7
D52: 12 ... b6

D51

12 ...   ♘d7
13 h3
Or:

a) After **13 ♖xb7?** ♘b6 threatens ... ♗c8, therefore the bishop must be expelled.

b) **13 a4** ♘b6?! (better is 13 ... b6 14 h3 ♗h5 see next var. d. 14 a4 b6) 14 a5! ♘c4 15 ♖b5 ♗c7 16 h3 ♗h5 17 ♗xc4 ♗xf3 18 ♕xf3 dc 19 ♗a3 ♖e8 20 ♖xb7± Filipenko - Kiselev, Moscow 1986.

13 ...   ♗h5
Or 13 ... ♗xf3 14 ♕xf3 ♘b6 15 g3! ♖c8 16 h4 ♖c7 17 h5± Dvoiris - Jakovich, Kiev Ch. 1986.

14   ♖b5
Or:

a) **14 ♖xb7** ♘b6 15 ♕d2! (15 ♗a6? ♕e8! 16 ♕c2 ♘c6 (... ♘c4) 17 ♕b5 ♕xc3 18 ♗b2 ♕c2∓ Sokolov - Rosentalis, Minsk 1986) and now:

a1) **15 ... ♕c8?!** 16 ♗xh7+ ♔xh7 17 ♘g5+ ♔g6 18 g4 ♕xb7 19 ♖e1!± △ gh+, ♕c2+; 16 ... ♔h8 17 ♖xb6 ab 18 ♗b1±.

a2) **15 ... h6!?** 16 ♖e1 ♕c8 17 ♗a6 ♕c6 (17 ... ♕f5? 18 ♘h4!±) 18 ♘e5 ♕xb7 19 ♗xb7 ♗xd1 20 ♗xa8 ♗xe5! 21 de ♗a4 22 ♗b7 ♗b5! 23 ♖b1 ♗c4 24 a3 (24 ♘e3) 24 ... ♖b8 25 ♗c6 ♖c8 26 ♗b5 ♖c5! 27 ♗xc4 ♘xc4 28 ♗f4 ♖a5! 29 h4 ½-½ Serper - Akopyan, Tbilisi 1989, 29 ... h5!∓

b) **14 a4** when:

b1) **14 ... b6** and now:

b11) **15 ♖b5** ♘f6 16 ♗g5 ♖c8! (16 ... ♗e7?! 17 g4! ♗g6, Glek - Raetsky, corr. 1988, 18 ♘e5 ♗xd3 19 ♕xd3±) 17 ♗xf6 ♕xf6 18 ♖xd5 ♗xf3 19 ♕xf3 ♕xf3 20 gf ♖xc3 21 ♖xd6(!) ♖xd3= Ivanchuk - Rosentalis, Lvov 1987

b12) **15 ♗f5!?** ♘f6 16 ♗g5 ♗c7 17 ♕d3 ♗g6 18 ♘e5

♗xf5 19 ♕xf5 ♖c8 20 ♗xf6 ♗xf6 21 ♘d7 ♖e8 22 ♖fe1 ♖xe1+ 23 ♖xe1 ♖xc3 24 ♕xd5± Kotronias - Arduman, Istambul 1988.

b2) **14 ... ♘b6** when:

b21) **15 a5** ♘c4 16 ♗xc4 (16 ♖b5?! ♘xa5 17 ♖xa5 ♗xf3! 18 ♕a4 ♗c7 19 ♖xa7 ♕d6∓ Ivanov - Kiselev, Moscow 1986) 16 ... dc 17 ♖b5 ♗g6 18 ♘e5 a6 19 ♖xb7 ♗xe5 20 de ♕xa5 21 e6 fe 22 ♕d4 ♖f7= Krugliakov - Kiselev, Moscow 1986.

b22) **15 ♔h1!?** ♖e8?! 16 a5 ♘c4 17 ♖b5 ♘xa5? (17 ... ♗b8!? 18 ♗xc4 ♗xf3 19 ♕xf3 ♕c7 20 ♗f4 ♕xc4 21 ♖fb1! ♗xf4 22 ♕xf4 ♖e1+ 23 ♖xe1 ♕xb5 24 ♕c7± Kiselev) 18 ♖xd5 ♗xf3 19 ♕xf3 ♕c7 20 ♖xd6! ♕xd6 21 ♕h5± Kozlov - Gorelov, Moscow 1986. We suggest 15 ... ♗g6!?, e.g. 16 a5 ♘c4 17 ♖b5 ♗c7 18 ♗xc4 dc 19 ♘e5 ♗xa5 (or 19 ... a6 c.f. var. b21).

b23) For **15 ♖b5** see next var. a 15 a4.

b3) **14 ... ♖b8** - *Schach Archiv*.

14 ...   ♘b6

a) **15 a4** a6 (⌐ 15 ... ♗g6 16 ♗xg6 hg 17 ♕b3 ♖e8 18 ♗g5 ♕d7 19 a5 ♘c4 Mestel - Miralles, Thessaloniki (ol) 1988, 20 ♖xb7 ♗c7! 21 ♕b5 ♕d6 22 ♖a1 a6 23 ♕b4 ♕c6∞ Miralles) 16 ♖b1 ♗xf3?! 17 ♕xf3 ♘xa4 18 ♖xb7 ♘xc3 19 ♗xh7+ ♔xh7 20 ♕xc3 (△ ♕c6, ♕d3+)± Kozlov - Gorelov, Moscow 1986; 16 ... a5!= (Rosentalis).

b) **15 c4!?** and now:

b1) **15 ... ♘xc4** 16 ♖xd5 (16 ♗xc4 ♗xf3) 16 ... ♗h2+ 17 ♘xh2! ♕xd5 18 ♗xc4 ♕xc4 19 ♕xh5± Dvoiris - Vladimirov, Barnaul 1988.

b2) **15 ... ♗xf3** 16 ♕xf3 dc 17 ♗c2 when:

b21) **17 ... a6?** 18 ♗g5! Belyavsky - Petursson, Reykjavik 1988.

b22) **17 ... ♖b8** 18 a4 a6? 19 ♗g5! ♕c7 20 ♗xh7+ ♔xh7 21 ♕h5+ ♔g8 22 ♗f6! ♗h2+! (22 ... gf? 23 ♕g4+ and mate) 23 ♔h1 ♕d6 24 ♗xg7!±± Kudrin - Machado, Thessaloniki (ol) 1988.

b23) **17 ... ♕d7** 18 a4 g6 (18 ... ♗c7 19 ♖c5! ♗d6 20 ♖g5, Adams - Anand, Oakham 1990, 20 ... g6∞; 19 g3 a6 20 ♖h5 g6 21 ♘h6 f5 22 ♗xf8 ♖xf8∞ Arakhamia - Akopyan, Oakham 1990; 18 ... ♖ab8 19 ♗g5!± Gavrilov - Frog, corr. 1989-90) 19 ♗d2 c3 20 ♕xc3 ♖ac8 21 ♕b3 ♖c7 22 ♗d3 ♖fc8 23 ♖e1 ♗f8 24 a5 ♘c4 25 ♗xc4 dc 26 ♖xb7

♛xd4= A Sokolov - B Fine-
gold, Reykjavik 1990.

b24) **17 ... ♛c7!?** - Gavrilov.

D52

12	...	**b6**
13	**♖b5**	**♗c7**

13 ... ♘c6? 14 ♖xd5! △
♗xh2+ 15 ♘xh2!±.

14 c4

Or 14 h3 a6! 15 ♖xd5 ♛xd5
16 hg∞ Short, e.g. 16 ... ♘c6!
17 ♘g5 h6 18 ♘e4 ♖ad8! 19
g5 ♖fe8 20 ♖e1 ♘xd4!=
Dvoiris - Rosentalis, Lvov
1990.

Alternatives after 14 c4:

a) **14 ... ♛d6** 15 ♖e1! (15
g3? ♛f6) ♗xf3 16 ♛xf3
♛xh2+ 17 ♔f1 ♘c6 18 ♖xd5±
♖ae8 when:

a1) **19 ♗e3?** g6? (19 ... f5!∓
△ ... ♘b4, ... ♘e7 or ... f4 -

Short) 20 a3!± (△ 20 ... f5 21
♛h3) Short - Salov, Am-
sterdam 1989.

a2) **19 ♖xe8!** ♛h1+ (19 ...
♖xe8? 20 ♖h5!) 20 ♔e2
♖xe8+ 21 ♗e3 ♛a1 (21 ... ♖e7
22 ♖d7!!±) 22 ♛f5! ♘xd4+
23 ♖xd4 ♛xd4 24 ♛xh7+
♔f8 25 ♛h8+ △ ♛xe8+!±±
Short.

b) **14 ... dc!** 15 ♗e4 ♘c6! 16
♖g5! (16 ♗xc6 ♛d6∓; 16 ♗a3
♛f6!∓) 16 ... ♗xf3 17 ♛xf3
♛d6 (17 ... ♘xd4?! 18 ♗xh7+!
♔xh7 19 ♛h5+ ♔g8 20 ♖xg7+
is equal - Timman) 18 ♖g3
(18 ♖h5 g6; 18 g3 ♘xd4 19
♛e3 ♖ae8 20 ♗a3 ♘e2+! 21
♔g2 ♛d4∓) 18 ... ♘xd4 19
♛g4 Short - Timman, Hil-
versum (m/4) 1989, 19 ...
♛e5 20 ♗f4 ♘e2+ 21 ♛xe2
♛xf4 22 ♗xa8 ♖xa8∓ Tim-
man.

29) 3 ♘xe5 d6: 6 ♗d3 ♗e7
Introduction

4	♘f3	♘xe4
5	d4	d5
6	♗d3	♗e7

One of the most popular lines.

7 0-0 *(88)*

Also to be considered:

a) **7 c4 ♗b4+** transposes to line A in Chapter 27.

b) **7 ♕e2 ♗f5** (for 7 ... ♘d6 c.f. line A) 8 ♘bd2 0-0! (8 ... ♘d6 9 ♗xf5 ♘xf5 10 ♕d3!±) 9 0-0 (9 ... ♘xe4?! de! 10 ♗xe4 ♗b4+ △ ... ♖e8) 9 ... ♘xd2=.

c) **7 c3** 0-0 8 ♕c2 f5 or 8 ... ♗d6 equalizes.

d) **7 ♘c3 ♘xc3** 8 bc c5=.

e) **7 ♘bd2 ♗f5** (best) 8 0-0 (8 ♕e2 0-0! see var. b) 8 ... ♘xd2 9 ♕xd2 ♗g6 10 ♘e5 0-0 11 ♖e1 ♘d7= as in Velikov - Spasov, Pamporovo 1981.

f) **7 h3** This is generally ignored, but the move fits into any structure and its advantage is that ... ♗g4 is prevented. For 7 ... 0-0 8

0-0 see 7 0-0 0-0 8 h3 line A in Chapter 30.

Now Black has:

A: 7 ... ♘d6
B: 7 ... ♗f5
C: 7 ... ♗g4

Or:

a) **7 ... 0-0** — see Chapter 30.

b) **7 ... ♘c6** — Chapters 31-35.

c) **7 ... ♘d7(?)** Irish master James Mason used to experiment with this. The knight is heading for f6. The disadvantage is that the e5 square will be weak. 8 c4 (also good is 8 ♖e1) when:

c1) **8 ... ♘df6** 9 ♘e5±.

c2) **8 ... c6** 9 ♘c3 ♘xc3 10 bc 0-0 11 ♖e1 ♗f6 (11 ... ♘f6!? ±) 12 ♗a3± Teichmann – Marco, Cambridge Springs 1904.

c3) **8 ... ♘ef6** 9 cd (also 9 c5) ♘xd5 10 ♘c3 ♘7f6 11 ♖e1 (11 ♘e5) 11 ... c6 12 ♗g5 ♗e6 13 ♘e5± Janowski – Mason, Hastings 1895.

A

```
7   ...      ♘d6
8   ♗f4
```

This rules out ... ♗f5. Other ideas:

a) **8 ♘c3** c6 9 ♖e1 0-0 10 ♘e2 ♘d7 11 ♘g3 ♖e8 12 c3 ♘f8 13 ♕c2 ♗g4? (⌓ 13 ... ♗e6 – Baranov) 14 ♘e5 ♗e6 15 f4 f6 16 ♘f3± Vasyukov – Bronstein, USSR Ch. 1972.

b) **8 ♘e5** 0-0 and now:

b1) Weak is **9 f4?!** f6 10 ♘f3 f5 or 10 ♕h5 ♘e4=.

b2) **9 ♕f3** c6 10 ♖e1± △ 10 ... f6? 11 ♘g6!

```
8   ...      ♗g4
```

Other interesting ideas:

a) **8 ... ♘c6** 9 ♖e1 (9 c3 is also good) 9 ... ♘b4? (Black falls for White's provocation) 10 ♗f1 ♗f5 11 ♘a3 ♘c4? 12 ♘xc4 dc 13 ♗xc4 ♘xc2 14 ♖e5 ♕d7 15 ♖c1 ♘b4 16 ♗xf7+ ♔xf7 17 ♖xe7+! 1-0 Salm – Garner, corr. 1959-62.

b) **8 ... 0-0** when:

b1) **9 ♘c3** c6 10 ♘e2! ♖e8 11 ♘g3 ♘d7 12 c3 ♘f8 13 ♕c2 ♘g6 14 ♗d2 ♗e6 15 ♖ae1± Torre – Balinas, Melbourne 1975.

b2) **9 ♖e1** ♗g4 (if 9 ... ♖e8 10 ♘e5) 10 ♘bd2 ♘d7 11 ♘f1 ♖e8± (Polugayevsky).

b3) **9 ♘bd2** ♘d7 10 c3 ♖e8! 11 ♕c2 ♘f8 12 ♖fe1 c6, Arnason – Karlsson, Iceland 1984, 13 ♖e2!?±.

```
9   ♘bd2     0-0
10  c3
```

A dual purpose move, reinforcing the d-pawn and permitting a choice of squares for the development of the queen at c2 or b3.

Or 10 ♖e1 ♘d7 11 ♘f1! ♘f6 (11 ... ♖e8!) 12 ♘g3 ♘h5 13 ♘xh5 ♗xh5 14 ♖e5 ♗xf3 15 ♕xf3± Dvoretsky – Schussler, Tbilisi 1980.

```
10  ...      ♘d7
11  ♕c2      g6
```

Benko suggests 11 ... h6.

```
12  ♖ac1     ♖e8
13  h3       ♗e6?!
```

Black's pieces become congested and get in each other's way 13 ... ♗xf3 must be correct here.

14 ♖fe1

♗xg6 is now threatened. The game Balashov - Benko, Lone Pine 1977 went: 14 ... ♘f8 15 ♘f1 c6 16 ♘g3 a5 (⊙ 16 ... b6 △ ... c5 - Benko) 17 h4!±. White has a slight initiative and his h4 pawn can hardly be captured as the black squares might remain without protection.

B

7 ... ♗f5
8 c4

8 ♖e1 ♘c6 is discussed, by transposition, in Chapter 32, line A: while 8 ... 0-0 in Chapter 30, line B2.

8 ... dc

9 cd ♕xd5 10 ♘c3 was threatened.

9 ♗xc4 ♘d7

Or 9 ... 0-0 10 ♖e1 ♘c6! 11 ♘c3 ♘d6 12 ♗d3 (if 12 ♗b3 ♗g4 13 ♘d5 ♗f6=, Tal) 12 ... ♗f6!= is Tal - Veingold, Tallinn 1981. We suggest 10 ♘e5.

10 ♖e1 0-0

11 ♗d5 (11 ♘c3 is also good) 11 ... ♘d6 12 ♘c3 ♖e8 13 ♘e5 ♘b6 14 ♗b3 ♗f6 15 ♗f4 ♗e6, Karpov - Panno, Buenos Aires 1980, 16 ♕f3±.

C

7 ... ♗g4 *(89)*

89
W

8 c4

Or:

a) **8 ♖e1** when:

a1) **8 ... f5?** 9 c4 c6 10 ♘c3 0-0 11 ♕b3±±.

a2) **8 ... ♘d6** 9 ♘c3 c6 10 ♕e2!± - Bilguer.

a3) **8 ... ♘c6(!)** see Chapters 32-35.

b) **8 h3** and now:

b1) **8 ... ♗xf3?** 9 ♕xf3 ♘c6 10 c3±.

b2) For **8 ... ♗f5** 9 c4 see line B, with White's 8 h3 as an extra tempo.

b3) **8 ... ♗h5** 9 c4 ♘f6 10 ♘c3 dc (10 ... 0-0? 11 cd ♘xd5 12 ♗xh7+! ♔xh7 13 ♘g5+!; ⊙ 10 ... ♘c6) 11 ♗xc4 0-0 12 g4! ♗g6 13 ♘e5 c5 14 dc ♕c7 15 ♗f4 ♕xc5 16 ♖c1± Ljubojevic - Handoko, Indonesia 1984.

8 ... 0-0

Or:

a) **8 ... c6?** 9 cd cd 10 ♕a4+/10 ♕b3±.

b) **8 ... ♘c6** and now:

b1) **9 ♖e1** transposing into Chapter 33.

b2) **9 ♘c3** See the game Ermenkov - Radulov (by transposition) in line C32 Chapter 31.

c) **8 ... ♘f6** 9 cd 0-0 transposes into the column, while 9 ♘c3 dc (9 ... 0-0) 10 ♗xc4 0-0 11 ♖e1 ♘c6, see line C2 Chapter 31.

> **9   cd   ♘f6!**

9 ... ♕xd5? 10 ♖e1 f5 11 ♕c2±±.

> **10   ♘c3   ♘xd5**
> **11   ♗e4**

Or:

a) **11 ♖e1 ♘c6** see (by transposition) line B in Chapter 33.

b) **11 h3 ♗e6!** (11 ... ♗h5? 12 ♗xh7+! ♔xh7 13 ♘g5+ wins).

After 11 ♗e4 Black may defend in three ways:

a) **11 ... ♘xc3** 12 bc (this position is much more favourable to White than after 9 ♘c3 ♘xc3) 12 ... c6 13 ♗f4!± ♕b1 is threatened, while 13 ... ♗d6? loses a pawn: 14 ♗xh7+! ♔xh7 15 ♗xd6 ♕xd6 (15 ... ♗xf3 16 d3+) 16 ♘g5+.

b) **11 ... c6** 12 ♕b3 ♘b6 13 ♗e3 ♘8d7 14 d5± (Sozin).

c) **11 ... ♗e6** when:

c1) **12 ♖e1 ♘c6** transposing into line B1 in Chapter 33.

c2) Only **12 ♕c2** is a promising alternative; after 12 ... f5 13 ♗d3! ♘c6 14 ♖e1 (threatening ♖xe6 and ♘xd5) 14 ... ♘db4 15 ♕e2 ♘xd3 16 ♕xe6+ ♔h8 17 ♖d1 ♘xc1 18 ♖axc1± Tseshkovsky - Dvoretsky, USSR 1975. The other alternative is 12 ... h6 13 ♖e1 ♘c6, see (by transposition) line B12, Chapter 33.

30) 3 ♘xe5 d6: 7 0-0 0-0
Mason's Defence

4	♘f3	♘xe4
5	d4	d5
6	♗d3	♗e7
7	0-0	0-0 *(90)*

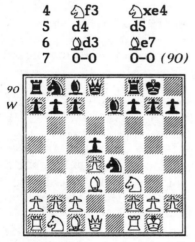

90
W

White has three tries for an initiative:

A: 8 h3
B: 8 ♖e1
C: 8 c4

Or 8 ♘c3 ♘xc3 9 bc c5! 10 ♖e1, Tukmakov - Meny, Leningrad 1974, 10 ... c4=.

A

8   h3
This prevents ... ♗g4,

though Black gains time.

8   ...   ♗f5

Or:

a) **8 ... ♘d7** 9 c4 c6 10 ♕c2 ♘df6 11 ♘c3 ♘xc3 12 bc h6 13 ♖e1 ♗e6 14 cd± Mednis - Paoli, Norristown 1973.

b) **8 ... ♗e6** 9 c4 c6 10 ♖e1 ♘f6 11 cd ♘xd5 12 ♘c3±.

c) **8 ... ♘c6** 9 ♖e1 and now:

c1) **9 ... ♘d6?!** 10 c3 ♗f5 11 ♗f4± Parma - Paoli, Reggio Emilia 1974.

c2) **9 ... f5** 10 c4±.

c3) **9 ... ♗f5** 10 c3 (10 c4 ♘b4=) 10 ... ♖e8 11 ♕c2 ♗g6 12 ♘bd2 ♘xd2 13 ♗xd2, Micheli - Toth, (m) Italy 1973, 13 ... ♕d6=.

d) **8 ... c5** 9 c4 (9 c3 ♘c6=) 9 ... cd 10 cd ♘f6 11 ♘xd4 ♘xd5 12 ♘f5 ♗xf5 13 ♗xf5 ♘c6= Estevez - Balshan, Graz 1972.

9   ♖e1
Or 9 ♘c3 ♘c6=.

9   ...   ♘d7?!
9 ... ♘c6 is best trans-

posing to above var. c. 8 ...
♘c6.

10 c4   c6

11 ♘c3 ♘xc3 12 bc ♗xd3
13 ♕xd3 dc 14 ♕xc4 ♖e8,
Mednis – Paoli, Reggio Emilia 1974, 15 ♗f4! and White
is slightly better.

B

8   ♖e1

Black's possibilities:

B1: 8 ... ♘f6
B2: 8 ... ♗f5
B3: 8 ... ♘d6

Not 8 ... f5 9 c4±.

B1

8   ...   ♘f6

And now White may de-
velop thus:

B11: 9 ♗f4
B12: 9 ♘e5

Or:

a) **9 ♗g5** ♘c6 10 c3 ♗g4 11
♘bd2 ♗h5 12 ♕b3, Sax –
Kapelan, Vrsac 1981, 12 ...
♖b8!± Sax.

b) **9 h3** c5 10 dc ♗xc5 11
♗e3 ♗xe3 with even chances
in Pyhala – M Markovic,
Kilton Cup 1986/87.

c) **9 ♘bd2** b6?! (9 ... c5) 10
♘f1 c5 11 c3 ♗g4? (△ 11 ...

♘c6±) 12 ♘e3! ♗xf3 13 ♕xf3
cd 14 ♘f5 ♖e8 15 ♕g3 g6 16
♗g5! ♘bd7 17 ♗b5±± Kuz-
min – Falkon, Nice (ol) 1974.

B11

9   ♗f4

Simple and good.

9   ...   ♗g4

a) 9 ... ♖e8 10 ♘bd2 ♘bd7
11 c4!? c5 13 ♕c2! dc 13
♗xc4± Marco – J Schwarz,
Vienna 1895.

b) 9 ... ♘c6 transposes to
line B in Chapter 32.

10 ♘bd2   ♗d6

Or 10 ... ♘bd7 △ ... ♖e8,
... ♘f8± is still playable.

11 ♗g3

⌐ 11 ♗e5

11   ...   ♗xg3

12 hg ♘c6 13 c3 ♕d6=
Lasker – Mason, London
1892.

B12

9 ♘e5   ♘c6!?

Recommended by Panov.
Others:

a) 9 ... c5?! 10 dc ♗xc5 11
♘c3 ♘c6 12 ♗g5 ♗e6 13 ♕f3
♗e7, Eisenberg – Pillsbury,
Monte Carlo 1902, 14 h3±.

b) 9 ... ♖e8 10 ♗f4 ♘bd7
11 ♘d2 ♗d6 12 c4!± Gaprindashvili – de Caro, Medellin
(ol) 1974.

10 c3

Or 10 ♘xc6 bc is equal.

10 ... ♘xe5

11 de ♘e8 12 ♕c2 g6 13
♗h6 ♘g7 14 ♘d2 ♖e8 15
♖ad1 ♗g4 or 15 ♘f1 ♗g5=.

8 ... ♘f6 is slightly passive.

B2

8 ... ♗f5
9 c4

Or:

a) 9 ♘c3 ♘xc3 10 bc ♗xd3
11 cd± Suetin.

b) **9 ♘bd2** ♘d6 10 ♘f1
♘d7 11 ♘g3 ♗xd3 12 ♕xd3
♖e8 13 ♗f4± Tseshkovsky -
Suetin, Dubna 1976.

9 ... c6
10 ♕c2!

Or:

a) **10 cd** cd 11 ♕b3 ♘c6! 12
♘c3 (12 ♕xb7? ♘b4∓) 12 ...
♗b4=.

b) **10 ♘c3** ♘xc3 11 bc
♗xd3 12 ♕xd3 dc 13 ♕xc4
♘d7 14 ♕b3!± Kavalek -
Pfleger, Montilla 1973.

c) **10 ♕b3** dc! 11 ♗xc4 ♘d6
when:

c1) **12 ♗f1** ♘d7 13 ♗f4 ♘b6
14 ♘c3 Tarrasch - Walbrodt,
(m) Nuremberg 1894, 14 ...
♗e6 15 ♕c2 ♘d5 nearly
equalizes - Panov.

c2) **12 ♗d3** ♗xd3 13 ♕xd3
♘d7, Timman - Stumpers,
Rotterdam 1969, Toth's 13 ...

♘a6 is close to equality.

10 ... ♘a6

11 a3 (threatens ♘c3) 11
... ♗g6 12 ♘e5±.

B3

8 ... ♘d6

Holding up c2-c4, but
the e5 square is weak.

9 ♗f4! ♘c6

Or 9 ... ♗g4 10 h3(!) ♗xf3
(10 ... ♗h5? 11 ♖e5±) 11 ♕xf3
c6 12 ♘d2 ♘d7 13 ♖e2 ♖e8
14 ♖ae1 ♗f8 15 ♕g3± Tim-
man - Hort, Bugojno 1978.

10 c3 ♗g4

This seems to be the
most accurate. After 11 h3
♗h5 12 ♘bd2 ♗g6 13 ♕c2
♕d7 14 ♘e5! ♘xe5 15 de
♗xd3 16 ♕xd3 ♘f5 17 ♘f3
slightly favours White,
Lanka - Mikenas, Riga 1978.

C

8 c4 (91)

And now:

C1: 8 ... ♘c6
C2: 8 ... ♘f6

Or:

a) **8 ... ♗g4** and now:

a1) **9 ♖e1** ♘f6 10 cd ♘xd5 11 ♘c3 ♘c6(!) transposes into Chapter 33.

a2) **9 cd** ♘f6 10 ♘c3 ♘xd5 11 ♗e4! see line D Chapter 29.

b) **8 ... c6** 9 ♘c3 (also strong 9 ♕c2) 9 ... ♘xc3 10 bc dc 11 ♗xc4 ♘d7 12 ♖e1 (12 ♗d3 ∠ c4, ♗b2, ♕c2 also good) 12 ... ♘f6 13 ♗d3 ♗e6 (⌐ 13 ... ♗g4) 14 a4± Mrdja - Paoli, Lublin 1978.

C1

8	...	♘c6
9	cd	

If 9 ♘c3 ♘xc3 (9 ... ♘f6 10 cd transposes to line C23 Chapter 31) 10 bc ♗e6!=.

9	...	♕xd5
10	♘c3	

Or:

a) **10 ♗xe4** doesn't gain a piece, e.g. 10 ... ♕xe4 11 ♖e1 ♕g6 12 d5 ♗h3 13 g3 ♖ad8 14 ♕b3 ♕f5! 15 dc ♖d3∓∓ Matulovic - Udovcic, Yugoslav Ch 1963.

b) **10 ♖e1** ♘f6 11 ♘c3 ♕d6 (11 ... ♕d8) 12 h3 a6 (12 ... ♗e6 △ ... ♖ad8) 13 ♗g5, Kupreichik - Mihalchishin,

Minsk 1985 13 ... ♗e6=.

10	...	♘xc3

11 bc ♗g4 12 ♖e1 (12 ♕e2) ♗xf3 13 ♕xf3 ♕xf3 14 gf±.

C2

8	...	♘f6

Black reinforces d5.

9	h3	

a) **9 cd** ♘xd5 10 ♘c3 when:

a1) **10 ... ♗g4** 11 ♗e4 see line C, Chapter 29.

a2) **10 ... c6** (passive) 11 ♘e4±.

a3) **10 ... ♘c6!** and now:

a31) **11 ♕b3** ♗e6= and not 12 ♕xb7? ♘db4∓∓.

a32) **11 ♗e4** is necessary, reaching (after ... ♗e6) one of the critical positions - see line D Chapter 29.

b) **9 ♘c3** when:

b1) **9 ... ♗g4?!** 10 h3 (10 cd ♘xd5 11 ♗e4± Tarrasch - Maroczy, Ostend 1905) and now:

b11) **10 ... ♗h5?** 11 cd ♘xd5 (⌐ 11 ... ♘bd7) 12 ♗xh7+! ♔xh7 13 ♘g5+ ♔g8 14 ♕xh5±± Tseitlin - Karasev, USSR Ch. 1971.

b12) Better is **10 ... dc** 11 ♗xc4 ♗xf3 12 ♕xf3 ♘c6 13 ♗e3 ♘xd4 14 ♕xb7, Schallopp - Mason, Breslau 1889, here we suggest 14 ... c5 ∠ ... ♖b8, ♕xa7 ♖a8 keeping the balance.

b2) **9 ... ♘c6!?** transposes into line C2, Chapter 31.

b3) **9 ... dc** 10 ♗xc4 ♗g4 11 ♖e1! ♘bd7 12 h3 ♗H5 13 g4 ♗g6 14 ♘e5± Ree – Langeweg, Amsterdam 1968.

9	**...**	**dc**
10	**♗xc4**	**♘bd7**
11	**♘c3**	**♘b6**

12 ♗b3 ♘bd5 (preventing ♗f4 – e5) 13 ♖e1 c6 14 ♗g5 ♗e6 15 ♖c1 ♖e8 (15 ... h6 16 ♘xd5 ♘xd5 17 ♗xe7 ♕xe7 18 ♗xd5 cd 19 ♕b3 ♖fc8±/= Kurajica – Ostojic, Belgrade 1978) 16 ♘e5 ♘d7 17 ♗xe7 ♖xe7 18 ♘e4! ♘f8 19 ♘c5 ♕e8 20 ♕f3 ♖d8?! (⌐ 20 ... ♖c8) 21 ♘xb7! ♖xb7 22 ♘xc6 ♖xb3 (22 ... ♖bd7 23 ♖c5!) 23 ♕xb3 ♖d7 24 ♕a3 ♕a8 25 b4± Sax – Korchnoi, Wijk aan Zee (m) 1991.

31) 3 ♘xe5 d6:
Jaenisch's 7 ... ♘c6

4	♘f3	♘xe4
5	d4	d5
6	♗d3	♗e7
7	0-0	♘c6! *(92)*

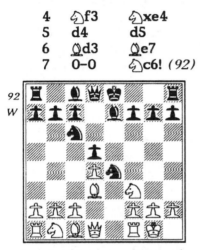

92
W

Jaenisch's recommendation from 1842. Black can undertake more active and demanding moves than castling, which is not that urgent.

With 7 ... ♘c6 Black contests the important d4 and e5 squares at once and threatens ... ♗g4. In addition, Black sometimes has ... ♘b4. Reflex responses like 8 a3 or 8 h3 are inferior at this particular stage of development.

White has tried:

A: 8 ♘c3
B: 8 c3
C: 8 c4

Other ideas:
a) For **8 ♖e1** see chapters 32-35.
b) **8 a3?** ♗g4 9 ♗e3 0-0 10 c4 f5∓ Penrose - Hooper, Buxton 1950.
c) **8 h3** This delays White's general development, e.g. 8 ... 0-0 9 ♖e1 (⌐ 9 c4 ♘b4=) 9 ... f5 10 c4 ♗e6 11 cd ♗xd5 12 ♘c3 ♗b4 13 ♕c2 ♘xc3 14 bc ♗xf3 15 cb ♗d5 16 ♕c3 ♕h4 17 b5, Teichmann - Hodges, Cambridge Springs 1904, 17 ... ♘xd4! 18 ♗b2 ♕g5∓∓.
d) **8 ♘bd2** ♘xd2 9 ♗xd2 ♗g4 10 c3 0-0 11 ♗f4, Mariasin - Dvoretsky, USSR 1979, and now one may transpose to line B by 11 ... ♗h5 12 ♖e1 ♗d6, giving equal chances

but with a more accurate move order.

A

8   ♘c3   ♗f5!?

Inferior are: 8 ... f5? 9 ♗b5±; or 8 ... ♘xc3 9 bc when:

a) **9 ... 0-0** 10 h3 (10 ♖b1) 10 ... ♗e6 11 ♖e1 ♕d7 (11 ... h6?! 12 ♘e5 ♘xe5 13 ♖xe5 ♗d6 14 ♖h5!? ♕f6? 15 ♗g5! hg 16 ♗h7+ Genova - Galobert, corr. 1956, mate in four moves follows) 12 ♗f4 ♖fe8 13 ♖b1 ♖ab8 14 ♗e3! ♗f6 15 ♘g5± Aronin-Zhilin, USSR 1959.

b) **9 ... ♗g4** 10 ♖b1 and now:

b1) **10 ... ♘a5?** 11 h3 ♗h5? (11 ... ♗xf3 is slightly better) 12 ♖e1 0-0 13 ♖e5! ♗g6 14 ♖b5 ♘c6 15 ♖exd5+±± Adorjan - Miles, Hastings 1973/74.

b2) **10 ... ♖b8** 11 ♖e1 0-0 12 ♗f4 ♕d7? (△ 12 ... h6 Adorjan =/±) 13 ♖e3! g5 14 ♗g3 f5 15 ♗e5 f4 16 ♖e1 ♗f6 17 ♗xf6 ♖xf6 18 h3! ♗h5 19 ♘e5 ♕e8 20 ♘g4 ♖e6 21 ♘f6+! ±± Browne - Murray, Vancouver 1971.

9   ♖e1

Or 9 ♕e1?! 0-0 10 ♘xe4 de 11 ♗xe4 ♗b4! 12 c3 ♖e8 13 ♗xf5 ♖xe1 14 ♖xe1 ♗d6 Bal-

ashov - Yusupov, Minsk 1982, 15 ♗g5 ∞.

9   ...   ♗b4
10 ♘d2

Or 10 ♗d2 ♗xc3 11 bc 0-0=.

10 ...   0-0
11 ♘dxe4 de
12 ♗xe4   ♘xd4=

B

8   c3

This seems harmless but needs to be treated with care.

8   ...   ♗g4

a) Simpler **8 ... ♗f5** 9 ♖e1 0-0 10 ♕c2, see 9 c3 in Chapter 32.

b) **8 ... ♕d6** 9 ♖e1 f5 10 ♘e5 ♘xe5 11 de ♕g6 12 ♗e3 0-0 13 f4 ♗e6 14 ♘d2 c5 ½-½ Rivera - Forintos, Benidorm 1983.

9   ♘bd2   ♘xd2

9 ... f5 (Keres) 10 ♕b3! ♖b8 11 ♘e1!±.

10 ♗xd2   0-0
11 h3   ♗h5
12 ♖e1

With alternatives:

a) **12 ... ♕d7?** Capablanca - Marshall, Havana 1913, and now 13 ♘e5! wins material, e.g. 13 ... ♘xe5 14 ♗xh7+! or 13 ... ♗xd1 14 ♘xd7 ♖fd8 15 ♘e5!

b) **12 ... ♗g6** 13 ♗xg6 hg 14

♛b3 ♘a5 15 ♕c2 ♖e8 (15 ...
♗d6) 16 ♗f4 ♗d6 17 ♖xe8+
♕xe8 18 ♗xd6± Efimov –
Zaura, Lvov 1976.

c) **12 ... ♗d6**=.

d) We suggest **12 ... ♕d6**.

C (Modern Treatment)
8 c4 *(93)*

White undermines Black's
central set up.

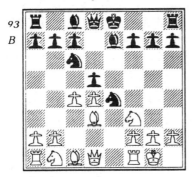

Black now has:

C1: **8 ... ♗e6**
C2: **8 ... ♘f6**
C3: **8 ... ♗g4**
C4: **8 ... ♘b4**

Or 8 ... 0-0 9 cd ♕xd5
and for 10 ♗xe4? or 10 ♘c3
see line C Chapter 30.

C1
8   ...   ♗e6
9   ♖e1 (!)
Feeble are:
a) **9 ♕b3 ?!** when:

a1) **9 ... dc?!** 10 ♕xb7! ♗d5
11 ♗xc4! ♘d6 12 ♗xd5 ♘xb7
13 ♗xc6+ ♔f8 14 ♗xb7 ♖b8
15 ♗c6± Jaenisch.

a2) **9 ... 0-0** 10 ♗xe4 (10
♕xb7? ♘b4 11 ♗xe4 ♖b8! 12
♕xa7 dc 13 ♘e5 ♖a8 14 ♕b7
♕xd4∓∓ Melignon – Sig-
walt, corr. 1958) 10 ... de 11
d5 ef 12 dc fg! 13 ♖d1 ♗d6 14
cb ♖b8 with a black king-
side attack.

b) **9 cd ♗xd5** 10 ♘c3 ♘xc3
(10 ... f5?! 11 ♕e2 ♘xc3 12 bc
0-0 13 ♖b1 ♕d7, Anderssen
– von Guretzky, Berlin 1865,
14 ♗b5!± △ c4 or ♘e5; however, 10 ... ♘f6 △ 11 ♘xd5
♕xd5! is good) 11 bc 0-0 12
♗f4± Löwenthal – Morphy,
London 1858 (m/13).
9   ...   ♘f6
Relatively best.
10   c5
Or 10 cd ♘xd5 11 ♘c3 0-0
12 ♗e4 ♗f6 and Black has
gained an extra tempo
compared to line B1 Chap-
ter 33!
10   ...   0-0
11   ♘c3   ♗g4
Or 11 h3 ♘e4! 12 ♘c3 f5=.
12   ♗e3   ♗xc5!
13   dc   d4
14   ♗xd4   ♘xd4
15 ♗xh7+ ♘xh7! 16 ♕xd4
♗xf3 17 ♕xd8 ♖fxd8! 18 gf
♘g5 19 ♖e7 ♖ac8 20 ♖e3 (20

♔g2? ♘e6!) 20 ... ♖d2 21
♘e4 ½–½ Short – Smyslov,
Hastings 1988/89.

C2

8   ...   ♘f6

A reliable defence al-
though analogous with the
previous line.

9   ♘c3

Or:

a) Kasparov's move order
9 h3 0-0 10 ♘c3 transposes
to line C22. For 10 cd see c.

b) 9 c5 0-0 10 ♗b5 ♘b8 11
♘e5 (11 a3) 11 ... c6 12 ♗d3 b6
13 cb ab= Chekhover –
Kamishov, Leningrad 1938.

c) 9 cd ♘xd5 10 ♘c3 ♗e6!
when:

c1) 11 ♖e1 0-0 12 h3 (12
♘e4 h6!=) and now:

c11) 12 ... ♖e8?! 13 ♔c2 h6
14 ♗b5± Ivanovic – Toth,
Catanzaro 1979.

c12) 12 ... ♗f6?! 13 ♘e4
♗xd4? 14 ♘eg5 h6 15 ♖xe6
hg 16 ♖xc6±± Adams –
Garcia Gonzalez, Lucerne
1989.

c13) 12 ... h6 13 a3 ♖e8 14
♘e4=.

c2) 11 ♘e4 ♘db4! (11 ... h6
12 a3 0-0 13 ♗c2!? ♕d7 14
♘g3 ♗d6 15 ♖e1 ♗xg3 16 hg
♗f5 17 ♗a4 △♘e5± van Mil
– Pujol, Amsterdam 1986) 12
♗b1 ♗g4 13 a3 ♘d5∞.

c3) 11 a3 0-0 12 ♕c2 h6 13
♖d1 can be considered.

d) 9 ♗g5 0-0 10 ♘c3 dc 11
♗xc4 ♘g4= Schmittdiel –
Hort, (m) Bad Neuenahr
1989.

9   ...   0-0

Other ideas:

a) 9 ... ♗g4 transposes to
line C3.

b) 9 ... dc 10 ♗xc4 and
now:

b1) 10 ... ♗g4? 11 d5! Ba-
logh – Keemink, corr. 1930.

b2) 10 ... 0-0 11 h3, Dvoiris – Klusevich, Leningrad
1979, we suggest 11 ... ♗f5.

c) 9 ... ♗e6 10 cd ♘xd5 11
a3 (⌂ 11 ♖e1 see line C23) 11
... ♕d7!?, where Black does
not rush to castle, 12 ♗b5
f6 Karpov – Larsen, Bugojno
1980.

Now White has a choice:

C21: 10 ♖e1
C22: 10 h3
C23: 10 cd

For 10 c5 ♗g4 11 ♗e3
♗xc5! compare line C1.

Or 10 ♗g5 see note d.

C21

10   ♖e1   dc

a) 10 ... ♗g4 11 cd see
Chapter 33.

b) 10 ... ♘b4?! 11 cd (11

♗f1) 11 ... ♘bxd5 12 ♕b3 c6 13 ♗g5± △ ♘e5 Pandavos - Jones, Thessaloniki (ol) 1988.

11 ♗xc4 ♗g4
12 ♗e3
12 d5 ♘a5 13 ♗e2 c6=.
12 ... ♗xf3
12 ... ♘a5?! 13 ♗d3 ♖e8 14 h3 ♗h5 15 a3 a6, Tal – Suetin, Sochi 1977, 16 b4 ♘c6 17 g4 ♗g6 18 ♗xg6 △ 19 d5± Suetin.

13 ♕xf3 ♘xd4
a) **14 ♕xb7 ♘c2 15 ♖ad1 ♖b8** Suetin, or even 15 ... ♗d6=.

b) **14 ♗xd4 ♕xd4 15 ♖xe7 ♕xc4 16 ♕xb7 c6! 17 ♕b3!? ♕xb3 18 ab ♖ab8! 19 ♖a3 ♖fe8=** Kasparov - Karpov, Moscow (m/30) 1984/85.

C22
10 h3
Good responses are:

C221: 10 ... dc
C222: 10 ... ♘b4

Not 10 ... ♗e6?! 11 c5± Averbakh and Taimanov.

C221
10   dc
11 ♗xc4 ♘a5
12 ♗d3 ♗e6
13 ♖e1

Or 13 ♗e3 ♘c4 14 ♕c2 ♘xe3 =/∞ Tal.
13 ...   ♘c6
13 ... c5 14 ♘g5 ♗c4 15 d5! h6 16 ♘ge4± Shamkovich; or 14 ♗g5 h6 15 ♗h4 c4 16 ♗xf6 ♗xf6 17 ♗e4± (van der Tak).

14 a3   a6
14 ... ♖e8? 15 ♗b5! ♕d6 16 ♗g5!± Lobron - Handoko, Zagreb/Rijeka 1985.

15 ♗f4
Or 15 ♗e3 ♘d5! 16 ♕c2 h6 17 ♖ad1 ♗d6= Ivanchuk - Romanov, USSR 1985.
15 ...   ♘d5
Feeble is 15 ... ♕d7 16 ♘e5! ♘xe5 17 de ♘d5 18 ♘xd5 ♗xd5 19 ♕c2 g6 20 ♖ad1± Kasparov - Karpov. Moscow (m/48) 1984/85.

16 ♗g3   ♗f6
17 ♗c2 ♘ce7 18 ♘e4 ♗f5 with even chances in Gufeld - Schüssler, Havana 1985; ⌐ 17 ♗e4.

C222
10 ...   ♘b4
11 ♗e2   dc
Other tries:
a) 11 ... ♗f5 and now:
a1) 12 ♗g5 dc 13 ♗xc4 c6 14 ♖e1! b5 15 ♗f1 ♖e8 (15 ... ♘c2? 16 ♘h4!) 16 ♖c1± Schlechter - Barry, Cambridge Springs 1904.

a2) **12 a3** ♘c6 **13** ♗f4 dc **14** ♗xc4± Dolmatov – Kjärner, USSR 1985.

b) **11 ... c5 12** a3 ♘c6 **13** dc dc **14** ♗e3 ± Velimirovic – Schüssler, Smederevska Palanka 1979.

12   ♗xc4   c6

Solid defence. More flexible:

a) **12 ...** ♘bd5 and now:

a1) **13** ♕b3 ♘b6!? **14** ♗d3 ♗e6 **15** ♕c2 h6 **16** ♖e1, Kislov – Manugaran, USSR 1987, 16 ... c5=; or 16 ♖d1!? c6!=.

a2) For **13** ♖e1 c6 see main line.

a3) If **13** ♘e5 c5.

b) **12 ...** ♘fd5 **13** ♖e1 (13 a3 ♘xc3! 14 bc ♘d5 15 ♕b3 ♘b6 or 15 ♕c2 ♗f6 keeps balance) **13 ...** ♘b6 **14** ♗b3 ♗f5 **15** ♘e5 ♘4d5± Hartmann – Gruen, Germany 1988.

13   ♖e1

Or 13 ♗g5 ♘bd5 (13 ... ♘fd5 simplifies) 14 ♕b3 ♘b6 15 ♗d3 ♗e6 16 ♕c2 h6 17 ♗d2 ♘bd5 18 ♘a4 ♕c8 19 ♘e5 ♖d8 20 ♘c5 ♗xc5 21 dc ♗xh3!? with counterplay in Gufeld – Andrianov, USSR 1980.

13   ...   ♘bd5

13 ... ♗f5 14 a3! ♘c2? 15 ♘h4!±±.

14   ♗g5   ♗e6

15 ♕b3 (15 ♕d2!?) and now:

a) **15 ...** ♖e8? **16** ♗xf6! gf (16 ... ♗xf6 17 ♗xd5 △ ♕xb7±) 17 ♘xd5 cd 18 ♗b5 ♖f8 19 ♘h4 ♔h8 20 ♗d3± Ornstein – Valkesalmi, Järvenpää 1985.

b) **15 ...** ♖b8 **16** ♘e5! ♖e8 **17** ♖ad1 ♕d6 **18** ♗h4± Hulak – Toth, Becici 1981.

c) **15 ...** ♕b6!? (Schwarz).

C23

10   cd   ♘xd5

Or 10 ... ♘b4 when:

a) **11** ♗c4 ♘bxd5 **12** ♖e1 c6 **13** ♗g5 ♗e6 **14** ♕b3 (compare 15 ♕b3 in main line C22) 14 ... ♘xc3? **15** ♗xe6± Unzicker – Rabar, Munich 1954; better was 14 ... ♕b6±.

b) **11** ♖e1 ♘bxd5 **12** ♕b3 c6 **13** ♗g5 h6 **14** ♗h4 ♘f4 **15** ♗f1 ♘e6, Belyavsky – Mascarinas, Lvov 1981, 16 ♖ad1±.

11   ♖e1

Or:

a) **11** ♕b3? ♗e6 **12** ♕xb7? ♘db4∓∓.

b) **11** ♗e4 ♗e6 **12** ♕d3 f5 equalizes, e.g. 13 ♘xd5 fe 14 ♘xe7+ ♘xe7 15 ♕xe4 ♗d5.

11   ...   ♗e6

11 ... ♗g4 see line B, chap 33.

12   a3

Or:

a) **12 h3** see var. c1 in line C2.

b) **12 ♘e4 h6=** Capablanca.

12	...	♗f6
13	♗e4	

If 13 ♘e4 ♗f5 is good.

| 13 | ... | ♘ce7 |

Inferior are:

a) **13 ... ♘xc3?** 14 bc ♗d5 15 ♗f4± Korbusov - Yuferov, Minsk 1983.

b) **13 ... ♘de7?!** 14 ♗g5! ♗xg5 15 ♘xg5 ♗f5? (⌐ 15 ... h6±) 16 d5 ♘xe4 17 ♖xe4 ♘b8 18 ♕h5 h6 19 ♖ae1 ♘d5 20 ♘xf7! ♘f6 21 ♘xh6+ ♔h7 22 ♕h3 1-0 Kudrin - Wolff, USA Ch. 1985.

| 14 | ♘g5 |

14 ... ♗xg5 15 ♗xg5 f6 16 ♗d2 ♕d7 17 ♕c2 f5 18 ♗f3 c6 Geller - Anand, India 1987, 19 ♘xd5 ♘xd5 20 ♖e5 (*Schach Archiv*) 20 ... h6!? △ ♖f6, ♗f7=. For 14 ♗g5, 14 ♕d3 or 14 ♕c2 compare with Chapter 33.

C3

| 8 | ... | ♗g4 |

One of the main lines.

The possibilities for White are:

C31: 9 cd
C32: 9 ♘c3

Or for 9 ♖e1 see Chapter 33 with transposition.

C31

9	cd	♕xd5
10	♘c3	♘xc3
11	bc	(94)

A critical position, now:

a) **11 ... ♗xf3** when:

a1) **12 ♕xf3!** ♕xf3 13 gf and now:

a11) After **13 ... 0-0-0**:

a111) **14 ♖b1!?** g6 15 ♖e1 ♗d6 (better is 15 ... f5) 16 ♗g5 ♖de8 17 ♖e3± Sax - Insham, Lugano 1984.

a112) We recommend: **14 ♗f5+ ♔b8 15 ♖b1** △ ♗e4.

a12) Or after **13 ... 0-0**:

a121) **14 ♗f4 ♗d6!** 15 ♗e3 ♘e7 (15 ... f5) 16 c4 ♘g6 17 ♖fb1 b6 18 a4 f5 with balanced chances as in Semenova - Ioseliani, USSR (m) 1983.

a122) **14 ♖b1 ♘a5** 15 ♖e1 ♗d6 16 ♗c3 b6 17 c4 ♖ad8 18

♗f1 ♖fe8 19 c5± Byrne -
Hector, Iceland 1984, better
is 14 ... ♖ab8, see next var
b1.

a2) **12 gf** 0-0 13 ♗f4 (better is 13 ♗e4 first) 13 ... ♗d6
14 ♗g3, Tarrasch - Bier,
Hamburg 1885, 14 ... f5 with
good counterplay.

b) **11 ... 0-0** when:

b1) **12 ♖b1** ♖ab8 13 ♖e1
♗xf3 14 ♕xf3 ♕xf3 15 gf
♗d6 16 f4± Purdy - Kerfil,
corr. 1948.

b2) **12 ♖e1** ♗xf3 13 ♕xf3
♕xf3 14 gf ♗d6 15 ♗e3 and:

b21) **15 ... ♖ad8** 16 ♖ad1
b6± Ehlvest - Yusupov, St.
John (m/4) 1988.

b22) **15 ... ♘e7** 16 c4 c6 17
♖b1 b6 18 a4± Timman -
Yusupov, Belfort 1988.

C32
9   ♘c3   ♘xc3
Or:

a) **9 ... ♗xf3?** 10 ♕xf3
♘xd4 11 ♕g4± Jurkov.

b) **9 ... ♘f6** 10 cd! ♘xd5
when:

b1) **11 ♖e1±** Sozin.

b2) On **11 ♗e4** Black has:

b21) **11 ... ♗e6** 12 ♕d3!
♘cb4 13 ♕e2 c6 14 a3 ♘a6 15
♘xd5 cd 16 ♗d3±.

b22) **11 ... ♘f6** 12 ♗xc6+ bc
13 h3 ♗xf3 14 ♕xf3 ♕d7 15
♗f4 0-0 16 ♗e5 ♖ab8 17 b3

♘e8 18 ♖fd1 f6 19 ♗g3 ♗a3
20 d5 c5 21 ♘e4 ♘d6 22
♗xd6 cd 23 ♖ab1 ♗b4 24
♕g3 ♖fd8 25 ♖bc1 ½-½
Chandler - Hort, German
League 1988/89.

b3) **11 h3** ♗e6 12 ♘e4 and
now:

b31) **12 ... ♘cb4** 13 ♗b1
♘f6 14 ♗g3 0-0 15 a3 ♘c6 16
♘f5 ♗xf5 17 ♗xf5 ♕d5 18
♗c2 ♖ad8 19 ♗e3, Byrne -
Henley, New York 1983, 19
... ♕d6 △ ... ♘d5=

b32) **12 ... h6** 13 a3 0-0 14
♗g3 ♗d6 15 ♗c2 ♘f4 16 ♖e1
♗d5 with level chances in
Kuczynsky - Handoko, Du-
bai (ol) 1986.

b33) **12 ... ♕d7** 13 a3 (13
♗b5 f6=) 14 ... ♗f5! 14 ♕b3
(⌐ 14 ♕c2) 0-0-0 15 ♕c2
♗g6 16 b4 ♘f6!= Hjartarson
- Mihalchishin, Hastings,
1988.

10   bc   0-0

10 ... dc can also be
played, and:

a) After Bilguer's **11 ♗e4**
gambit, we suggest 11 ...
♘a5∞.

b) **11 ♗xc4** 0-0 12 ♖e1
when:

b1) **12 ... ♘a5** 13 ♗d3 c5 14
♗a3!, Ermenkov - Radulov,
Vratsa 1975, 14 ... ♖e8 15
♗b5±.

b2) **12 ... ♕d6** 13 h3! ♗h5

14 ♖b1, Diaz – Lepeshkin, Managua 1984, 14 ... ♖ab8±.

b3) **12 ... ♗d6** 13 ♖b1 ♕f6 14 ♗d3 ♖ae8? 15 ♗g5! ♕xg5 (15 ... ♗xf3? 16 ♕d2!) 16 ♘xg5± Nicholson – Condie, London 1986.

b4) **12 ... ♖c8** 13 ♖b1 ♘a5 14 ♗d3 c5 15 ♕e2 ♗e6 16 ♘e5± Pyhala – Valkesalmi, Finland 1988.

11   ♖b1

Or:

a) **11 cd** ♕xd5 12 ♖e1 ♖fe8 13 ♗e4 ♕d6 14 ♖b1 ♖ab8 15 h3 ♗d7 16 ♕c2 h6± Matulovic – Capelan, Vrsac, 1981.

b) For **11 ♖e1** dc 12 ♗xc4 see earlier var. b 11 ♗xc4.

11   ...   dc

If 11 ... ♖b8? 12 ♖e1 ♗e6 13 ♕c2 h6 14 ♗f5± Steinitz.

12   ♗xc4   ♘a5

13 ♗d3 (or 13 ♗e2) 13 ... c5 14 d5 and White has a bit more space.

C4

8   ...   ♘b4 *(95)*

C41: 9 cd
C42: 9 ♗e2

C41

9   cd   ♘xd3
10   ♕xd3   ♕xd5

10 ... ♘f6? 11 ♕b5+ ♗d7 12 ♕b3! 0-0 13 ♘c3 b5 14 ♗g5

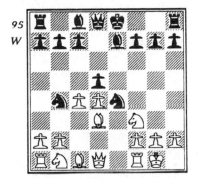

b4 15 ♗xf6!± Timman – Vl Kovacevic, Zagreb 1985.

11   ♖e1   ♗f5!
12   ♘e5

Or 12 ♘c3 ♘xc3 13 ♕xc3 when:

a) **13 ... c6?** 14 ♗h6! (Browne) and now:

a1) **14 ... gh** 15 ♖e5 ♕d7 16 ♖ae1 ♗e6 17 d5! cd 18 ♖xe6 fe 19 ♕xh8+ ♗f8 20 ♕f6±.

a2) **14 ... ♗e4** 15 ♗xg7 ♖g8 16 ♖xe4! ♕xe4 17 ♖e1 ♕xe1+ (17 ... ♕g4 18 ♕b4±) 18 ♕xe1 ♖xg7 19 ♕e5± Byrne and Mednis.

a3) **14 ... ♖g8** 15 ♖e5 ♕d7 16 ♖ac1 ♗e6 17 ♘g5!! 0-0-0 (◯17 ... ♗xg5±) 18 ♘xf7! ♗xf7 19 ♖xe7 ♕xd4 20 ♖xf7 ♕xc3 21 bc gh 22 ♖b1!± Browne – Bisguier, Chicago 1974.

b) **13 ... ♕d6?!** 14 d5! 0-0 15 ♗f4 ♕xf4 16 ♖xe7 ♖ac8 17 ♘d4± (if 17 ... ♗g6 18 ♘e6! wins) Todorovic –

Lalic, Yugoslavia 1989/90.

c) **13 ... ♗e6!** and now:

c1) **14 ♕xc7 ♗d6** 15 ♕c2 0-0 16 ♗d2 ♗f5 (16 ... ♕h5) 17 ♕b3 ♕xb3 18 ab f6⯑ Hübner – Smyslov, Velden, (m) 1983.

c2) **14 ♖e5** and:

c21) **14 ... ♕d7** 15 d5 ♗xd5 16 ♖xe7+! ♕xe7 17 ♗g5 f6 18 ♖e1 ♗e6 19 ♘d4 0-0-0= Gik – Baikov, USSR 1982.

c22) **14 ... ♕c6** 15 ♕e1 (15 ♕xc6 bc=) 15 ... 0-0-0 16 ♗g5 ♗xg5 17 ♖xg5 ♗d5 18 ♘e5 ♕b6 19 ♖xg7 ♖hg8= van der Wiel – Short, Biel (m) 1985.

12 ... g6

a) **12 ... ♗h4?** 13 g3 ♘xg3 14 ♕f3! ♘e4 15 ♘c3! ♘xc3 16 bc± Zuidema – Barendregt, Amsterdam 1967.

b) **12 ... 0-0-0?!** 13 ♕f3 g6 14 g4 ♗h4!, Halasz – Arhipov, Kecskemet 1984, 15 ♘c3! ♘xc3 16 bc ♗e6 17 ♕xd5 ♗xd5 18 g5± Arhipov.

c) **12 ... ♘d6?!** 13 ♘c3! ♕a5 14 ♕e(f)3± Gik.

d) **12 ... f6** when:

d1) **13 ♕f3** (Keres) 13 ... g6! 14 ♘d3! ♖d8 15 ♗e3 ♘c3 16 ♘d2 ♕xf3 17 ♘xf3 ♘e2+!∓ Carvalho – D Costa, Brazil corr. 1989.

d2) **13 ♘c3 ♘xc3** 14 ♕xf5 ♘b5 and now:

d21) **15 ♕h5+** g6 16 ♕h3 fe 17 ♖xe5 ♕xd4 18 ♕e6 ♕d1+ 19 ♖e1 ♕d7 20 ♗g5 0-0-0= Makropoulos – Toth, Budva 1981.

d22) **15 ♕g4 ♘xd4!** (15 ... fe? 16 ♖xe5 ♕xd4 17 ♖xe7+! ♔xe7 18 ♗g5+ ♔d6 19 ♖d1 c5 20 ♗e3 ♕xd1+ 21 ♕xd1 ♔c7 22 ♕c2±± Baulin – Glianetz, USSR 1986) 16 ♘d3 ♔f7! (16 ... ♘c2? 17 ♘b4! ♘xb4 18 ♕xb4± de Firmian – Plaskett, Copenhagen 1985) 17 ♖xe7+? ♔xe7 18 ♕xg7+ ♕f7 19 ♕g4 ♖d8 20 b3 ♕g6!∓∓ Ulibin – Serper, Sochi 1986.

13 ♕f3

Or:

a) **13 g4?** ♗h4 or ♘xf2! – Gik.

b) **13 ♘c3 ♘xc3** 14 ♕xc3 0-0-0= but not: 15 ♘xg6?! hg 16 ♖xe7 when Black plays 16 ... ♕d6!∓.

c) If **13 f3 ♘f6!**

13 ... ♕xd4

14 ♘c3 ♕xe5 15 ♗f4 (15 ♘xe4 0-0 16 ♗h6 ♖fe8 17 ♘g3 Grosar – Sifrer, Yugoslavia 1988, 17 ... ♕b5=) 15 ... ♕a5 16 b4! ♕a3! (16 ... ♕xb4? 17 ♘d5) 17 ♘d5 ♕xf3 18 gf ♗d8! 19 fe ♗e6 20 ♘xc7+ ♗xc7 21 ♗xc7 f6 22 a3 ♖c8 23 ♖ac1 ♔f7 ½-½ Belyavsky – Smyslov, Reggio Emilia 1986/87.

C42

9 &e2

Alternatives:

C421: 9 ... dc
C422: 9 ... 0-0

Or 9 ... &e6 when:

a) **10 ♘c3 0-0** transposes to line C422.

b) **10 c5 ♘c6 11 ♕a4** (Matsukevich's suggestion) **11 ... 0-0 12 b4 a6** is the best defence.

c) **10 a3 ♘c6 11 cd &xd5 12 ♘c3 ♘xc3 13 bc 0-0** see line C422.

C421

9 ... dc
10 &xc4 0-0
11 ♘c3

Or **11 ♘e5** and now:

a) **11 ... c6 12 ♘c3 ♘xc3 13 bc ♘d5**, Puc – Rabar, Sarajevo 1957, **14 ♕d3** △ **&b3 – c2±**.

b) **11 ... c5** can be considered.

c) **11 ... ♘c6?! 12 ♘xc6 bc 13 ♘c3 ♘d6 14 &b3 ♘f5 15 d5 c5 16 ♖e1 ♘d4 17 &e3±** Sindik – Iannaccone, Italy 1985.

d) **11 ... ♘d6!? 12 &b3 ♘f5 13 a3 ♘d5 14 ♘c3 &e6 15 ♖e1 c6 16 &c2 ♘c/=** Sindik – Zysk, Baden Baden 1985.

11 ... ♘d6

Kasparov's move. Feeble are:

a) **11 ... ♘f6 12 ♘e5±**.

b) **11 ... &f5 12 ♘e5 ♘c6 13 ♘xc6 bc 14 &e3±**.

c) **11 ... ♘xc3 12 bc ♘d5 13 ♕d3 c6 14 &b3 ♖e8 15 ♘e5 &f8 16 &d2 &e6 17 ♖ae1 g6 18 ♕f3±** Popovic – Kapelan, Vrsac 1989.

12 &b3 &f6

a) **12 ... &g4 13 h3 &h5 14 g4 &g6 15 ♘e5±** Vasyukov.

b) If **12 ... ♔h8** 13 h3 or 13 a3.

13 ♘e5

Or **13 h3 &f5 14 &e3 ♖e8** (14 ... ♘e4!?) **15 a3 ♘d3!?** (15 ... ♘c6 16 &a2/&a4±** Schach Archiv**) 16 ♖b1 c5 17 dc ♘e4** (17 ... ♘xb2? 18 ♖xb2 &xc3 19 cd!) **18 &c2! ♘xb2!∞** Karpov – Kasparov, Moscow 1985 (m/41).

13 ... ♘c6

a) **13 ... ♘f5? 14 ♘xf7! ♖xf7 15 &xf7+ ♔xf7 16 ♕b3+±±**.

b) **13 ... &xe5? 14 de ♘f5 15 &xf7+ ♔xf7 16 ♕b3+±±**.

c) **13 ... c5 14 &f4! c4! 15 ♘xc4 ♘xc4 16 &xc4 &xd4 17 ♘b5 ♘c6 18 ♘xd4!±** Kuznetsov – Matsukevich, corr. 1985.

14 &f4

14 ♘xc6 bc 15 &f4 ♘b5−.

14   ...   ♘f5
15   ♘xc6   bc
16 d5 Sokolov - Agzamov, Riga 1985, 16 ... ♗b7 (16 ... cd 17 ♘xd5±) 17 ♖c1 ♘d4 18 ♗e3 ♘b5 19 ♘xb5 cb 20 ♖c2 △ 21 ♕f3 with a slight advantage for White.

C422
9   ...   0-0
10   ♘c3
Or:
a) 10 ♘e5?! c5! 11 ♗e3 ♗f5 12 a3 ♘c6 13 ♘xc6 bc 14 cd cd 15 dc ♗xc5 16 ♗xc5 ♘xc5 17 ♘d2 d4∓ Nunn - Yusupov, Reykjavik 1988.
b) 10 a3 ♘c6 11 cd ♕xd5 12 ♘c3 ♘xc3 13 bc ♗f5 (13 ... ♗f6 14 ♖b1 a6 15 ♗f4 ♕a5 16 d5 ♘e7 17 c4 ♘g6 18 ♗d2 ♗c3 19 ♗c1 ♖b8 20 ♕c2 ♖e8 21 ♗d3 ♗d7= Saltayev - Forintos, Novi Sad 1990) 14 c4 ♕d6 (14 ... ♕e4?! 15 ♖a2! ♗f6 16 ♖d2 ♖ad8 17 ♗b2± Sznapik - Tischbierek, Warsaw 1990) 15 d5 ♘e5 16 ♘d4 ♗d7 17 ♖b1 b6 18 ♘b5 ♗xb5 19 ♖xb5 ½-½ Hjartarson - Yusupov, Barcelona 1989.
10   ...   ♗e6 (96)
10 ... ♗f5 is also good, e.g. 11 a3 ♘xc3 12 bc ♘c6 13 ♖e1 and now:
a) 13 ... ♗f6 14 ♗f4 ♖c8 15 ♕a4 a6 16 ♕b3 ♘a5 17 ♕b4

96
W

c5= 18 dc ♘c6 19 ♕b3 ♘a5 20 ♕b4 ♘c6 21 ♕b3 ♘a5 22 ♕b4 ½-½ Ljubojevic - Yusupov, Belgrade 1989.
b) 13 ... dc 14 ♗xc4 ♗d6 15 ♗g5 ♕d7 16 ♘h4 ♘a5 17 ♗a2 ♗g4= 18 ♕c2 ♖ae8 19 h3 ♗e6 20 c4 (20 d5? ♗xh3!∓) 20 ... ♗e7 21 ♗xe7 ♕xe7 22 ♘f3 ½-½ Ljubojevic - Yusupov, Barcelona 1989.
11   ♗e3
Or:
a) 11 a3 ♘xc3 12 bc ♘c6 13 cd ♗xd5! 14 ♕c2 (14 ♖e1 ♘a5 15 ♘d2 ♗f6 ½-½, Short - Seirawan, Biel 1985) 14 ... ♕d6 15 ♖e1 ♖ae8= Nunn - Halifman, Groningen 1988.
b) 11 ♘xe4 de 12 ♘e1 c6=
c) 11 ♖e1 ♗f5 (△ ... ♘xc3) 12 ♘xd5 ♘xd5 13 cd ♗b4!= Sherzer - Anand, London 1987.
d) 11 cd ♘xc3 12 bc ♘xd5 13 ♕c2 (13 ♗d2 ♘b6= Karpov) 13 ... c5! 14 c4?! ♘b4 15

♕e4 ♕d7, Ljubojevic – Seirawan, Brussels 1986, 16 ♗b2!
with even chances.

   11   ...   ♘xc3

Other moves:

a) **11 ... ♘f6** and then:

a1) **12 cd?!** ♘xc3 13 bc
♘xd5∓ Karpov.

a2) **12 a3** ♘xc3 13 bc ♘c6
14 cd ♗xd5= Karpov.

a3) **12 ♘xe4** de 13 ♘e1 c6
14 ♕b3 ♕e7 15 a3 (Karpov's
suggestion 15 ♖d1 △ a3, d5
can be met by 15 ... b5!?, e.g.
16 a3 ♘d3!) 15 ... ♘a6 16 ♘c2
♖fd8 (16 ... ♕d7 17 ♖fd1 ♘c7
∠ ... b5 – Karpov) 17 ♖fd1
♖ac8 18 ♕a4 c5! 19 ♖ac1 cd
20 ♘xd4 ♘c5! 21 ♕xa7
Ljubojevic – Karpov, Bu-
gojno 1986 with complica-
tions and slight advantage
for White – Karpov.

a4) **12 ♕b3** a5 13 ♘xe4 de
14 ♘e1 ♗xd4 15 a3 ♗xe3 16
♕xe3 ♘c6 17 ♕xe4 ♕f6∓
Kuczynski – Garcia Gonza-
lez, Polanica Zdroj 1987.

a5) **12 ♕a4** ♘xc3 (12 ... a5)
13 bc ♘c6 14 ♖ab1 (14 ♖fd1
a6 △ 15 cd b5) when:

a51) **14 ... ♖b8** 15 ♖fd1 ♖e8
16 cd ♗xd5 17 c4 ♗e4 18
♖bc1 ½–½ Chandler – Ribli,
German League, 1986/87.

a52) **14 ... ♕d7** 13 ♕a3 (15
♖xb7? ♘xd4!, but 15 ♔h1!?)
15 ... b6 (15 ... ♖b8) 16 cd

♗xd5 17 c4 ♗xf3 18 ♗xf3
♖ad8 19 d5 ♘e5 20 ♗e2 ♕d6!
21 c5! ♕xd5 22 ♕xa7 ♖a8 23
♕xc7 ♕xa2 24 ♖fe1 bc=
Kudrin – Seirawan, New
York 1987.

a6) **12 ♖c1** c5!? 13 a3 cd 14
♘xd4 ♗xd4 15 ♗xd4 ♘xc3
16 ♖xc3 ♘c6 17 cd ♘xd4±/=
Ljubojevic – Christiansen,
Linares 1985.

b) after **11 ... ♘f5**:

b1) **12 ♕b3** when:

b11) **12 ... dc** 13 ♗xc4 a5!
14 a3 (14 ♘e5 ♘d6!) 14 ...
♘d2! 15 ♗xd2 (15 ♘xd2 ♗c2
16 ab – Timman) 15 ... ♗c2 16
♗xf7+ (◠ 16 ab!? ♗xb3 17
♗xb3 ♗xb4 18 ♗g5!±) 16 ...
♖xf7 17 ♕e6 ♗f5 18 ♕b3 (18
♕e5 ♗d6) 18 ... ♗c2 19 ♕e6
½–½ Efimenko – Vzdvizkov,
corr. 1989; inferior is 14 ...
♘xc3?! 15 ab! b5 16 ba bc 17
♕xc3± Timman – Hjartar-
son, Rotterdam 1989.

b12) **12 ... c6** and now:

b121) **13 c5!?** ♘xc3 (13 ...
a5 14 ♖ac1 ♕c7 15 ♘a4 ∠
a3± Timman) 14 bc ♘c2 15
♖ac1 ♘xe3 16 fe ♗e4! △ 17
♕xb7 ♗g5!∓.

b122) **13 ♖ac1** dc 14 ♗xc4
b5?! 15 ♗xf7+! ♖xf7 16 ♘e5,
Halifman – Arhipov, Mos-
cow 1985, and now 16 ...
♕e8 doesn't help because
of 17 g4!

b123) **13 cd** cd 14 Racl a5 15 a3 Nxc3 16 Rxc3 a4 17 Qd1 Nc6 (Mazukevich) 18 Bb5!?± van der Vliet.

b2) **12 a3** Nxc3 13 bc Nc2 14 Ra2 Nxa3 (14 ... Nxe3 15 fe±) 15 Rxa3! Bxa3 16 c5 A Ivanov – Arhipov, USSR 1985, 16 ... b5! 17 Qb3 (17 Bxb5?! Rb8 18 Qa4 Bb2 19 Bd2 Bc2!∓) 17 ... Bxc5 18 dc c6 19 Nd4 Bd7 20 Bf4 a5∞ Ivanov.

b3) **12 Rc1** dc (12 ... Nxc3 13 bc Nxa2 14 Rc2! Bxc2 15 Qxc2 Nxc3 16 Qxc3 c6 17 Rb1 a5! 18 Rxb7 a4 19 Ne5 Bd6 20 Nxc6 Qc8 21 Rb6 Ra6 22 c5 Rxb6 23 cb Qb7± Short – Timman, Hilversum (m/6) 1989) 13 Bxc4 c6 14 Ne5! Nxc3 15 bc Nd5 16 Qf3± Hubner – Timman, Sarajevo 1991.

c) **11 ... f5** and:

c1) **12 Qb3** (12 Ne5 dc!) Nxc3 13 bc dc 14 Bxc4 Bxc4 15 Qxc4+ Qd5 16 Qe2 Nc6 17 c4 Qe4!∓ Zagrebelny – Agzamov, Tashkent, 1988.

c2) **12 cd** Nxd5 13 Nxd5 Bxd5 14 Bf4 (△ Be5), Dvoiris – Sorokin, USSR 1990, 14 ... Bd6=.

c3) **12 a3** Nxc3 13 bc Nc6 when:

c31) **14 cd** Bxd5 and now:

c311) **15 c4** Bxf3 16 Bxf3 f4 17 Bd5+ Kh8 18 Bc1 Nxd4! 19 Rb1 Bc5 20 Rxb7 f3! 21 Bxf3 Nxf3+, ½-½ Hübner – Yusupov, Rotterdam 1988, 22 gf Bd6∞.

c312) **15 Qc2** Kh8 16 Rfd1 Qd7! (16 ... Nf6? 17 Ne5±) 17 Bf4 Bd6 18 Ne5 (⌐ 18 Bxd6=) 18 ... Bxe5 19 de Qe6 20 c4 Be4 21 Qc3 Ne7 22 Rd4 Rae8∓ Belyavsky – Yusupov, Barcelona 1989. The e5 pawn is feeble.

c313) **15 Bf4** Bd6 (15 ... Bf6!?) 16 Bxd6 (16 Qd2 Bxf4 17 Qxf4 Qd6!=) 16 ... Qxd6 17 Nd2, Dvoiris – Mihalchishin, Lvov 1990, 17 ... Na5 18 Qa4 b6 19 Bf3 c5= Mihalchishin.

c32) After **14 Qa4** f4 (14 ... Rb8∞ Madl – Solomon, Sydney 1990):

c321) **15 Bd2** Kh8 16 Rab1 (16 Rfe1 dc 17 Bxc4 Bg4 18 Be2 a6 19 h3 Bh5 20 Nh2 Bxe2= Bönsch – Tischbierek, Germany 1989) 16 ... Rb8 17 Rfe1 dc 18 Bxc4 Bg4 19 Be2 a6= (19 ... Bd6 20 h3 Bh5 21 Rb5! Be8 22 Qc2 a6 23 Rf5!± Karpov – Seirawan, Brussels 1986) 20 h3 Bh5 21 Ng5? (21 Rbd1) 21 ... Bxe2 22 Ne6 Qd5! 23 Rxe2 f3!∓ Rohde – Seirawan, USA Ch. 1986.

c322) **15 Bc1!?** a6 (15 ...

♚h8 16 ♖b1 ♖b8 17 ♖e1 a6 18
♗d3± Kayumov – Serper,
USSR 1987) 16 ♖e1 ♚h8 17
♗d3 ♗g4 18 cd ♗xf3= Mar-
tin del Campo – Guill. Garcia, Santa Clara 1990.

c33) **14 ♖b1** f4 (14 ...
♖b5!?) 15 ♗c1 ♖b8 16 ♖e1 dc
17 ♕a4 ♚h8 18 ♗xc4 ♗f5 19
♖b2 a6 20 ♗f1 b5∞ Zapata –
Guill. Garcia, Santa Clara
1990.

d) **11 ... ♘f6** 12 a3 ♘c6 13 b3
♘e4 14 ♘xe4 de 15 d5 ef 16
♗xf3 ♗d7 17 dc ♗xc6 18
♗xc6 bc 19 ♕f3 ♕d3! 20
♖ab1 ♕g6 21 a4 a5 22 ♗f4
♗d6= Sokolov – Smyslov.
Moscow 1987.

12	**bc**	**♘c6**
13	**cd**	**♗xd5!**

14 ♕c2 (14 ♘d2 f5) 14 ...
♗f6 15 ♘d2 ♖e8 16 ♖ae1 ♗e6
17 ♗d3 g6, Ehlvest – Yusupov, St. John (m) 1988, 18
♘e4±; better is 14 ... f5 –
Yusupov, transposing to
var. c13 above 15 ♕c2.

32) 3 ♘xe5 d6:
Löwenthal's 8 ♖e1

4	♘f3	♘xe4
5	d4	d5
6	♗d3	♗e7
7	0-0	♘c6
8	♖e1	(97)

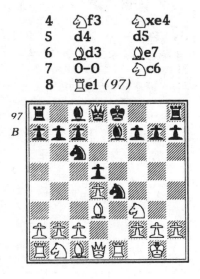

97
B

A: 8 ... ♗f5
B: 8 ... ♗g4

Or:

a) **8 ... f5?** 9 c4! ♗e6 (9 ... ♘b4 10 ♗f1±) 10 cd ♗xd5 11 ♘c3 ♘xc3 12 bc 0-0 Löwenthal - Morphy, London 1858, 13 ♘e5 ♘xe5 14 ♖xe5 △ ♕e2± Maroczy.

b) **8 ... ♘f6** and now:

b1) **9 c3** ♗g4 10 ♗g5 0-0 11 ♘bd2 ♗h5 12 ♕b3 Sax, - Kapelan, Vrsac 1981, 12 ... ♖b8!± Sax.

b2) **9 ♗f4** 0-0 10 c3 ♗d6 (⌐10 ... ♘g4) 11 ♘e5± Tarrasch - Walbrodt, Nuremberg 1894.

b3) **9 c4** ♗g4 see Chapter 33.

c) **8 ... ♘d6** (Directed against c2 - c4 and preparing ... ♗f5. But it is passive and gives up the e5 square, just as 7 ... ♘d6 does) 9 ♗f4 (also 9 ♘c3 ♗e6 10 ♘e2 {Steinitz} 10 ... ♗f5 11 ♘g3 ♗xd3 12 ♕xd3 0-0 13 ♘e5±) 9 ... 0-0 10 c3 and now follows:

c1) **10 ... ♗g4** 11 h3 ♗h5 12 ♘bd2 ♗g6, Lanka - Mikenas, Riga 1978, 13 ♗xg6 hg 14 ♕b3!±.

c2) **10 ... ♗e6** 11 ♘bd2 ♕d7 12 ♘f1 f5? (⌐12 ... ♖e8± - Byrne) 13 ♕e2! ♘e4 14 ♘e5 ♘xe5 15 ♗xe5 ♗f6 16 ♗xf6 ♖xf6 17 f3± R Byrne - Reshevsky, USA Ch. 1972.

A

8   ...   ♗f5 *(98)*

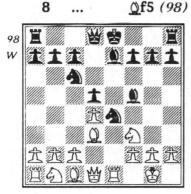

Transposed   positions
(e.g. after 7 ... ♗f5 8 ♖e1
♘c6; 7 ... 0-0 8 ♖e1 ♗f5) are
also discussed here.

White may try:

A1: 9 ♘bd2
A2: 9 a3
A3: 9 c4
A4: 9 ♗b5

Or:

a) **9 c3** 0-0 10 ♕c2 (10
♘bd2? ♘xf2!) 10 ... ♖e8 11
♗f4 ♗d6 12 ♗xd6 ♕xd6 13
♘bd2 ♘xd2 14 ♕xd2 ♗xd3
15 ♕xd3 a6= Fedorowicz –
Reshevsky, USA Ch. 1981.

b) **9 ♘c3!?** ♘xc3 10 bc
♗xd3 when:

b1) **11 cd** (Kasparov's
suggestion) 11 ... 0-0 12 ♕b3
♖h8 13 ♘e5 ♘xe5 14 ♖xe5
c6 15 ♗a3 ♗f6 16 ♗xf8
♗xe5= Kristensen – Schüss-

ler, Scandinavian Ch. 1981.
We suggest 13 ♖e2.

b2) **11 ♕xd3** 0-0 and now:
b21) **12 c4** ♗f6!? 13 ♗a3?
♘xd4! – Adorjan.
b22) **12 ♖b1** now ♖b8 is
best.

A1

9   ♘bd2   ♘xd2

9 ... ♘d6?! 10 ♘f1 0-0 11
♘g3 ♗g6 12 c3 ♗f6 13 ♗f4±
Akopyan – Sorokin, USSR
1985.

10   ♕xd2

Or 10 ♗xf5 ♘xf3+ 11 gf
0-0 △ ... ♗d6∓.

10   ...   ♗xd3
11   ♕xd3   0-0
12   c3

Or 12 ♗d2 ♗f6 13 ♘e5
(Lasker).

If 12 ♗f4:

a) **12 ... ♕d7** 13 ♖e2 a6 14
♖ae1 ♖ae8 15 c3 ♗d8 16
♖xe8 transposes to note to
column's 16th move.

b) **12 ... a6** 13 ♖e3 ♕d7 14
♖ae1 ♖fe8 15 ♕e2 ♗f8 16 c3
♗d6 17 ♗xd6 cd 18 ♘g5±
Hazai – Plaskett, Plovdiv
1984.

c) **12 ... ♗d6** 13 ♗xd6 (13
♘g5 g6 14 ♕d2 ♕f6= Kava-
lek – Reshevsky, USA Ch
1981) 13 ... ♕xd6= Gipslis –
Tal, Tallinn 1981.

12   ...   ♕d7

After 12 ... ♛d6:

a) **13 ♕f5!** ♖ad8 14 ♗f4, ½-½ Adorjan – Hübner, (m/8) 1980, 14 ... ♛d7 15 ♕xd7 ♖xd7 16 ♖e2±.

b) **13 ♘e5** is also good.

13 ♗f4   a6

a) If **13 ... ♖fe8**:

a1) **14 h3?!** a6 15 ♖e3 ♗d6 16 ♘g5 g6 17 ♗xd6 ♛xd6 18 ♖ae1 ♛d7= Adorjan – Hübner, (m/10) 1980.

a2) White by **14 ♛b5**, can fight for an opening advantage.

b) **13 ... ♗d6** seemingly good but not right, e.g.:

b1) **14 ♘e5** ♗xe5 15 de± or

b2) **14 ♘g5!** g6 15 ♗xd6 ♛xd6 16 ♛h3 h5 17 ♛f3 (17 ♘e6!? – T Horvath) 17 ... ♛d7 18 ♘h3! ♖ae8 19 ♘f4!± Lukov – Govedarica, Belgrade 1982.

14 ♖e3   ♖ae8
15 ♖ae1   ♗d8
16 h3

Or:

a) **16 ♖xe8** ♖xe8 17 ♖xe8+ ♛xe8 18 ♛f5 ½-½ Ljubojevic – Hort, Amsterdam 1981.

b) **16 ♘e5** ♘xe5 17 de ♛b5= Kavalek – Smyslov, Amsterdam 1981.

c) **16 ♛e2** ♖xe3 17 ♛xe3 ♛f5=.

16 ...   ♖xe3
17 ♖xe3

If 17 ♛xe3 ♛f5! with counterplay.

Kasparov – Karpov, Moscow 1981 continued 17 ... f6 18 ♖e2 ♖f7 (18 ... ♖e8?! 19 ♖xe8+ ♛xe8 20 ♛f5±) 19 ♘d2!±/=.

A2

9 a3   0-0

Or 9 ... ♘d6 10 ♗xf5 ♘xf5 11 ♛d3 ♛d7 12 ♘c3 (△ 13 ♘e5) 12 ... g6 13 b4 f6 14 ♗f4 0-0-0 15 b5 ♘a5 16 g4 ♘g7 17 ♘xd5∞ Hulak – Henley, Surakarta/Denpasir 1982.

10 c4   ♗f6

If 10 ... ♖e8?! 11 ♘c3!

After 10 ... ♗f6 11 ♘c3 ♘xc3 12 bc ♗xd3 13 ♛xd3 dc 14 ♛xc4 ♘a5 15 ♛a4 b6 16 ♗f4 ♛d5 17 ♗xc7 ♖ac8 18 ♗e5 ♖xc3 19 ♗xf6 gf 20 ♖ac1 ♖xc1 21 ♖xc1 ♖d8! 22 h3 (22 ♖c3) 22 ... ♛b3! ½-½ Kavalek – Karpov, Torino 1982.

A3

9 c4   ♘b4

9 ... 0-0 also deserves attention when:

a) **10 cd** ♛xd5 11 ♘c3 (11 ♛e2 ♘f6 12 ♘c3 ♗xd3 13 ♛xd3 promises more – *Schach Archiv*; 11 ♗xe4=) 11 ... ♘xc3 12 bc and now:

a1) **12 ... ♗xd3** (12 ... b5!?)

13 ♕xd3 b5 (13 ... ♗f6!) 14
♗f4 ♗d6 15 ♘g5 g6 16 ♕h3
h5 17 ♘e4 ♔g7 18 ♕e3±
Abramovic - Radulov, Vrn-
jacka Banja 1983.

a2) **12 ... ♖fe8** 13 ♗f4!
♗xd3 (13 ... ♗d6? 14 ♖xe8+
♖xe8 15 c4±) 14 ♕xd3 ♕d7
15 ♖b1 b6 16 d5 ♖ad8 17 c4
♗f6 18 ♗g5! ♘b4 19 ♕d2±
Matulovic - Kapelan, Vrsac
1985.

b) **10 ♘c3 ♘xc3** 11 bc
♗xd3 12 ♕xd3 dc 13 ♕xc4
♗d6 (13 ... ♕d7 14 ♖b1±
Timman) 14 ♖b1 ♖e8 15 ♗e3!
Timman - van den Sterren,
Dutch Ch. 1983, and now 15
... ♕d7 holds Black's position.

10 ♗f1! (99)

If 10 cd? ♘xf2!∓.
Now Black can choose:

A31: 10 ... dc
A32: 10 ... 0-0

Or 10 ... ♘f6?! 11 ♘h4!
♗e4 12 ♘c3±.

A31

10 ...   dc?!
11 ♘c3

Feeble is 11 ♗xc4? 0-0 12
a3, e.g. 12 ... ♘d6! 13 ♗b3
♘d3∓ Reshetnikov - Gaiser,
corr. 1981.

11 ...   ♘f6

11 ... ♘xc3?! 12 bc ♘d5 (13
... ♘c2? 13 ♖e5 ♕d7 14 ♕e2!
♘xa1 15 ♗a3±± Karpov; 13
... ♘d3? 14 ♗xd3 cd 15
♗a3±±) 13 ♗xc4 ♗e6, Braga
- Sariego, Manzanillo 1983,
14 ♕b3!± Karpov.

12 ♗xc4   0-0
13 a3   ♘c6

13 ... ♘c2? 14 ♘h4!
Karpov - Portisch, Til-
burg 1982 went 14 d5 ♘a5 15
♗a2 c5 16 ♗g5! ♖e8 (⌐ 16 ...
h6) 17 ♕a4! (△ 18 d6) 17 ...
♗d7 18 ♕c2 h6 19 ♗h4 ♘xd5
20 ♘xd5 ♗xh4 21 ♖xe8+
♗xe8 22 ♕e4? ♗f6 ∞/∓;
better is 22 ♖e1!±.

A32

10 ...   0-0
11 a3   ♘c6
12 ♘c3

Or 12 cd ♕xd5 13 ♘c3
♘xc3 14 bc when:
a) **14 ... b5?** 15 ♘e5! ⌐
♘xc6 or g4, ♗g2±.

b) **14 ... ♗g6?!** 15 c4 ♕d7
(15 ... ♕d6) 16 d5 ♗f6 17 ♖a2
♘a5 18 ♗f4± Karpov - Por-
tisch, Lucerne 1982.

c) **14 ... ♕d6** 15 a4 ♖fe8 16
♕b3 b6 17 ♗a3 ♕f6 18 ♗xe7±
Lobron - Schüssler, Ger-
many 1983.

d) **14 ... ♗f6** 15 ♗f4 ♕d7
(15 ... ♘a5?! 16 ♗xc7 ♖ac8 17
♗e5!±) 16 ♗g5 ♗xg5 17 ♘xg5
♖ae8 18 ♕b3 ♘a5 19 ♕b4 b6
20 ♘f3 f6!= Glek - Antonov,
USSR 1984.

| 12 | ... | ♘xc3 |
| 13 | bc | dc |

13 ... ♗e6? 14 cd ♗xd5 15
♘d2!± (Karpov).

13 ... ♗f6 is good and
after 14 cd transposes into
var. d 14 ... ♗f6.

| 14 | ♗xc4 | ♘a5 |

Prepares c5. Others:

a) **14 ... ♗d6** 15 ♗g5 ♕d7 16
♘h4 ♘a5 17 ♗a2 b5 (If 17 ...
♗g4 18 ♕d3 {18 f3 ♗e6 19 d5
♗f5= Hübner} 18 ... ♖fe8 19
h3! ♗h5 20 ♕f5±) 18 a4!±
Karpov - Portisch, Torino
1982.

b) **14 ... ♗f6** 15 ♗f4 ♕d7 16
♘g5 ♘a5 17 ♗a2 c5! 18 ♖c1
(we prefer 18 ♘e4) 18 ... c4!
19 ♘e4 ♗e7 20 a4 ♖fe8=
Yurtayev - Makarichev, Jurmala 1983.

| 15 | ♗a2 | c5! |

16 ♘e5! ♗f6 17 g4! ♗d7 18

♗f4± Ehlvest - Halifman,
Minsk 1987.

A4

| 9 | ♗b5 | ♗f6! |

9 ... 0-0 10 ♗xc6 bc 11
♘e5 ♗h4! 12 ♗e3 and now:

a) **12 ... ♕d6?** 13 ♕h5±
Timman - Portisch, Mos-
cow 1981.

b) **12 ... ♖e8!?** (Makarichev) △ ... ♖e6 or ... c5
equalizes.

| 10 | ♘bd2 |

Leading to nothing are:

a) **10 ♘e5** (10 c4 0-0=) 10
... ♗xe5 11 de 0-0 12 f3
♘c5=.

b) **10 ♗f4** 0-0 11 ♗xc6 bc
12 ♗e5 ♗e7!∓ Lepeshkin and
Plisetsky.

| 10 | ... | 0-0 |

11 ♘f1 ♘e7 12 c3 ♘g6 13
♗d3 ♘d6 (not 13 ... ♗e7 14
♕c2 △ 15 ♘e3 - Tal) 14 ♗xf5
♘xf5 15 ♕b3, Karpov -
Korchnoi, (m/4) Meran 1981,
15 ... ♕d6!=.

B

| 8 | ... | ♗g4(!) |

An earlier 7 ... ♘c6 was
reasonable with the later ...
♗g4. Then, Black intends
the sacrifice of his central
pawn.

| 9 | ♗xe4 |

Or:

a) **9 c4** is discussed in Chapter 33.

b) For **9 c3** see Chapters 34 and 35. If 9 ♘c3 ♘f6 is recommended.

c) After **9 ♘c3 ♘f6** is best.

9   ...   de
10   ♖xe4   ♗xf3

10 ... f5? 11 ♖e1 ♗xf3 12 ♕xf3 ♘xd4 13 ♕xb7 0-0 14 ♗e3! ♗f6 15 ♗xd4 ♗xd4 16 c3 ♖ab8 17 ♕f3 ♗f6 18 ♕e2± Zinkl - M Weiss, 1896.

11   ♕xf3

11 gf? f5 12 ♖f4 0-0! 13 d5 ♗g5 14 ♖a4 ♗xc1 15 ♕xc1 ♕xd5∓ Bilguer.

11   ...   ♘xd4
12   ♕d3

12 ♕c3 ... ♘e6 13 ♘d2 0-0 14 ♘f3 ♗f6 15 ♕c1 ♕d5∓ Berry - Napier, Cambridge Springs 1904.

12   ...   ♘e6
13   ♕e2   0-0

14 ♘c3 ♗f6 15 ♗d2 c6 16 ♖d1 ♕c7= was Langenberg - Düsseldorf, Intercities corr. 1875.

33) 3 ♘xe5 d6: 8 ♖e1 ♗g4 9 c4 Modern Method

4	♘f3	♘xe4
5	d4	d5
6	♗d3	♗e7
7	0-0	♘c6
8	♖e1	♗g4!
9	c4 *(100)*	

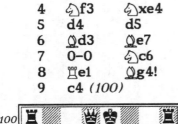

100
B

White intends to undermine the e4 knight by attacking its prop at d5.

9 ... ♘f6

Feeble are:

a) **9 ... ♘xd4??** 10 ♗xe4 de 11 ♕xd4 ef 12 ♕xg4.

b) **9 ... f5?** 10 ♘c3!±.

c) **9 ... ♗xf3** 10 ♕xf3 ♘xd4 11 ♕e3 ♘f5 12 ♕h3 ♘fd6 13 cd ♘f6 14 ♗g5 ♕d7 (14 ... ♘xd5? 15 ♘c3 ♔f8 16 ♖xe7!±

Lobron - Handoko, Indonesia 1983) 15 ♕h4 0-0-0 16 ♘c3 h6 17 ♕d4! ♔b8 18 ♗e3 b6 19 a4± Chigorin - Schiffers, (m) St. Petersburg 1879.

10 cd

White can also choose:

a) **10 ♗e3** 0-0 11 ♘c3 and now:

a1) **11 ... dc** transposes to var. b1 10 ... dc.

a2) **11 ... ♘b4** 12 ♗f1 dc 13 ♗xc4 c6 seems best.

b) **10 ♘c3** keeps the tension. 10 ... 0-0 11 cd then transposes to the column and the only other tries are discussed here:

b1) **10 ... dc** 11 ♗xc4 0-0 12 ♗e3 see line C31 White's 12th in Chapter 31.

b2) **10 ... ♗xf3** 11 ♕xf3 ♘xd4 when:

b21) **12 ♕e3?!** dc! - Bottlik, and:

b22) **12 ♕g3** dc 13 ♗xc4 (13 ♕xg7? ♘f3+! 14 ♔h1 ♖g8∓) 13 ... 0-0 (13 ... ♘f5?

14 ♕h3 ♘d6 15 ♗g5! ♘xc4 16
♖ad1 ♕c8 17 ♕h4± Kavalek)
14 ♗g5 ♗d6 15 ♕h4?! (⌐ 15
♕h3 ♕d7 16 ♕xd7 ♘xd7 17
♖ad1 ♘c6= Sternberg –
Voronkov, USSR 1976) 15 ...
h6! 16 ♗xf6 ♕xf6 17 ♕xf6 gf
18 ♖e4?! (18 ♖ad1 ♘c6=
Karpov) 18 ... c5! 19 ♖h4
♔g7 20 ♘e4 ♗e7 21 ♘g3 f5∓
Lobron – Karpov, Hannover
1983.

b23) **12 ♕d1 ♘e6** 13 cd
♘xd5 14 ♗b5+ c6 15 ♘xd5 cb
16 ♕b3 (16 ♗f4?! ♗d6 17 ♕g4
0-0 18 ♖xe6 ♗xf4= Karpov
and Zaitsev while 16 ♕h5!?
0-0 17 ♗e3 ♗g5 18 ♖ad1±
Keene and Goodman) 16 ...
0-0 (16 ... a6? 17 ♖d1±) 17
♘xe7+ ♕xe7 18 ♕xb5 a6 19
♕b3 ♖fd8= Kasparov – Kar-
pov, Moscow (m/15) 1985.

b3) **10 ... ♘xd4!?** 11 cd
♗xf3 12 gf (12 ♕a4+? c6! 13
♕xd4 ♗xd5∓) 12 ... 0-0 13
♗xh7+ (13 ♗e3 c5 14 ♗c4
♗d6!) 13 ... ♘xh7 14 ♕xd4
♗f6 15 ♕c4 ♗xc3 16 bc c6! 17
dc ♖c8! with enough com-
pensation for the material
in Hazai – Forintos, Budapest 1986.

After 10 cd Black has:

A: 10 ... ♕xd5
B: 10 ... ♘xd5
C: 10 ... ♗xf3

A

10 ...   ♕xd5 *(101)*

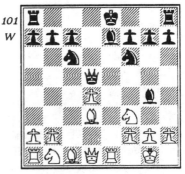

101
W

11   ♘c3
If 11 ♗e2 (Toth) 0-0 12
♘c3 ♕d6.
11   ...   ♗xf3
a) **11 ... ♕h5** 12 ♗b5!± Vitolins – Heida, Riga 1972. .
b) **11 ... ♕d8** 12 ♗b5 0-0 13
♗xc6 bc 14 h3± Browne –
Medina, Las Palmas 1974.
c) **11 ... ♕d7** 12 ♗b5 a6 13
♗xc6 bc! 14 ♗f4 0-0 15
♗e5±.
12   ♘xd5   ♗xd1
13   ♘xc7+!
Or:
a) **13 ♘xe7 ♘xe7** 14 ♖xd1
0-0-0 15 ♗c4 ♘fd5 Valenti
– Toth, Haifa (ol) 1976.
b) **13 ♘xf6+** gf and now:
b1) **14 d5 ♘e5** (14 ... ♗a4
15 dc ♗xc6 16 ♗f4± Honfi)
15 ♖xd1 ♘xd3 16 ♖xd3
0-0-0±/=.
b2) **14 ♖xd1 ♘xd4** 15 ♗e3
♘e6 16 ♗e4! c6 17 ♖ac1± (⌐

♖xc6) King - Becx, Bern 1986.

13 ...   ♔d7
14 ♗f4!

White gains time to attack the black king while the black minor pieces are insecure.

14 ...   ♗g4

If 14 ... ♘h5?! 15 ♗f5+! ♔d8 16 ♗e5! ♘xe5 17 ♘xa8 ♘c6 18 ♖axd1 ♗d6 19 ♖e5! ♘e7 20 ♖a5 b6 21 ♖xa7 ♘xf5 22 ♘xb6± (Kavalek).

15 d5   ♘d4

Dubious is 15 ... ♘xd5 16 ♘xd5 ♗d6 17 ♗e4 △f3±.

16 ♘xa8   ♖xa8

17 ♗e5! ♗f5! 18 ♗f1! ♗c5! (18 ... ♘c2 19 ♗b5+ ♔d8 20 d6 ♘xe1 21 ♖xe1 ♗e6 22 de+ ♔xe7 23 ♗d4!± Kavalek - Toth, Haifa (ol) 1976) 19 ♖ad1! ♘c2 20 ♗b5+ ♔e7, Makarov - Rosentalis, Leningrad 1982, 21 d6+ ♔f8 22 ♖e2 ♖d8 23 d7 ♘xd7 24 ♗xd7 △ 25 ♗d6+! or 25 ♖ed2±.

B

10 ...   ♘xd5
11 ♘c3   0-0

11 ... ♗e6 may be premature:

a) **12 ♗e4** 0-0 leads to var. B1, while 12 ... ♕d7?! is met by 13 ♘g5±.

b) **12 ♘e4** h6 13 ♘c5! ♗c8 14 a3 0-0 15 b4, Vitolins - Mikenas, Riga 1978, 15 ... ♗f6±.

c) **12 a3** 0-0 when:

c1) **13 ♕c2** h6 14 ♗h7+ ♔h8 15 ♗f5 ♘xc3! 16 bc ♗d5= Privara - Bresrak, corr. 1981.

c2) **13 ♗b5** ♘a5! with level chances.

c3) **13 ♘e4** h6 14 ♗c2 (14 ♘g3?! ♘f6! 15 ♗c2 ♕d5 16 ♗f4 ♗d6∓ Barnsley - Wason, corr. 1939-40; 14 ... ♘c5) 14 ... ♗f5, Wolf - Teichmann, Monte Carlo 1903, 15 ♘e5!?. Better is 14 ... ♘f6.

After 11 ... 0-0:

B1: 12 ♗e4
B2: 12 h3

Weaker is 12 ♘xd5 ♕xd5 13 ♗e4 ♕d6 14 ♗xc6 bc= Honfi - Bednarski, Bern 1975.

B1

12 ♗e4   ♗e6! *(102)*

Best. Feeble are:

a) **12 ... ♗b4?** 13 ♘xd5 ♗xe1 14 ♕xe1 f5 15 ♗g5! ♕d7 (15 ... ♕d6? 16 ♘e7+!± consultation game, Chigorin/Schiffers - Alapin/Petrovsky, St. Petersburg 1882) 16 ♗c2 ♗xf3 17 gf ♘xd4 18 ♕d1± (Sozin).

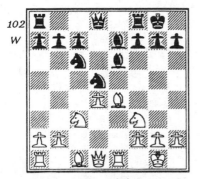

b) **12 ... ♘xc3(?)** 13 bc ♘a5 14 ♖b1 c6 15 h3 ♗e6! 16 ♕c2 h6 17 ♘e5 ♕c7 18 ♕e2! △ ♕h5± R Haag – Copliv, corr. 1984–85.

c) **12 ... ♘f6** 13 d5! ♘b4 14 a3 ♘xe4 15 ♖xe4 ♗xf3 16 ♕xf3, Teschner – Schuster, Berlin 1953, 16 ... ♘a6±.

After 12 ... ♗e6!

B11: 13 ♕d3
B12: 13 ♕c2
B13: 13 a3

Or 13 ♘a4 ♖e8 14 ♘c5 ♗xc5 15 dc ♘f6 equalizes.

B11

    13 ♕d3   h6

13 ... f5? 14 ♘xd5 ♗xd5 15 ♗xf5 ♗xf3 16 gf ♘xd4 17 ♗xh7+ ♔h8 18 f4± Mortensen – Solomon, Thessaloniki (ol) 1984.

    14 ♗h7+
Or:

a) **14 ♕b5** ♘cb4! 15 ♕xb7 ♖b8=.

b) **14 a3** ♗f6 see var. b line B13.

c) **14 ♗f5** see var. c2 at B12.

    14 ...   ♔h8
    15 ♗f5   ♘cb4

a) **15 ... ♘db4?!** 16 ♕e4! ♗c4 17 ♕g4! ♘d3 18 ♖d1 ♘xc1 19 ♖axc1 ♘b4 20 ♗b1± Belyavsky – Yusupov, USSR Ch. 1981. For 19 ... ♗g5 see line B21.

b) **15 ... ♗xf5** 16 ♕xf5 ♘f6 17 ♗f4 ♗d6 18 ♗e5 ♘e7 when:

b1) **19 ♕h3** ♘g6 20 ♖ad1 ♖e8 21 ♖e3 ♔g8! 22 ♕g3 ♘h5 23 ♕g4 ♘f6 24 ♕g3 ♘h5 ½–½ Tal – Karpov, Moscow 1983.

b2) **19 ♕c2!?** ♘g6 c.f. note b1.

    16 ♕b1   ♗xf5
    17 ♕xf5   ♘f6

a) **18 ♗d2** ♘bd5 19 ♘e5 ♕c8 (⌓ 19 ... ♔g8) 20 ♕f3± Mortensen – Jakobsen, Denmark 1984.

b) **18 ♗f4** ♘bd5 19 ♗e5 c6= Psakhis – Schüssler, Tallinn 1983 and Lobron – Toth, Rome 1983.

B12

    13 ♕c2

This can interchange with

13 ♕d3.

Exceptions up to var. c2:

a) **13 ... f5?** 14 ♗d3 ♘db4 15 ♕e2± Tseshkovsky – Dvoretsky, USSR Ch. 1975.

b) **13 ... g6?** 14 ♗h6 ♖e8 15 ♖ad1 △ ♘e5±.

c) **13 ... h6** and now:

c1) **14 a3** ♗f6 15 ♗e3 ♘ce7 16 ♖ad1 c6 17 ♗c1, Poulsen – Johansen, corr. 1979, 17 ... ♕c8±.

c2) **14 ♗f5** when:

c21) **14 ...** ♘xc3 15 bc ♗d5 (15 ... ♗xf5 see var. c22) 16 ♗e4 ♖e8 17 ♖b1, Tseshkovsky – Dvoretsky, USSR Ch. 1976, 17 ... ♗f6! – △ 18 ♖xb7 ♖xe4! and ... ♘xd4.

c22) **14 ...** ♗xf5 15 ♕xf5 ♘xc3 16 bc ♗f6 17 ♕g4 ♕c8 18 ♕g3 ♘e7! 19 ♘e5 ♗xe5 20 ♖xe5 ♘g6 ½–½ Kasparov – Yusupov, USSR 1977.

c23) **14 ...** ♘cb4 15 ♕b1 ♗xf5 16 ♕xf5 ♘f6 (16 ... ♗f6 17 ♘e4 ♕c8 18 ♕h5 c6= Korsunsky – Yusupov, Baku 1979) 17 ♗f4 ♗d6 18 ♘e5 ♕d7 19 ♕xd7 ♘xd7 20 ♖ad1 ♗xe5 21 de ♘c5= Kasparov – Mayorov, USSR 1978.

c3) **14 ♗h7+** ♔h8 15 ♗f5 transposes to line B11.

B13

13 a3(!)

A multi-purpose move.

---

13 ... ♗f6!

Other tries:

a) **13 ... f5?** 14 ♗d3±.

b) **13 ... ♖e8** 14 ♕d3 h6 15 ♗d2 ♕d7 16 ♖ad1 (16 ♖ac1!), Gerigk – Ivanov, corr. 1975. 16 ... ♖ad8±.

c) **13 ... h6** 14 ♕c2 ♗f6 15 ♖d1 and White has greater freedom, but Black's position is solid.

d) **13 ... ♕d7** 14 ♗g5! f6?! (14 ... h6? 15 ♗xd5!±; ⌐ 14 ... ♖fe8) 15 ♗h4 g6 16 ♗g3 ♖ac8 17 ♕e2! ♗f7 18 ♕b5 ♖fd8, Sax – Kurajica, Vrbas 1980, 19 ♖ac1±.

14 ♕d3

Or:

a) **14 h3** see 14 ♗e4 in line B222.

b) **14 ♘a4** and now:

b1) **14 ...** ♖b8 15 ♕d3 h6 16 ♘c5 ♗c8 17 ♘e5 (17 b4) 17 ... ♘de7 (⌐ 17 ... ♘ce7) 18 ♗f4 ♗xe5 19 de ♕xd3, Sax – Bednarski, Vraca 1975, 20 ♗xd3± (Barcza).

b2) **14 ...** ♗g4! when:

b21) **15 ♕d3** ♗xf3 16 ♕xf3 ♘ce7 17 ♘c5 b6 18 ♕h3 ♘g6 19 ♘d7 ♖e8 20 ♗d2 c6 21 ♗xd5 ♖xe1+ 22 ♖xe1 cd 23 ♘xf6+ ½–½ Adorjan – Yusupov, Vrbas 1980.

b22) **15 h3** ♗xf3 16 ♕xf3. A critical position. The d5 knight is hanging and the d4 pawn cannot be taken because ♕h5 would win a piece. The game Ljubojevic - Vlado Kovacevic, Bugojno 1984 went: 16 ... ♖e8 (⌂ 16 ... ♘ce7= Kovacevic) 17 ♗d2 ♘de7 (17 ... ♘ce7? 18 ♗xd5 ♕xd5 19 ♖xe7! ♕xd4 20 ♗c3!±) 18 d5 ♘e5 (18 ... ♘d4 19 ♕d3±) 19 ♕b3 ♘c8! and now 20 g3 ♘d6 21 ♗g2± was necessary.

14 ... h6
15 ♗d2

Or:

a) 15 ♘a4 b6 16 ♘c3 ♖c8 17 ♗d2 ♘de7= Ljubojevic - Henley, Indonesia 1983.

b) 15 ♘e5!? ♗xe5 16 de ♘xc3 17 ♕xc3 ♘d4 18 ♗e3 c5, Bengfort - Erlach, Dortmund 1986, 19 ♗xd4!±; better is 15 ... ♘ce7=.

c) 15 ♗e3 ♘ce7 16 ♖ad1 ♕d6, Kondali - Przevoznik, corr. 1985, 17 ♗c1 △ 18♘e5±.

15 ... ♕d7

Kristiansen - Schneider, Söndersö 1987.

Or:

a) 15 ... a6, Meyer - Lirgl, corr. 1952-53, 16 ♘e5±.

b) 15 ... ♘ce7 as in Decsi - B Szabo, corr. 1983, 16 ♖ad1 △ ♗c1±/=.

16 ♘e5! ♗xe5

White keeps the edge with 17 de ♖ad8 18 ♕g3±.

B2

12 h3 ♗e6

a) 12 ... ♗h5? 13 ♘xh7+!± Olafsson - Persitz, Hastings 1955/56.

b) 12 ... ♗xf3?! 13 ♕xf3 ♘db4 14 ♗b1 (14 d5!? - Flesch) when:

b1) 14 ... ♘f6 15 a3 ♘a6 16 d5 ♘d4 17 ♕d3 g6 18 ♗h6± A Sokolov - Yusupov, Moscow 1981.

b2) 14 ... ♖e8 15 d5 ♘d6 16 ♖xe8+ ♕xe8 17 ♗e3 ♘e5 18 ♕e4± Dolmatov - Yusupov, USSR 1981.

After 12 ... ♗e6, the choice is between:

B21: 13 ♕c2
B22: 13 a3
B23: 13 ♘e4

B21

13 ♕c2 h6
14 ♗h7+

Or 14 ♗f5 ♘cb4 15 ♕b1 ♗xf5 16 ♕xf5 ♗f6, Chiburdanidze - Barua, Delhi 1984. 17 ♘e4 c6 18 ♗d2 ♘a6 19 ♖ad1 ♘ac7 20 ♗c1±.

14 ... ♔h8
15 ♗f5 ♘cb4

Or 15 ... ♘db4 16 ♕e4 ♗c4 17 ♕g4 ♘d3 18 ♖d1± Autenrieth - Rabiega, Germany 1988.

16 ♕b1 ♗xf5

17 ♕xf5 and now:

a) **17 ... ♗f6** 18 ♗d2 ♕c8 19 ♕e4 c6 20 ♘e5 ♗xe5 (Capturing on e5 rarely equalises) 21 de ♖d8 22 f4± Schüssler – Eng, Germany 1983.

b) **17 ... ♘f6** 18 ♗f4 ♘bd5 (weaker is 18 ... c6, e.g. 19 ♖ad1 ♘bd5 20 ♗c1 ♕c8 21 ♕d3 ♕c7 22 ♘e5± Chandler – Schüssler, Germany 1983) 19 ♗e5 c6 20 ♖ad1 ♔g8 21 ♘h2 ♕c8 22 ♕f3 ♕d7 23 ♘f1 ♖fe8 24 ♘e3 ♗f8 with a solid position for Black in Lobron – Toth, Rome 1983.

B22

13 a3   ♗f6

Other tries:

a) **13 ... h6?** 14 ♗c2! ♖e8 15 ♕d3 ♘f6 16 ♗xh6! ♕d7 (16 ... gh 17 ♖xe6!± Chandler – Fries Nielsen, Germany 1981).

b) **13 ... ♘xc3?!** 14 bc ♗f6 when:

b1) **15 ♕c2** g6 (15 ... h6) 16 ♖b1 ♗d5 17 ♘d2! b6 18 ♘c4 (∠ 19 ♘e3) 18 ... ♘e7 19 ♘e5± Vasyukov – Vladimirov USSR 1981.

b2) **15 ♗f4** h6?! (⌐ 15 ... ♕d7) 16 ♗c2, Lewis – Nascimento, Thessaloniki (ol) 1988, 16 ... ♗c4±.

c) **13 ... ♖e8** 14 ♗c2 (14 ♕c2 h6 15 ♗e3 a6?! 16 ♕d2 ♗f8 17 ♗c2 ♘xc3 18 bc ♗d5 19 ♘h2± Pyhala – Handoko, Thessaloniki (ol) 1988; 14 ♘e4!?) 14 ... ♘xc3 15 bc ♗f6 and now:

c1) **16 ♖b1** b6 17 ♘d2 ♘a5 18 ♘e4 ♗f5! keeps balance Balashov – Kochiev, USSR Ch. 1977.

c2) **16 ♗f4** g6 17 ♕d2 ♕d7= Ivanov – Kochiev, USSR 1983.

c3) **16 ♘d2** can be considered.

d) **13 ... ♕d7** 14 ♕c2 h6, Bauer – Autenrieth, Germany 1986, 15 ♘e5±.

After 13 ... ♗f6 White has:

B221: 14 ♘e4
B222: 14 ♗e4

Or:

a) **14 ♗c2** when:

a1) **14 ... ♘xc3** 15 bc ♖e8 and now:

a11) **16 ♖b1** and for 16 ... b6 see var. c1 in B22.

a12) **16 ♗f4** ♘a5 17 ♘e5, Pyhala – G Hernandez, Thessaloniki (ol) 1988, 17 ... g6 equalizes.

a2) **14 ... ♘b6** 15 ♘e4 ♗f5, Tal – Schüssler, Tallinn 1983, 16 ♗e3 ♘c4 17 ♕d3 ♘xe3 18 fe ♗g6 with even chances.

b) 14 ♗b5 ♘xc3 15 bc ♘e7
16 ♘g5 ♗f5 17 ♘e4 ♗xe4! 18
♖xe4 c5 19 ♗e3 ♘d5= Lukin
– Yusupov, USSR 1981.

c) 14 ♘a4 ♘xd4! 15 ♘xd4
♗xd4 16 ♗xh7+ ♔xh7 17
♕xd4 b6 18 ♘c3 ½–½ Psak-
his – Karpov, USSR 1983.

B221

　　14　♘e4

When:

a) 14 ... h6 and now:

a1) 15 ♗c2 ♗f5! Gufeld –
Haritonov, USSR 1981.

a2) 15 ♘c5 ♗c8 16 ♘e5
♗xe5 (16 ... ♘xd4∞) 17 de b6
18 ♕a4± A Sokolov – Andrianov, Sochi 1980.

b) 14 ... ♗f5 15 ♕b3! ♖b8
16 ♘xf6+ ♕xf6 17 ♗g5 ♕g6
18 ♕xd5! ♗xd3 19 ♘h4 ♕d6
20 ♕xd6 cd 21 d5± Lobron –
Schüssler, 1984 and Hellers
– Schüssler, Malmö 1987/88.

B222

　　14　♗e4

It is worthy of note that
this continuation, occurring
even after 12 ♗e4, seems
best. There h3 is neglected.

a) 14 ... a6(?) 15 ♕d3±
Vitomkis – Salmisch, corr.
1984–86.

b) 14 ... ♘ce7 15 ♗g5 c6 16
♕d2 ♕d6 17 ♗c2 ♕c7 18

♗xf6 ♘xf6 19 ♘g5 ♗d5 20
♖e5± Westerinen – Schüss-
ler, Malmö 1986.

c) 14 ... h6 15 ♗c2 ♘de7
(15 ... ♘b6 16 ♕d3±) 16 ♗e3
♘f5 17 ♗xf5! ♗xf5 18 d5±
Gipslis – Sieiro, Havana
1984.

B23

　　13　♘e4 (Keres)

a) 13 ... ♘f6 14 ♘fg5 h6 15
♘xf6+ ♗xf6 16 ♘xe6 fe 17
♕g4 ♘xd4 18 ♗xh6± Lob-
ron – Kavalek, Hannover
1983.

b) 13 ... ♗f5 14 a3 ♗f6 15
♕b3! see var. b 14 ... ♗f5
line B221.

c) 13 ... h6 (Toth) 14
♘g3±.

C

　　10　...　　♗xf3 *(103)*

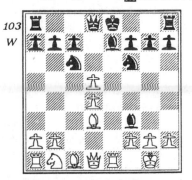

This is regarded as the
best move.

　　11　♕xf3　　♕xd5

Not 11 ... ♘xd4? 12 ♕e3±; 11 ... ♘xd5? 12 ♘c3±.

Now White can choose:

C1: 12 ♕xd5
C2: 12 ♕g3
C3: 12 ♕h3

C1

12 ♕xd5 ♘xd5
13 ♘c3

Feeble is 13 ♗e4 0-0-0 14 ♘c3 ♗b4!, e.g.:

a) **15 ♗g5** (△ 15 ... f6 16 ♗xd5±) 15 ... ♘xc3!∓, e.g. 16 ♗xd8 ♖xd8 or 16 a3 ♖xd4!

b) **15 ♗xd5** ♖xd5! 16 ♘xd5 ♗xe1 17 ♘xc7 (17 ♗e3 ♗a5∓) and now:

b1) **17 ... ♗xf2+** 18 ♔xf2 ♕xc7 19 ♗f4+ ♔d7 20 ♖c1 ♔e6∓ Ljubojevic - Tal, Bugojno 1984.

b2) **17 ... ♗a5** 18 d5 ♘d4 19 ♗e3 ♘c2 20 ♖c1 ♘xe3 21 ♘b5+! ♔b8! 22 fe ♗d2 23 ♖d1 ♗xe3+ 24 ♔f1 ♖d8! 25 ♔e2 ♗f4 26 ♔f3 ♗e5 27 ♘c3 f5 28 h3 ♔c7∓ Borsavölgyi - Forintos, Budapest 1990.

c) **15 ♗d2** when:

c1) **15 ... ♘xd4** 16 ♘xd5 (16 ♗xd5?! ♗xc3 17 bc ♘c2!∓) 16 ... ♗xd2 17 ♖ed1 c6 18 ♖xd2 cd=.

c2) **15 ... ♘f6** and now:

c21) **16 a3** ♘xe4 (16 ... ♖xd4∞) 17 ♖xe4 ♗xc3 18 bc

♘a5= Ehlvest - Mihalchishin, Dortmund 1984.

c22) **16 ♗xc6** bc 17 ♗e3 (17 a3?! ♖xd4! 18 ab ♖xd2 19 ♖xa7 ♖e8!∓ Lobron - Mihalchishin, Dortmund 1984) 17 ... ♘d5 18 ♖ac1 ♖he8 19 ♖e2 ♘xe3 20 fe c5= A Rodriguez - Seirawan, Biel 1985.

c3) **15 ... ♘b6** planning ... ♘c4 or ... ♘xd4 seems strongest.

13 ... ♘db4

13 ... 0-0-0 14 ♗e4 ♗b4! transposes to the above 13 ♗e4 variations. In our opinion there is a slight defect to this - if White interpolates 14 ♗f5+! and plays 15 ♗e4 only after ... ♔b8 the evaluation of some alternatives may well be altered. However, with precise counterplay Black might nevertheless equalize.

14 ♗e4 ♘xd4
15 ♗e3

Or:

a) **15 ♗f4?** ♘e6 — van der Sterren.

b) **15 ♖b1** c6 16 ♗e3 ♘e6 17 a3 ♘a6 18 b4 0-0 19 b5 ½-½ Sax - Ristic, Smederevska Palanka 1982.

15 ... c5!

a) Weaker are: **15 ... ♘dc2?** 16 a3!; **15 ... ♘bc6?** 16 ♗xd4 ♘xd4 17 ♗xb7 ♖b8

18 ♘d5!± Wiedenkeller – Schüssler, West Germany 1984; 15 ... ♘bc2? 16 ♗xd4+ as above.

b) 15 ... ♖d8?! 16 ♗xd4 ♖xd4 17 a3 (17 ♗xb7 ♔d7 △ ... ♖b8) 17 ... ♘c6 18 ♘b5 ♖d2 when:

b1) 19 ♗xc6+ bc 20 ♘xa7 ♔d7 21 ♘xc6 ♗c5! 22 ♘e5+ ♔c8∓.

b2) 19 ♘xc7+ Abramovic – Rukavina, Yugoslav Ch. 1985, 19 ... ♔d7! 20 ♘b5 ♖d8 21 ♖ad1 ♖xd1 22 ♖xd1+ ♔c8=.

b3) 19 ♖ad1! ♖xd1! (19 ... ♖xb2?? 20 ♗xc6+ bc 21 ♘xc7+ ♔f8 22 ♖d8+! and mate) 20 ♖xd1 h5 21 ♘xc7+± Ivanovic – Rukavina, Yugoslav Ch. 1985.

16 ♗xd4

Or:

a) 16 ♘d5? ♘xd5 17 ♗xd5 ♘c2 18 ♗xb7 (18 ♗xc5? ♘xe1 19 ♖xe1 0-0-0!∓) 18 ... ♖b8 19 ♗c6+ ♔f8 20 b3 h5∓ Perenyi – Forintos, Hungarian Ch. 1986.

b) 16 ♗xb7 ♖d8! 17 ♖ad1 ♘bc2 18 ♖f1 ♖b8 19 ♗e4 ♖xb2 20 ♗c1 ♖b8 21 ♗f4 ♖d8 22 ♖d2 ♘b4 23 ♖e1 0-0! 24 ♗xh7+ ♔xh7 25 ♖xe5∓ Belyavsky – Timman, Bugojno, 1984.

16 ... cd

17 ♘b5 ♖d8!
a) 17 ... 0-0? 18 a3! ♘c6 19 ♗xc6 bc 20 ♘c7±.

b) 17 ... ♔f8?! 18 a3! ♘c6 19 ♖ac1 d3 20 ♗xd3 ♘f6 21 b4 g6 22 ♗e4± P Popovic – Kurajica, Yugoslavia 1984.

18 a3 ♘c6

19 ♗xc6+ bc 20 ♘xa7 ♖d6! 21 ♖ac1 ♔d7 22 ♘xc6 ♘f6! 23 ♘b4 d3 24 ♖cd1 d2! 25 ♖e2 ♖e8! 26 ♖exd2 (26 ♔f1 ♖xe2 27 ♔xe2 ♗xb2 28 a4 ♘c3) 26 ... ♖e1+ 27 ♖xe1 ♖xd2 and the activity of Black pieces was enough compensation for the sacrificed material in L A Schneider – Forintos, Boras 1986.

C2

12 ♕g3 ♕xd4
13 ♘c3 0-0
a) 13 ... 0-0-0 is risky:
a1) 14 ♗f5+ ♔b8 15 ♗f4±.
a2) 14 ♘b5 ♕b6!∞, e.g. 15 a4 ♗c5 16 ♗f5+ ♔b8 17 ♗f4 ♘d5; also unclear is 17 b4.
b) 13 ... ♖d8 14 ♗b5! ♖d7 when:
b1) 15 ♗g5 ♕g4 16 ♕xg4 ♘xg4 17 h3! (17 ♘d5 f6!) 17 ... ♘f6 (17 ... f6 18 ♗f4±) 18 ♗xf6 gf 19 ♘e4±.
b2) 15 ♕xg7 ♖g8 16 ♕h6 ♘g4?! 17 ♕f4 ♔d8 18 ♕xd4 ♖xd4 19 ♗xc6 bc 20 h3?! ♘xf2! with good counter-

play in Hübner – Smyslov, Velden (m/1) 1983. Better is 20 f3! ♘f6 21 ♗e3 ♖b4 22 ♖ad1+ ♗d6 23 b3± (Kavalek).

14   ♘b5

Or:

a) **14 ♕h3** ♖ad8∞.

b) **14   ♖d1 ♕g4!** 15 ♕xc7 ♗c5 16 h3 ♕h4 17 ♕f4 ♕xf4 with equality, Mihalchishin – Halasz, Budapest 1984.

14   ...   ♕g4

a) **14 ... ♕b4** ½–½ in Abramovic – Kurajica, Yugoslavia 1984.

b) **14 ... ♕d7** 15 ♖d1, Kasparov – Wolff, simultaneous exhibition, London 1988, 15 ... ♗d6 △ 16 ♕h4 ♘e5=.

15   ♕xg4

Better is 15 ♘xc7 ♖ad8 16 ♕xg4 ♘xg4 17 ♗e2 ♘f6 or 15 ♗f4 ♕xg3 16 ♗xg3 ♗d6! 17 ♘xc7 ♗xg3=.

The game Sax – Yusupov, Thessaloniki (ol) 1984 went 15 ... ♘xg4 16 ♗f5?! (16 ♗e2=) 16 ... ♘f6 17 ♘xc7 ♖ad8 18 ♗e3 a6! 19 ♖ac1 (△ 19 ♖ed1 – Sax) 19 ... ♗b4! 20 ♖f1 ♘d4 with comfortable play for Black.

C3

12   ♕h3 (104)

12   ...   ♘xd4

Riskier is the capture 12

... ♕xd4. After 13 ♘c3:

a) If **13 ... ♕d7?** 14 ♗f5.

b) **13 ... 0–0?** 14 ♗g5 h6 15 ♖ad1!±.

c) After **13 ... ♖d8!** 14 ♗f5:

c1) **14 ... h5** 15 ♕g3 ♔f8:

c11) **16 ♗e3?!** ♕b4 17 a3 ♕a5 18 ♕f3 g6 19 ♗c2 h4∓ Velimirovic – Kurajica, Bela Crkva 1984.

c12) Better is **16 ♕xc7** ♗d6 17 ♕xb7 ♘e7 and here we suggest 18 ♗h3 (18 ♕f3?! ♘g4∞) 18 ... ♘g4 19 ♗xg4 hg 20 g3±.

c2) **14 ... g6** 15 ♗e3 ♕b4 16 a3 ♕b3?! (△ 16 ... ♕c4) 17 ♗h6 gf (17 ... ♖g8? 18 ♘e4!) 18 ♗g7 ♖g8 19 ♗xf6 ♕c4 20 ♖e3 ♖g6 21 ♗xe7 ♘xe7 22 ♖ae1 ♖e6 23 ♕xh7± Ivanovic – Forintos, Metz 1988.

c3) **14 ... 0–0** 15 ♗e3 ♕b4 ½–½ Korchnoi – Smyslov, Beer Sheva 1990.

13   ♘c3   ♕d7

14   ♕xd7+

Or 14 ♕g3 0-0 15 ♗h6 ♘e8!∓ (Taimanov) △ ... ♔h8, ... c5.

14 ... ♔xd7

14 ... ♘xd7? 15 ♘d5 ♘e6 16 ♖xe6!

15 ♗e3 ♘e6

16 ♖ad1 ♗d6 17 ♗f5 ♔e7 18 ♘b5 (18 g4 g6!) 18 ... ♖hd8 19 ♘xd6 cd 20 h3 b6 21 g4 h6 22 ♗d4 ♖ac8 23 ♗c3 g6 24 ♗c2 h5 25 f3 ½–½ Kasparov – Karpov, (m/28) Moscow 1984/85.

34) 3 ♞xe5 d6: Berger's 9 c3 Introduction

4	♞f3	♞xe4
5	d4	d5
6	♗d3	♗e7
7	0-0	♞c6
8	♖e1	♗g4(!)
9	c3 *(105)*	

First of all White elects to strengthen his d4 pawn.

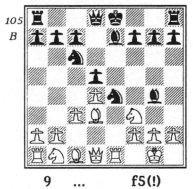

9	...	f5(!)

The e4 knight, strengthened in this way, is hardly ever removable and secures Black equality. The power of the usual c4 move can only be realised by a loss of tempo. Less effective are:

a) **9 ... ♗f5?** Moving the same piece twice in succession cannot go unpunished in the opening – 10 ♗b5!± △ ♗xc6, ♞e5 is inconvenient for Black.

b) For **9 ... ♞d6** see note c 8 ... ♞d6 in Chapter 32.

c) **9 ... ♞f6** 10 ♗g5! when:

c1) **10 ... 0-0** 11 ♞bd2 ♗h5 12 ♕b3± Sax - Kapelan, Vrsac 1981. White is two tempi up compared with the Exchange Variation of the French Defence.

c2) **10 ... ♕d7?!** 11 ♞bd2 0-0-0? (11 ... 0-0±) 12 ♕a4 h6 13 ♗h4 g5 14 ♗g3 ♗xf3 15 ♞xf3 g4? 16 ♞e5 ♞xe5 17 ♗f5!! ♕xf5 18 ♖xe5 ♕d3 19 ♖xe7 ♖d7 20 ♖e3 ♕a6 21 ♕xa6 ba 22 ♗e5 1-0 Keres - Alexander, Hastings 1954-55.

After 9 ... f5:

A: 10 c4
B: 10 ♞bd2

Or:

a) **10 ♕b3** — the best line, discussed in Chapter 35.

b) **10 h3** when:

b1) **10 ... ♗h5** 11 ♕b3! 0-0 12 ♕xb7 ♖f6 see Chapter 35; while 11 ♘bd2 ♕d6 or 11 ... 0-0=.

b2) **10 ... ♗xf3!?** is an interesting idea: 11 gf (11 ♕xf3 0-0 planning ... ♗d6 and ... ♕h4 with good chances) 11 ... ♘f6 12 ♗xf5 0-0 13 ♕d3 ♗d6 14 ♗g5 ♘e7! 15 ♗e6+ ♔h8 16 ♘d2 ♘g6 17 ♗f5 (17 ♘f1) 17 ... ♗f4! 18 ♗xf6 ♕xf6 19 ♗xg6 ♗xd2 20 ♖e2 ♗f4 21 ♗xh7 ♕g5+ 22 ♔h1 ♕h5 0-1 Enklaar - Dvoretsky, Wijk aan Zee 1975.

c) **10 ♕c2** 0-0 11 ♘fd2? (11 ♘bd2=) 11 ... ♘xf2! 12 ♖xe7?? (12 ♔xf2 ♗h4+ 13 g3 f4∓) 12 ... ♗d1! 0-1 Kugayevsky - Kmielevsky, corr. 1897-98.

d) **10 ♗e2?!** ♕d6∓.

e) **10 ♗b5?!** 0-0 11 ♗f4 ♗d6 12 ♗xd6 ♕xd6 13 ♕d3 ♗xf3 14 ♕xf3 ♖f6 15 ♘a3 ♖af8∓ Torre - Handoko, Indonesia 1983.

A

        10   c4   dc!
Not:

a) **10 ... ♘xd4?** 11 ♗xe4 de 12 ♕xd4 ef 13 ♕xg7±.

b) **10 ... ♗xf3?** 11 gf ♘f6

12 cd! ♕xd5 (12 ... ♘xd5 13 ♗xf5±) 13 ♘c3+.

c) **10 ... ♕d6?** when:

c1) **11 ♘c3** and now:

c11) **11 ... ♘xc3** 12 bc 0-0 13 ♖b1± Bilguer.

c12) **11 ... ♗xf3** 12 ♕xf3 ♘xd4 13 ♕e3± Berger.

c13) **11 ... dc** 12 ♘xe4 fe 13 ♗xe4 0-0 14 ♗e3± Bilguer.

c2) **11 cd** ♗xf3 12 ♕xf3! ♘xd4 13 ♕e3! △ ... ♕xd5 14 ♘c3±.

d) **10 ... ♗b4?** 11 ♘c3!±.

e) **10 ... 0-0?!** 11 cd ♕xd5 (11 ... ♘xd4? 12 ♗xe4 fe 13 ♕xd4!±) 12 ♘c3 ♘xc3 13 bc ♗xf3 (△ 13 ... ♗d6 Bilguer) 14 ♕xf3 ♕xf3 15 gf ♗d6 16 ♖b1 ♖ab8 17 ♖b5± Maroczy - Pillsbury, Monte Carlo 1902.

f) **10 ... ♗h4** Discovered by Maroczy in 1902. Now it is White who has difficulty demonstrating equality:

f1) **11 cd?** ♗xf2+ 12 ♔f1 ♗xe1 13 dc ♗xf3! 14 gf (14 ♕xf3 ♕xd4 {14 ... ♗h4 is also good} 15 cb ♖d8 16 ♗b5+ c6! 17 ♗xc6+ ♔e7 18 ♗xe4 fe 19 ♗g5+ ♔e8 20 ♕e3 ♖f8+ wins - Krause 1903) 14 ... ♕xd4 15 ♕e2 0-0-0 16 ♗c2 (16 cb+ {16 ♗a6 ♗h4!∓} 16 ... ♔b8 17 ♗xe1 ♖hc8! 18 fe ♖xe4!∓ Maroczy and Teichmann 1903) 16 ... ♗a5!

17 fe ♗b6 18 ♕g2 fe 19 ♘c3 ♖hf8+ (20 ♔e1 ♖f2 21 ♕xe4 ♖xf1+!) 0-1 Ernst - L A Schneider, Swedish Ch. 1986.

f2) **11 ♖f1?** dc (11 ... 0-0 12 cd ♗xf3 13 gf ♘xf2∓) 12 ♗xc4 ♕f6 △ ... 0-0-0∓ Vignoli/Krause.

f3) **11 ♗e3?** and now:

f31) **11 ... f4?!** 12 ♗xe4 de 13 ♗xf4 0-0 14 ♖xe4 ♗xf3 (14 ... ♗f5? 15 ♗xc7!±) 15 gf ♗xf2+! with a quick draw in Teichmann - Napier, London 1904.

f32) **11 ... 0-0** 12 cd (12 g3? f4! 13 gf ♘xf2 14 ♗xf2 ♗xf2+ 15 ♔xf2 ♖xf4 △ ... ♘xd4, ... ♕h4+ Vignoli) 12 ... ♘b4 13 d6 (13 ♘c3 ♗xf3 14 gf ♘g5∓) 13 ... ♘xd3 14 ♕xd3 ♗xf3 15 gf ♘xd6!∓ Keres.

f4) **11 ♗xe4** de 12 d5 when:

f41) **12 ... 0-0** 13 dc ef (△ 13 ... ♕xd1 14 ♖xd1 ef - Maroczy) 14 ♕xd8 ♖axd8 15 cb ♖fe8 16 ♖xe8+ ♖xe8 17 h3= Tarrasch - Maroczy, Monte Carlo 1903.

f42) **12 ... ♘e5!** 13 ♕a4+ (13 ♗f4 ♘g6∓) 13 ... b5! 14 ♕xb5+ c6! 15 dc ♘xf3+ 16 gf ♗xf2+! 17 ♔xf2 ♕h4+ 18 ♔f1! 0-0!∓ Bilguer.

f5) After **11 g3**:

f51) **11 ... ♗xf3** 12 ♕xf3 ♘xd4 and then:

f511) **13 ♕e3?!** ♘f6 14 cd (14 f3 0-0! 15 fe fe∓) 14 ... 0-0 15 ♗xe4 ♖e8∓ *Modern Chess Openings*.

f512) **13 ♕d1** (Cafferty/Hooper) 13 ... 0-0! 14 gh ♕xh4 15 ♗xe4 (15 ♘e3 f4! 16 ♗xd4 f3∓) 15 ... de 16 ♕xd4 ♕g4+ 17 ♔f1 ♕h3+ is equal.

f52) **11 ... ♘xd4** 12 ♗xe4 de 13 ♕xd4 ♗xf3 14 ♕e5+! and:

f521) Not **14 ... ♗e7?** 15 ♗g5 ♖f8 16 ♘d2± Black - Schroeder, New York 1918.

f522) **14 ... ♕e7!** 15 ♕xf5 g6 16 ♕h3 ♗g5 17 ♗xg5 ♕xg5 18 ♕e6+ ♔f8=.

f53) **11 ... ♗f6** (Hooper) 12 cd ♘xd4 13 ♕a4+ (13 ♗xe4 0-0!∓) 13 ... ♕d7 14 ♕xd7+ ♔xd7 15 ♘xd4 ♗xd4 16 ♗xe4 ♖ae8 and Black has slightly better chances.

11 ♗xc4 ♕d6!

11 ... ♗xf3 is also good: 12 gf ♕xd4 (12 ... ♘f6? 13 d5 ♘b8 14 ♕b3± Bilguer) 13 ♕xd4 ♘xd4 14 fe ♘c2 15 ♖e2 ♘xa1 16 ef ♖d8! (16 ... 0-0-0? 17 ♖xe7! ♖d1+ 18 ♔g2 ♖xc1 19 ♘c3± Schlechter) 17 ♘c3 c6!, e.g. 18 ♗g5 ♖d7∓ △ ... ♔d8 (19 ♗e6? ♗xg5!).

12 ♘c3 0-0-0!

Now 13 ... ♗xf3 is threat-

ened. Not 12 ... ♗xf3?! 13 gf
♘xf2 14 ♕c2! ♘h3+ 15 ♔g2
♘f4+ 16 ♗xf4 ♕xf4 17 ♘d5
♕g5+ 18 ♔h1 ♔d8 19 ♖g1± Mihalchishin.

13   ♘xe4

▱ 13 ♗e3 ♕g6 14 ♗e2 - Bikhovsky.

13   ...   fe
14   ♖xe4   ♕g6!∓

The game Holmov - Mihalchishin, Minsk 1985 went 15 ♖f4? (▱ 15 ♗d3) ♘xd4! 16 ♖xd4 ♖xd4 17 ♕xd4 ♗xf3! 18 ♗f1 ♖d8 19 ♕e3 ♗xg2! 20 ♕xe7 ♗xf1+ 21 ♕g5 ♖d1! 22 h4 ♗e2+ 23 ♔h2 ♕e4 0-1.

B

10   ♘bd2 *(106)*

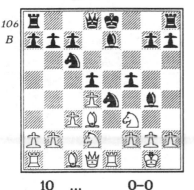

10   ...   0-0

A traditional move. Alternatives:

a) 10 ... ♕d6!? when:

a1) 11 ♘f1 0-0 12 ♘g3 (12 ♘e3 ♗h5 13 ♗e2∞ ½-½

Westerinen - L A Schneider, Järvenpää 1982) 12 ... ♔h8 (12 ... ♗h4!? - Schwarz) 13 ♕b3 ♖ae8 14 ♕xb7 ♘xf2! 15 ♔xf2 f4 16 ♘f1! ♗xf3 17 ♔xf3 ♕h6∞ Stean - Toth, France 1976.

a2) 11 ♕a4?! (△ 12 ♗b5) 11 ... 0-0! 12 h3?! (weakens the king's position) 12 ... ♗h5 13 ♕b3 ♔h8 14 ♕xb7 ♖ab8 15 ♕a6 ♖b6 16 ♕a4 g5 with a strong attack in Sharif - Chow, New York 1984.

a3) 11 ♕b3 0-0-0! 12 ♗b5 ♗f6 13 ♕a4 and now:

a31) 13 ... ♖he8 14 ♗xc6 ♕xc6 15 ♕xc6 (15 ♕xa7 ♘xf2!? - see a32) 15 ... bc 16 ♘xe4 ♖xe4 17 ♗g5! ♖de8, Pokojowczyk - Sinkovics, Budapest 1984, 18 ♗xf6 gf 19 ♔f1!± △ ♘g1; so we recommend 16 ... fe 17 ♘d2 h6 18 ♘b3 ♗e7 △ 19 ♗f4 ♗d6=.

a32) 13 ... ♖de8 14 ♗xc6 ♕xc6 15 ♕xa7 (15 ♕xc6 bc - cf a31) 15 ... ♘xf2!? (15 ... ♘g5?! 16 ♘e5!) 16 ♔xf2 ♖xe1 17 ♘xe1 ♖e8 18 ♘df3 ♕b5 19 c4! ♕xc4 20 ♗e3, Pacioni - Castellano, Italy 1980, 20 ... ♗xf3!? 21 ♘xf3 ♕c2+ 22 ♘d2 ♕d3 23 ♖e1 f4∓; or 22 ♗d2 ♗g5! 23 ♕a8+ ♔d7 24 ♕a5 ♗e3+ 25 ♔g3 f4+∓.

a33) 13 ... ♘xd2 14 ♘xd2! (14 ♗xd2? ♗xf3 15 gf a6 16

♗d3 ♔b8! 17 ♗xf5 ♗h4 18 ♗h3 ♕f6 and Black's play is at least worth the sacrificed material, Mukhin - Dolmatov, USSR 1977) 14 ... ♖he8 15 ♖f1 ♗e2= Mestel - Wolff, London 1985.

a4) **11 ♕c2** 0-0 13 b4 a6 14 ♞e5 ♞xe5 15 de ♕g6 16 ♞f1, Armas - Halasz, Dortmund Open 1989, 16 ... c6 with mutual chances.

b) **10 ... ♞xd2** (Haag) 11 ♗xd2 0-0=, e.g. 12 ♕b3 ♗xf3 13 gf ♕d6 or 12 ♗e2 ♕d6 13 ♞e5 ♞xe5 14 de ♕e6= △ ... ♗xe2 and ... f4.

11 ♕b3

This is best, transposing to lines discussed in Chapter 35, after 10 ♕b3 0-0 11 ♞bd2. Other ideas for White:

a) **11 h3 ♗h5** 12 ♕b3 ♖b8 13 a4 (13 ♞xe4 ♞a5 14 ♞f6+ ♖xf6 15 ♕a4 ♗xf3 is also good) 13 ... ♔h8 14 ♕c2 ♗d6 15 b4 ♕f6 with comfortable play for Black in Planinc - Benko, Hastings 1974/75.

b) **11 ♕c2** ♖f6?! (11 ... ♔h8 or 11 ... ♗d6 ∠ ... ♕f6) 12 b4

♗d6 13 b5 ♞xd2 14 ♗xd2 ♗xf3 15 bc ♖g6 16 g3 ♕h4 17 cb ♖f8 18 ♖e5!± f4? 19 ♗xf4! Halifman - Kartanaite, USSR 1979; or 18 ... ♗xe5 19 de ♗e4 20 ♗e3±.

c) **11 ♗e2 ♗d6** 12 h3 ♗xf3 (⌐ 12 ... ♗h5) 13 ♞xf3 ♞e7 14 ♞e5 c6 15 f3, Mason - Napier, Monte Carlo 1902, 15 ... ♞g3∞.

d) **11 ♞f1?!** when:

d1) **11 ... ♗d6** 12 ♞e3? (12 ♗e2∓; 12 h3∓) 12 ... ♗xh2+! 13 ♔xh2 ♞xf2∓∓ Janovsky - Schlechter, (m/1) Carlsbad 1902, after the exchanges ... ♕h4+ and ... ♕xe1 wins.

d2) **11 ... ♗h4!?** and now:

d21) **12 ♞g3?!** ♞xf2! 13 ♔xf2 f4 14 ♕c2 ♕f6∓ Hamid - Stewart, British Ch. 1989.

d22) **12 g3 ♗g5** (12 ... ♗e7 13 ♞e3 {13 ♗e2!?} 13 ... ♗h5 14 ♞g2 ♗d6∓ {△ ... g5} Mason - Napier, London 1904) 13 ♗xg5 ♞xg5 14 ♗e2 ♞h3+ (14 ... f4!?) 15 ♔g2 f4 16 ♞3d2! ♗xe2 (14 ... ♗c8) 17 ♕xe2 ♞g5 18 ♕g4± Ljubojevic - Hjartarson, Belgrade 1989.

35) 3 ♘xe5 d6: Berger's 9 c3 with 10 ♕b3

4	♘f3	♘xe4
5	d4	d5
6	♗d3	♗e7
7	0-0	♘c6
8	♖e1	♗g4
9	c3	f5!
10	♕b3	*(107)*

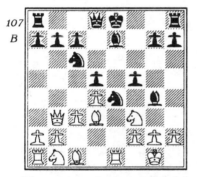

107
B

The queen is unpinned by the g4-bishop. However the attacked b7 pawn is often sacrificed by Black.

10	...	0-0

Or:

a) **10 ... ♘a5?** 11 ♕a4+ c6 12 ♘e5± Bilguer.

b) **10 ... ♖b8?!** 11 ♘fd2!±.

c) **10 ... ♕d6** (△ ... 0-0-0) when:

c1) **11 ♕xb7?!** ♖b8 12 ♕a6 ♗xf3! 13 gf and now:

c11) **13 ... ♕g6+** 14 ♔f1 0-0! 15 ♗c2 (15 fe fe∓) and:

c111) **15 ... ♗h4** 16 ♖e2 ♖f6 17 fe fe 18 ♗e3 ♘xd4 19 ♕xf6 ♕xf6 20 cd, Hübner – Borik, Cologne 1980, 20 ... c5! with powerful attack.

c112) **15 ... ♖b6!** 16 ♕d3 ♘xf2!∓; or 16 ♕e2 ♗h4 17 fe fe 18 ♗e3 ♘e7∓ △ ... ♘f5 – Reefschläger.

c12) **13 ... 0-0** 14 ♗b5? (14 ♗c2) ♖b6 15 ♕a4 ♗h4 16 ♖e2 ♗xf2+ 17 ♖xf2 ♘xf2 18 ♔xf2 ♖e8∓ Ernst – L A Schneider, Swedish Team Ch. 1986.

c2) **11 ♘e5?!** ♘xe5 12 de ♕xe5 13 ♕xb7 (13 f3 ♗d6 △ 14 fg ♕xh2+ 15 ♔f1 0-0-0∓) 13 ... 0-0 14 c4 ♗c5!? 15 ♗e3 ♘xf2! 16 ♔xf2 ♗xe3+ 17 ♖xe3 ♕f4+ 18 ♖f3 ♗xf3 19 gf ♕d4+∓ Gizynski – Heintze, Halle 1985.

c3) For **11 ♘bd2** see move order 10 ♘bd2 ♕d6 var. a3 11 ♕b3 in line B, Chapter

34.

c4) **11 ♘fd2** when:

c41) **11 ... ♘xd2** 12 ♘xd2 0-0 and:

c411) **13 h3** ♗h5 14 ♘f1 f4! 15 ♘h2 ♗h4∓ Sax – Handoko, Zagreb 1985.

c412) **13 f3** ♗h4 14 ♖f1 ♗h5 15 ♕xb7 ♖ab8 16 ♕a6 f4 17 ♕a4 ♗g6 18 ♕c2, Yudasin – Tischbierek, Leipzig 1986, 18 ... ♕f6 △ ... ♗g3 or ... ♘xd4∞.

c413) **13 ♕xb7!?** ♖b8 14 ♕a6 f4 15 ♗e2! f3?! 16 ♘xf3 ♗xf3 17 ♗xf3 ♘xd4 18 ♗xd5+! ♕xd5 19 cd ♗d6 20 ♕e2 ♕xd4 21 ♕e6+ ♔h8 22 ♗e3± Ernst – Schüssler, Malmö 1987/88.

c42) **11 ... ♗h5** 12 f3 ♘xd2 13 ♘xd2 0-0 14 ♘f1 f4 15 ♕xb7 ♖ab8 16 ♕a6 ♗h4 17 ♖e2 ♗g6 18 ♗xg6 ♘xd4 19 ♗xh7+! ♔h8 (19 ... ♔xh7 20 ♕d3+ ♘f5 21 b4±) 20 ♗d3 ♖b6 (△ 20 ... ♘xe2+ 21 ♗xe2 ♕c5+ 22 ♔h1 ♕f2 △ 23 ♗d2 ♖xb2) 21 ♕a4 ♘xe2+ 22 ♗xe2 ♕c5+ 23 ♗e3!± Ehlvest–Forintos, Tallinn 1986.

c43) **11 ... 0-0-0** 12 f3 and now:

c431) **12 ... ♗h3** 13 ♖e2 ♕g6 14 ♘f1 ♗g5 (14 ... ♗g5 15 ♕c2 ♖he8 16 ♘a3 △ ♔h1±) 15 ♗xg5 ♕xg5 16 ♔h1 ♕c1 17 ♖d2± △ ♕d1 or ♖d1 Ernst –

L A Schneider, Swedish Ch. 1988.

c432) **12 ... ♗h4** 13 ♖f1 ♗h3 (13 ... ♗h5 14 fe fe 15 ♗xe4!± Yusupov; or 13 ... ♗f2+ 14 ♖xf2 ♘xf2 15 ♔xf2 ♕xh2 16 ♘f1 ♕h4+ 17 ♔g1 ♖hf8 18 ♕c2 ♗h5 19 ♗e3 f4 20 ♗f2 ♕g5 21 ♘bd2 ♖d6 22 ♖e1± Ernst – L A Schneider, Göteborg 1988) 14 ♕c2 ♕g6 15 ♘b3 ♖hf8 16 ♘a3 ♖de8 17 ♔h1? ♘f2+ 18 ♖xf2 ♗xg2+! 0-1 Ivanchuk – Anand, Reggio Emilia 1988/89. Better is 17 ♗f4! Yusupov.

f) **10 ... ♕d7** strengthens the f5 pawn 11 ♘fd2 0-0-0 12 f3 ♘xd2 13 ♘xd2 ♗h5 14 ♕a4 and now:

f1) **14 ... ♖de8** 15 ♘b3 ♗d6?! (⌐ 15 ... a6 see var. f2 16 ♗d2 ♖xe1+ 17 ♖xe1 ♖e8 18 ♘c5± Oll – Mihalchishin, Kuybishev 1987.

f2) **14 ... ♖he8** 15 ♘b3 a6 16 ♗d2 (△ ♘c5) 16 ... ♗g6 17 ♗f4 (17 ♘c5 ♗xc5 18 dc ♘e5=) 17 ... ♘b8?! 18 ♕xd7+ ♘xd7 19 ♔f2 ♗f6 20 g3 ♖f8 (20 ... h6 21 g4!) 21 a4 ♗f7 22 a5 h6 23 ♘c5± Ehlvest – Yusupov, Rotterdam 1989. We suggest 17 ... g5, planning ... ♗g6, e.g. 18 ♘c5 ♗xc5 19 dc f4 20 b4 ♗g6! △ ... ♘e5 and Black keeps the balance.

After 10 ... 0-0:

A: 11 ♘fd2
B: 11 ♕xb7
C: 11 ♘bd2

A

11 ♘fd2? ♘xf2!
12 ♔xf2

Slightly better 12 ♗f1 ♘e4 13 ♕xb7∓ Makarichev.

12 ... ♗h4+
13 g3

13 ♔f1? ♗xe1 14 ♔xe1 ♕h4+ 15 ♔f1 ♖ae8∓∓.

13 ... f4
14 ♔g2

Or:

a) **14 gh** ♕xh4+ 15 ♔f1 f3!

b) **14 ♔g1** fg 15 h3 ♗xh3 16 ♗e4 g2! 17 ♕xd5+ ♔h8 18 ♕xd8 ♖axd8 19 ♖d1 ♗g4 20 ♗c2 ♖de8∓∓.

14 ... fg
15 hg

15 ♗e4 ♗h3+! 16 ♔g1 (16 ♔xh3 ♕d7+!) 16 ... gh+ 17 ♔xh2 ♕d6+ 18 ♔h1 ♗xe1∓∓ Ljubojevic – Makarichev, Amsterdam 1975.

15 ... ♕d6!

16 gh ♖f2+! 17 ♔xf2 ♕h2+ 18 ♔e3 ♕g3+ 19 ♘f3 ♖e8+ 20 ♔d2 ♖xe1! 21 ♕xd5+ ♗e6∓∓ Schlechter.

B

11 ♕xb7?!

By the time the queen returns from pawn hunting, Black has gained two to three tempi, and Black's pieces reach optimal attacking positions.

11 ... ♗xf3!?

Also 11 ... ♖f6 12 ♕b3 (12 ♗f4 ♗xf3 13 gf ♖b8 14 ♕xc7 ♕e8 15 fe ♘d8∓) 12 ... ♖g6 13 ♘bd2 ♖b8 14 ♕a4(!) ♗d6 15 ♔f1∞ Yudasin – Jakovich, Kiev 1986.

12 gf

12 ♕xc6? ♖f6! △ ... ♖g6∓.

12 ... ♗h4!
13 ♗xe4 fe

14 ♕xc6 ♖f6 15 ♕b5, Zuidema – Hort, Jun. World Ch. 1961, 15 ... ♖xf3 16 ♗e3 ♗xf2+! 17 ♗xf2 ♕g5+ wins – Averbakh.

C

11 ♘bd2 ♔h8!?

Other ideas:

a) **11 ... ♖b8** 12 ♘xe4 ♘a5 13 ♕a4 (13 ♘f6+ ♖xf6 14 ♕a4 ♗xf3 15 ♕xa5 ♗c4=) 13 ... fe (13 ... ♗xf3? 14 gf fe 15 fe± Michimata – Grech, Thessaloniki (ol) 1988) 14 ♘e5 (14 ♗xe4 ♘c4∞) 14 ... ed 15 ♘xg4 ♘c4 16 ♕d1 ♗g5 and Black can keep his position, Ernst – Forintos, Malmö 1988-89.

b) **11 ... ♘a5!?** 12 ♕a4 ♘c6

13 ♕b3 ♘a5 14 ♕a4 ♘c6 15 ♗b5 ♘xd2 (15 ... ♖f6 16 ♗xc6 ♖xc6 17 ♘e5 ♖a6= Botvinnik) 16 ♘xd2 ♕d6 17 ♘b3 f4 18 ♘c5 ♕g6 19 ♗d3 ♗f5 20 ♗xf5 ♖xf5 21 f3∞ ½–½ Yudasin - Halifman, Simferopol 1988.

After 11 ... ♔h8:

C1: 12 ♕xb7
C2: 12 h3

Not 12 ♘f1? ♗xf3! 13 gf ♘xf2! 14 ♔xf2 ♗h4+ 15 ♘g3 f4∓ Capablanca.

C1

12   ♕xb7 *(108)*

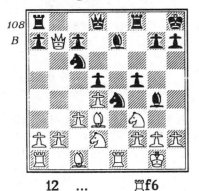

108
B

12   ...   ♖f6

Not 12 ... ♕d6? 13 ♗b5! ♘a5 14 ♕a6 ♘xd2 15 ♘xd2 c6 16 ♗f1±± Petrushin - Timofeyev, USSR 1979.

13 ♕b3   ♖g6

For the pawn Black has the initiative and a strong

knight base on e4.

Other tries:

a) **13 ... ♗d6** 14 g3 ♕g8 15 ♗e2 ♖e8 16 ♘xe4 ♖xe4 17 ♗e3 f4 18 ♘g5!± P Blatny - Kuczynski, Groningen 1985/86.

b) **13 ... ♖b8** when:

b1) **14 ♕c2 ♗d6!?** 15 ♘f1 ♖g6 16 ♔h1 ♕f6 with compensation in Arahamija - Chelushkina, Kiev 1984.

b2) **14 ♕d1 ♖g6** 15 ♘f1, Ribli - Bonner, Skopje (ol) 1972, 15 ... ♗d6 with enough compensation for the pawn.

b3) **14 ♕a4 ♗d6!** 15 h3 (15 g3) 15 ... ♘xd2! 16 ♘xd2 ♗xh3! 17 gh ♖g6+ 18 ♔f1 ♕g5 19 ♕xc6? ♕g2+ 20 ♔e2 ♗g3 21 ♕d7 ♕xf2+ 22 ♔d1 ♕xe1+ 23 ♔c2 ♗f4 24 ♕xf5 ♗xd2 0-1 Storland - Ernst, Gausdal 1987.

14   ♗b5!

This disturbs the co-operation of the black pieces while preparing ♘f3 - e5.

Some other tries:

a) **14 ♘e5?** ♘xe5 15 de ♘xf2! 16 ♔xf2 ♗c5+ 17 ♔f1 ♕h4∓∓ Savereide - Milligan, Thessaloniki (ol) 1988

b) **14 ♗f1** when:

b1) **14 ... ♖b8** 15 ♕c2 ♗d6 16 b3? ♘xd2 17 ♘xd2 ♗xh2+! 18 ♔xh2 ♕h4+ 19 ♔g1 ♖h6

20 f3 ♕xe1∓∓ Greensite – Baugh, corr. 1976. 16 g3!∞.

b2) **14 ... ♕d6** 15 ♕c2, Unzicker – Alexander, Biel 1960. 15 ... a5∞.

b3) **14 ... f4!?** 15 ♘xe4? de 16 ♘e5 ♘xe5 17 de e3!∓ (△ 18 fe ♗h4) Muchnik – T Chekhova, Minsk 1981. Better is 15 ♕c2∞.

14 ...   ♘xd2!
15 ♘xd2   ♗d6!
16 g3

16 ♗xc6? ♗xh2+! 17 ♔xh2 ♕h4+ 18 ♔g1 ♖h6∓.

16 ...   ♘e7!

Black has compensation for the pawn.

C2

12 h3   ♗h5

Karpov first chases the bishop, and only then captures on b7. So Black has the opportunity to change plan and not sacrifice the b7 pawn, e.g. 12 ... ♗xf3 13 ♘xf3 ♖b8 (R. Byrne). The two bishops are restrained by the e4 knight.

13 ♕xb7   ♖f6!

13 ... ♘a5? 14 ♕b5 c5, Ligterink – Dvoretsky, Wijk aan Zee 1975, 15 b4±.

14 ♕b3   ♖g6

a) **14 ... ♕d6?** 15 ♗b5 ♖b8 16 ♕a4± Botvinnik.

b) **14 ... g5** Botvinnik's

suggestion based on weakening h3, e.g. 15 ♘xe4 fe 16 ♘xg5 ♖b8 17 ♕c2 ♕f8 18 ♘f1 ♗g6 △ ... e3 or ... h6: 15 ♘e5 can also be considered, e.g. 15 ... ♘xe5 16 de ♖b6 17 ♕c2 △ c4.

15 ♗e2   ♗d6

a) **15 ... ♘xf2?** 16 ♔xf2 ♗h4+ 17 ♔f1! Botvinnik.

b) **15 ... ♕d6?** 16 ♘e5±; or 16 ♘xe4 fe 17 ♘g5! ♗xg5 18 ♗xh5 ♖h6 19 ♗g4 ♗xc1 20 ♖axc1± Garwell – Shterenberg, Thessaloniki (ol) 1988.

c) **15 ... ♖b8** 16 ♕d1 ♗d6 17 ♘xe4! fe 18 ♘e5 ♘xe5 19 ♗xh5 ♘d3 20 ♗xg6 ♕f6 (20 ... ♘xe1 21 ♕h5) and White is better, Steig – Mende, corr. 1976.

d) **15 ... ♗h4** 16 ♖f1! ♗xf3 17 ♘xf3 ♗xf2+?! (Korchnoi had only four minutes here) 18 ♖xf2 ♘xf2 19 ♔xf2 ♕d6 20 ♘g5! ♖f8 21 ♕a3!±± Karpov – Korchnoi, (m/6) 1974.

16 ♘e5

Or 16 ♕d1, Garwell – Milligan, Thessaloniki (ol) 1988, for 16 ... ♖b8 see c 15 ... ♖b8; 16 ... ♕f6 is possible.

16 ...   ♘xe5

17 ♗xh5 ♖xg2+ 18 ♔xg2 ♕g5+ 19 ♔f1 ♕h4! 20 ♘xe4 ♕xh3+ 21 ♔g1 de 22 de ♗xe5 23 f4 ♕g3+ gives perpetual check – O'Kelly.

Index of Variations

1 e4 e5 2 ♘f3 ♘f6
3 d4 ed

3 d4 ♘xe4

3 ♘xe5